INSIDERS' GUIDE® SERIES

MYRTLE BEACH AND THE GRAND STRAND

SIXTH EDITION

by

Lisa Tomer Rentz

and

Kimberly Allyson Duncan

AN IMPRINT OF THE GLOBE PEQUOT PRESS
GUILFORD, CONNECTICUT

•

Front cover photo: sandcastle, courtesy of the Myrtle Beach Area Chamber of Commerce
Back cover photo: fireworks, courtesy of Cotton Company
Photo band, from left: beach, courtesy of Brandon Advertising;
boat, Lisa Tomer Rentz; underwater tunnel, courtesy of Cotton Company;
golf course, Michael Slear, courtesy of Brandon Advertising;
roller coaster, courtesy of Cotton Company
Spine photo: dock, courtesy of Lesnik Himmelsbach Wilson Hearl & Hirsch

•

ISBN 1-57380-151-8

•

Manufactured in the United States of America

•

Sixth Edition/First Printing

Preface

Don't think of your trip to Myrtle Beach in terms of how long it will take you to get here—the few hours from Columbia or the all-day drive from Pennsylvania. Rather, think of what you are gaining on this sandy adventure: incomparable ocean views and sultry breezes, mounds of all-you-can-eat crab legs, your highest score on a video game or lowest in golf, a perfect memento to wear back home or (and probably most of all) a touch of that Southern sunshine that will slow you down to the comfortable pace of the local drawl.

As you've probably heard by now (with over 13 million visitors annually, word can't help but spread), the Grand Strand has a lot more to offer than its wide, fun-filled beach. You should definitely spend your afternoons there, laying out, reading, crabbing, shelling and swimming—you know, all the traditional beach things Myrtle Beach provides so well. But what should you do in the cool mornings? What if it's raining? What if your child asks about the area's flora and fauna or history? Which golf courses allow walking? With your special tastes in consideration, where should you stay? And, where should you eat?

When you arrive, you'll see plenty of signs pointing you in many different directions; the multitude of businesses along U.S. Highway 17 compete with each other in everything from price to visibility. But with The Insiders' Guide®, you'll be prepared for, if not knowledgeable of, the new surroundings. As Insiders we have crafted a guide to the Grand Strand specifically for people who want to enjoy themselves; even though we're not necessarily on vacation here, we heartily agree the Grand Strand is about enjoying yourself.

There are many ways to accomplish this, from strolling the beach and eating grilled meals to playing the most exclusive golf clubs and experiencing fine dining. With this Insiders' look at the Grand Strand, we hope we are helping you come up with the right combination and ensuring that you'll come back to try out a new one next year.

We looked at all the possibilities, trying to think of the most significant Insiders' tip to make your excursion as comfortable as possible, and this is the one that leapt to our minds first: Do not underestimate the value of a good sunscreen!

About the Authors

Lisa Tomer Rentz

Transplanted to South Carolina when she was 17, Lisa Tomer Rentz has since eaten her weight in hushpuppies, walked miles of Strand with her dogs, and married a true Southern gentleman. Her background in marketing and her husband's family's hundred-year-old beach house in Ocean Drive drew her to the Grand Strand, where Lisa works as a freelance writer. Locally, for *Yikes!* magazine, she has written about what Grand Stranders want for Christmas, local charities, local artists and bands, Harley bikers, the Long Bay symphony, and juggling bus boys.

Kimberly Allyson Duncan

Kimberly Allyson Duncan, a native of the Carolina Lowcountry, graduated from the University of South Carolina. She is president and owner of The Altman Group, a business communications firm that provides outsourcing solutions for a wide variety of marketing and public relations needs. Specialties include copywriting, special events planning, and consumer show production/promotion. Kimberly also co-publishes The Lowcountry Companion, a popular magazine that focuses on the area's wealth of art, ecotourism and history resources.

Acknowledgements

Lisa Tomer Rentz

It's been too much fun working on this book; the Insiders' Guide® gave me the opportunity, and Grand Stranders gave me all the help and inspiration, thoughts and tips.

Grand Strand residents have a lot of practice sharing their beach, festivals, creativity, food and culture with everyone who decides they want to see what this part of the coast is about. I've only recorded their efforts here like a message in a bottle.

Kimberly Allyson Duncan

Boundless gratitude is extended to those who worried with me, overlooked my acid moods and made me laugh when I didn't feel like laughing: Kelly—the most wise and wonderful friend of all; Sherri, Holly, Troi, Gail, Myra, Amy—cherished friends who encourage me in ways they do not know; and the countless others who have always been there when I needed them: Bob, Chip, Danny, David, Hugh, Lee, and L.R.

Thanks to my father for teaching me to love words. My life is infinitely richer because of his gift. And, thanks to Mother for a genetic dose of creativity that helps me weave those words together in ways that delight and comfort me when nothing else can.

Last of all, and most importantly, I'd like to acknowledge Madison and Kaela—the world's most remarkable little girls—I hope to make both of you proud.

And . . .

We would like to thank Holly Lumpkin for her fact-checking and proofreading on the sixth edition of this book.

Born and raised in South Carolina, mid-state and in the Lowcountry, M. "Holly" Lumpkin earned a doctorate from the University of Georgia and is the author of a forthcoming book, *Trick or Treatment: How to Avoid Harm from Your Therapist*, (NewJoy Press). She currently is at work freelance writing, editing, and consulting with agencies and organizations which need a grant-writer.

Brookgreen displays a huge variety of flora.

Table of Contents

Directory of Maps

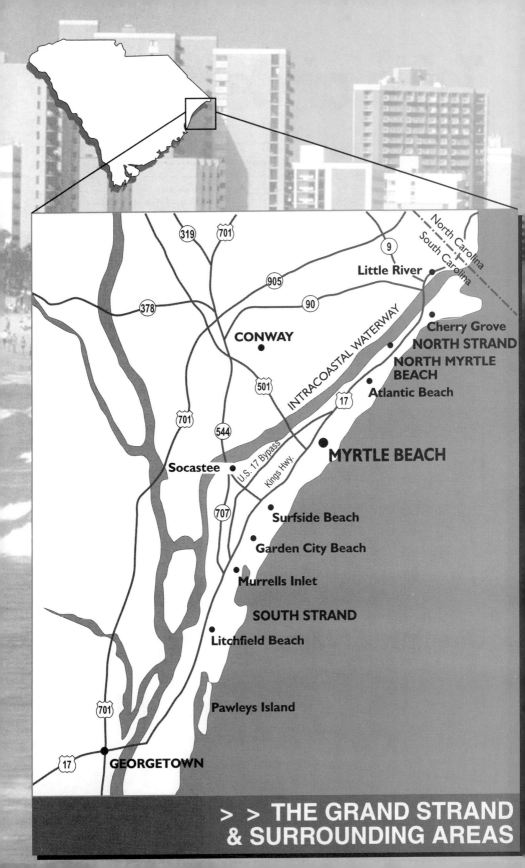

> > THE GRAND STRAND
& SURROUNDING AREAS

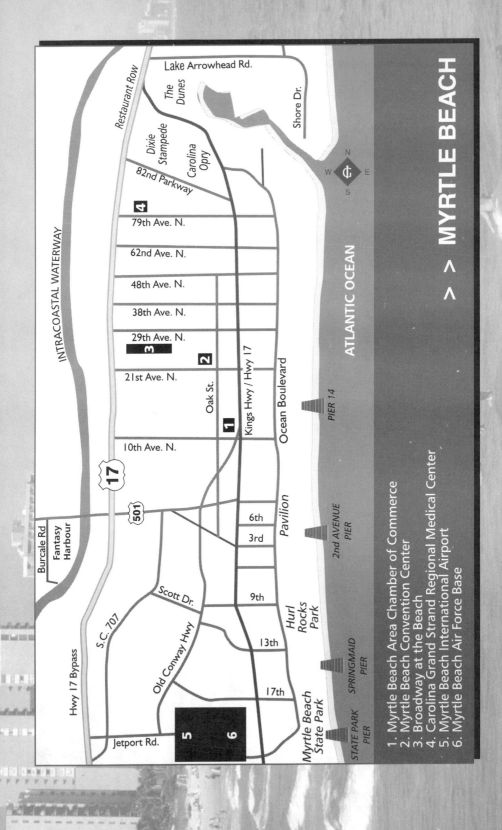

>> MYRTLE BEACH

1. Myrtle Beach Area Chamber of Commerce
2. Myrtle Beach Convention Center
3. Broadway at the Beach
4. Carolina Grand Strand Regional Medical Center
5. Myrtle Beach International Airport
6. Myrtle Beach Air Force Base

Broadway at the Beach fireworks.

Photo: Courtesy of Cotton Company

How to Use This Book

This incredible 60-mile stretch of beach from Little River to Georgetown, appropriately dubbed the Grand Strand, is a vacationer's mecca. There's so much going on in any given area that, oftentimes, people need not wander beyond a 2-mile radius from their hotel to keep busy all day and night. We hope that this guide to South Carolina's favorite coastal resort will help you effectively plan your next visit here, your relocation or your retirement. One thing is sure, this guide will give you a true Insider's view of the Grand Strand from those of us who live, work and play here.

In producing *The Insiders' Guide® to South Carolina's Myrtle Beach & the Grand Strand*, we have tried to lead you through the dizzying options of things to see and do. The chapters on Shopping, Restaurants, Nightlife, Annual Events, Entertainment, Attractions, Kidstuff and Arts and Culture should be good starting points for planning your activities. If you still have time and energy, the chapter on Daytrips can direct you to nearby sites of interest. The last thing we want is for you to get lost around here, so we've provided a Getting Here, Getting Around chapter as well as a variety of maps of the overall area, including main arteries and roadways.

We also have used the regional headings of the North Strand, Myrtle Beach and the South Strand in the chapters to orient you and save you travel time. By breaking out these areas, you can pinpoint people, places and things closest to you. Basically, the North Strand is anywhere from the village of Little River to Myrtle Beach proper. Lake Arrowhead Road and the Restaurant Row section of the Grand Strand will be your landmarks of note that you have passed from the North Strand into Myrtle Beach proper.

The Myrtle Beach section of the Strand continues southward until you see the signs denoting Surfside Beach. Surfside marks the starting point of the South Strand entries in this book, encompassing Garden City Beach, Murrells Inlet, Litchfield Beach, Pawleys Island and Georgetown. Road signs let you know that once you've hit the Murrells Inlet area, you've traveled from Horry County into Georgetown County.

This guide contains several listings from sister regions, which we call Beyond the Strand. As a geographical heading, Beyond the Strand lends itself to areas within Horry or Georgetown counties that are considered inland and usually denote areas west of the Intracoastal Waterway.

Whether you're staying for a weekend, a week or permanently, this guide will help you find suitable accommodations or a roof over your head; check out the chapters on Accommodations and Real Estate.

To make financial planning easier, we've coordinated a dollar-sign key to give you a price range for places to eat and stay. However, prices quoted in this guide are subject to change, and each establishment reserves the right to make those changes without prior notice. Also we do apologize here and now if you should contact any place mentioned in this guide only to find it out of business. As is typical of a resort area, there is so much new market competition here that it's not unusual for a certain percentage of businesses to close their doors each year.

Other chapters provide vital information on child care, education, local laws, retirement and medical care.

When using the Insiders' Guide, you'll come across a lot of cross-referencing. We do this to give you the most complete information possible. For example, you may be reading an entry in the Attractions chapter that refers you to the Kidstuff chapter for more information. The Kidstuff chapter may include the same entry, but it's written from the perspective of relating to children's interests. In this way you'll be able to get the whole scoop on a place, what there is for adults and for children.

Please note that the area code for the Coastal and Pee Dee regions of South Carolina is 843 (which replaced an 803 code in 1998).

This (843) area code includes the South Carolina counties of Beaufort, Charleston, Chesterfield, Colleton, Darlington, Dillon, Florence, Georgetown, Horry, Jasper, Marion, Marlboro and Williamsburg. It will also take in most of Berkeley County and parts of Bamberg, Clarendon, Dorchester, Hampton, Kershaw and Lee counties.

We welcome and appreciate your comments and suggestions. Just drop us a line and let us know how we're doing.

Insiders' Guide to Myrtle Beach
c/o The Globe Pequot Press
P.O. Box 480
Guilford, CT 06437-0480
www.insiders.com

We hope *The Insiders' Guide® to Myrtle Beach and the Grand Strand* will give you a real feel for this area and the opportunity to experience it to the fullest. With this information in hand, you'll fit right in as if you've been beachcombing all your life.

Area Overview

Most people think of the Grand Strand as the coast of South Carolina; technically The Strand is an island with a 60-mile oceanfront and three roads connecting it to the mainland (four, if you count U.S. Highway 17 connections in both the North and South strands.) Surrounded on the north and the west by the Intracoastal Waterway, a Roosevelt-era shipping lane, the east by the Atlantic Ocean and on the south by Winyah Bay, the Grand Strand can be basically shut off from the outside motoring world by closing four bridges.

LOOK FOR:
• Vital Statistics
• North Strand
• Myrtle Beach
• South Strand

The Grand Strand is named so for a reason: The wide strand accommodates people of every type at various activities including swimming, sunbathing, sea-shelling, volleyball playing, Sea-Dooing, fishing, parasailing, boating and more. The communities are first and foremost beach oriented. All the houses and buildings are designed for optimum views of the water. One street inland, Myrtle Beach goes beyond sand in your shoes and provides restaurants, shopping, golf and many other diversions.

Since *Southern Living* magazine began doling out its prestigious Readers Choice awards three years ago, the Grand Strand has consistently been spotlighted as one of the South's finest resort destinations. *BY-WAYS* magazine, a publication of the National Motor Coach Network, ranked Myrtle Beach as the favorite destination of motor coach carriers and tour operators. Good Morning America has televised part of its shows here, as was a QVC (television shopping network) telecast. More permanently, Crook & Chase, a popular talk show airing on TNN, moved into Fantasy Harbor. The accolades keep pouring in, matching the expectations of more than 13 million visitors every year.

The Grand Strand directly generates more than $2.5 billion annually; combining direct expenditures with indirect expenditures totals $4.9 billion, which accounts for 34.9 percent of the state's total revenues from travel and tourism.

According to the Myrtle Beach Area Chamber of Commerce, leisure travelers spend an average of $101 a day, per person; business travelers spend an average of $178. 84 percent of visitors arrive in their own car and 56 percent stay in hotels or condos, 30 percent in timeshare units. Most visitors like to take their time and stay for a week—the average visit is 6.7 days as opposed to the United States average of 2.2 days for leisure travel.

More than 19 percent of all visitors to the beach area are senior citizens. And many of those visitors retire here; it's not only cheaper than Florida, but the area also has a much lower crime rate than some larger Florida cities.

Stretching far beyond just the city limits of Myrtle Beach, the Grand Strand reaches from the North Carolina border, beachcombing southward more than 60 miles to the historic, oak-lined avenues of Georgetown,

Myrtle Beach and the Grand Strand Vital Statistics

Nicknames:
"The Grand Strand"—the extra wide beach and grouping of all the beach towns such as Little River, Windy Hill, Myrtle Beach, Garden City, and Pawley's Island.
"The Independent Republic"—Horry County, because of historical events such as the signing of secession papers in Conway (the county seat), and Horry County's geographic separation, with rivers and marshes separating it from the rest of the state.

Mayor of Myrtle Beach:
Mark S. McBride

Population:
(Horry & Georgetown County) 234,600 (permanent residents)

Area:
The Grand Strand—60 miles of coast, from Little River to Georgetown

Average Temperatures:
July—air 88, water, 80; January—air 56, water 50

Average Days of Sunshine:
Sunny, 216; rainy, 72; average humidity at 1 PM, 57 percent

Major University:
Coastal Carolina University

Important Dates in History:
1730: The city of Georgetown is planned.
1779: South Carolina joins Union.
1900: Burroughs and Collins Company constructs a railway to the beach.
1901: First hotel, the Seaside Inn, is built.
1936: Intracoastal Waterway is opened to boaters.
1954: Hurricane Hazel
1989: Hurricane Hugo
1997: Beach Renourishment Project begins; area's first museum of art opens.

Major Area Employers:
Burroughs and Chapin, AVX

Famous Sons and Daughters:
Vanna White, Alabama (started as Wild Country at the Bowery)

Major Airport:
Myrtle Beach International Airport

Major Roadways:
Ocean Boulevard: runs parallel to ocean throughout most of Grand Strand
U.S. Highway 17 Business (King's Highway) and Bypass: also runs parallel to the ocean a little farther inland
U.S. Highway 501: from Florence, into Conway and on into the heart of the Grand Strand. To get to North Strand leave U.S. 501 to take S.C. Highway 90
Interstate 40 East (to U.S. 17 S.): for travelers coming from eastern North Carolina
Interstates 95 and 20: for those coming from the west into Florence

Driving Laws:
To obtain a driver's license you must be at least 18 years of age; to obtain a permit, age 14; new residents may use old licenses for up to 90 days. Seat belts and child safety restraints required. Headlights must be on when use of wipers is necessary.

Alcohol Laws:
Drinking age is 21. Sale of alcohol prohibited on Sundays. Beer and wine available at grocery stores; liquor sold at ABC stores marked with large red dots.

Sales Tax:
5 percent South Carolina sales tax; 16 cents per gallon gasoline tax; maximum of $300 tax on purchase of vehicles.

Hospitality Tax:
2.5 percent hospitality fee charged on prepared food, admissions, and overnight accommodations of less than 90 days.

Tourism Information:
Myrtle Beach Area Chamber of Commerce
1200 N. Oak St.
Myrtle Beach, SC 29577
(800) 356-3016

Welcome centers at 213 Hwy. 17 N., North Myrtle Beach, 29582;
3401 Hwy. 17 S. Business, Murrells Inlet, 29576;
2090 501 E., Horry-Georgetown Technical College, Conway 29526

North Myrtle Beach Chamber of Commerce
220 Surfwood Plaza, Hwy. 17 N.
North Myrtle Beach, SC 29582
(877) 332-2662

Pawleys Town Square
Hwy. 17, Pawleys Island, 29585

Georgetown Chamber of Commerce
100 Front St., Georgetown, 29440
(843) 546-8437

AREA OVERVIEW

Pelicans are a common sight on the waterfront.

Photo: Lisa Tomer Rentz

where five rivers meet to form Winyah Bay. This 60-mile stretch includes the latest high-tech amusements to more than 106 golf courses to world-class entertainment theaters and superstars to family beaches to almost-untouched beach wilderness. Amazingly, one can drift just slightly off the beaten path and find salt marshes, classic Spanish moss, hammocks, ghost tales and historic legends that make The Disney Channel seem dull.

So you've got plenty to do. Visit the world-famous Pavilion and ride every ride. Smell the salt water dancing with the scents of fresh cotton candy and mustard-coated corn dogs. Sift your toes into the sand as the surf laps at your ankles. Take a marsh cruise, go deep-sea fishing or windsurf. Fall asleep in the sun. Swim and sail and dine and dance. Play a few rounds of golf. Hob-knob with country music stars, or just relax and enjoy what the poet called "God's Country."

North Strand

Tourist development of the North Strand began around 1937 with a log cabin-type motel. Except for some serious destruction from Hurricane Hazel in 1954, these little beach communities have maintained their individual identities while creating a greater presence as North Strand entities.

INSIDERS' TIP

Pay attention to North and South indicators on numbered street names. For example: Not only is 30th Avenue N. 60 streets north of 30th Avenue S. in Myrtle Beach, but there is also another set of 30th avenues, North and South again, in North Myrtle Beach.

Although minimal but steady erosion has prompted a renourishment project on a 25-mile stretch of beach between North Myrtle Beach and Garden City Beach (see the related Close-up in our Beach Information chapter), many folks who call the North Strand home boast that they still have the world's widest beach. While the claim is disputable, no one will deny that their beach is remarkably wide—especially when the tide is at low ebb. Unlike many South Carolina beaches, this section of sand still offers plenty of room to bask in the sun, take long walks, mastermind sandcastles and play volleyball and paddle ball, even when the tide is high.

The sand of the North Strand is packed firm; driving cars on the beach used to be popular but is now prohibited. But bikes are allowed and make for a breezily enjoyable ride. Bicycles and a three-wheeled, low-riding style of bike can be rented along the North Strand, so avoid the hassle of bringing your own. The three-wheelers are a comic and attention-getting mode of travel; you sit in a semi-reclined position and pedal with your feet out front. It's awkward at first, but with a little coordination and some concentration, you'll get the knack quickly. Although these big trikes have hand grips, you steer using your feet and the sway of your body. Attachments allow you to pull the kids along.

Little River

Where the Carolinas meet, the sun smiles on the charming fishing village of Little River. Nestled beneath the twisted arms of weathered oaks, you'll discover an unhurried and uncommon side of the Grand Strand. From clutches of cheerful shops, an unexpected array of merchandise spills forth. You can also schedule a deep-sea fishing excursion, take a cruise down the Intracoastal Waterway or hang around and chat with tanned dock workers while they haul in a day's catch. Restaurants, marinas and fresh seafood abound. Water is the undisputed king, and everyone is subject to its rule. Like the rest of the North Strand, Little River is growing rapidly, but it's still possible to discover marvelous pockets of solitude in this historic fishing village.

Each spring, thousands of people make a pilgrimage to Little River on the weekend in May when the horseshoe area of the beloved waterfront hosts the famous Blue Crab Festival (see our Annual Events chapter). This day-long event—Little River's finest—showcases live entertainment, oodles of arts-and-crafts displays and an abundance of fresh, delectable seafood.

North Myrtle Beach

North Myrtle Beach, proud home of the state's shimmy-in-your-well-worn-Weejuns dance, the Shag, makes up the largest section of the North Strand. The city was established in the 1960s after legendary South Carolina Congressman John Jenrette (then a state legislator) argued that the four smaller communities of Cherry Grove, Ocean Drive, Crescent Beach and Windy Hill would prosper if they merged into a single municipality.

Condominiums and small motels are typical oceanfront accommodations, but you can still find front-row cottages. Their suitability for house parties, coupled with North Myrtle Beach's

AREA OVERVIEW

The beautiful salt marshes and waterways of the North and South Strand provide a multitude of views.

Photo: Lisa Tomer Rentz

long-standing party-hearty reputation, make it a mainstay for Shaggers, collegiate men and women and arcade-loving kids.

From mid-May, when exams end at many institutions, until mid-June, you'll find North Myrtle overflowing with celebrating students from far and wide. On Easter weekend alone, an estimated 75,000 to 90,000 kids flock to the beach for dancing and romancing. Over the years, police have been forced to become especially strict about public drinking. Consequently, many college kids have found themselves singing the jailhouse blues instead of dancing on the Strand. Jenrette, who served as the first town judge, still enjoys telling of his escapades trying not to jail many a young drinking party-seeker in the early days of North Myrtle. Even today, for those willing to demonstrate a little self control, one visit will confirm an irrefutable truth: There's no better place on the eastern seaboard to celebrate the end of another school year.

Cherry Grove, just south of Little River, is one of several communities that compose North Myrtle Beach. Sea Mountain Highway is the only way into Cherry Grove from U.S. 17, so watch the signs carefully. Cherry Grove has its share of oceanfront condominiums and motels, but away from the

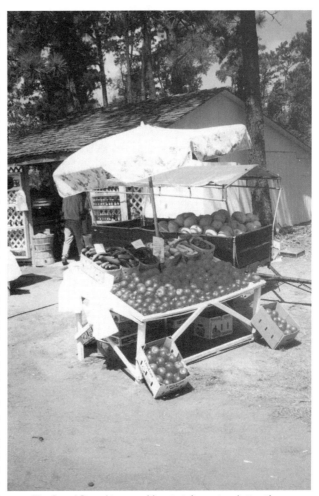

The Grand Strand teems with entertainment and attractions, but cruise "off-the-beaten-path" and you'll find a slow, sweet side of South Carolina's Lowcountry.

Photo: Courtesy of The Lowcountry Companion

ocean you'll find rows of houses on pilings lining serpentine channels and inlets. Many Cherry Grove residents and tourists handpick this section of the Strand because they relish the joys of catching, cleaning and cooking their own seafood.

From dawn to dusk, Cherry Grove's Hogg Inlet bustles with folks shrimping and fishing, crabbing with chicken necks and dutifully tending their fish pots. Patient anglers troll, seeking out the day's best fishing spots. At night they gig for flounder. You'll be glad to know Hogg Inlet has a public boat landing, so you don't have to own a home on the creek to partake of the Inlet's bounty. In recent years Hogg Inlet has also become a late-night hangout and parking spot for young locals wanting a secluded smooching area.

Along U.S. 17, the communities known as Ocean Drive, Crescent Beach, Atlantic Beach and Windy Hill run together in a hard-to-distinguish blur. In fact, if you're not a local, it's nearly impossible to know when you've passed from one community into the next. On the ocean you'll find more motels and condominiums in Ocean Drive and Crescent Beach. Ocean Drive is best known as the place where the world-famous dance the Shag originated. Accordingly, Main Street Ocean Drive boasts several clubs where beach music will never go out of style.

Although not technically a part of the city of North Myrtle Beach, Atlantic Beach sits between the Windy Hill and Crescent Beach communities. Historically, Atlantic Beach was known as the "black beach" because during Jim Crow years it was the only beach on the southern Atlantic seaboard open to African Americans. Separated for years from the rest of North Myrtle Beach by oceanfront chain-link fences, today Atlantic Beach has a few small motels, nightspots and lots of cottages, and it is still primarily an African-American community.

Where North Myrtle ends Briarcliffe Acres begins, sheltered by a wall of tall pine trees. Moderately upscale and almost solely residential, you're likely to miss this tiny town if someone doesn't point it out. The easy way to find it is to look for Colonial Mall on the west side of the highway.

One of the North Strand's many delights is Barefoot Landing, a top-ranked tourist attraction. On U.S. 17 and inland from Windy Hill Beach, this charming variation of a shopping center includes shops nestled around a 20-acre freshwater lake. Barefoot Landing is home to more than 100 specialty and retail shops, factory direct stores, more than 1,000 feet of floating dock, a boardwalk and a handful of waterfront restaurants. Attractions include the Barefoot Carousel, *Barefoot Princess Riverboat*, Alligator Adventure, The Alabama Theatre and the House of Blues.

The North Strand wraps up with the Grand Strand's famed Restaurant Row. Like a string of fine pearls, an impressive selection of restaurants lines either side of U.S. 17. Seafood, of course, is the natural specialty, but hearty steaks, spicy ribs, Italian favorites, Japanese options and even down-home country cooking can be found along this renowned strip. During summer dinner hours, nearly every restaurant sports a long line of eager patrons, but you're sure to find the food worth the wait. Highway traffic is especially heavy during that dinner rush, which starts as early as 5 PM and continues until around 8 PM.

Closest to Myrtle Beach is the unincorporated Shore Drive community. Highly developed and densely populated, this is an area of high-rise hotels and condominiums, retiree homes, a nearly constant flow of renters and timeshare purchasers and a couple of upscale residential communities.

Myrtle Beach

The Grand Strand revolves around the city of Myrtle Beach. The resort area first became popular here, and everything seems to spiderweb outward from Myrtle Beach. Though Pawleys Island was a long-standing resort for the wealthy, it was Myrtle Beach that made the Strand accessible to the general population. The largest, most developed and most popular of the beaches, Myrtle Beach is so dominant that most locals refer to it simply as "The Beach." Even folks living south in Surfside or Garden City and those living north in Ocean Drive or Cherry Grove still tell outsiders that they live "at Myrtle Beach."

In years past the area has been billed the Seaside Golf Capital of the World, the Campground Capital of the World and the Miniature Golf Capital of the World—on top of all the other hoopla about the Strand.

Myrtle Beach once was even home to the world's largest sand sculpture. As part of a Sun Fun Festival (see our Annual Events chapter) promotion, Myrtle Beach challenged the city of Long Beach, Washington, to a sandcastle-building competition. Hundreds of volunteers rallied Southern pride to create a sand sculpture that stretched for 86,536 feet—more than 16 miles! The feat landed the city in the Guinness Book of World Records in 1991 (Long Beach has since recaptured the record).

The tourism experts say that Myrtle Beach's greatest attractions are still the Atlantic Ocean and the beautiful beaches. But in the past few years so many other things have sprung up that it is hard for even Insiders to keep track of the latest attraction. In addition to shopping, amusement parks, miniature golf, water parks, waterway cruises, golf and the live-entertainment theaters, there is a constant quest among promoters to find even greater ways to satisfy visitors and residents alike. Whether it's the golfer's paradise, the country music and live-entertainment haven, family

INSIDERS' TIP

Always take time to stop at visitors centers or chamber of commerce offices when you're new in town or just visiting. The staff can point you in the direction of fun and may know of special events or have coupons for you to use.

beach, the food, the shopping, the amusements, the attractions . . . whatever the draw, Myrtle Beach seems to provide something for everyone.

Even old-timers are amazed at the development that has transformed Myrtle Beach.

The Wall Street Journal recently declared that the state bird of South Carolina is evolving into to the "construction crane" because of Myrtle Beach. Myrtle Beach once was a summer vacation resort catering to blue-collar factory workers primarily in North and South Carolina and Tennessee. In fact, even Generation-X locals can remember when the only real tourist season was during July when the textile mills closed for vacation. But the face of Myrtle Beach has rapidly changed, becoming a mixture of blue-collar workers, northern mid-management retirees, upscale golfers, families and a whole new demographic of white-collar vacationers.

During the past 10 years, the Strand's 100-plus golf courses have helped expand the spring and fall shoulder seasons in the tourism industry to make Myrtle Beach a nine-month resort. Nearly 4.28 million rounds of golf are played in the area each year. Little wonder—Myrtle Beach is the self-proclaimed seaside golf capital of the world.

Still, the average visitor to the Myrtle Beach area is an ocean-seeking vacationer. Almost 40 percent of the 13.5 million annual visitors live within a day's drive to the beach. Myrtle Beach is approximately halfway between New York City and Miami.

Myrtle Beach's main drag is Ocean Boulevard (known locally as the Boulevard), the street that literally runs along the ocean. The Boulevard is divided east-west by numbered streets (30th Street S. to First Street S. and then First Street N. to 82nd Street N.).

Unofficially, Myrtle Beach is divided into four areas. The south end of the Boulevard is a solid line of accommodations—some large, some small. The mid-portion of the Boulevard features venues for entertainment and activities, including the Myrtle Beach Pavilion and Ripley's Believe It or Not! Museum. Beginning around 32nd Avenue N., there is an exclusive residential district where permanent and summer residents coexist in beautiful homes. From 52nd Avenue northward, motels and condominiums dominate the beachfront.

Heading directly west from the mid-portion of the Boulevard, along 21st Avenue N., you will cross U.S. Highway 17 Business, also called Kings Highway and the primary home for shopping centers, a mall and regular non-resort businesses. Further west is Oak Street, primarily a business district. About 3 miles from the ocean you will hit U.S. Highway 17 Bypass; locals know it as simply the Bypass, and many have come to call it the "former Bypass" because of recent traffic

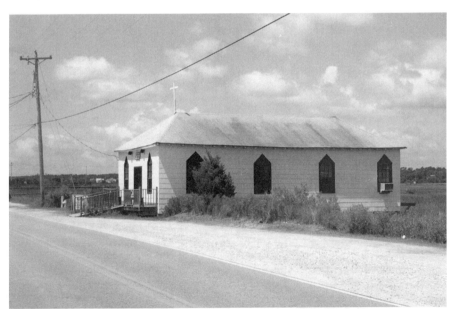

The south end of the Grand Strand boasts plenty of historic attractions like this pretty little chapel on the creek in Pawleys Island's historic district.

Photo: Courtesy of Lowcountry Companion

INSIDERS' TIP

If you're flying to your destination, pack a change of clothes in your carry-on, so if your luggage gets lost, you'll have something to wear until they find your suitcase.

backups. On 21st Avenue N., between Oak Street and the Bypass, you will find Broadway At The Beach, one of the most significant developments at Myrtle Beach during the past decade.

The beaches of the Grand Strand are public; in fact, law specifically designates how many feet apart public access areas must be, based on development density. Thanks to the vision of Myrtle Beach officials, many of the city's public access areas have parking available. The city has erected blue and yellow signs along the Boulevard to help visitors recognize these access sites. Handicapped access to the beach is also provided; through the efforts of several area civic clubs, beach services now offer specially designed wheelchairs that are easy to maneuver on the sand.

Myrtle Beach hosts many annual festivals. Two of the most popular are the Sun Fun Festival, usually held the first full weekend in June, and the Canadian-American Days festival, held in March to coincide with spring break for Canadian students.

The 46-year-old Sun Fun Festival originally served as an official kickoff for the summer season. Even now that Myrtle Beach is a nearly year-round tourist destination, the traditional Sun Fun Festival continues to offer four days of nonstop fun in early June. The famous festival frequently attracts national media attention to the beauty and bikini contests, sandcastle-building, a huge parade, children's games, musical and theatrical performances, cookouts, sailing regattas and much more.

Canadian-American Days offers a jam-packed agenda too. "Can-Am," as locals call it, was developed in recognition of thousands of Canadian tourists who were already visiting the beach every spring. About 39 years ago the Chamber of Commerce decided to launch a Canadian advertising campaign to extend the beach season by encouraging even more northern visitors during the otherwise slow time. During this 10-day festival, banks willingly exchange currency, and some businesses even offer an exchange rate at par. Radio, television and newspapers headline Canadian news.

See the Annual Events chapter for details on both of these events.

South Strand

The South Strand includes Surfside Beach, Garden City Beach, Murrells Inlet, Litchfield Beach and Pawleys Island. Compared with the rest of the Grand Strand, the South Strand subscribes to a more leisurely pace and lifestyle, with less neon and glitter as well as a low key nightlife with just as much allure. Many praise this stretch of land, with its rich marshland, uninhabited beaches, bountiful inlets and maritime forest, as the Carolina coast's finest treasure. For those same reasons, South Strand residents cherish their privacy and work vigilantly to protect the area's resources.

The town of Surfside was incorporated in 1964 with 881 residents. Today, having officially changed its name to Surfside Beach and billing itself as "the family beach," the town's year-round population is more than 4,000. Immediately adjacent to Myrtle Beach and most like it in nature, Surfside Beach has become a destination unto itself—mostly for RV park visitors and hotel guests who like a little more solitude than Myrtle Beach offers.

U.S. 17 in Surfside is lined with restaurants, beach shops and attractions, including the Legends In Concert show of celebrity impersonators. Accommodations along Surfside's oceanfront differ somewhat from those in Myrtle Beach. Fewer high-rises tower above the sun-drenched beaches, and cottages and condominiums treasure comfort.

Directly south of Surfside Beach, Garden City Beach is a family-oriented retreat sporting hundreds of residential homes, summer cottages and condominiums. Surf fishing reels in many participants along this beach, which is also a favorite retreat for beachcombers. Garden City Beach is also one of the Grand Strand's most popular retirement destinations, with large controlled-access senior-citizen communities dominating the area.

The point where Atlantic Avenue punctuates Ocean Boulevard is the only area in Garden City that resembles the glittery expanses of Myrtle Beach. Here you'll find arcades and carnival-style food vendors. As for quieter pursuits, walking Garden City's pier is a popular pastime, particularly when a silvery Carolina moon is riding high.

The North Jetty of Garden City was built in 1979 with rocks weighing up to 200 pounds each. It extends 3,445 feet from the shore and stabilizes the inlet across the ocean so commercial and recreational boats won't bog down. The jetty ensures ideal boating conditions, regardless of tidal action, which is especially important for those who fish commercially and rely on the sea's bounty to make a living.

South of Garden City is Murrells Inlet, the oldest fishing village in South Carolina. Murrells Inlet is home to anglers, writers, poets and more legends and ghost stories than any other part of the Grand Strand. Mickey Spillane, who created the detective character Mike Hammer, lives in the Inlet as do a dozen other nationally known novelists, poets and musicians, all of whom love the small-town atmosphere of being able to walk into a fish market or a barber shop without being mobbed.

Fishing in the creeks and waterways of Murrells Inlet has been a way of life for generations, and the quiet community trumpets itself as the Seafood Capital of South Carolina. Best known to tourists for almost 40 seafood restaurants in a 3-mile stretch, Murrells Inlet also is home to numerous antiques shops, fresh seafood markets and Captain Dick's, one of the Grand Strand's best marinas (see our Boating chapter).

The journey south on U.S. 17 from Murrells Inlet to Litchfield is a quick, pretty trip. Densely wooded areas line the highway and give a sense of traveling back in time, a sensation deliberately cultivated by locals. Carefully manicured landscapes adorn the median along the main highway. Once known as Magnolia Beach, the popular resort of Litchfield Beach takes its name from Litchfield Plantation, a rice plantation on the Waccamaw River. The manor house is one of the few still-standing plantation homes surrounded by majestic oaks. Open as a country club and a bed and breakfast, Litchfield Plantation is now classified as a small world-class luxury hotel.

Litchfield's quaint shops, outstanding restaurants and various accommodations are reasonably new compared to the historic resort of Pawleys Island, slightly south of Litchfield. The beaches of Litchfield and Pawleys are among the widest, most litter-free and best-preserved on the South Carolina coast; however, much of the property is private, and you'll find only a few points of public beach access. Though the points are clearly marked, parking is limited.

Pawleys Island proclaims itself the oldest resort area in America. Even in the 1700s the tiny barrier island was a summer retreat for wealthy plantation owners and their families. Despite storms and the ravages of time, many of their cottages, weather-worn and rustic looking, still remain. Hence, for many years, locals have termed their island "arrogantly shabby." As a matter of fact, bumper stickers, T-shirts and tourism brochures for Pawleys Island all have adopted that description.

Today Pawleys is known for its low-key lifestyle, handmade hammocks and sightings of the Gray Man, a friendly ghost who warns of impending hurricanes. The cherished lifestyle is carefully protected by islanders. The 2-mile island was incorporated as a town in 1984 and in recent years has made for one of the most colorful political stories in South Carolina's history, with their struggle to restrict local building codes and prevent construction of high-rise condominiums and hotels. They have been successful. A few bed and breakfast inns flourish, offering a taste of beach living as it used to be: simple, unassuming and perfectly tranquil.

South of Pawleys Island and at the foot of the Grand Strand is Georgetown, a one-time rice-plantation and shipping community that was often called Little Charleston. With a Revolutionary War-era flavor, the narrow, brick streets and its well-preserved, two-centuries-old churches and homes, the flavor of the town really is colonial. A bell-towered Rice Museum dominates the center of town and features exhibits that track the antebellum history of the plantation heyday.

In recent years the little community has grappled with pollution problems stemming from wastewater discharge from International Paper and a steel mill that have long replaced the shipping, slaving and rice industries. Still, there is enough flavor left of the old colonial town and enough old-style bed and breakfast residences that the visitor seeking to step back in time will find a paradise in Georgetown.

Getting Here, Getting Around

A vacation in Myrtle Beach is wonderful. It can calm even the most tense soul. So while you're sitting in traffic with the kids squabbling in the back seat, just remind yourself how nice your vacation is going to be.

Close your eyes and think about those gorgeous beaches with the sun shimmering on the water; feel that cool salt air wafting across your face; and imagine yourself floating over the crisp clear waves. Now say to yourself every five or 10 minutes, "It really is worth it." Because it is.

Most likely, the only distasteful part of your trip will be getting here and, possibly, getting around in places once you're here. Don't fret—this chapter should help.

Getting Here . . .

By Automobile

The popularity of the Grand Strand has soared, with an estimated 13 million visitors pouring in every year. The problem is that Horry County's roads just haven't kept up with the Grand Strand's popularity. But take it from those of us who have lived here for years: It's easy to avoid traffic snarls if you travel at the right times of day and night. Plan your trip so that you will be driving U.S. Highway 501 into Myrtle Beach before 7 AM or after 7 PM Monday through Thursday. Another rule of thumb is to stay off beach exit roads right after hotel checkout time on Saturdays and Sundays. You will be much better off to check out of your room, put the bags in the car and hang around town until late afternoon. That way, you can also get in one extra afternoon on the beach, which is far more pleasant than bumper-to-bumper driving.

If you're coming to the Grand Strand from eastern North Carolina, you might want to try Interstate 40 east or U.S. Highway 17 south to Wilmington, North Carolina. At Wilmington, head southbound on U.S. 17. You should expect traffic to be moving pretty slowly along that stretch, unless you heed our previous advice and travel it early morning or late evening.

From Charleston, take U.S. 17 north. It could be crowded at peak traffic times.

If you're traveling north on Interstate 95, take Exit 170 (clearly marked "Myrtle Beach"), near Florence. Take U.S. Highway 76 to U.S. 501 and follow it the rest of the way. Vacationers heading to North Strand beaches—Little River, Crescent Beach, Ocean Drive, Atlantic Beach and Windy Hill—should veer to the left at Marion, cross two lanes of U.S. 501 and continue on U.S. 76. At Nichols, take a right onto S.C. Highway 9.

If you're traveling Interstate 20, follow the signs toward Florence. The road will merge into I-95 north and bypass Florence. Then take Exit 170, same as if you'd come the whole way on I-95.

If you're traveling south on I-95, take Exit 193 at Dillon. Head toward Latta, then take U.S. 501. If you're going to North Myrtle Beach, you can take S.C. 9 all the way from Dillon.

If you're going to the South Strand, you might want to take S.C. Highway 544. You'll turn to the right off U.S. 501 about 4 or 5 miles out of Conway. Note that S.C. 544 is a two-lane road; it's curvy, dangerous and frequently slowed by campers headed to the South Strand. The good news is that the new stationary bridge over the waterway is complete (it's now a straight overpass drive), so there's no more waiting for boats to pass through. You have the option of taking S.C. 544 or continuing on U.S. 501 and then connecting with U.S. 17 Bypass at the overpass about 10 miles out of Conway, just after the bridge at the Waccamaw Pottery complex. U.S. 501 and the U.S. 17 Bypass are much easier roads to travel than S.C. 544, but they'll add a few miles to your trip, and traffic is usually bad between 7 AM to 7 PM or when it's raining. It's a toss-up. The route you pick will probably depend on what kind of road you prefer.

From Conway, most people will take U.S. 501. You'll find it most frustrating on Saturdays between about 11 AM and 3 PM.

The first segment of the new Conway Bypass opened in the summer of 1999. This section connects S.C. Hwy. 90, just east of Conway, with U.S. 17 near Briarcliff Acres and makes visitors access to North Myrtle Beach easier when coming from the west.

When completed, the Conway Bypass will be a 28-mile stretch of highway connecting U.S. 17 near Briarcliffe Acres to U.S. 501 between Conway and Aynor. By 2018, the S.C. Department of Transportation estimates between 60,000 and 67,000 vehicles will travel the route daily. The highway's second segment, from S.C. 90 to S.C. 905, is scheduled to open between January and March of 2001. The third segment, connecting S.C. 905 to S.C. 701, is scheduled for a midsummer completion in 2001. The last bit, scheduled for December 2002, will connect to U.S. 501.

Coming South Via I-77?

Coming to the Grand Strand via Interstate 77 from western North Carolina, West Virginia, Ohio, western Pennsylvania, Michigan and, possibly, Canada can be a trying time. We've consulted a couple of travel-service offices for their best directions; but, when we tried those routes, we wound up spending a lot of time sitting in traffic. So, here's a favored route of some transplanted Northerners who call Myrtle Beach home: Travel I-77 S. through Charlotte, North Carolina, to Rock Hill, South Carolina. Just past Rock Hill, take Exit 77 onto U.S. Highway 21 S. Stay on U.S. 21 for about 5 miles and exit east onto S.C. Highway 5. Stay on S.C. 5 for about 5 miles until you reach U.S. Highway 521. Head south on U.S. 521 to Lancaster. Outside of Lancaster, take S.C. Highway 9 for about 3 miles to S.C. Highway 903. Take S.C. 903 east for about 20 miles to S.C. Highway 151 and turn right. Stay on S.C. 151 for about 40 miles to Darlington. Just outside of Darlington, take U.S. Highway 52 toward Florence until it junctions with I-95. Take I-95 north and follow the instructions included in this chapter (see previous section) from that point.

It sounds confusing, we know, but pull out your map and highlight the route in advance. Even though the roads look like two-laners on most maps, you actually will travel four-laners most of the way, with the exception of the 60-mile or so stretch between Lancaster and McBee, South Carolina. Following these directions, it should take about 3½ hours to get from Charlotte to Myrtle Beach. If you don't want to bother with the back roads, we understand. If you prefer interstate highways, stay on I-77 to Columbia, South Carolina, then take I-20 to Florence and follow the directions included in this chapter from that point. The advantage is traveling all interstates, but it might take a little longer.

Some relief possibly is in sight: West Virginia is building its first segment of what will be Interstate 73. This $31 million addition to the state's interstate system will run from Detroit to Charleston, South Carolina, and is expected to become a major thoroughfare for northern tourists traveling to the Grand Strand. But, don't escalate your hopes just yet, the South Carolina portion isn't slated for construction for another 20 years and other obstacles have recently come up. While West Virginia is busy with its portion of the highway, other states are still debating its route. Ohio is currently conducting impact studies. Conservationists are up in arms in South Carolina since the proposed route would cut a swath through the Francis Marion National Forest, and other sections infringe on historic sites and natural wetlands. In fact, at a public hearing held in Georgetown in November 1997, opponents were strong in attendance,

The Conway Bypass is one example of the many improvements being made to the area's system of roadways.

Photo: Courtesy of Fluor Daniel, Conway Bypass Project

holding up stickers that proclaimed "No 73." Besides overcoming public objection, the state of South Carolina will have to cough up about $6 billion for its end of this interstate deal.

By Plane

In addition to services offered at the Myrtle Beach International Airport and the Grand Strand Airport (listed subsequently), private planes and corporate jets can access the Conway-Horry County Airport, off U.S. Highway 378, outside Conway, (843) 397-9111. The airport is home of the North American Institute of Aviation, an international pilot training school. Overnight tie down is $2.50. (See our Child Care and Education chapter for more information.)

Myrtle Beach International Airport
Between U.S. Hwy. 17 Bus. and
U.S. Hwy. 17 Bypass, Myrtle Beach
• (843) 448-1589

An $18-million renovation project put Myrtle Beach International Airport into the big-city league. The terminal grew from 50,000 square feet to 120,000, and an upper-level concourse was added.

Rainy days no longer bring a polite attendant with an umbrella out to the planes to walk passengers into the terminal. Two jetways now connect the planes to the terminal, so passengers need never get wet nor cold. For additional information, you can link to Myrtle Beach International via a link at www.horrycounty.org.

Service to Myrtle Beach is offered by: US Airways, (800)428-4322; ASA, Comair and Delta, (800)282-3424; Continental Connection, a commuter carrier for Continential Airlines, (800)525-0280; Spirit Airlines, a non-stop carrier to Philadelphia, Detroit and New York City, (800)772-7117; Jet Express, (800)FUN 2 SUN; Midway Connection, (800)446-4392; Midway/Corporate, (800)555-6565; and Vanguard, which flies direct to Atlanta twice each day (800)826-4827. (Jet Express can get you to the Strand in a jiffy from Newark (N.J.) International LaGuardia, Detroit's Metro and Cleveland's Hopkins airports.)

For private or charter aircraft, Myrtle Beach Aviation, the general fixed base operator at Myrtle Beach International Airport, can be reached at (843)477-1860.

You should be able to get to Myrtle Beach by air from just about anywhere in the United States. Unless you can book an express flight, you'll have to take a smaller commuter flight, probably from a major air terminal in Charlotte, North Carolina, or Atlanta.

Grand Strand Airport
33rd Ave. S. and Terminal Ave., North Myrtle Beach
• **(843) 272-5337**

Horry County operates the Grand Strand Airport, where private aircraft and corporate jets can land. It's open 24 hours a day. You don't have to notify anyone that you're coming, but be aware that all services close for business at 10 PM.

You can leave your craft for several days while you enjoy the beach. The airport is about one block west of U.S. 17, pretty much in the heart of North Myrtle Beach.

The fixed-base operators at Grand Strand Airport is Ramp 66 which can be reached via telephone at (843) 272-5337 or (800) 433-8918 or via e-mail at ramp66@aol.com. Overnight tie-down is $5 per night. Fuel is also available.

If Ramp 66 staffers have time, and your accommodations aren't too far away, they will take you to your motel.

Ramp 66 also has its own car rental service, featuring all new cars. Customers can use a car for an hour for free. After that, it's $8 per hour. It also has weekly rates. If you're coming into the airport at odd hours, you need to take care of your car rental ahead of time. Ramp 66 is at your service seven days a week, 24 hours a day.

Loris-Twin Cities Airport
U.S. Hwy. 301

This is a public and unattended airport for training and landings for private aircraft.

Rental Cars

Eight companies including National, (800)227-7368; Avis, (800)331-1212; Hertz, (800)654-3131; Budget, (800)527-0700; Payless, (800)729-5377; Dollar, (800)800-4000; and USave at (800)441-3741, rent cars and vans at Myrtle Beach International. Other rental car offices in the Myrtle Beach area include Alamo, (800)327-9633 or (843)626-8166; Thrifty, (843)626-6527; Rent-A-Wreck, (843)626-9393; CarTemps USA, (843)444-0044 and Zippy Car Rental, (843)448-1991. Coastal Cabs can take you to your hotel and provide a van by request; inquire at the Executive Coach Service booth.

By Bus

You should be able to get to Myrtle Beach on a Greyhound bus from just about any point in the United States. You'll find it easier during the summer when more buses are scheduled. The station, Oak Street and Seventh Avenue N., Myrtle Beach, is open from 8 AM to 1 PM and 3 to 7 PM. Call (843) 448-2471 or (800) 231-2222 for details.

By Train

Don't count on riding the train to your Grand Strand vacation destination; Florence and Dillon are the two closest places Amtrak serves. The problem is you can't get to the Grand Strand from either of those cities unless you arrange for a vehicle or have friends who'll pick you up. If you decide to take the train to Florence or Dillon and then rent a car, there are two outlets that, with advance notice, can arrange for a vehicle to be at the station when you arrive. In Florence, contact Carolina Car Rentals, (843) 665-0802; in Dillon, call Dillon Used Auto Parts Inc., (843) 774-5301.

Some folks used to ride Amtrak to Florence and catch the Greyhound bus to Myrtle Beach. However, bus service from Florence to Myrtle Beach was discontinued because not enough people used it.

Greyhound officials say it is possible that the Florence to Myrtle Beach bus will be put back into action during the tourist season, but don't count on it. They recommend calling ahead before you buy your train ticket.

By Boat

The most scenic and perhaps most peaceful way to get to the Grand Strand is by boat. The Intracoastal Waterway generally parallels the Atlantic Ocean for 1,200 miles from Boston to Key West, Florida.

In 1932, the Army Corps of Engineers dug a 20-mile canal, connecting Little River to the Waccamaw River. This portion goes right through the Grand Strand.

Boaters can tie up at Barefoot Landing for a day of shopping and dining and an evening of country music at the Alabama Theatre. There are numerous marinas along the waterway and the Waccamaw River where boaters can spend the night, eat in a nice restaurant, buy groceries or have their motors tuned up.

Many of the marinas have signs along the waterway telling you what CB radio channel to tune in to contact them.

Marinas along the Grand Strand include Hague Marina, just before Socastee, (843) 293-2141; Bucksport, a very popular docking spot, (843) 397-5566; Wacca Wache at Wachesaw Landing, (843) 651-2994 or (843) 651-7171; and Cedar Landing, in the Murrells Inlet area, (843) 651-5805. (See our Boating chapter for details about marinas.)

There is a city-owned marina in Conway, (843) 248-1711, on the Waccamaw River. If you're traveling south on the waterway, turn right at Enterprise Landing at Channel Marker 25. Then head north for about 9 miles. Some boaters choose this course to enjoy the river's beauty. It winds and has some sharp turns, so if your boat's length is 40 feet or more, you might not want to try it.

To navigate the waterway, it's a good idea to have a nautical chart. Such charts point out dangerous spots, marinas and buoys and describe available services at the marinas.

You won't find the waterway as crowded as U.S. Highway 501, but it is a popular artery for travelers, recreational boaters and water skiers. Water routes can get crowded on weekends—especially the Waccamaw River.

The stretch between Conway and Bucksport is especially charming—a wonderful place to get back in touch with nature. Egrets build nests on the channel markers, and beautiful old trees overhang the water. If you're fortunate enough to travel at night, the moon glistens on the water on clear nights, and you can spot campfires back in the woods. At times, campers come to the river bank and shout hearty hellos to the boaters.

Getting Around . . .

Navigating the Strand Like a Local

Trying to navigate the Grand Strand can be a frustrating venture at first because there seem to be so many names for the same routes. You'll hear "17 Bypass," "Kings Highway," "the Boulevard" and a host of others. We're going to try to make sense of all this for you.

The first thing to remember is that all main arteries along the Grand Strand parallel the Atlantic Ocean. Closest to the beach is Ocean Boulevard (a.k.a. the Boulevard or the 'Vard). Ocean Boulevard officially runs from Garden City Beach northward, breaks for 5 to 7 miles of private land and state park and ends at Dunes Golf and Beach Club, 9000 Ocean Boulevard. It picks up again at 48th Avenue S., at Windy Hill beach, and continues northward to Cherry Grove beach.

Westward from Ocean Boulevard, the next main roadway is Kings Highway—commonly referred to as U.S. 17 or Business 17 (in Myrtle Beach). Kings Highway is the proper name for this road in Myrtle Beach. To make a mental note, just remember that Kings Highway is also called "Business 17" because shops, restaurants and attractions galore line both sides of this main artery. Kings Highway (U.S. 17) stretches the length of the Strand to Georgetown, then southward all the way through South Carolina. (Ed. note: For our purposes, we only use Kings Highway to refer to U.S. 17 Business in Myrtle Beach; otherwise, we defer to U.S. 17.)

Still moving west, you'll come across the racing traffic of U.S. 17 Bypass or Alternate 17. True to its name, this highway's purpose is to bypass traffic from Kings Highway. The Bypass reaches from Murrells Inlet northward until it merges with Kings Highway at Dixie Stampede just south of the Restaurant Row district. Once you've merged here, the road becomes U.S. 17.

If you really want to skip through town like a true native—anywhere from the Myrtle Beach International Airport to 48th Avenue N., in Myrtle Beach—here's how:

Leaving the Myrtle Beach International Airport, take the first right turn onto S. Broadway (road signs read S.C. 15). As you proceed, S. Broadway will turn into W. Broadway at the stoplights. Keep in the center lanes that allow you to travel straight through this original downtown section of Myrtle Beach until you reach the third set of stoplights; then get in the left-turn lane. Turning left will put you on Oak Street; you'll wind through town to 38th Avenue N. Go straight through the 38th Avenue stoplights onto Pine Lakes Drive and pass through a lovely old residential section of Myrtle Beach all the way to 48th Avenue N.

INSIDERS' TIP

If you're traveling with your dog, your furry companion must be kept on a leash. In North Myrtle Beach the only beach access restrictions for pets are during the summer days, from 9 AM to 5 PM. In Myrtle Beach and Surfside, sections are out of bounds for four-footed friends year round.

Getting around in Myrtle Beach is easier thanks to the widening of 21st Avenue N. between Kings Highway and U.S. 17 Bypass. Another project widened Oak Street to five lanes—four travel lanes and a turn lane—from 21st Avenue N. at the Myrtle Beach Convention Center to 29th Avenue N. From 29th Avenue N. to 38th Avenue N., the road was widened to three lanes—two travel lanes and a turn lane. The project also included the addition of curbs, gutters and sidewalks.

Several years ago, the state pledged more than half a million dollars for road construction in Horry County. Portions of the Conway Bypass are already open the following projects are slated for the near future:

• completing the Conway Bypass;
• constructing a Carolina Bays Parkway that will add four lanes from S.C. 9 to a bridge across the Intracoastal Waterway near 62nd Avenue N.;
• constructing a Conway Perimeter Road between U.S. 378 and U.S. 501;
• completing a cloverleaf bypass from U.S. 501 to U.S. 17 Bypass;
• converting S.C. 544 to five lanes from Socastee to Conway;
• installing intersection improvements on U.S. 501, S.C. 90 and Secondary roads 31 and 66;
• adding frontage roads from Forestbrook Road to the Intracoastal Waterway; and
• completing Central Parkway and an overpass above U.S. 501 at Waccamaw Pottery.

Taxis

For easy, accessible travel it's always best to have an automobile when exploring the Grand Strand. Let's face it, to cover 60 miles of territory, any other mode of transportation will take considerable time. But there's nothing more expedient than a cab to simply get from point A to point B in good time. We warn you that taxi fares are not cheap around here. To give you an idea of the usual cost, a trip from Myrtle Beach International Airport to a Myrtle Beach destination around 21st Avenue N. costs approximately $10 to $15. Try any of the following companies for service: Carolina Cab, (843)448-9999; City Cab, (843)448-5555; Coastal Cab, (843)448-4444; Southern Flyer Taxi, (843)361-2464 or Yellow Cab (843)448-3181.

Public Transit

Once you're in Myrtle Beach, you might want to walk or ride the Coastal Rapid Public Transit Authority (CRPTA) bus whenever you can, (843) 626-9138. As of October 1996, CRPTA established a three-year franchise with Myrtle Beach to cruise the city. In years past, CRPTA has run buses along five routes as outlined below. However, try as we may, we could not get CRPTA representatives to confirm or deny their current routes. Call (843) 626-9138 for updated information about routes and times.

Route 1 runs between Myrtle Square Mall and U.S. 501 in southern neighborhoods, with service scheduled every 40 minutes between 9 AM to 6:40 PM Monday through Saturday from the day after Labor Day through Memorial Day. From Memorial Day through Labor Day it runs from 7:30 AM to 10:15 PM.

Route 2 is scheduled to run from Myrtle Square Mall north to Pinewood Road, serving the northwestern neighborhoods. This trolley runs every 30 minutes between 9 AM and 10 PM Monday through Friday.

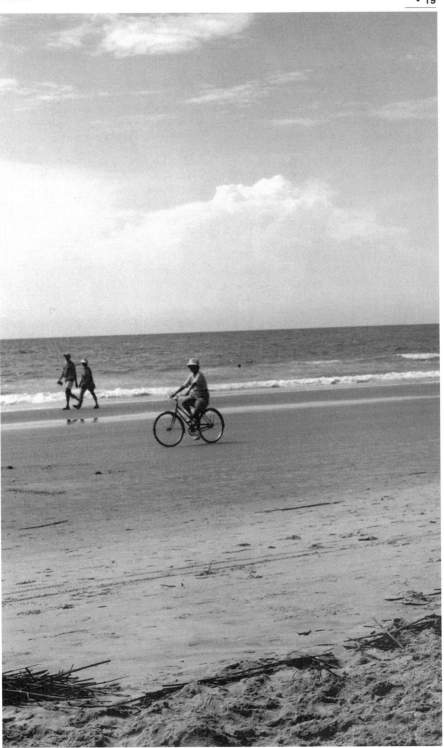

When the tide is low, rent a bike and enjoy a cruise down the sun-scrubbed shoreline.

Photo: Courtesy of Lowcountry Companion

Route 3 ranges from Myrtle Square Mall east to Kings Highway, west to Seaboard Commons and back to the mall along 10th Avenue N. and Oak Street. It runs every 30 minutes from 10 AM to 9 PM daily.

Route 4 involves a trolley at Broadway At The Beach that runs the circumference of Celebrity Circle. It's free to riders and runs every 15 minutes from 10 AM to 9 PM, every day of the week.

Route 5 takes passengers from U.S. 17 Business and 29th Avenue S., east and north to 17th Avenue N. at U.S. 17 Business.

Depending on destination, riders on routes 1 through 3 and 5 pay between $1.10 and $2.10 each; transfers from one route to another are included. If you stand out near the road and wave, the bus driver will stop and pick you up.

Another option is to catch a ride with the Great American Trolley Company, (843) 236-0337, from March 1 to October 1. These San Francisco-style, open-air vehicles trundle along Ocean Boulevard from 29th Avenue S. to 79th Avenue N. as the regular route, but they also offer a variety of packages to accommodate groups and school classes.

The South Ocean Boulevard Route rides from 29th Avenue S. to Myrtle Square Mall and Broadway At The Beach. Daily service starts at 8:30 AM and trolleys run every 30 minutes; evening cars operate until midnight and run every 20 minutes. Drivers will stop on any corner to pick up passengers en route. Fares are $1.50 per person (adult or child), one-way. Transfers are $1 and babes in arms ride free.

A North Ocean Boulevard Route starts at 79th Avenue N. and moves along to Myrtle Square Mall and Broadway At The Beach. This route runs daily from 8:30 AM to 4 PM, every 30 minutes. The same fares and pick-up procedures apply as with the South-end travel.

Specialty trips on the trolley cars can be reserved at any time of the year, including entertainment packages, shopping sprees, field trips and even passage to destinations like Charleston and Wilmington, North Carolina. Prices depend on the size of a group and specifications.

History

LOOK FOR:
• 20th Century
  Myrtle Beach
• Vacation Time

Even though the name Myrtle Beach has been around for less than 100 years, people have been enjoying the Grand Strand area for a few centuries, from the original Native American inhabitants to visiting dignitaries such as George Washington, to today's vacationers. Despite all the new development that obscures much of this history, you could say we're keeping up a historic seaside tradition by maintaining the Grand Strand as one of the East Coast's favorite getaways.

Long before Europeans landed on these shores, what is now U.S. Highway 17 and the section of it known as Kings Highway, began as an Indian trail. It then evolved into a stagecoach route from Northern colonies (eventually states) to Charleston and Savannah. After his election, George Washington used the route and lodgings along the way (for more details about his journey, see the Close-up in this chapter). The Waccamaw and Winyah Indians were the area's first inhabitants and now lend their names to the rivers and bays here. The Indians called this land *Chicora*, which means the Land. The Horry County Museum in Conway (see the Attractions chapter for more details) has exhibits detailing their way of life. Additionally, an Indian burial mound is on Waites Island near Little River, and the remains of an Indian village have been excavated near Murrells Inlet.

As early as the 1520s, Europeans were attempting to settle this area, but it wasn't until the 1700s that things got exciting. Even before the American Revolution, pirates made good use of the bays and inlets of the Grand Strand. To this day locals relish stories about Blackbeard marauding local shippers and rumors that Captain Kidd buried treasure somewhere around Murrells Inlet. Edgar Allen Poe's novella *The Gold Bug* is a fantastic account of good old South Carolinian treasure hunting.

Georgetown is the state's third oldest city. The city was planned by

Bikers and shaggers and classic cars have been crowding the Ocean Drive section of North Myrtle Beach in the spring for over 50 years.

Photo: Lisa Tomer Rentz

English colonists in 1730 and quickly became the center of America's colonial rice empire. *A Woman Rice Planter* is a fascinating personal account by Elizabeth Allston Pringle of her struggles to maintain her rice plantation after the Civil War ended and changed the plantation system irrevocably. The colonial spirit of Georgetown is preserved in many still-standing plantations; Hopsewee Plantation is the birthplace of Thomas Lynch Jr., a signer of the Declaration of Independence.

Pawleys Island, just north of Georgetown, is the original vacation spot for this area and one of the first resorts in the United States. A half-mile wide and 4-miles long, the island is abundant with oleander and oak trees pressed in between the old summer cottages. Pringle wrote of Pawleys Island, "To me it has always been intoxicating, that first view each year of the waves rolling, rolling, and the smell of the sea, and the brilliant blue expanse."

Also in the south end of the Grand Strand, Murrells Inlet is the oldest fishing village in the state. It is home to anglers, writers, poets and more legends and ghost stories than any other part of

Alice's resting place is well tended.

Photo: Lisa Tomer Rentz

the Grand Strand. The area's history, much like a Southern romantic novel, recounts stories of pirates patrolling the seaside, aristocratic plantation owners accumulating immense wealth, the daughter of a U.S. vice president being forced to walk the plank of a pirate ship, phantom lighthouses steering ships from storms and cemetery-walking ghosts searching for centuries-missing lovers. The Spanish moss laden oak trees do nothing but encourage these stories.

The story of Alice Belin Flagg is probably the most romantically tragic. Alice was caught in the traditional dilemma of the upper-class belle in love with a beau her family did not approve of. Her beau presented her with an engagement ring, but since she couldn't wear it on her finger, she wore it on a ribbon around her neck where it was eventually discovered by her brother, who ripped it off and threw it into the creek on their plantation. Of course, Alice pined away for the ring of her forbidden beau and died for want of true love. She now rests at All Saints Church in Pawleys Island under a simple marble slab—marked only by her first name. The local superstition is that if you walk around her grave 13 times backwards, you will evoke her spirit. Many people claim to have felt tugs on their own rings.

Until the 1900s the beaches north of Murrells Inlet were practically uninhabited because of geographical inaccessibility and the poor economy. In what is now Restaurant Row at the north end of Myrtle Beach, a salt making operation with more than 30 buildings was destroyed during

George Washington Tours the Grand Strand

Just as millions of people do every year now, George Washington toured the Grand Strand in 1791. Two years after he was elected president, George Washington wanted to visit the new states "to become better acquainted with their principal characters and internal circumstances as well as to be more accessible to numbers of well-informed persons who might give useful information and advice on political subjects." He also wished "to acquire knowledge of the face of the country, the growth and agriculture thereof; and the temper and disposition of the inhabitants toward the new government."

As you read Washington's comments, note that many of the family names he mentions are still in use today: Mrs. Horry (Horry County), Vereen (Vereen Marina and Vereen Park), Pawley (Pawleys Island). Also, we've preserved the president's spelling for historical flavor.

Washington followed the same road we take almost every day; in fact, the section of U.S. Highway 17 that runs through Myrtle Beach is known as Kings Highway in his honor (the former colonists weren't quite comfortable with the new title of president). While he toured the coast, he saw the condition of the people at all levels of society, staying at public houses when possible and paying for his accommodations when allowed. When William Washington of South Carolina offered him use of a Charleston townhouse, President Washington declined. "I cannot," he wrote, "without involving myself in inconsistency; as I have determined to pursue the same plan in my Southern as I did in my Eastern visit, which was not to incommode any private family by taking up my quarters with them during my journey. It leaves me unencumbered by engagements, and by uniform adherence to it, I shall avoid giving umbrage to any, by declining all such invitations."

Even though it's the same road, the Carolina coast was much different for Washington: "... the country from Wilmington through which the road passes ... is pine barrens with very few inhabitants ... a perfect sameness seems to run through all the rest of the Country. On [the rivers] especially the swamps and low lands on the rivers, the soil is very rich; and productive when reclaimed. ... " Obviously, this president did not need to travel with a motorcade.

His accommodations were equally as rural. "Excepting the Towns (and some Gentlemens Seats along the Road from Charleston to Savanna) there is not with in view of the whole road I travelled from Petersburgh to this place, a single house which has anythh. [sic.] of an elegant appearance- They are altogether of Wood and chiefly of logs- some indd. [sic.] have brick chimneys but generally the chimneys are of split sticks filled with dirt. ... The accommodations on the whole Road (except in the Towns and even there, as I was prepared for I had no opportunity of Judging, lodgings having been provided for me in them at my own expence) we found extremely indifferent the houses being small and badly provided either for man or horse; though extra exertions when it became known I was coming, wch. was generally the case, were made to receive me."

Washington found his constituents to be prospering. "The people however appear to have abundant means to live well the grounds where they are settled yielding grain in abundance and the natural herbage a multitude of mean with little

(Continued on next page)

HISTORY

or no labr. to provide food for the support of their stock. . . . The manner of the people, as far as my observations, and means of information extended, were orderly and Civil. and they appeared to be happy, contented and satisfied with the genl. [sic.] government under which they were placed."

Washington's first stop in South Carolina was at James Cochran's house, which stood in what is now the town of Little River near the intersection of Minneola Avenue and U.S. 17. Of course, most of the places where Washington stopped at are now gone, but a few in the South Strand do remain—keep reading to find out where.

"April 27 . . . lodged at Mr. Vareens 14 miles more and two miles short of the long bay. To his house we were directed as a Tavern, but the proprietor of it either did not keep one, or would not acknowledge it. We were therefore entertained (& very kindly) without being able to make compensation."

The house of Jeremiah Vereen Sr. stood near the intersection of what is now U.S. 17 and Lake Arrowhead Road in Restaurant Row. The Vereens kept a public house for many years—possibly the progenitor of all the restaurants to follow?

"April 28, Mr. Vareen piloted us across the Swash (which at high water is impassable, & at times, by the shifting of the Sands is dangerous) onto the long Beach of the Ocean; and it being at a proper time of the tide we passed along it with ease and celerity to the place of quitting it which is estimated at 16 miles. . . . "

This swash referred to by Washington is probably Singleton's Swash, which enters the ocean just north of Myrtle Beach at the Dunes Golf and Beach Club.

"April 28 ... Five Miles farther we got dinner & fed our horses at a Mr. Pauleys a private house, no public one being on the road. . . . "

Five miles past Singleton's Swash, Washington stopped at George Pawley's house. Pawley was also a government official; he had been in the First and Second Provincial Congresses (1775, 1775-76) and in the First General Assembly (1776). He served as justice of the peace in 1765 and 1774 and as a colonel in the militia around 1775.

"April 28 . . . being on the Road, & kindly invited by a Doctor Flagg to his house, we lodged there; it being about 10 miles from Pauleys & 33 from Vareens."

Dr. Henry Collins Flagg (1746-1801) married Rachel Moore Allston, the widow of William Allston of Brookgreen Plantation on Waccamaw Neck, in 1784. The site of the house in which Washington stayed is now occupied by the Alligator Pool fountain at Brookgreen Gardens.

"April 29 . . . We left Dr. Flagg's about 6 oclock and arrived at Captn. Wm. Alstons' on the Waggamaw [sic.] to Breakfast."

Clifton Plantation, the home of William Alston (1756-1839), stood on the banks of the Waccamaw River on Waccamaw Neck. He and his new wife, Mary Motte, entertained Washington for breakfast at Clifton Plantation.

Now part of Arcadia Plantation, Clifton then "looked like fairyland" to Washington. "His house which is large, new, and elegantly furnished, stands

George Washington traveled to the people to better understand those he lead.

on a sand hill, high for the Country, with his Rice fields below; the contrast of which with the lands back of it . . . is scarcely to be conceived."

"April 30 . . . Crossed the Waggamaw to Georgetown by descending the River three miles. At this place we were recd. under a Salute of Cannon, & by a Company of Infantry handsomely uniformed. I dined with the Citizens in public and in the afternoon, was introduced to upwards of 50 ladies who had assembled (at a Tea party) on the occasion." This is a party we would have loved to attended.

"Seven captains of vessels, dressed in round hats trimmed with gold lace, blue coats, white jackets . . . in an elegant painted boat" rowed George Washington across the river to Georgetown. Thirteen rounds of fire, one for each state of the Union, saluted his arrival, and he was escorted to his lodgings, reportedly the house of Benjamin Allston on Front Street. Locals now maintain that this is the same Adam-style brick house with a hipped roof that stands on a raised basement and faces the Sampit River at 1019 Front Street in Georgetown. First Federal Bank of Georgetown owns the house now, and the grounds are open to the public.

"May 1 . . . Left Georgetown about 6 Oclock, and crossing the Santee Creek [Sampit River] at the Town and the Santee River 12 miles from it . . . we breakfasted and dined at Mrs. Horry's about 15 Miles from Georgetown. . . . "

Another historic site you can visit, Hampton Plantation, was the home of Daniel Horry II. The original house was a 1½-story central-hall structure. After 1757 Daniel Horry enlarged the house to its present size, and the wide portico and pediment were added to the front of the house around 1790. Called Hampton by 1769, it was a working rice plantation. Harriott Pickney Horry and her mother, Eliza Lucas Pickney, greeted Washington in 1791 when he stopped at Hampton for breakfast. The ladies "were arrayed in sashes and bandeaux painted with the general's portrait and mottoes of welcome."

Hampton Plantation State Park is open to the public; see the Attractions chapter for more details.

From there Washington continued this inaugural journey to Charleston and Savannah. The South Carolina Department of Archives and History in Columbia has a more detailed record of this momentous journey; while you're in the Grand Strand, however, you can take the time to enjoy the same splendors of the coast that George Washington did.

the Civil War. The area later became the first campground in the area, mostly for people from Conway, and is still used as a campground today.

20th Century Myrtle Beach

The creation of Myrtle Beach as we know it began during the first part of the 20th century when F.A. Burroughs bought some timberland several miles inland from the South Carolina coast. In a story that rings with as much irony as buying Manhattan Island for beads and trinkets, the owners of the timberland would only agree to sell if Burroughs would agree also to buy the "worthless" coastal land as part of the same deal. So Burroughs was stuck with that property too. Confounded at the worthlessness of the area, called Long Bay, Burroughs sought to find a way to add value to the sandy strip.

Meanwhile, the towns of Cherry Grove and Windy Hill had been well-established. In an effort to find funding to develop the beach area into a resort to outclass Pawleys Island, Burroughs contacted a New York stockbroker named S.G. Chapin. To help with the effort, Burroughs's wife gave the area a more attractive name: Myrtle Beach, for the rows of myrtle trees growing along the coast line. Chapin was at first interested, but his wife was so adamant about not wanting to live in the wilderness that he was prepared to reject the idea outright. But after meeting, the two men became such good friends that they decided to go forward with the project. Thus in 1912 Myrtle Beach Farms Inc.—and the future of the Grand Strand—was born.

Although the area's first motel, Seaside Inn, was constructed in 1901 (under the direction of F.A.'s son, F.G. Burroughs), the rich and famous were not flocking to the beach. In fact, except for members of the Burroughs or Chapin extended families, there were very few visitors; Burroughs did convince some relatives to buy lots from him (at $25 each) to build resort cottages.

Following the Pawleys Island lead, the two entrepreneurs coaxed a wealthy textile magnate to build a resort playground hotel for the rich and famous. This 1925 venture, which included Myrtle Beach's first golf course, fizzled with the stock market crash of 1929. The result was the luxurious Ocean Forest Hotel, featuring chandeliers and an enormous ballroom in a classic high-rise (for the time) Old World hotel. The Ocean Forest ultimately was demolished in 1974.

The corporation continued to operate small hotels and cottages, rent and sell land and develop beachfront attractions until the 1954 destruction wrought by Hurricane Hazel, and the dream to attract the rich and famous went on a back shelf in favor of survival … a survival that was supported by becoming an inexpensive beach for working-class families.

Vacation Time

From 1954 through the 1980s, a rebuilt Myrtle Beach—with a new boardwalk and a new pavilion replacing the 1909 bath houses and 1912 amusements building—remained a small summer beach resort for a few hundred thousand blue-collar families from North and South Carolina. Myrtle Beach was a minor destination dotted with small mom-and-pop hotels, amusement parks and minor regional attractions. Myrtle Beach had indeed grown into a modest and pleasant resort.

Hurricane Hugo hit in 1989, but again the Grand Strand rebounded. Building and rebuilding has become more than a hobby around here, and in the '90s quite a few ambitious projects were undertaken. The number of golf courses has reached more than 100. Barefoot Landing, formerly Village of the Barefoot Traders, expanded over a scenic marsh and set the precedent for a new, natural Myrtle Beach as opposed to the harsh neon that glowed in the '80s. Broadway At The Beach opened in 1995 and successfully combines both glitzy and charming features for an all-day experience. This growth has anchored the Strand even more solidly as a major tourist destination and has been accompanied by many smaller and just-as-worthwhile establishments opening up throughout the Grand Strand area.

And now in 2000 more than 13 million visitors relax here annually. People still come to get away from their busy, landlocked lives just as generations before have. Though we now have all the modern conveniences (some days you just can't do without air conditioning) and distractions (using up a roll of quarters at the arcade can be so satisfying), we're still here for the same reason: those rolling, rolling waves.

Accommodations

Considering that the Grand Strand offers literally thousands of accommodations for visitors, we have tried to narrow the scope to those establishments that consistently get positive reviews from the public. That's not to say that all others are dank tenements, but the numbers are far too vast to bring all the players into this arena. Lodging is in such demand along the Grand Strand that new facilities are being built as fast as you can turn these pages, and smaller mom-and-pop hotels are abundant here. Some locals have quipped that the construction crane should be designated the official bird of the Grand Strand.

It's safe to say that 95 percent of the hotels, motels and condominiums on the Grand Strand line both sides of Ocean Boulevard, the road that parallels the Atlantic Ocean from North Myrtle Beach to Surfside Beach and becomes Waccamaw Drive in Garden City. Don't be confused if you're riding along, in awe of the hundreds of lodging marquees, and the road suddenly jogs west to U.S. Highway 17 Business. A couple of miles of private property separate North Myrtle Beach from Myrtle Beach, and you'll find several campgrounds between Myrtle Beach and the end of the South Strand.

LOOK FOR:
• A Room with a View
• About Pets . . .
• Regarding Reservations . . .
• Hotels and Motels
  - North Strand
  - Myrtle Beach
  - South Strand
  - Other Featured Accommodations
• RV and Camping Facilities
  - North Strand
  - Myrtle Beach
  - South Strand

A Room with a View

Properties closest to the beach are considered oceanfront. Properties with an oceanview refer to rooms that might have a view of the ocean but do not directly face it (on the side of the building) or, in some cases, rooms not on the east side of Ocean Boulevard. Rooms with a balcony or walkway are referred to as rooms with a sideview. You might also run across terms such as poolside or streetside that denote a room's location within the property. Be sure to ask specific questions about the location of your room when confirming your reservation.

About Pets . . .

Those of you who travel with your pets might find it difficult to rent a room.

The City of Myrtle Beach passed an ordinance that prohibits animals of any kind in the downtown area from March 1 through September 30. It seems there was a problem with folks bringing their pets and other exotic animals (boa constrictors, ferrets, iguanas) down to the heavily populated Pavilion area, causing quite a stir with other pedestrians. The law was passed to mitigate any potential accidents or incidents caused by the animals.

Regarding Reservations . . .

Like most resort areas, be prepared to make a deposit when calling in your reservation. It is required by the majority of properties and will be credited to your bill. Generally, a deposit equals a day's rent. To avoid hassles, use credit cards, cash or traveler's checks to pay for everything; most local banks will not cash out-of-town personal checks unless you

Price Code

The dollar-sign key used with each listing is based on the average room rate for two people (at least two double beds) per night in the middle of July, when hotel and motel rates are at their highest. This average rate was determined by taking into account all the types of lodging available at each property. Weekends and holidays always command a higher room rate.

$	$68 to $93
$$	$94 to $120
$$$	$121 to $145
$$$$	$146 to $171
$$$$$	$172 and up

have an account with them or enough picture identification to satisfy the FBI on a manhunt. Vital reservation information includes the time you plan to arrive, the number in your party, the length of your stay and the date you plan to depart.

Although rooms are plentiful, the Strand's population swells to almost four times its year-round size in the heat of summer, and all of these people need a place to lay their weary heads. Think twice about driving to the beach and "finding" a room, especially in the middle of the night. The tourism season blooms like the flowers each spring and peaks like the hot noonday sun each summer. As the autumn leaves fall, so do lodging rates; and in wintertime, snowbirds flock to the beach for cheap, cheap rates. In the 1960s and '70s, most businesses rolled up the sidewalk from Labor Day until Easter. That is a practice of the past. As the Grand Strand is quickly becoming a year-round resort, the majority of properties remain open throughout the year.

Hotels and Motels

These accommodations are listed according to location, beginning on the North Strand and ranging southward through Myrtle Beach and the South Strand. In accordance with the Americans With Disabilities Act, all of these properties should be handicapped-accessible; establishments must comply to stay in business. Keep in mind when making reservations that most accommodations offer at least a 10 percent discount if you're staying a week or longer. Most also offer senior citizen, travel club and group discounts as well. Always ask about any special rates or entitlements.

On any given evening, there are approximately 60,000 rooms available on the Grand Strand—ranging from hotels, motels and condos to timeshare units. But, even with so much capacity, there's apparently still room for more growth in the market. Annual occupancy rates are still on the rise and new accommodations continue to climb skyward.

Unless otherwise indicated, all accommodations listed in this chapter accept at least Visa and MasterCard as methods of payment. Inquire about alternative options when you make your reservation.

Please note that we have also indicated establishments that provide babysitters or referrals for such services.

Have a pleasant and comfortable stay.

North Strand

Blockade Runner Motor Inn
$ • 1910 N. Ocean Blvd.,
North Myrtle Beach
• (843) 249-3561

On the oceanfront in the popular Ocean Drive section of North Myrtle Beach, the Blockade Runner offers 72 two-bed units, including efficiencies, all overlooking the ocean. In addition to an oceanfront pool and kiddie pool, guests can also enjoy the Jacuzzi and a delicious meal in the on-premises restaurant. The restaurant is open from 6 AM to 2:30 PM every day. Golf specials are offered from Labor Day through June 1.

Buccaneer Motel
$ • 401 S. Ocean Blvd., North Myrtle Beach
• (843) 249-1466, (800) 548-7552

Ahoy mates, you've landed at the Buccaneer Motel, a very affordable place for families looking for one-room efficiencies or two-room apartments on the beach. If the ocean isn't for you, then splash around in the pool or in the hot tub. The Buccaneer has 37 rooms.

Colonial Inn
$$ • 1630 U.S. Hwy. 17, Little River
• (843) 249-9894

The Colonial Inn is a family owned and operated property with 12 rooms, and these folks take pride in adding their personal touch. Generations of families have been vacationing here and enjoying the year-round amenities such as swimming pools and king-size beds. If you're looking for an alternative to beach recreation, charter a boat at one of the nearby marinas or ask about the golf packages.

Helms Vista Family Motel and Apartments
$ • 300 N. Ocean Blvd.,
North Myrtle Beach
• (843) 249-2521, (800) 968-8986

This small, friendly looking oceanfront property offers 77 rooms, suites and apartments

From stem to stern, the Grand Strand abounds with accommodations to suit every taste and budget.

Photo: Courtesy of Litchfield Beach & Golf Resort

to guests looking for an affordable place to lay their heads. Each room has a refrigerator. Special package deals include golf, live entertainment, deep-sea fishing and dinner cruises. In addition to two kiddie pools, the motel has two regularly sized pools and a hot tub. The Helms Vista is within walking distance of North Myrtle Beach's finest restaurants and dance clubs.

Ocean Creek Plantation Resort & Conference Center
$$$$$ • 10600 N. Kings Hwy., North Myrtle Beach
• (843) 272-7724, (800) 845-0353

Ocean Creek Plantation is one of the grandest resorts along the beach. The luxurious accommodations (435 in all) include studios and one-, two- and three-bedroom condominiums in six separate complexes. The resort's oceanfront beach club features a large outdoor pool, sun decks and a poolside bar. In 1996 the resort's beach club added a kiddie pool, playground and volleyball court.

Guests can enjoy fine dining at the Four Seasons restaurant if they don't want to leave the property. Supervised activities for the kids are available in summer months, freeing parents for a little private vacation time. The resort also features seven on-site lighted tennis courts and extends guest privileges at a major-ity of area golf courses. Ocean Creek staff consider the finest details whether hosting a family of four or a conference for hundreds.

San-A-Bel Resort
$$$$ • 1709 S. Ocean Blvd., North Myrtle Beach
• (843) 272-2079, (800) 387-7714

San-A-Bel offers 97 two-bedroom, two-bath condominiums. Each unit has a full kitchen with microwave and dishwasher as well as a washer and dryer adjoining the kitchen area. The beautiful indoor heated pool features expansive skylights and glass walls for unobstructed views of the ocean. Outside, a large wooden sun deck surrounds the whirlpool—a relaxing haven after a workout in the fitness room.

Sea Trail Resort & Golf Links
$$$ • 211 Clubhouse Rd., Sunset Beach, N.C.
• (843) 272-2185, (800) 624-6601

Not many resorts in the coastal region can offer three golf courses in their backyards. Sea Trail offers this and much more. The resort, midway between Myrtle Beach and Wilmington, North Carolina, welcomes guests looking for exclusive living. You can rent any one of the 324 villas, either with one, two, three or four bedrooms. Each is complete with two

ACCOMMODATIONS

ACCOMMODATIONS

*Whether you stay in a cozy oceanside inn or a fancy downtown hotel,
you can always expect a hearty dose of Southern hospitality.*

Photo: Courtesy of Brandon Advertising

full bathrooms, a fully equipped kitchen, living and dining areas and a balcony overlooking the fairways.

Sea Trail is a perfect venue for biking, jogging and nature walks. The swim and tennis club—new and improved in 1997—provides swimming pools, a sauna, whirlpool spas, a fitness room and lighted tennis courts. A year-round activities director coordinates events for adults and children alike. Sea Trail keeps an updated list of reliable babysitters in the area, which the staff can refer you to.

Sea Trail can accommodate up to 700 guests in its meeting facilities. This off-the-beaten-path getaway spans more than 2,000 acres and offers two restaurants. Golf packages and an on-site golf school are also available.

The Seaside Inn
$$ • 2301 S. Ocean Blvd.,
North Myrtle Beach
• (843) 272-5166, (800) 433-5710

The Seaside Inn provides about 56 units; half are oceanfront. The rooms are clean and modest but provide all the comforts of home: microwaves, refrigerators, card tables and remote-control TVs. Some Seaside units have sleeper sofas as well. Golf packages are available, and there's a bonus for golfing group leaders. The group leader who brings 10 players gets free lodging; one who brings along 20 players also receives a free golf package. By the way, there are about 25 golf courses within a 15-minute drive. Other features include a pool and hot tub, both of which are covered for comfortable use during the cooler temperatures of winter. The Seaside Inn is close to Barefoot Landing and also offers show packages at various theaters throughout town.

Myrtle Beach

Anderson Inn
$ • 2600 N. Ocean Blvd., Myrtle Beach
• (843) 448-1535, (800) 437-7376

You'll enjoy a stay at the Anderson Inn, a family owned and operated property. On the oceanfront, it houses 112 units ranging from efficiency rooms to suites and singles. Rooms with fully equipped kitchens are available. The children will be amazed at the custom-built kiddie pool—the largest of its kind in the area. Other features include two more oceanfront pools, an indoor heated pool, an indoor Jacuzzi and an exercise room, too.

Anderson Inn is in the center of Myrtle Beach, close to grocery stores, malls, entertainment and restaurants. If you'd rather not venture out, don't worry: You won't go hungry with the Magnolia Cafe on the premises. The staff at the Anderson Inn also coordinates golf packages.

Atlantic Paradise Inn
$ • 1401 S. Ocean Blvd., Myrtle Beach
• (843) 444-0346, (800) 992-0269

Nothing fancy, but the 74 two-room apartments and efficiencies of Atlantic Paradise offer your family an affordable vacation at the beach. Amenities include an oceanfront pool with deck, kiddie pool and indoor whirlpool. Golf and country music packages are available.

Beach Colony Resort
$$$ • 5308 N. Ocean Blvd., Myrtle Beach
• (843) 449-4010, (800) 222-2141

This resort has everything you'll need for a great vacation. Beach Colony is home to 240 vacation units that include oceanfront suites, two-, three- and four-bedroom condominiums and ocean-view studios. Guests may dine in the restaurant or relax in the lounge. For water other than the ocean, the resort has a kiddie pool, two outdoor pools, an indoor pool and indoor and outdoor whirlpools for winding down. An exercise room, saunas and a racquetball center offer you options for working up a sweat. The Carolina Room at Beach Colony can accommodate up to 175 people for meeting or event purposes, and the Azalea Room can take in up to 50 guests. The resort also has a multilevel, covered parking garage.

In summer 1995 Beach Colony opened another tower that features 77 two-bedroom, oceanview condominiums. While they were at it, they added an outdoor Lazy River water ride and an arcade.

This resort is home to Fusco's, a wonderful Italian restaurant that serves one of the area's

INSIDERS' TIP
Before going out on the town, check with the front desk of your hotel or motel about free passes or discount coupons. For promotional purposes, many Grand Strand clubs and attractions supply accommodation properties with thousands of these to give to guests. There's no harm in asking!

only Sunday brunch buffets. The folks at Beach Colony can refer guests to reputable babysitters.

Breakers Resort Hotel & North Tower
$$$$ • 2700 N. Ocean Blvd., Myrtle Beach
• (843) 626-5000, (800) 845-0688

Staying at the Breakers has been a family tradition for generations; now the Breakers has an adjoining North Tower to accommodate even more vacationing families and golfers in brand-new two- and three-bedroom abodes. This property boasts more than 387 units based on more than 20 room plans. Typical rooms feature two beds facing the ocean, or you can choose from two- or three-room suites with fully equipped kitchens. Honeymoon, golf and family packages are house specialties. During the summer season, kids can take part in various planned activities while their parents enjoy oceanfront dining or drinks in the Top-of-the-Green Lounge. This resort also sports one indoor and three outdoor swimming pools.

Near downtown Myrtle Beach, the Breakers is accessible to numerous shops, restaurants and attractions. Ample parking is available, and that's hard to come by at most uptown places. Handicapped-accessible facilities are provided in the main tower only. The front desk can assist families with a babysitting referral service.

Cadillac Court
$$ • 2202 N. Ocean Blvd., Myrtle Beach
• (843) 448-5143, (800) 525-1371

Choose from an array of units at the Cadillac (82 in total), including one- and two-bedroom efficiencies, two-room suites and three- or four-bedroom apartments. A small cafe on the premises opens at 9 AM for breakfast and stays open until the last appetite of the night is satisfied. Amenities include an outdoor oceanfront pool, a kiddie pool and a rooftop pool and Jacuzzi. The exercise room is open to all guests, and a game of shuffleboard can be scared up across the street.

Captain's Quarters Resort
$$$ • 901 S. Ocean Blvd., Myrtle Beach
• (843) 448-1404, (800) 843-3561

Although the Captain's Quarters Resort has been around for many years, the management continues to keep up with the times by expanding and renovating the property when

INSIDERS' TIP

During the winter months, traffic on Ocean Boulevard is especially light, making it a pleasant option to Kings Highway.

needed. (Many of the newer hotels should look this good on their opening day!) There are 328 units: efficiency apartments, one-bedroom and two-room suites. The family can splash about in the large oceanfront outdoor pool, indoor pool or one of three whirlpools. The resort's recreation center features an extra-large arcade, so bring lots of quarters. The on-site Captain's Restaurant serves breakfast, lunch (until 1 PM) or dinner. Guests also have access to laundry facilities. Golf privileges are offered at more than 70 championship courses in the area, so pack your clubs. The staff of Captain's Quarters will happily refer families to trusted babysitters.

Caravelle Resort Hotel & Villas
$$$ • 6900 N. Ocean Blvd., Myrtle Beach
• (843) 918-8000, (800) 845-0893

To accommodate the ever-increasing demand for places to stay, the Caravelle added the Villas tower about six years ago. The main hotel offers about 100 units, and the tower has 56 efficiencies. The two-room oceanfront executive suites feature kitchens and queen-size beds. Efficiencies include full kitchens with microwaves and queen- or king-size beds. In June 1997 Caravelle opened a new tower with 170 oceanview deluxe suites and oceanfront rooms and efficiencies.

Amenities featured between both buildings include several pools, a game room, exercise room and restaurant. Adults and children love the Lazy River pool, where you grab an oversized inner tube and glide along the course of the ride. Now the complex has two kid-friendly Lazy Rivers and a kiddie pool. Golf and entertainment packages are available.

Carolina Winds
$$$ • 200 76th Ave. N., Myrtle Beach
• (843) 449-2477, (800) 523-4027

Carolina Winds is known for its fine condominiums and guest suites—145 units in all. This oceanfront property is away from the hustle and bustle of downtown and features everything you'll need for a luxurious visit. Guests can take a dip in the 120-foot-long oceanfront pool and wind down in the Lazy River. An on-site sauna is available for visitors. Jacuzzis and hot tubs are added attractions, as are golf packages. If guests require babysitting services, the staff has a list of referrals.

Chesterfield Inn & Motel
$$ • 700 N. Ocean Blvd., Myrtle Beach
• (843) 448-3177, (800) 392-3869

Just a block from the Myrtle Beach Pavilion, the venerable Chesterfield Inn has maintained a tradition that comes with being one of the oldest hotels along the beach. For more than 60 years, this property of vintage elegance has been family owned and operated. Guests have the option of including breakfast in the price of the room. The charming and inviting dining room yields a perfect view of the ocean. The 57 units feature various floor plans. Unfortunately, the Chesterfield Inn closes for a short time in winter, but plenty of repeat guests plan their vacations around the closing. Golf and entertainment packages are available. The Chesterfield staff is happy to help coordinate group events such as family reunions.

Compass Cove Ocean Resort
$$$ • 2311 S. Ocean Blvd., Myrtle Beach
• (843) 448-8373, (800) 228-9894

The Swamp Fox Ocean Resort is a spacious complex that overlooks the ocean. It features 377 units, seven indoor and outdoor pools, a Jacuzzi, sauna and a restaurant and lounge. An added bonus for the budget-conscious family: Children younger than 14 stay free with parents. Golf and entertainment packages are also available.

Coral Beach Resort
$$$$ • 1105 S. Ocean Blvd., Myrtle Beach
• (843) 448-8421, (800) 843-2684

With 301 units and plenty of amenities, Coral Beach is definitely one of the trendiest and largest resorts on the beach. Accommodations include standard rooms, efficiencies and two-room suites.

Coral Beach is one of the only resorts on the beach that houses an arcade complete with a bowling alley. Children are entertained with supervised activities offered from June through August. Other amenities include in-room safes, complete kitchens in all efficiencies and suites, a steam room, saunas and three whirlpools.

Did we say pools? How about two outdoor heated pools, kiddie pools, a Lazy River ride and a pool bar. In addition to a full-service restaurant, guests may enjoy cocktails and entertainment in MacDivot's Clubhouse lounge.

Most of the area's accommodations boast plenty of amenities for fun away from the ocean.

Photo: Courtesy of Brandon Advertising

ACCOMMODATIONS

Court Capri
$$ • 2610 N. Ocean Blvd., Myrtle Beach
• (843) 448-6119, (800) 533-1338

If for no other reason, we had to include this motel since it's the only one along the Grand Strand with a rooftop heart-shaped whirlpool and sun deck! Needless to say, Court Capri offers honeymoon packages. Rooms and one- or two-bedroom efficiencies can be booked as well as extensive golf packages. The Capri also offers guests an indoor pool, indoor whirlpool, Jacuzzi, kiddie pool, exercise facilities and a full-service restaurant.

Crown Reef Resort
$$$$ • 2913 S. Ocean Blvd., Myrtle Beach
• (843) 626-8077, (800) 405-7333

All 514 units in this beautiful motel are oceanfront, with balconies overlooking 125 feet of beach and the Atlantic. Efficiencies, rooms, deluxe suites and Jacuzzi suites are for let. The property offers 21 pools and whirlpools, convention facilities, a fitness center, a game room, 575 feet of Lazy River (the largest on the beach), Jacuzzis, hot tubs, three full-service restaurants and an express restaurant. During the summer lots of activities for kids—fitness walks, arts and crafts, face painting, seashell searches—keep the younger set busy so grown-ups can lounge by the pool or indulge in an afternoon nap. Entertainment packages can be booked from this resort.

Days Inn Grand Strand
$ • 806 S. Ocean Blvd., Myrtle Beach
• (843) 448-8261, (800) 448-8261

This modest property could be perfect for a family looking for bargains. Only 18 blocks to the Pavilion area, the Oasis rents 58 double rooms and efficiencies. It's across the street from the ocean and offers guests an outdoor pool, 27-channel televisions and a free continental breakfast.

Dayton House Best Western
$$$ • 2400 N. Ocean Blvd., Myrtle Beach
• (843) 448-2441, (800) 258-7963

For more than 30 years, the Thomas family has been rolling out the red carpet for families, senior citizens and vacationing couples. In the last six years, four new buildings have been added to the property—now offering 327 units, including 96 two-room oceanfront suites. Amenities include a large outdoor spa, an oceanfront lawn and sunning area, a Lazy River, indoor and outdoor pools and whirlpools, an exercise room and golf packages at over 90 courses.

Driftwood On The Oceanfront
$$ • 1600 N. Ocean Blvd., Myrtle Beach
• (843) 448-1544, (800) 942-3456

All of the 90 accommodations at Driftwood have refrigerators, microwave ovens and remote-control TVs, whether you're staying in a room or efficiency unit. Just six blocks from the downtown Pavilion area, this hotel offers an on-site game room, fitness room and two outdoor pools.

Firebird Motor Inn
$$ • 2007 S. Ocean Blvd., Myrtle Beach
• (843) 448-7032, (800) 852-7032

The Firebird Motor Inn specializes in two-bedroom apartments for families. Single rooms and efficiencies are also available on the oceanfront, poolside or along the sideview. Children will love the Lazy River, the video-game room and supervised summer activities. You can even fire up a grill in the cookout area.

Just south of the busy downtown area, the Firebird is still close to restaurants and attractions. Inquire about golf and entertainment packages.

Forest Dunes Resort
$$$ • 5511 N. Ocean Blvd., Myrtle Beach
• (843) 449-0864, (800) 845-7787

This resort, across the boulevard from the beach in the Cabana section, houses 134 oceanfront or oceanview units, which are one-bedroom and three-bedroom condominiums. Once you've unpacked, take advantage of the wide sandy beach in front of this resort, or float along the Lazy River. (The Lazy River is enclosed during the winter months, so it's always available to guests.) Other features include indoor and outdoor pools, a kiddie pool, whirlpool, exercise room, video game room and an independently leased bar and grill. Comforts of home include laundry facilities and spacious rooms. Golf and entertainment packages are available.

Four Seasons Beach Resort
$$ • 5801 N. Ocean Blvd., Myrtle Beach
• (843) 449-6441, (800) 277-7562

In the Cabana section, the Four Seasons Beach Resort offers 74 single and double rooms and fully equipped condominiums. Winter rates are outrageously low ($400 to $610 per month) for the caliber of accommodations and amenities offered here, it's an especially appealing lodging option for many senior citizens. The Four Seasons offers its guests exercise and steam rooms and an expansive outdoor pool.

Whether you're traveling for business or pleasure, solo or with a family, a wide variety of accommodations are easy to come by.

Photo: Courtesy of Brandon Advertising

The resort is just across the street from the beach and offers an unobstructed view of beachfront cabanas.

Grand Strand Motel
$$ • 1804 South Ocean Blvd., Myrtle Beach • (843) 448-1461, (800) 433-1461

The Grand Strand Motel is located across the boulevard from the ocean and is a property that mainly caters to families and couples. Grand Strand staff takes pride in the cleanliness and value of their property.

Ninety-six units are available, ranging from single rooms to one, two, three and four-bedroom efficiencies, on up to luxury penthouse suites. There's even a 3-bedroom, fully equipped cottage, which can be perfect lodging for an extended family vacation.

A large sundeck beckons guests to partake of the renowned Carolina sunshine—take a quick dive into the swimming pool for instant cool-offs. Just ask the front desk and they will be happy to arrange a scuba, golf or entertainment package for you. The Grand Strand Motel also offers its guests laundry facilities.

Hampton Inn
$$$ • 4709 N. Kings Hwy., Myrtle Beach • (843) 449-5231, (800) 833-1360

The Hampton Inn is a family-oriented hotel with 150 units where children stay free with parents. A couple of blocks from the ocean, the Hampton Inn is somewhat of a landmark around these parts and is a favorite of local seniors. Guests may start the day with a free continental breakfast, and then you're on your own to explore the area. This Hampton Inn also houses a huge indoor swimming pool and a fitness room.

Hampton Inn Northwood
$$$$ • 620 75th Ave. N., Myrtle Beach • (843) 497-0077, (800) 543-4286

This new addition to Myrtle Beach's Hampton Inn lineup opened in August 1995. Like its sister on N. Kings Highway, the Northwood is within walking distance of the beach and serves guests a complimentary deluxe continental breakfast. Among its 122 rooms are 21 two-room suites, four with Jacuzzis. Guests can enjoy a pool, exercise room and sauna here.

ACCOMMODATIONS

Holiday Inn Downtown Oceanfront
$$$$ • 415 S. Ocean Blvd., Myrtle Beach
• (843) 448-4481, (800) 845-0313

Located right in the middle of all the action, this oceanfront Holiday Inn hosts one of the liveliest, continuous pool-bar parties—it lasts all season long. There are 306 rooms, and all oceanfront units boast private balconies to watch either the poolside happenings or the ocean. Amenities include a second bar in the lobby, indoor and outdoor pools, a sauna, a Jacuzzi, a video game room, an exercise room, a full-service restaurant and a gift shop.

Fall of 1997 finally brought the completion of a yearlong, $5 million renovation of this property. All of the guest rooms were gutted, redesigned and given new carpet, paint, draperies and furniture. A larger lobby now sports its own bar—the very popular Port O'Call lounge.

Holiday Inn Express
$ • 9551 U.S. Hwy. 17
(Restaurant Row area), Myrtle Beach
• (843) 449-5348, (800) 222-5783

Holiday Inn Express was voted the Best Budget Hotel Chain by *Entrepreneur* magazine. Guests receive a free continental breakfast each morning. You'll find 85 rooms plus five Jacuzzi suites and an outdoor heated pool. Special packages include golf, entertainment, romance, Christmas and New Year's options. Room rates are considered low during peak season but are relatively high during the winter months, as the hotel aims for consistent pricing rather than extreme fluctuations from one season to another. This hotel is 1.5 miles from the beach.

Jonathan Harbour
$$ • 2611 S. Ocean Blvd., Myrtle Beach
• (843) 448-1948, (800) 448-1948

Two- and three-room efficiency units with fully equipped kitchens and laundry facilities are what you'll find here. Enjoy recreation or relaxation in the indoor or outdoor pool, one of two whirlpools, the kiddie pool, an exercise room, sauna or steam room. Guests have ample parking facilities across the street.

Kingston Plantation
$$$$$ • 9800 Lake Dr., Myrtle Beach
• (843) 449-0006, (800) EMBASSY

Kingston Plantation is a multimillion-dollar resort with more than 700 hotel rooms (in-cluding 255 oceanview suites), condominiums, townhomes and villas set in a richly designed atmosphere. The grounds span 145 oceanfront acres east of Restaurant Row. The resort features conference centers, several pool decks, a year-round bar and seasonal pool bar, on-premise restaurant and lush foliage. A visit here isn't complete if you don't take advantage of the $4 million Sport and Health Club that includes racquetball courts, aerobics classes, state-of-the-art tennis courts, cardiovascular and weight-training machines and massage services. With an on-site golf department, arranging a round is easy here.

A renovation project changed this former Raddison hotel into the Embassy Suites, so the 20-story property is now under new ownership. Art deco furnishings have redecorated all of the suites, and Caribbean accents have been added to the exterior. The price code listed for Kingston Plantation reflects Embassy Suites rates only. Other units are privately owned and rented separately.

This is more than a place to store your luggage; it's a vacation destination and group-meeting attraction—an exceptional choice as evidenced by two years of Gold Key Awards.

La Quinta Inn & Suites
$$ • 1561 21st Ave. N., Myrtle Beach
• (843) 916-8801, (800) 687-6667

If you're not particular about staying near the ocean, then you might try this brand-new, prototype La Quinta. The fresh design is one of the chain's first hotels to feature two-room suites and extended-stay facilities.

Across the street from Broadway at the Beach, this 128-room hotel treats guests to a continental breakfast every morning and accepts small pets. Amenities include an outdoor pool, exercise room, telephones with computer dataports, refrigerators, microwave ovens and coffee makers. Each room sports a 25-inch television and Super Nintendo games.

Landmark Resort Hotel
$$$ • 1501 S. Ocean Blvd., Myrtle Beach
• (843) 448-9441, (800) 845-0658

Everything you need for a great vacation is right here at this oceanfront property. This accommodation includes 327 single and double rooms as well as penthouse suites. In 1996 the

Landmark completed construction of a new tower of one-room suites, bringing the total room count to 570. This hotel is the only Grand Strand property to have a covered pedestrian bridge across Ocean Boulevard that links its accommodations with the parking lot across the road. Completed in 1997, the walkway cost an estimated $750,000, while the parking facility was part of a $40 million expansion.

Entertainment includes an English-style pub and dining in the Gazebo restaurant. Families can play in the video game room, relax in the sauna or splash about in the indoor pool complex that includes Jacuzzis. The Landmark also specializes in hosting group tours and conferences. Golf packages are available. As of summer 1997 The Landmark added two 300-foot Lazy Rivers and full laundry facilities.

Meridian Plaza Resort
$$$ • 2310 N. Ocean Blvd., Myrtle Beach
• (843) 626-4734, (800) 323-3011

The Meridian Plaza is a tall, sleek building that rents out 90 ultramodern one-bedroom suites, each of which has a fully equipped kitchen and two televisions. Parking in the downtown area is normally crowded; however, the Plaza provides spaces for its guests in the five-level garage. Amenities include indoor and outdoor pools and whirlpools, an exercise room and video arcade. Special golf packages are available from September through May.

Myrtle Beach Martinique Resort Hotel
$$$$$ • 7100 N. Ocean Blvd., Myrtle Beach
• (843) 449-4441, (800) 542-0048

The motif might be called "Come to the island, mon," but the beach is definitely Myrtle. All 204 units here face the ocean, and each has a private balcony with a view of the Grand Strand. All of the Martinique's rooms have been renovated and upgraded with new decor and furniture. Near the northern end of a Myrtle Beach residential section, the Martinique exudes a sense of exclusivity. The resort features an oceanfront swimming pool, sun-deck whirlpool, exercise room, oceanfront restaurant, lounge and a game room. You'll find another swimming pool and whirlpool indoors. Banquet and meeting facilities are large enough to accommodate 400 people. Golf packages and referrals to bonded babysitters are coordinated through the staff.

Ocean Dunes Resort & Villas
$$$$$ • 201 75th Ave. N., Myrtle Beach
• (843) 449-7441, (800) 845-0635

The twin towers of this huge resort provide 400 rooms, suites, one-, two- and three-bedroom villas plus three-bedroom oceanfront penthouses. On-site features include oceanfront pools with bars, indoor pools and whirlpools, a steam room, saunas, massage therapy, weight room, game room, gift shop and convenience store. But wait, there's much more. Entertainment options feature restaurants, a lounge and a Lazy River.

During the summer, supervised programs are offered for children, and kids get a free T-shirt and identification bracelet. The Ocean Dunes staff can also refer you to reputable babysitters. Children younger than 18 also stay free in the same room with an adult. Golf, entertainment and specialty packages are available. Courtesy airport pickup is provided.

Ocean Forest Villa Resort
$$$$$ • 5601 N. Ocean Blvd., Myrtle Beach
• (843) 449-9661, (800) 845-0347

All of the Forest's 243, two-bedroom villas face oceanfront, oceanview or poolside. Each villa is conveniently designed to house two full baths, an equipped kitchen, living room, dining room and balcony.

This is a vacation place with children in mind. On-premise are two outdoor pools and two heated whirlpools. On top of that, special programs for kids and babysitting services run from Memorial Day through Labor Day.

Golf packages at 100-plus area courses can be arranged plus entertainment tours. Privileges to an off-premise fitness center and tennis courts can be had for the asking. Ocean Forest provides airport shuttle transportation.

The Palace Resort
$$$ • 1605 S. Ocean Blvd., Myrtle Beach
• (843) 448-4300, (800) 334-1397

The Palace condominiums are fit for kings and queens. You'll feel like royalty in any of the 298 suites at this plush resort that towers over the ocean. Featured amenities include Jacuzzis, hot tubs, enclosed pools, a sauna and steam room. Although many of the condominiums are privately owned, there are numerous units available for weekly rentals. The Palace only rents to couples and families.

Patricia Grand Resort Hotels
$$$ • 2710 N. Ocean Blvd., Myrtle Beach
6804 N. Ocean Blvd., Myrtle Beach
• (843) 448-8453, (800) 255-4763,
(888) 255-4763

From the moment you step into the plush setting of the Patricia Grand, you'll know you're some place special. The 501 luxurious accommodations include double rooms, efficiencies and executive suites designed to pamper those with the most discriminating tastes. The oceanfront restaurant and lounge are relaxing retreats after you've had enough of the pool, whirlpool, Lazy River or sauna. When it's time for more active pursuits, arrange a golf outing through the front desk. Hotel staff are happy to arrange golf and entertainment packages as well as group tour and travel excursions. The Patricia Grand's central location means shopping malls, attractions and restaurants are within easy reach.

Poindexter Family Resort
$$$ • 1702 N. Ocean Blvd., Myrtle Beach
• (843) 448-8327, (800) 248-0003

This resort obviously caters to families. The Poindexter, set on 300 yards of white, sandy beachfront, is walking distance to the Pavilion area. Oceanview and oceanfront rooms and efficiencies are available. Poindexter offers guests the use of 10 pools (both indoor and outdoor), whirlpools and a gigantic kiddie pool. There is an on-site restaurant for all meals, a meeting room and exercise facilities.

Special package plans run the gamut from golf and amusement park to honeymoon and entertainment. Supervised children's activities are planned every day during summer.

Riptide Beach Club
$$ • 2806 N. Ocean Blvd., Myrtle Beach
• (843) 448-1486

The Riptide offers 80 one- and two-bedroom condos, most of which are rented out with permission of the owners. All have sleeper sofas or a set of twin or bunk beds for plenty of places to rest weary heads. Amenities include two pools, hot tubs, a game room and an exercise facility. During the summer there are activities planned for the entire family including wine and cheese get-togethers, craft workshops and trips to a water park.

Sandcastle Resorts
$$$ • Sandcastle North,
1802 N. Ocean Blvd., Myrtle Beach
• (843) 448-7101,
(800) 626-1550 (reservations only)
• Sandcastle South,
2207 South Ocean Blvd., Myrtle Beach
• (843-448-4316)

The Sandcastle people run two properties in Myrtle Beach, both of which offer 240 accommodations each. Sandcastle North is located within nine blocks of the action-packed

Myrtle Beach Pavilion area. Here, guests can choose from oceanfront and oceanview rooms, suites and efficiencies, many of which have separate sleeping and living quarters.

Amenities abound with a winding river, oceanfront pool, kiddie pool plus another swimming pool and whirlpool inside. There is also an on-premise cafe.

Sandcastle South was brand new in 1998. All of its units are oceanfront. Here, you'll find rooms, suites and efficiencies offering two queen-size beds. This new Sandcastle has all the amenities of its northern cousin, but has added Jacuzzis, a lounge and gift shop. Both locations arrange an extensive array of golf packages.

Sands Beach Club All-Suite Resort
$$$$$ • 9400 Shore Dr., Myrtle Beach
• (843) 449-1531, (800) 845-6999

This centrally located resort is on a point of land at the end of Shore Drive, overlooking both the Atlantic Ocean and the Dunes Club marsh. It's in the middle of everything, yet secluded. With 125 units, Sands Beach Club gives guests the option of a two-bedroom oceanfront suite or a one-bedroom unit with views of the ocean and marsh. Regardless of the number of bedrooms, each Sands suite is spacious and includes a separate living room, dining room and full kitchen.

Topper's Restaurant and Topper's Lounge, on the premises, are totally encased in glass to take advantage of the spectacular seascape. A gourmet pizza shop, game room and mini-convenience store are also on-site. Meetings for up to 200 people can be arranged by the staff.

For recreation, Sands Beach Club offers a sports deck with hoops and nets for impromptu basketball and volleyball matches. Here you'll also find two lighted tennis courts, indoor and outdoor pools and whirlpools for guests. Supervised programs for the kids and a child-care service for toddlers are available from Memorial Day through Labor Day. A roster of specialty packages includes golf, entertainment and honeymoon options. Sands also offers a free shuttle service from Myrtle Beach International Airport.

Sand Dunes Resort Hotel
$$$$$ • 201 74th Ave. N., Myrtle Beach
• (843) 449-3313, (800) 845-1011

Once you've checked into the Sand Dunes, you'll only have to leave the hotel to sightsee. The 250 accommodations here range from double rooms and efficiencies to two-bedroom executive suites and oceanfront penthouses.

Overlooking the Atlantic Ocean is the hotel's steakhouse, The Flying Machine, and a sports lounge called Team Spirits. For a quick bite, there's a sidewalk pizza shop, ice cream parlor and beach bar and cafe.

This is an arena of activity with indoor and outdoor pools, a fitness facility, a Lazy River and Bogey's Back Alley game room and entertainment center. From Memorial Day through Labor Day, the hotel coordinates programs for children and offers babysitting services. The Sand Dunes also treats its guests to courtesy airport pickup. Golf and entertainment packages can be arranged at any time.

Sands Ocean Club Resort
$$$$$ • 9550 Shore Dr.
(near Restaurant Row), Myrtle Beach
• (843) 449-6461, (800) 845-2202

Treat yourself to a one-, two- or three-bedroom suite or efficiency along the oceanfront at the Sands Ocean Club Resort. This upscale facility offers numerous on-site amenities including several pools, lounges, Ocean Annie's Beach Bar, restaurants (including a delicatessen), gift and golf shops, an exercise room and golf privileges at more than 100 area courses. During summer months, children's programs and a toddler service are available to guests. Kids will be happy to know that a Lazy River flows at the Sands Ocean Club Resort. Courtesy airport transportation is always available to guests of Sands.

Sea Crest Resort
$$$ • 803 S. Ocean Blvd., Myrtle Beach
• (843) 913-5800, (800) 845-1112

With nine oceanfront pools and both an indoor and outdoor Lazy River ride, you would think all you'd have to do is splish and splash all day. But there's much more to do at the Sea Crest near the heart of downtown Myrtle Beach. The Sea Crest property boasts 1½ acres of oceanfront lawn and lounging, with a pool bar within crawling distance.

There are 360 units in all, with 28 different room types to choose from; all accommodations at Sea Crest feature in-room voice mail for messages.

Relax in the on-premise cafe and lounge,

pick up the sundries you left at home at the convenience store or work out in the exercise room. Sea Crest also sports a game room and six-hole children's miniature golf course. Golf and entertainment packages are available.

Sea Dip Motel
$$ • 2608 N. Ocean Blvd., Myrtle Beach
• (843) 448-7971, (800) 334-1467

Sea Dip is a small but friendly establishment that specializes in family vacations. Reservation options include single rooms, efficiency apartments, two-room suites and efficiency suites with three double beds. Sea Dip offers guests two oceanfront pools, two whirlpools, sun deck, a kiddie pool, a Lazy River and laundry facilities. The ever-smiling staff is always happy to arrange golf, entertainment, honeymoon or motor coach packages. This motel is about a 12-block walk from the Pavilion and amusement areas.

Sea Mist Resort
$$ • 1200 S. Ocean Blvd., Myrtle Beach
• (843) 448-1551, (800) SEAMIST

The Sea Mist is a complete world within itself, sprawling along both sides of Ocean Boulevard. The resort houses more than 800 rooms, efficiencies, suites, townhouses and bungalows for families and tour groups. As if that weren't enough to choose from, the Sea Mist turned some of its units into Jacuzzi suites for the 1998 season. And if you stay six paid nights at standard rates, the seventh night is free.

This expansive complex features eight adult swimming pools, six kiddie pools and a large on-site water park with an inner-tube slide, an activity pool and a Lazy River that stretches more than 500 feet. And that's not all. Guests can putter around on the resort's miniature golf course, work out in the health club or dine in one of several restaurants. The kids really seem to go for the ice cream parlor, doughnut shop and video arcade. Organized activities focus on keeping the kids occupied. Adults enjoy golf privileges and the glorious Carolina sunshine.

The Sea Mist is smack-dab in the middle of downtown Myrtle Beach, and parking and traffic can be hectic. But once you've parked the car, you won't have to leave until it's time to

INSIDERS' TIP
After unpacking your bags in the room, it's always a good idea to discuss an emergency evacuation and meeting plan with the family in the event of fire, earthquake or other disaster. Make sure the kids know where the emergency exits are located.

ACCOMMODATIONS

pack up and go home; just about anything you'll need can be found in the resort complex.

Sheraton Four Points Resort
$$$ • 2701 S. Ocean Blvd., Myrtle Beach
• (843) 448-2518, (800) 842-1871

The Sheraton continues its tradition of quality service at its Myrtle Beach Resort. More than 200 rooms overlook the ocean, including family suites and efficiencies. During the 1996 off-season, the Sheraton spent $1 million on room and lobby renovations.

Geared more to the adults, Kokomo's oceanfront bar and restaurant attracts guests from the pool deck during the summer and provides fun for everyone. Other amenities include an exercise room and sauna. Honeymoon, golf and entertainment packages are available.

Super 8 Motel
$ • 1100 S. Ocean Blvd., Myrtle Beach
• (843) 448-8414, (800) 448-7577

Across the street from the ocean, you'll find this humble motel that offers 41 one-room efficiencies with refrigerators and three two-bedroom units. An outdoor pool, picnic area and shuffleboard are available to guests. Golf packages can also be arranged by the staff.

Tropical Shores
$$$$$ • 703 S. Ocean Blvd., Myrtle Beach
• (843) 626-3610, (800) 255-5954

This oceanfront hotel has a great location within a short walking distance to the Family Kingdom Amusement Park area, stores, bars and restaurants. With 122 units in all, Tropical Seas offers sideview rooms and efficiencies, two-room suites, oceanfront accommodations that include efficiencies and three-room penthouses.

There's an indoor pool, kiddie pool and whirlpool, an oceanfront sun deck, social area and video game room. Golf and entertainment packages are available.

Wyndham Myrtle Beach Resort
$$$$$ • 10000 Beach Club Dr.,
Myrtle Beach
• (843) 449-5000

Get ready for a one-stop vacation experience at the Wyndham, which offers 374 oceanview guest rooms and 11 full suites. Each has a private balcony, refrigerator, coffee maker and in-room safe.

The hotel is set on the 18-hole Arcadian Shores championship golf course, and guests are privy to reduced greens and cart fees at this course. You'll also find four on-site lighted tennis courts exclusively for guests. Tennis clinics and lessons are available for a fee. Other recreational options include volleyball, a fully equipped fitness room and, when you've had enough exercise, a resident masseuse.

The Wyndham is home to an oceanfront restaurant that serves breakfast, lunch and dinner daily as well as Beachcomber Bob's, a small seasonal cafe that whips up sandwiches, finger foods and pizza.

Wyndham's popular pool deck usually pays tribute to beach music, with live bands playing favorite shagging and dance tunes from 1 to 5 PM daily all summer.

The Yachtsman Resort Hotel
$$$$ • 1400 N. Ocean Blvd., Myrtle Beach
• (843) 448-1441, (800) 868-8886

The Yachtsman's twin towers house more than 142 all-suite units in the very heart of the downtown area. Exclusive packages cater to golfers, honeymooners and tour groups. One of the closest attractions to the resort is Pier 14, a restaurant that extends over the ocean.

The studio and one-bedroom suites feature whirlpool baths big enough for two people and fully equipped kitchens. Inside you'll find one pool; outside are two pools, Jacuzzis, hot tubs, a miniature golf course and shuffleboard. The Yachtsman was voted one of South Carolina's favorite getaways by The State newspaper.

South Strand

Barnacle Inn
$ • 115 S. Waccamaw Dr.,
Garden City Beach
• (843) 651-2828, (800) 272-1222

From September through March, a small deposit makes families with small pets welcome. Even students, who are often hardpressed to find accommodations if visiting without adults, are welcome if they are willing to pay a deposit. Barnacle Inn is just steps from Garden City Beach and has thirty modest but comfortable units for a simple, affordable vacation. Guests can access an on-site swimming pool and laundry facilities. Winter rentals are a specialty. Entertainment packages can be arranged by management.

Days Inn Surfside Pier Resort
$$$ • 15 S. Ocean Blvd., Surfside Beach
• (843) 238-4444, (800) 533-7599

The Days Inn Surfside Pier offers the same affordable rates as most area Days Inns. This hotel overlooks the Surfside Pier (hence the

When it comes to accommodations, the Grand Strand has exactly what you're looking for—from oceanfront highrises with a view to quaint cottages tucked along the creeks and marshes.

Photo: Courtesy of Brandon Advertising

name), which was restored after sustaining severe damage during a 1995 storm. This area tends to be more crowded than others on the South Strand because of the pier. Guests enjoy sampling the restaurant's home-style cuisine and sipping their favorite beverages at Scotty's Beach Bar on the property's oceanfront. All 158 units offer a sideview of Surfside Beach. There's an outdoor heated pool and a Jacuzzi too.

Litchfield Beach & Golf Resort
$$$$$ • U.S. Hwy. 17 S., Litchfield Beach
• (843) 237-3000, (800) 845-1897

There is no other resort in the historic Lowcountry that compares to Litchfield Beach & Golf. Set amid 4,500 acres of marshlands and oceanfront property, the complex features an array of accommodations including villas, condominiums and cottages. The grounds are enhanced with avenues of century-old oaks, flowering gardens and uncrowded beaches. Although the resort is about 15 minutes from Myrtle Beach, there is no hint of either neon or a hectic pace.

Ranked one of the top-five tennis vacation destinations in the country by *Tennis* magazine, Litchfield's 26 on-site courts attract tennis lovers from far and wide. Three signature golf courses grace this resort: River Club, Willbrook Planta-

tion and Litchfield Country Club. Guests are exempt from golfing surcharges. A comprehensive summer children's program appeals to many families looking for accommodations a cut above those at traditional resorts. In addition to the spa, indoor and outdoor pools and racquetball courts, the resort offers a sauna, beauty salon and the ever-popular restaurant and lounge known as Webster's.

Royal Garden Resort
$$$$$ • 1210 N. Waccamaw Dr.,
Garden City Beach
• (843) 651-1929, (800) 446-4010

In the midst of the weather-worn beach houses and cottages of Garden City Beach is the Royal Garden Resort, with more than 206 condominium units and suites. The oceanfront property features golf packages. Enjoy Royal Garden's indoor and outdoor pools, a Jacuzzi, sauna, game room and gift shop. Restaurants and attractions are within walking distance, and there's a seasonal snack bar too.

Water's Edge Resort
$$$$$ • 1012 N. Waccamaw Dr.,
Garden City Beach
• (843) 651-0002, (800) 255-5554

With 135 spacious condominiums boasting

one-, two- and three-bedrooms, this resort is larger than its neighbor, the Royal Garden Resort, but offers the same features, including pools, Jacuzzis and an oceanfront lounge and deck with a perfect view of the beach. Golf, entertainment and honeymoon packages are offered. Supervised activities for the kids are available during the summer months.

Other Featured Accommodations

The Atlantica
$$$ • 1702 N. Ocean Blvd., Myrtle Beach
• (843) 448-8327, (800) 248-0003

The Atlantica is located minutes from the Pavilion and offers anything your heart desires in condominiums ranging from one-bedroom efficiencies to a two-floor apartment with three separate sleeping rooms and a rooftop sundeck. All units have private, beachfront balconies and contemporary décor.

The property offers indoor and outdoor pools and spas. The staff will gladly arrange entertainment and golf packages with your reservations or upon arrival in slower seasons.

Days Inn Beachfront
$$ • 1403 S. Ocean Blvd., Myrtle Beach
• (843) 448-1636, (800) 826-2779

If you're looking for an affordable, convenient stay for the family, Days Inn is just the ticket. This oceanfront inn rents 54 sideview and oceanfront efficiencies, double and king-size rooms. All have private oceanfront balconies.

The property offers a swimming pool and kiddie pool. It's located about 11 blocks from the popular Family Kingdom Amusement Park, and one mile south of the Pavilion area.

Entertainment and golf packages are available with reservations.

Myrtle Beach Resort
5905 U.S. Hwy. 17 S., Myrtle Beach
• (800) 803-7303

Myrtle Beach Resort is an all-in-one vacation destination, sprawling more than 33 acres of oceanfront. Condominium and villa-style accommodations can be found here, ranging from studios to one- and two-bedroom units.

Here you'll discover a recreational wonderland that offers 6 swimming pools (2 indoors), 4 whirlpools, 3 saunas, basketball, shuffleboard and tennis courts. The resort also sports arcade games and a kiddie playground. Twenty-four hour security keeps all of Myrtle Beach Resort's guests safe and sound.

Staff are always happy to arrange great golf packages for visitors. On average, a week's stay in mid-July will cost $800.

Ocean Lodge
$$ • 604 N. Ocean Blvd., Myrtle Beach
• (843) 448-6770, (800) 757-1580

Ocean Lodge is only a short walk to the Pavilion area, centrally located and oceanfront. It is a smaller property with 27 oceanfront, sideview and poolside double rooms with full kitchens. Ocean Lodge also rents out two apartments that can accommodate up to six people.

Laundry facilities are available to guests and the staff can arrange golf packages.

Pan American Resort
$$$ • 5300 N. Ocean Blvd., Myrtle Beach
• (843) 449-7411, (800) 845-4501

Pan American Resort's features and amenities include indoor/outdoor pools, on-site tennis courts, lazy river and exercise facility. The rooms are spacious and well-decorated and the staff is friendly and helpful. Golf packages can be arranged upon request.

RV and Camping Facilities

Myrtle Beach-area campgrounds offer more than 9,000 individual campsites with all the comforts of home for a perfect family vacation. Each campground offers basic services plus a variety of recreational activities.

Summer is the area's most popular camping season; most children are out of school, and families can plan their vacations together. However, camping is quickly becoming a year-round activity along the Grand Strand, so don't roll into town during October through March and expect to find accommodations easily. The fall and winter seasons attract many campers due to the mild climate and off-season rates. All of the campgrounds are within walking distance of grocery stores, restaurants and attractions.

North Strand

Barefoot RV Resort
U.S. Hwy. 17 and 48th Ave. S.,
North Myrtle Beach
• (843) 272-1790, (800) 272-1790

Barefoot RV Resort offers 250 recreational

vehicle campsites for a less crowded camping adventure on the oceanfront. Although smaller than most campgrounds in the Myrtle Beach area, the Barefoot RV Resort still offers all the comforts of the larger campgrounds including utility hookups, bathhouses, laundry facilities and a convenience store. The resort boasts a clubhouse complete with a game room, whirlpool, fitness center and indoor pool. Outside you'll find another swimming pool, a kiddie pool and Lazy River.

The Park Model rentals are equipped for up to six people, with two bedrooms and a sofa sleeper. Bring your own sheets, pillow cases, washcloths and towels.

Depending on site location, the summer daily rate ranges from $34 to $38.

Myrtle Beach

Apache Family Campground
9700 Kings Rd., Myrtle Beach
• (843) 449-7323, (800) 553-1749

You can select from 277 rental sites from the total inventory of more than 700 spacious campsites (the remainder are annual rentals or permanently booked) nestled beneath towering pines and oaks at Apache Family Campground.

All sites have sewage hookups (except for the handful close to the ocean), free cable TV and picnic tables. Amenities include a large swimming pool, laundry facilities and a fully stocked trading post. Apache Campground is home to the longest and widest fishing pier in the Southeast—Apache Pier (see our Fishing chapter)—complete with a restaurant and seasonal live entertainment.

Depending on site location, the summer daily rate is about $35.

KOA Kampground
613 5th Ave. S., Myrtle Beach
• (843) 448-3421, (800) 255-7614

Nestled in this densely wooded area, campers at the KOA might have trouble believing that the heart of Myrtle Beach is just 700 yards away.

More than 500 campsites are available in this 60-acre complex that offers log cabin-style rentals—called Kamping Kabins—in addition to its large, shaded tent sites. Free cable TV is included with utility hookups, and KOA provides bathhouses with showers. You and the family can splash about in the two pools or rent a bike for recreation. Other amenities include a convenience store with gas station, game room and Laundromat.

Depending on site location and hookups, the summer daily rate ranges from $26 to $38. Kabins run from $45 to $55.

Myrtle Beach State Park
4401 S. Kings Hwy., Myrtle Beach
• (843) 238-5325

The Myrtle Beach State Park is just 3 miles south of downtown Myrtle Beach and is one of the most popular public beaches in the area. It was the first state park opened to the public in South Carolina; it's also the site of the first campground and fishing pier on the Grand Strand.

The park offers 350 campsites, picnic areas with shelters, a swimming pool, nature trails, playground equipment, a park store and snack bar. Campsites are rented on a first-come, first-serve basis. Only 40 sites are available each year for advance reservation. Each site has water and electrical hookups and is convenient to hot showers and restrooms.

The summer daily rate is $22 per site, $23 for reserved spots, and there is an additional $4-per-vehicle admission charge to enter the park.

Myrtle Beach Travel Park
10108 Kings Rd., Myrtle Beach
• (843) 449-3714, (800) 255-3568

Only 10 miles north of downtown Myrtle Beach, the Travel Park offers more than 1,100 campsites in a variety of locations: oceanfront, wooded or lakeside, all complete with utility hookups. Furnished villas and 35-foot travel trailers are also available for rent. Campers can enjoy a variety of swimming activities, rent paddleboats or fish for freshwater game from surrounding lakes.

The summer daily rate starts at $40.

South Strand

Huntington Beach State Park
U.S. Hwy. 17 S., Murrells Inlet
• (843) 237-4440

Huntington State Park is a nature lover's dream come true. About 3 miles south of Murrells Inlet, the diverse natural environment of the South Carolina coast awaits at the freshwater lagoon, salt marsh and nature trail. The view of the beach from Huntington Beach State Park is one of the most breathtaking you'll find along the Grand Strand. The park is also the site of the historic castle Atalaya, the former winter home and studio of American sculptress Anna Hyatt Huntington.

Park facilities include about 186 campsites,

Another beautiful day along the Grand Strand.

Photo: courtesy of Brandon Advertising

52 of which can be reserved in advance; the rest are rented on a first-come, first-serve basis. There are picnic areas with shelters, a boardwalk, a park store and nature programs directed by park staff. Each site has water and electrical hookups, and hot showers and restrooms are nearby. Sewage hookups are available at about 22 sites. The summer daily rate, from April through October, is $22; from November through March, $19.

Lakewood Camping Resort
5901 U.S. Hwy. 17 S., Surfside Beach
• (843) 238-5161, (800) 258-8309

Lakewood is among the largest oceanfront campgrounds in the South Strand area, with more than 1,900 campsites complete with utility hookups. It is also home of *High Steppin' Country*, a musical and variety show featuring professionally trained talent, local to the community. Each summer, from June to August, the entertainers perform a couple of nights a week before packed houses, singing and dancing country favorites mixed with a few contemporary numbers.

The 3-acre recreation complex provides a variety of activities, including an 18-hole miniature golf course. Four freshwater lakes are stocked with fish just begging for a hook. When it's time to cool down, kids of all ages will love rushing into the Olympic-size pool from the sliding board built into a tropical rock formation. Campers can also enjoy a heated pool and a Jacuzzi.

Beach Villa rentals are available in addition to camper storage and annual leases. Depending on site location, the summer daily rate ranges from $36 to $41.

Ocean Lakes Family Campground
6001 South Kings Hwy., Surfside Beach
• (843) 238-1451, (800) 722-1451

Like many Grand Strand campgrounds, Ocean Lakes is a world within itself, providing campers with everything from convenient shopping, meeting rooms and laundry facilities to a chapel, a book-exchange library, a post office and telephones. Daily programs for children are available during the summer months.

Ocean Lakes is the largest campground facility on the east coast. Of nearly 3,500 sites, less than 1,000 are transient sites. Ocean Lakes offers 250 rental units (ideal headquarters for an affordable vacation), and the remaining sites are permanently leased.

From 1997 through 1999, Ocean Lakes was awarded the National RV Park of the Year award by the National Association of RV Parks and Campgrounds. In addition to a beachfront location, Ocean Lakes boasts an indoor pool and an observation deck that enables a breathtaking view of the Atlantic.

Depending on site location, the summer daily rate ranges from $40.50 to $42.50.

PirateLand Family Campground
5401 U.S. Hwy. 17 S., Surfside Beach
• (843) 238-5155, (800) 443-CAMP

Set among 140 acres of stately oak trees, private lagoons and oceanfront property, PirateLand is a real treasure. More than 25 years of business has garnered PirateLand several generations of family vacationers whose visits turn into neighborhood block parties. Each of the 1,100 oceanfront and lakeside campsites is fully equipped with a picnic table and hookups for utilities and free cable TV. Trailer storage space is also available. Keep in mind that you don't have to be a camper to enjoy the surroundings at PirateLand. The campground also offers fully furnished, two- and three-bedroom Lakeview Villas for weekly and monthly rental.

Campground amenities include a heated indoor pool and spa, an Olympic-size outdoor pool, playgrounds, tennis courts, a miniature golf course and an arcade. The staff organizes activities including beach volleyball, deep-sea fishing, golf, Bible school, arts and crafts and neighborhood cookouts. The campground's general store is stocked with practically everything you can imagine or forgot to pack. There is also a coin-operated laundry facility for campers' convenience.

Depending on site location, the summer daily rate ranges from $34 to $40.

Vacation Rentals

Group Accommodations

LOOK FOR:
• Group
  Accommodations
  - North Strand
  - Myrtle Beach
  - South Strand

Want to take the whole gang, be it family or friends, on a little extended vacation? You may want to consider renting a large condominium or beach house. The kids, young and old, can be entertained by the sand and surf. The grown-ups looking for true rest and relaxation can pull a chair and a glass of lemonade on to the deck for a little wave-watching and snoozing. These accommodations combine the comfort, convenience and semi-privacy of home with the carefree existence of vacation. These short-term rentals have their own kitchens but some have restaurants on-site for the evening when you just don't feel like cooking. Others are equipped with laundry facilities.

The vacation rental option is great for large parties and events (such as family reunions) and are often more affordable than resort hotels once the cost is divided. The option of bringing and preparing your own food helps the cost factor, as well as catering to the all-day snackers of all sizes!

The hard part of vacation rentals is finding one. Group accommodations tend to be rather elusive, since most are under the thumb of rental management companies or real estate firms. Still, you can expect a wide variety of design, décor and amenities. It's wise to try and book a group accommodation well in advance of your stay, again depending greatly on the season you plan to visit. Have a good idea of the amenities you'd like to have, whether you're looking for a cabin without phones or the full suite with recreation center and Jacuzzi or maybe your needs are more along the lines of a playpen and crib. We've uncovered a few that might be worth looking into.

North Strand

Century 21 Thomas
625 Sea Mountain Hwy.,
North Myrtle Beach
• **(843) 249-2100, (800) 249-2100**

Strictly serving the North Myrtle Beach and Little River areas, this company maintains more than 400 units, condos, houses and oceanfront or channel homes. One- to seven-bedroom accommodations can be rented, and as many as 20 people can stay in one of the larger homes. Ninety-five percent of the condos offer pools, and all of the homes are oceanfront or second row from the Atlantic. Staff can arrange golf and entertainment packages for guests. Prices start at $505 per week for a one-bedroom unit and range all the way up to $4,290 for a six-bedroom oceanfront beach house.

Shore Crest Vacation Villas
4709 S. Ocean Blvd.
(Windy Hill section),
North Myrtle Beach
• **(843) 361-3600, (800) 361-8141**

Beautifully decorated and outfitted, Shore Crest Villas offer

Opt for a creekside rental and enjoy the joys of crabbing and fishing from your own private dock.

Photo: Courtesy of Lowcountry Companion

one- and two-bedroom condo units with full kitchens, two baths each and extra sofa beds. The one-bedroom villa accommodates four people easily; the two-bedroom can sleep six guests. The property sports an indoor pool and Jacuzzi, exercise room and video-game arcade.

On the oceanfront is another pool, Jacuzzi and a Lazy River. A week's stay at Shore Crest in the middle of July costs approximately $715.

Myrtle Beach

Arcadian Dunes
351 Lake Arrowhead Rd., Myrtle Beach
• **(843) 449-6611, (800) 446-4010**
Staying in any of the two-bedroom, two-bath condos at Arcadian Dunes places you one block from the Atlantic Ocean and smack-dab in the middle of the Restaurant Row area. Initial linens are furnished, and each unit has a washer and dryer to keep them fresh.

Harry The Hat's is on premise, providing visitors with a full-service restaurant and bar that's open every day for breakfast, lunch and dinner.

Arcadian Dunes offers guests a sauna, steam room, two outdoor pools, whirlpools and tennis courts. Children will love the on-site playground. Golf and theater packages are also available. In midsummer you'll pay $893 per week.

Barefoot Vacations
3405 N. Kings Hwy., Myrtle Beach
• **(843) 626-7457, (800) 845-0837**
Spanning the length of the sunny Grand Strand, Barefoot manages 100-plus properties, including one-room sun suites, one-bedroom condos, cottages and apartment complexes. Barefoot Vacations' staff members are experienced coordinators of family reunions and large-scale affairs. All properties have swimming pools available to guests and some include a clubhouse for events. The staff can also arrange dining, show and golf packages. The weekly cost of a Barefoot Vacations property in mid-July is $750 to $1,500.

Beach Vacations
357 Lake Arrowhead Rd., Myrtle Beach
• **(843) 449-8900, (800) 449-4005**
The staff of Beach Vacations promises to accommodate any size group,

INSIDERS' TIP

As you're reserving your vacaton rental be sure to ask if bed linens and towels are provided or if you need to bring your own.

anywhere along the Strand. This company has a large inventory of one-, two- and three-bedroom units, condos, cottages and golf course villas. All of the properties have access to swimming pools. Entertainment and golf packages can be arranged. Peak season prices start at $600 per week and range to $1,500.

Booe Realty
7728 N. Kings Hwy., Myrtle Beach
• (843) 449-4477, (800) 845-0647

Booe's inventory of 130 rental properties consists of condominiums and townhomes that sleep four to eight persons and beach houses that accommodate nine to 21 guests. Except the condos, no other units include swimming pools. But keep in mind that most beach houses are oceanfront or just across the street from the blue Atlantic. In mid-July condos and townhouses start at $545 per week, and oceanfront beach houses range from $1,495 to $3,100 weekly.

Chicora Beach Holiday
603 Briarwood Dr., Myrtle Beach
• (843) 272-7070, (800) 845-0833

All along the Grand Strand, Chicora manages hundreds of vacation villas, condos and cottages. Studios, efficiencies and up to four-bedroom accommodations are available, most of which are within comfortable walking distance to the beach or offer an on-site pool. Chicora also arranges golf, tennis and entertainment packages for guests. During peak season, rentals run anywhere from $675 to $1,065 a week. A four-bedroom, three-bath oceanfront villa costs about $2,545 for a week's stay.

Endless Summer Vacations
1800 N. Oak St., Myrtle Beach
• (843) 448-2381, (800) 476-1760

Approximately 200 units, efficiencies, cottages and penthouse suites are available for rent through this company. Some of the properties are large enough to accommodate 10 people under one roof. All include access to swimming pools. Summer rentals began at $575 per week for an efficiency, $1,975 a week for a fancy penthouse suite.

LITUS* To Let
1551 21st Ave. N., Ste. 24, Myrtle Beach
• (843) 448-9000, (800) 365-4887

A state-of-the-art reservation and customer-service center at LITUS* can put you in touch with a huge inventory of rentals all over the Grand Strand, from efficiencies to luxurious oceanfront homes suitable for 25 people. Prices

This creekside cottage is a charming example of the many summer homes available for rental on the Grand Strand . . . especially on the northernmost and southernmost ends of the Strand.

Photo: Courtesy of Lowcountry Companion

VACATION RENTALS

range from $50 per night to $6,000 for a week's stay. The staff encourages potential guests to call their customer-service center at any time, since last-minute cancellations often provide visitors with the perfect place at big savings.

The Noble Company
1211 48th Ave. N., Myrtle Beach
• **(843) 449-6625, (800) 358-6625**

Since 1980 The Noble Company has arranged vacation packages for families in some of the nicest condominium properties in North Myrtle Beach and Myrtle Beach. One- to four-bedroom condos can be rented along with a limited number of large beach homes. Garnering a select group of vacation properties over the years, Noble prefers to rent to families, married couples and singles older than 25. No house parties are permitted in any of the company's rental units, so look elsewhere if you want to have a beer-bash. Prices in mid-July range from $625 a week for a two-bedroom, two-bath unit across the street from the ocean to $1,375 a week for a four-bedroom, three-bath oceanfront condo.

South Strand

Dunes Beach Vacations
128 Atlantic Ave., Garden City Beach
• **(843) 651-2116, (800) 845-8191**

All up and down Surfside Beach and Garden City Beach, along canals, inlets and channels, Dunes Realty manages a large inventory of condominiums, cottages and beach houses. This company rents almost exclusively to family groups. The smallest accommodation starts at $500 a week in mid-July, and a seven bedroom beach house will cost $4,900. Dunes Beach Vacations does not accept credit cards.

Garden City Realty Inc.
608 Atlantic Ave., Garden City Beach
• **(843) 651-2121, (800) 395-5930**

Staying in its own neighborhood, this company handles about 300 rental properties in the Garden City Beach and Surfside Beach areas. Garden City Realty offers one-, two- and three-bedroom condos, homes and oceanfront beach houses. Most units sport pools and some offer hot tubs. In mid-July a three-bedroom condo starts at $1,100 per week; a six-bedroom oceanfront home, $4,500.

Golf Colony Resort
1841 Colony Dr., Surfside Beach
• **(843) 650-7651, (800) 654-6522**

Golf Colony offers 11 colonies of three to five buildings each. Each has its own pool, Jacuzzi and barbecue area.

Set on the 1,500-acre Deer Track Golf Resort (see our Golf chapter), the colony offers guests 470 condos, which range from studios to one- and two-bedroom accommodations. All have fully equipped kitchens and washers and dryers. The resort is just 1.5 miles from the ocean.

In July weekly rates run from $511 to $721; nightly stays are $75 to $105. There is a three-night minimum, six-person maximum for all reservations and a onetime cleaning charge of $35 to $45. Separate golf packages to stay at Golf Colony and play the 36 holes at Deer Track can be arranged by calling (800) 624-6886.

Pawleys Island Realty Company
88 N. Causeway, Pawleys Island
• **(843) 237-2431, (800) 937-7352**

This company's properties are concentrated in the Pawleys Island and Litchfield Beach areas. Choose from two-bedroom duplexes from about $350 per week to a four-bedroom home for $700 per week. If you have a really large group, ask about the $3,000-per-week beach house rentals. On the average, Pawleys Island Realty handles accommodations for groups of about eight people but unfortunately does not accept credit cards.

Plantation Resort
1250 U.S. Hwy. 17 N., Surfside Beach
• **(843) 238-3556, (800) 845-5039**

Although a little ways from the beach, this resort is nestled among the 36 championship fairways of Deer Track Golf Course (see our Golf chapter). Three-bedroom villas are available with three bathrooms, towels and linens, fully equipped kitchens and washer and dryer. Staying here entitles you to free summertime shuttle service to and from the beach and access to a 70,000-square-foot health and swim club. The $1 million club includes a heated pool, sauna, steam rooms, weights and aerobics. The staff can arrange golf and entertainment packages. Mid-July rates run $120 to $180 per night, with discounts applied to reservations of at least seven nights.

INSIDERS' TIP

Sunscreen is important year round. When packing for your trip, don't forget the SPF.

Surfside Realty
213 S. Ocean Blvd., Surfside Beach
• (843) 238-3435, (800) 833-8231

If you're looking at Surfside Beach or Garden City Beach as your vacation destination, this company maintains more than 400 apartments, condos, duplexes, cottages and houses. This company has been arranging vacations since 1962 and has a strict policy of booking families only. Golf packages can also be arranged through Surfside Realty.

During the summer, a one-bedroom apartment rents for $430 per week, and a house with a pool runs about $2,800. Special off-season discounts apply from post-Labor Day in September through May.

Bed and Breakfast Inns

LOOK FOR:
• Myrtle Beach
• South Strand
• Beyond the Strand

Price Code

This price code indicates the average one-night cost for two people during peak season.

$	$70 to $95
$$	$96 to $120
$$$	$121 to $145
$$$$	$146 and up

Besides the burgeoning number of hotel and motel suites springing up all over the Grand Strand, bed and breakfast establishments have also been making their mark. Most likely due to the incredible amount of competition from other accommodations from Little River through Garden City Beach, you'll find the majority of bed and breakfast inns have put down roots south of Murrells Inlet and especially in Georgetown.

It's not surprising that Georgetown should become the region's hub of bed and breakfast lodging, since the area is home to its fair share of sprawling, historic homes that lend themselves perfectly to the concept. Georgetown is a woman with a past—fascinating and mysterious—and is known as the "Ghost Capitol of the South." Founded in 1729, by 1840 Georgetown was not only an ideal port for shipping vessels, but also produced more than half of all the rice grown in the United States.

As the rice plantations flourished, so did the townspeople and antebellum life. Culling incredible wealth in a relatively short period of time—from 1840 through the 1850s—well-appointed homes began to line the oak-shaded tunnels of streets in town. Gracious plantations entertained and farmed along the shores of Winyah Bay, the Waccamaw, Black, and Pee Dee Rivers.

Georgetonians have worked hard to preserve their heritage, and their town remains a lovely step back in time with an intact historic district, preserved homes and original churches and storefronts. Today, historic tour companies run a brisk business by boat, by tram, or by horse-drawn carriage.

Each of the bed and breakfast inns we have listed in this chapter has a distinct personality that seems to have evolved from the property itself and its proprietors. The owners also operate their bed and breakfasts, taking great pride in what they consider to be their labor of love.

Myrtle Beach

The Brustman House
$$, no credit cards
• 400 25th Ave. S.,
Myrtle Beach
• (843) 448-7699, (800) 448-7699

Although the Brustman House's architecture is Colonial, its decor is Scandinavian. This bed and breakfast inn has three guest rooms with white onyx oval whirlpool tubs for two. One suite has a separate entrance and cooking facilities to accommodate a group or family. The house is 300 yards from the beach, situated on two quiet acres in the heart of Myrtle Beach.

Wendell C. Brustman, who holds a Ph.D. in clinical psychology, created the breakfast recipes that include a stack of 10-grain pancakes, French toast made with gourmet bread and vegetarian delights. Guests are served high tea from 4 to 6 PM daily, consisting of sweets, wine and gourmet coffee and tea. Fresh roses from the carefully tended gardens adorn the

Antiques and atmosphere abound at the 1790 House in Georgetown, SC. The house is post Revolutionary War, and the sheer dimensions of its West Indies style command attention.

Photo: courtesy of the 1790 House Bed and Breakfast

rooms, and hand-picked herbs lend flavor and aroma to wonderful recipes. The Brustman caters to honeymooners and romantic anniversary celebrations.

Sea Island, An Inn on the Beach
$$$ • 6000 N. Ocean Blvd., Myrtle Beach • (843) 449-6406, (800) 548-0767

Sea Island looks like a regular oceanfront hotel from the outside, but inside its ambiance and food plan made us consider it a bed and breakfast inn. Its 113 oceanfront units range from full rooms to efficiencies to deluxe accommodations with Colonial decor. Guests may partake of a full breakfast and a five-course dinner in the quaint dining room. Chefs change the menu daily to keep palates pleasantly surprised, never bored.

Sea Island offers two outdoor swimming pools and two kiddie pools. The staff here has a list of preferred babysitters that they are happy to share with guests.

Serendipity Inn
$$ • 407 71st Ave. N., Myrtle Beach • (843) 449-5268 , (800) 762-3229

A short, 300-yard walk from the beach, Serendipity is completely enclosed by dense foliage and a wraparound wall. This 16-year-old

property was built to offer guests separate entrances and baths.

Fifteen appointed rooms are available; a few noted as King suites with three rooms. Visitors are treated to a private pool and hot tub in the central courtyard, shuffleboard, table tennis and bicycles.

Breakfast is served fresh every morning. The menu changes daily but always includes a large fruit tray and steaming baked goods.

Owners Kay and Phil Mullins are happy to coordinate and cater special events like family reunions, gatherings and weddings. They can also make provisions for babysitting services on an as-needed basis. Smoking is permitted outside in the courtyard only.

South Strand

1790 House Bed and Breakfast
$$ • 630 Highmarket St., Georgetown • (843) 546-4821, (800) 890-7432

Yes, the home was built more than 200 years ago and is historically and architecturally significant. Listed on the National Register of Historic Places, this West Indies-style post-Revolutionary War home was Georgetown's social center in the late 1700s and early 1800s,

Overlooking a marina in the Conway's charming riverfront, just fifteen miles from Myrtle Beach, The Cypress Inn offers luxury accommodations and personal service.

Photo: courtesy of The Cypress Inn

when the rice plantation culture was at its peak. Six lovely guest rooms with private baths are turned out in early Colonial furnishings. Three of the rooms are adorned with fireplaces. Public rooms include a large drawing room with fireplace, a dining room, parlor/game room and a large wraparound veranda facing other historic homes and gardens. A separate cottage complete with Jacuzzi is housed in the original kitchen carriage house, which is a favorite for honeymooners.

A gourmet breakfast is served daily on the veranda or in the dining room, as are afternoon refreshments. In December 1997 owners John and Patricia Wiley started the Angel's Touch Tea Room in the parlor and have enjoyed great response. Every Tuesday, Thursday and Saturday at 12:30 PM and 2:30 PM an authentic high tea is served to 1790 House guests and the public alike. Two menus are offered for $12 or $6.50 per person. The high tea serves up a combination of assorted tea sandwiches, quiche, scones, home-baked goods and a sorbet in between courses to cleanse the palate. Reservations are not just recommended but required.

Games and Ping-Pong are available to guests. Smoking is permitted on the veranda and patio only.

Alexandra's Inn
$$ • 620 Prince St., Georgetown
• (843) 527-0233, (888) 557-0233

Surrounded by manicured gardens, flower beds and scented magnolia trees, Alexandra's Inn was built in 1880 as an overflow for guests of the Winyah Inn (now the Masonic Lodge). The main house was dramatically restored . Special detail was given to enhancing the gracious home's original pine floors, moldings, 11-foot ceilings and fireplaces that come with every room.

Because the home resembles Tara from *Gone With The Wind*, each bedroom is named after a character in the famous story and decorated with that person in mind. Here you'll find Scarlett's, Bonnie's, Ashley's, Melanie's and Rhett's rooms. Each room has cable TV and telephone as well as a private bath with either shower, tub or Jacuzzi. The main house rooms are designed for two people only; young children cannot be obliged.

Standing poolside, the carriage house is a private accommodation with two bedrooms, a large bath, living room, dining room and full kitchen. Decorated in light, breezy colors, it is a favorite for families or the business traveler looking for longer stays.

A gourmet breakfast is served every day for

guests staying in the main house. The front porch hosts a full army of rockers. Innkeepers, Vit and Diane, welcome small weddings or other special events. They can even coordinate and/or cater functions for you.

DuPre House Bed & Breakfast Inn
$$ • 921 Prince St., Georgetown
• (843) 546-0298, (877) 519-9499

The charming atmosphere, enchanting artwork throughout, warm hospitality and historical significance of DuPre House has earned this bed and breakfast inn a three diamond rating by the American Automobile Association.

Records of the house date back to 1734 when Elisha Screven first laid plans for her dream home on town lot 53 in Georgetown. The home changed ownership several times, the last surviving chronicle showing that Susannah Gignilliat lived there and filed a claim in 1776 for reimbursement for supplies given to American troops during the American Revolution. The inn is named after Susannah's mother, Mary Magdalen DuPre. Unfortunately, all other documents of ownership for the next 60 years were destroyed by Sherman's Advance during the Civil War.

Now in the hands of Richard and Judy Barnett, DuPre House has been extensively altered over the course of the 20th century, but its second floor wall overhang on the northwestern facade remains a rare example of an old building technique, uncommon to the southeastern states.

Each of DuPre's five rooms boast queen-size poster beds and private baths. Three of the suites include fireplaces. A full breakfast is served every morning to guests that includes a private roast coffee, blended especially for the DuPre House. Afternoon and evening refreshments are also served. Without leaving the grounds of the inn, you can take a refreshing dip in the pool or bubble away in the hot tub.

DuPre House accepts bookings for weddings, receptions, small meetings and family gatherings. Business travelers and children are accepted. Smoking outside only.

Harbor House Inn
$$ • 15 Cannon St., Georgetown, SC
• (843) 546-6532, (877) 511-0101

Harbor House Inn (circa 1765) is located di-rectly on Geogetown's working waterfront. Sailors say its distinctive red roof is visible three miles out across the bay. Harbor House has welcomed seafarers from across the globe for over two centuries. The imposing 3-story Georgian house is listed on the National Register of Historic Places, gracing the banks of the Sampit River from a bluff amid magnolia trees, camellias and venerable live oaks. Harbor House is within walking distance to main street stores, restaurants and the Historic District of Georgetown.

The house is accompanied by another monument of South Carolina history—The Red Store. This circa 1740 shipping warehouse formerly stored silks, indigo and imported wines. From shaded rockers on the inn's porch, visitors can view sailing ships and the blue waters of Winyah Bay—a view that has remained unchanged for centuries.

Innkeeper Meg Tarbox runs the immaculately restored house, keeping the original heart pine floors gleaming and dust off family antiques, eight fireplaces and oriental carpets. Meg is a Georgetown native with an intimate knowledge of her area.

The inn offers four beautifully appointed rooms with private baths. In addition to the popular porch rockers, guests can share the joggling board, piano, bicycles, games and books. Smoking is permitted on the open-air porches.

Litchfield Plantation
$$$$ • Kings River Rd., Pawleys Island
• (843) 237-9121, (800) 869-1410

At the end of a quarter-mile avenue lined with live oaks draped in Spanish moss, you'll find the stately Litchfield Plantation Manor House (c. 1750). The home overlooks fields where Carolina long-grain rice flourished in the early 1800s.

The inn tariff includes lodging in one of the four gracious rooms, a daily continental breakfast, use of the private heated pool and cabana, a private beach club at Pawleys Island , on-site tennis courts and access to the award-winning, on-premise Carriage House Club Restaurant. The Plantation boasts additional suites and villas for a total of thirty eight rooms and suites to accommodate couples, families and small groups. Non smoking rooms are available.

Litchfield Plantation is a member of the prestigious society for Small Luxury Hotels of the World.

INSIDERS' TIP
Many bed and breakfasts do not allow pets but if you call ahead your host or hostess may be able to recommend a boarding facility where you can board your pet.

Mansfield Plantation
$$ • 1776 Mansfield Rd., Georgetown
• (843) 546-6961, (800) 355-3223

A national historic landmark on the site of many archaeological digs, Mansfield is an authentic antebellum plantation of the Old South, offering bed and breakfast stays and historical tours. Especially for Civil War buffs, the plantation offers the retracing of the footsteps of Dr. Francis S. Parker, a signer of the South Carolina Ordinance of Secession, who planted rice here from 1842 to 1862. Parker was forced to leave his beloved Mansfield in April 1862 when Federal gunboats crossed into Winyah Bay and raided plantations along the Black River. However, the Mansfield innkeepers Sally and Jim Cahalan are astute historians who love to share this history with their guests.

Situated on 900 idyllic acres of pine forest, ricefields and dikes, Mansfield retains the original Plantation House, avenues of 220 live oaks draped with Spanish moss, more than 100 blooming camellia bushes, the antebellum slave village, chapel, school house, winnowing tower and parts of the rice threshing mill. The unspoiled environment plays host to alligators, beavers, fox, deer, otters and birds, including an occasional bald eagle.

Eight charming and comfortably outfitted rooms in historic guest houses, featuring hand-carved woodwork and mantelpieces, are for let. Private baths and air-conditioning keep each room comfortable. A full breakfast is served every morning in the elegant dining room of the plantation house.

Mansfield Plantation was featured in the April 1997 issue of *Charleston Magazine* as one of the "Ten Great Romantic Getaways" and received the coveted 5-Paw rating from Pets Welcome travel guide. Needless to say, family pets are welcome here.

This site is also home to the Mansfield Duck Hunting Club, and guests have the opportunity to fish for bream and bass or play golf on the adjacent 18-hole Wedgefield Plantation course. Weekend getaway packages are also offered at the plantation. Smoking is permitted outside on the grounds.

Sea View Inn
$, no credit cards
• 414 Myrtle Ave., Pawleys Island
• (843) 237-4253

This place is a Pawleys Island tradition. Sea View's 20 rooms overlook the ocean and the salt marshes of the inlet. As bed and breakfast inns go, this is among the most rustic. For more than 40 years, families have dined on authentic Lowcountry cuisine and have relaxed in the privacy of the traditional wraparound porch.

Beautiful views and salt-borne breezes make the porch of any area bed & breakfast an enviable place to be.

Photo: courtesy of The Cypress Inn

This is the ideal vacation destination for anyone who wants to get away from it all and have it all at the same time.

For a week in April, the Sea View hosts a Wellness Week where guests participate in a myriad of activities that include a daily massage, readings by psychics and astrologists, creative writing instruction, yoga, meditation and healing touch. They dine on food prepared by chefs who specialize in nutritional healing. At other times of the year, Sea View is the home of a week-long artists' workshop and a nature program.

In addition to your swimsuit, shorts and T-shirts, the other things you'll need are a good book and a fishing pole. Your stay includes three meals daily. From Memorial Day through Labor Day, Saturday to Saturday reservations are required. During other times of the year, a two-night minimum stay is required. Children three and younger are not allowed. Smoking is not permitted in the living or dining rooms.

The Shaw House Bed and Breakfast
$ • 613 Cypress Ct., Georgetown
• (843) 546-9663

Mary and Joe Shaw operate this refuge that overlooks Willowbank Marsh, considered by many to be a bird watcher's paradise. Getting to the Shaw House requires a jog through town, since it's set off the beaten paths of Georgetown, yet within walking distance of its historical district, shops and restaurants.

Three spacious rooms can be rented here, all furnished in antiques and offering a king- or queen-size Rice bed. Bicycles, games and an extensive library are extended to guests. Nightly turn down and chocolates are mainstay luxuries at the Shaw House.

A Southern home-cooked breakfast is served each morning that includes fresh baked bread and pots of rich coffee. Many guests of Shaw House have written that Mary is the ultimate hostess and personification of Southern hospitality.

Smoking is permitted on the outside porches.

Beyond The Strand

The Cypress Inn
$$ • 16 Elm St., Conway
• (843) 248-8199, (800) 575-5307

Just twelve miles from the heart of Myrtle Beach, in the charming town of Conway, this AAA Four Diamond Bed & Breakfast offers a welcome change of pace. Overlooking the Waccamaw River, this newly constructed Inn boasts twelve guest rooms, each with its own personality. The Carolina Room offers a king-sized mahogany four-poster bed, fireplace and a two-person Jacuzzi with a 12-inch French showerhead above.

The Miss Marple Room, featuring Country English decor, is home to over sixty Agatha Christi novels. Other amenities found in the rooms are plush bathrobes, luxurious bed linens, herbal soaps and shampoos and comfortable beds.

The business traveler will find the amenities and comfort of a luxury hotel—in-room desk, telephone with dataport, TV/VCR, private baths, fax and copier on-site—along with the personal service a bed and breakfast provides.

Each morning, breakfast is served in the sunny breakfast room. Wonderful, specially blended coffee, Tazo teas, homemade breads and muffins, fruit and a hot entree are presented to the guests. Some guest favorites include Sweet Potato Pancakes, Cypress Eggs, and Peachy French Toast.

The Inn is ideally located on Conway's Riverwalk. Guests can spend a leisurely afternoon rocking on the porch, renting a boat and cruising the Waccamaw River, biking around town or playing tennis just across the street.

The Cypress Inn serves an English Afternoon Tea the second and fourth Sunday each month. Teatime at the Inn is a time to relax and let the gentility of a bygone era sweep over you. Although the menu varies each week, some of the items served include scones, tea sandwiches, sweets and baked savories. There are two seatings at 2 PM and 3 PM and the cost is $10 per person. Reservations are required.

INSIDERS' TIP

The owners of local bed and breakfasts usually know a lot about local history, activities, and events. Be sure to spend some time talking with your hosts.

Restaurants

LOOK FOR:
• North Strand
• Myrtle Beach
• South Strand

We all work so hard to have a good time, strolling the beach in that soft sand, fighting the waves, spiking volleyballs, spotting and picking up all those pesky shells, stretching out on beach towels and working on a tan. Whatever you do here on the Grand Strand, you're going to work up an appetite whether you like it or not.

More than 1,500 restaurants accommodate our various palates. If you want to try every one of them on your next visit, plan on staying and eating three square meals a day for one year, five months. With this many restaurants from which to choose, this chapter can't begin to do justice to all the area's offerings. So we've opted to highlight a handful of favorites—mostly individually owned restaurants unique to the Strand. Of course, there are lots of good places we don't have room to cover, so our best advice for you is to explore!

One caveat: you might have to look a little harder to find a selection of exotic ethnic cuisine. Grand Strand restaurants have easy access to fresh seafood and therefore rightly emphasize the fresh catch and local nettings; you'll definitely find more family-style seafood buffets here than any single genre, followed closely by pancake houses. But as Myrtle Beach grows, so do our tastes, and restaurant owners are branching out into Thai, Fusion, Australian and Mediterranean, establishing some of the finest restaurants in America right in our biscuit-and-country-ham kind of town.

And the number is growing almost weekly. The village of Murrells Inlet, on the South Strand, is billed as the "seafood capital of South Carolina" with its nearly four dozen restaurants; the town of Calabash, North Carolina (on the North Strand), is credited with inventing Southern-fried seafood; and the stretch of U.S. Highway 17 between Myrtle Beach and North Myrtle Beach has been dubbed "Restaurant Row" because of its historical concentration of eateries. The opening of Broadway at the Beach and downtown Myrtle Beach establishments' efforts to be competitive have brought even more restaurants into the mix.

What to wear? What to wear! Yes, you can dine in long dresses and dark suits in some of the Strand's establishments; but you also can wear shorts and even bathing suits in others. From candlelight elegance to beer bashes in flip-flops, it's all here.

Don't think even for a minute that the phenomenal number of restaurants or the incredible choices of cuisine are johnny-come-lately ventures for tourism's sake. The dining heritage of the Grand Strand goes back two hundred years and is deeply entwined with the ghost stories, pirate adventures and folklore of this historic strip.

Hush puppies, the deep-fried and seasoned dollops of cornmeal-fish breading served with most Southern seafood dishes, are delivered as baskets of delicious little Ping-Pong-ball-size treats. The tasty morsels were invented more than 150 years ago, when it was fashionable for families to let dogs sleep under the table while they were eating. It was at one particular Murrells Inlet plantation that the cook decided to do something about the dogs that weren't sleeping as much as they were begging for treats from the table—especially when the meal was full of the aroma of fresh-cooked fish. This cook decided to take some leftover

INSIDERS' TIP

During June, July and August, Brookgreen Gardens offers the most soothing dinners available on the Grand Strand. Open until 9:30 PM Wednesday through Friday, Brookgreen offers a gourmet summer supper amidst their spectacular, manicured gardens. Adult admission is $8.50 plus the cost of dinner. Additionally, the Terrace Cafe is open for lunch and dinner. Call Brookgreen at (843) 235-6000 for more information.

breading, add a little sugar and make some quick-fried dough balls to set in baskets on the table. The idea was that when the dogs began begging, diners would toss a couple of dough balls under the table to "hush" the puppies. Of course it wasn't long before the humans at the table took a taste, and soon the dog pacifiers were "hushing" people too.

Over the years many seafood restaurants nationwide have offered hush puppies, but it is only in Murrells Inlet that the original sweet-flavored treats retain that unique plantation recipe. The cook at one Inlet restaurant today claims that his hush puppy recipe was handed down through eight generations. Even restaurants along the North Strand are often baffled by the South Strand flavor that seemingly no one has been able to duplicate; most Calabash-style restaurants serve hush puppies with onions in place of the sugar-sweet flavor.

"Calabash" is a word you'll see a lot when you go cruising for restaurants along the Strand. Calabash is a little fishing village in North Carolina, just across the state line, where Myrtle Beach vacationers since the 1930s have driven the 25 or so miles north on U.S. Highway 17 to enjoy the delicious fresh seafood meals. But in the past 10 or so years more than half the seafood buffet restaurants in Myrtle Beach have incorporated the word "Calabash" into the menus or signs describing their seafood. It has come to refer to the style of cooking that made tourists flock to the town: oily seafood dipped in a light cornmeal batter, deep fried and smothered with seasoned butter, then delivered to your table golden brown and piping hot.

Also in the Grand Strand's gastronomic mix are plenty of regionally and nationally known restaurants whose quality you can always count on: Cracker Barrel, Shoney's, Quincy's, Red Lobster, The Olive Garden, Pizza Hut, Fuddrucker's, T.G.I. Friday's ... the list is nearly endless. And we haven't even considered the fast-food regulars, all of which are present here.

Please note that many Grand Strand restaurants don't accept reservations, and long lines are common at the more laid-back walk-in places. The best bet here is to call before going or just drop in and see. As Insiders, one thing we have learned is that half the fun of eating at the beach is the adventure of finding a new favorite.

North Strand

Greg Norman's Australian Grille
$$$ • Barefoot Landing
• (843) 361-0000

Greg Norman's Australian Grille is the Grand Strand's most exciting and exquisite dining addition of 2000. This Greg Norman is the same Greg "the Shark" Norman of golfing fame, and the same Greg Norman of the Norman Course, which you can view from your table at his Australian Grille.

The flavors and seafood-heavy selection of the Australian Grille perfectly complement a stay on the Carolina coast, and the lively, aboriginal decor of the Grille goes well with our own Lowcountry stylings. The menu is amazing: pan fried lobster dumplings, Tasmanian sea mussels, miso and cane sugar marinated seabass, habanero-rubbed tenderloin, yellow fin tuna, even the classic Aussie pot pie, and spoon bread, an egg-rich Lowcountry specialty. Tables

are hard to get, and reservations are recommended. The bar is just as spacious and elegant as the dining rooms and includes a few TVs for sporting events (hmm, wonder which ones). It has its own satisfying menu: fried calamari tossed in a sweet-and-sour chili glaze, Queensland cut fries, and wood-grilled Yabbys (otherwise known as Australian crawfish) served in a Thai lobster broth.

Benito's Ristorante Italiano
$$$ • 1596 U.S. Hwy. 17 S.,
North Myrtle Beach
• (848) 272-1414

"Roma, Napoli and Venezia just got a little closer," proclaims Benito's, and they show it off, not only in their exquisitely fresh menu but with the stylish Italian setting.

There can't be a more delicious way to learn Italian than through Benito's extensive menu; pizetta al rosamarino, insalata Mediterranea, fusilli al pesto, osso bocco, pollo alla francese, penne con melenzane al forno, fettuccine alfredo ... don't worry, all are English subtitled, though there's no better dictionary than your own taste buds.

The Brentwood Restaurant
$$ • 4269 Luck St., Little River
• (843) 249-2601

The Brentwood is a feast for all your senses. The first floor of this remodeled Victorian-style restaurant, built in 1910, is reserved for dining. Upstairs there is a European "salon" where guests can retire after dinner for dessert and drinks, including espresso and cappuccino. It's also the perfect place to relax and leisurely enjoy a bottle of wine with cheese. Toss in a game of backgammon, and you've got the makings of a splendid interlude.

The food is, quite simply, excellent. Prior to opening The Brentwood, chef and owner Bill Stublick worked at two of the North Strand's best-loved restaurants: The Parson's Table and Oak Harbour Inn. Those in the know realize the value of those credentials. In addition to homemade desserts, the gourmet menu includes fresh veal, rack of lamb, fresh local seafood (the soft-shell crabs are extraordinary!), beef, pork and duck. Entrees include fresh-baked bread, a crisp salad, your choice of rice pilaf or Chantilly potatoes and a guaranteed-tasty vegetable of the day. There is also a delicious vegetarian menu available.

The Brentwood is open for dinner Monday through Saturday. Seatings begin at 5 PM, and reservations are suggested but not required.

Cappuccino's
$$ • 1531 U.S. Hwy. 17, Little River
• (843) 280-8999

Open for lunch and dinner, Cappuccino's feeds you well before you get to sit back and relax with a cup from their extensive list of coffees. Taking advantage of their proximity to the inlet, Cappuccino's emphasizes the fresh catch of the day or, as they state it on the menu, "what Bryan has selected from the local market." As with many locally run restaurants, the chef often makes it a point to get to know the customers, and Bryan Pearch is often seen—in full culinary regalia—checking on the dining room. We have enjoyed the green salads and the pasta of the day, usually seafood flavored,

at Cappuccino's. They also serve some tasty alternatives like crisp roast duck and spinach-walnut ravioli. The coffees, lattes, espressos and cappuccinos are complemented by the wallpaper, aprons and art depicting the same theme.

Down Under
$$ • 4310 McCorsley Ave., Little River
• (843) 249-5910

Unless he's too busy with his various skillets and pots, owner and chef Alan Pratt "G'days" everyone who walks through his door. This little hideaway is actually right on U.S. Highway 17 next to Toby's Old World (see the Shopping chapter for details) and The Parson's Table (also listed in this chapter), though partially obscured by a gazebo.

Inside and out, the cabin-like building is decked in smoothly worn wood, stained-glassed windows and vintage ski equipment Alan has placed about the rooms. The floor inside is heavily lacquered and complements the antiques. Bigger-than-life tropical fish hang from the ceiling to offset the stuffiness of antiques, and of course posters and mementos of Australia (watch out for that boomerang!) cover the walls. Alan maintains a blackboard menu in order to offer the freshest meals possible; the front patio has two porch swings to accommodate diners trying to make up their minds as they read the extensive list posted outside. We had a hard time—who can choose between pork tenderloin in apricot marsala glaze, salmon with Portobello mushrooms or oysters on the half-shell with fresh vegetables? These gourmet dinners, and the many more creations Alan thinks up, are served with the soup du jour (which also usually makes a perfect lunch,) salad, rice or potato and homemade bread.

Joe's Bar & Grill
$$$ • 810 Conway Ave.,
North Myrtle Beach
• (843) 272-4666

Owner and chef Joey Arakas wanted to give the Grand Strand a restaurant that would make diners feel as though they never left the comforts of their own homes. Fine dining in a rather rustic atmosphere is what has kept Joe's one of the busiest establishments in town for 13 years.

Joe's is the not the place to go if you have a

> **INSIDERS' TIP**
>
> One easy way to pack a picnic is to stop by the Grecian Corner in the Galleria Shopping Center in Restaurant Row. There's not much sitting room inside, but the menu covers all the Greek favorites like gyros and souvlaki, and they serve pizza too. Call ahead, (843) 449-9243.

Many area restaurants offer live entertainment—making dinner and dancing a delightful option.

Photo: Courtesy of Litchfield Beach & Golf Resort

craving for something fried: There is no such thing on this menu. The cuisine is definitely continental, including steak, seafood, veal and poultry dishes. All marinades, sauces, soups and dressings are made fresh daily. For seafood lovers, be sure to try the char-grilled swordfish with a jalapeno-lime cream sauce or the teriyaki tuna bites. Joe's is open for dinner only.

Oak Harbour Restaurant
$$ • 1407 13th Ave. N.,
North Myrtle Beach
• (843) 249-4737

Owners Phil and Theresa Annie, originally from Charleston, West Virginia, opened Oak Harbour Restaurant in 1990. Nestled alongside the Marina at Dock Holidays, Oak Harbour offers a casual yet intimate fine-dining experience. Enjoy a cocktail before (or after) dinner in the aquarium lounge. Then choose a table by the double-sided fireplace during cooler months; or, on warmer evenings, ask to sit on the outside deck overlooking the marina.

As for the food, the menu includes an array of fresh seafood, veal, pork and beef entrees. Try the strawberry shrimp appetizer followed by a sumptuous filet mignon entree. Or, if you're a true seafood lover, don't pass up the Grouper Crustacean, a fillet encrusted in Oriental bread crumbs, baked in a cream sauce and served with sauteed shrimp, scallops, mushrooms and onions. Save room for any of the delectable desserts and/or a cappuccino.

The Annies do their utmost to make every guest, from locals to travelers just passing through, feel at home. Dinner is served daily, and reservations are accepted.

Sante Fe Station
$$ • 1101 U.S. Hwy. 17 N.,
North Myrtle Beach
• (843) 249-3463

The single most distinctive thing about Sante Fe Station is the menu. It's bound to remind you of a metropolitan area phone book . . . it's enormous!

Sante Fe Station is fun—very youthful in atmosphere but not at all trendy. This restaurant has a great bar; have the bartender whip you up a fabulous specialty drink. There are 18 items on the appetizer menu alone! (Skip the reading: Order stuffed jalapenos or blackened lobster bites.) Entrees run the gamut, from healthy salads and fresh seafood to fat sandwiches, steaks, burgers, chicken and ribs. There's a kid's menu too. For dessert, the Key lime pie will soothe your sunburn. Better still, order a pitcher of Long Island iced tea and forget your worries. Sante Fe Station is open seven days a week for dinner only.

Theme Restaurants

A glass-cased, cyborg Arnold Schwartzenegger, armed and dangerous, watches you. A lobby is filled with lockers of personal items belonging to Andre Agassi, Tiger Woods and Monica Seles. Batman's suit stands at the ready. A huge pyramid covered with mysterious hieroglyphics rises out of a palm tree-studded parking lot. The $50,000, vintage choppers gleam with chrome. The Chevrolet that Jeff Gordon drove to win the Winston Cup Championship is parked out front. One of the country's largest collections of Folk or "Outsider" art by artists in the rural South fills walls with shoes, bottle caps, license plates and memorials to artisans. Bullwinkle pulls a rabbit out of his hat.

Myrtle Beach restaurants have all this and more.

So many restaurants compete for our attention that every single one strives for that niche that will make you crave its own specialized menu. But quite a few restaurants are getting a little more aggressive than hanging wacky antiques on the walls or letting you draw on the paper tablecloths with crayons. From outlandish architecture to glass-encased collections to celebrity owners, quite a few restaurants along the Grand Strand are rewriting the recipe for a fun, new-experience-filled and bedazzling dining experience.

House of Blues, Hard Rock Cafe, NASCAR Cafe, Easyriders Cafe, Planet Hollywood, the Official All Star Cafe and Bullwinkle's are the best examples of this new restaurant trend. They're also the most popular, so they are easy to recognize and find but, then again, parking might not be. They put on an elaborate show, though, and work hard for their money.

House of Blues in Barefoot Landing, North Myrtle Beach, is visible from U.S. Highway 17, but you might mistake it for a massive barn that someone forgot to tear down. *Don't* keep on driving—the House of Blues means to present this elegantly shabby image, and once you're a little closer you will not only agree with their decision, you will be entranced. The 43,000-square-foot structure looks like it is one of the originals in Myrtle Beach, but it just opened in the spring of 1997. To achieve this effect, the House of Blues went around the country buying not only the art and artifacts that fill the place, but also actually used and worn architectural and construction material, then carefully pieced it all together into the 700 capacity restaurant, outdoor "Sugar Shack" deck and 1,800 capacity concert hall that stands today.

The grand opening of the House of Blues was the biggest yet of all the splashes these restaurants put on, and we had the opportunity to attend. Instead of the formal, roped off runway of stars and the many celebrity investors, the House of Blues hosted a casual affair where we all enjoyed the courtyards and patios together. Dan Aykroyd, James Belushi, the then South Carolina Governor David Beasley and John Goodman rode right in on their loud Harleys; Cheech Marin brought all his kids; Alice Cooper showed up, as did quite a few bands worth of musicians, including James Brown.

Inside and out, the House of Blues is covered with more than 5,000 original paintings and sculptures by more than 60 self-taught creators. The art is almost primitive and rough but at the same time inspirational and full of expression. Every time we walk through we notice a new favorite. The deep porches and covered walkways serve as an open-air gallery; there's even plenty of wicker to rest on in the spacious Charleston-influenced courtyard shaded by live oak trees. You don't have to spend any money for this cultural experience, just walk through the welcoming, 11-foot wrought iron gates.

However, don't expect to get off without spending a few pennies. The restaurant, with its Southern pit cooking smells and ceiling embossed with portraits of blues legends, will draw you in. Every time we go, much as we try to order something else, we can't stay away from the Mississippi Cat Bites and the mashed sweet potatoes. Of course there's a lot more, from the Blues Brothers Salad to jambalaya to the smoked double-cut pork chops.

But even more irresistible is the House of Blues' Sunday gospel brunch. Every Sunday morning gospel groups from around the South perform at the House of Blues concert hall. It is an invigorating, soul-stirring experience. The elaborate banquet of grits, biscuits, roast beef, shrimp and rice, sausage and delicious bread pudding almost gets in the way of all the napkin waving, foot stomping and hallelujah-ing. By the end of the performance your tummy is full, your spirit renewed and half the audience members are up on stage singing their hearts out. As you can imagine, kids love it.

For more information on the musical talent that appears at the House of Blues, see our Entertainment chapter.

Hard Rock Cafe at Broadway at the Beach is probably the most recognized and picturesque; at any sunny moment, the sphinxes that guard the Hard Rock entrances are a favorite snapshot point. This international Pharaoh of restaurants occupies a huge pyramid surrounded by palm trees along the U.S. Highway 17 Bypass. It's hard to miss; at night it is lit up with spotlights, and around the clock it blares good old rock 'n' roll. When you enter the structure, you're a floor above the dining room—from this vantage point you get a bird's eye view of everyone else's meals and the cafe's collection of historic rock memorabilia.

The interior is covered with a stone finish, more hieroglyphics and mementos of rock and roll. The walls vibrate with echoes from the guitars of Hank Williams Jr., The Who, Joe Walsh, the Allman Brothers, Black Crowes, Black Sabbath, Pearl Jam, Guns and Roses, Jimi Hendrix, Bob Dylan and Jerry Garcia. These instruments were once in the hands of legends, and now they're out in the open to enjoy as you dine. A myriad of displays fill every nook, even at the phone booth and in the restrooms: Nancy Sinatra's made-for-walkin' boots, gold lamé shorts from Rocky of the *Rocky Horror Picture Show*, Brian Jones' fur coat and countless gold and platinum records from the likes of Buddy Holly, Nirvana, the Osmonds and the Beatles.

(Continued on next page)

RESTAURANTS

Hard Rock Cafe in Myrtle Beach rocks like an Egyptian.

Photo: Lisa Tomer Rentz

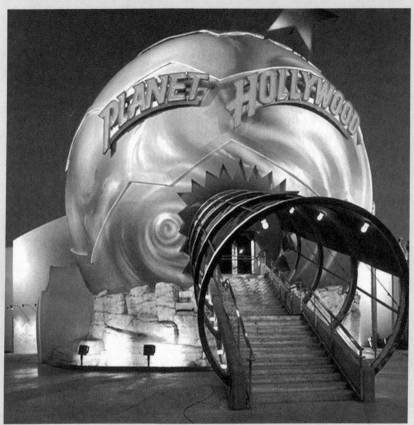

Planet Holly's outlandish architecture causes you to wonder what awaits inside.

Photo: Courtesy of Planet Hollywood

Of course, the menu can't be outdone by the elaborate interior, and you have your choice of almost 50 items. The Hard Rock, with its "Love All, Serve All" philosophy, has cooked up a selection for every lifestyle, from the Hard Rock Natural Veggie Burger to the Hickory Chicken 'N Ribs Combo. If you're just old fashioned, you can top it all off with a thick, cold milk shake or malt.

Immediately across the bypass from the Hard Rock is the NASCAR Cafe festooned in checkered flags. NASCAR has definitely transcended the restaurant category by adding a 20-acre racetrack—please see the Attractions chapter for more details. The designers couldn't even stop thinking about the track when they designed the restaurant; upon entry to the building you have to look both ways to cross Bill France Boulevard, which is busy with people checking out the displays and playing the many interactive video games. The boulevard is a walk through NASCAR history; Mr. France, whose life-size wax figure starts off the course, founded NASCAR in 1948. Huge sections of wall are dedicated to the icons of the racing world: Richard Petty, Dave Marcis, Dale Earnhardt, Chad Little, even Speed Racer. Throughout the restaurant 13 race cars are suspended from the ceiling, providing you with a novel, not to mention slowed-down, look at the machines.

Inside the circle of Bill France Boulevard is the NASCAR Cafe proper. Booths form another circular track around a massive bar that is crowned with David Pearson's Mercury Purolator, which won the 1976 Daytona Championship. Even the wait staff is groomed for speed; everyone wears a sleek red jumpsuit for ease of movement and a headset for quick communication; all the sooner to zip out platefuls of Thunder Road Burgers, Longtrack Chili Dogs, Bill France Pork Chops or a chocolate fudge tire.

For more motor madness, back in Celebrity Square at Broadway at the Beach is Easyriders Cafe, paying tribute to that other loud and fast machine, the motorcycle. This is a pretty tough-looking place, but everyone is here for a good time. Expect loud, live music, often in the form of tribute bands honoring classic rock legends like Led Zeppelin and AC/DC. Easyriders takes music seriously, almost as seriously as the bikes. The cafe has a few displays of its own accented by a slew of provocative *Easyriders* magazine covers, Peter Fonda's and Dennis Hopper's bikes from (what else) *Easyrider* the movie and the first V8 drag bike, which is owned by Joe Teresi, publisher of *Easyriders* magazine.

Everything inside the restaurant is chrome, black leather, steel studded or detailed in flames and racing stripes. Each barstool is the saddle of a bike, complete with leather fringe; don't mistake the staff's clothing for uniforms, most people that visit and work here have a serious interest in motorcycles and dress accordingly. In addition to the laid-back atmosphere, Easyriders Cafe hosts many community events such as free concerts in Celebrity Square, a Valentine's Day oyster roast and bike rally, and Labor Day and Christmas runs benefitting local charities.

For all this riding and partying, the menu is hearty. Nacho Mamma is drowning in cheese and beans, the V Twin is a monster double burger and the Chunk of Beef and Bread is "like a steak sandwich, only better." We recommend the barbecue oysters and Rips Chips with spicy carrots as a snack. Easyriders rounds off its services with the most impressive line of merchandise of all the restaurants around—it retails and services the full line of American Eagles Motors. You can ride out of there on two wheels for $17,000 to $24,000.

The Official All Star Cafe and Planet Hollywood share a parking lot across 25th Avenue from Broadway at the Beach. After visiting these two you'll feel like you've broken bread with your favorite luminaries. Both restaurants have highly recognizable owners who very publicly promote the establishments.

Planet Hollywood does everything to fulfill its name; the building itself is a blue and green planet, and the cement foundation is imprinted with the handprints and signatures of Bruce Willis, Demi Moore, Sylvester Stallone, Arnold Schwartzenegger, Melanie Griffith, Don Johnson, Jean Claude Van Damme and others. The wait at Planet Hollywood begins right here since most visitors love to compare their own hands with those of the stars.

Inside Planet Hollywood is a panorama of blockbuster movie hits. Throughout all the display cases, between booths, around pillars and covering an entire two-story wall is a collage of superstar faces a la the Sgt. Pepper's Lonely Hearts Club Band album cover. George Clooney looks mischievous, Elvis croons, Melanie hugs Don, Demi looks captivating in an evening gown as does Bruce in his muscle T, Mel Gibson and Wesley Snipes compete for a toughness award and, for some reason, Antonio Banderas is bowling but still manages to look smooth as can be.

In unmistakable Hollywood kitsch, animal print is the upholstery of choice, lending a stylish appeal to the fun restaurant. So settle in and unfold the 4-foot-long menu. Start off with a cocktail—a Ghost or a Cliffhanger or, if you're brave, The Terminator (catch that pattern?). As an appetizer we recommend the Chicken Crunch, which is tender chicken strips coated with CAP'N CRUNCH™ cereal and served with creole mustard. For the main course the menu offers a fusion of West Coast, Italian and Asian: the Pizza Margherita is savory and the Thai shrimp pasta is an adventure.

At the Official All Star Cafe you'll get hungry from just taking in the many

(Continued on next page)

displays of athletic accomplishment. Built to be a miniature stadium and topped with Olympic-like torches, the sports theme is extreme like the pro owners themselves. Inside the walls are broken up into sections honoring the careers of Andre Agassi, Joe Montana, Shaquille O'Neal, Monica Seles, Tiger Woods, Wayne Gretzky and Ken Griffey Jr. Their accomplishments are depicted larger than life: an endearing cutout of Agassi as a kid swinging an adult-size racquet, a list of facts about Tiger Woods at the age of 6 playing with Sam Snead, a growth chart for Shaq and a lesson in anatomy through all of Montana's injuries.

With true sportsmanship, the athletes share the playing field with their peers. Additional displays highlight the accomplishments of Coastal Carolina University's teams, a history of baseball players in the army, Chuck Norris' black belt and, of course, many signed jerseys.

But since you don't have any goals to defend or any balls to hit during the meal, sit down in one of the booths shaped like a giant baseball mitt and read the menu instead. The All Star has made a conscientious effort to combine the healthy with the tasty: The Vegadilla is a low-fat alternative to the quesadilla, filled with a chilled julienne vegetable medley, chopped cilantro and Southwest Vinaigrette. Or you can go all out with Joe's three cheese ravioli, a rib steak and Swiss sandwich or a serving of buffalo shrimp with bleu cheese sauce.

Tiger Woods greets the Grand Strand

Photo: Lisa Tomer Rentz

Bullwinkle's Family Food and Fun joined the Broadway at the Beach menagerie in 1998. The Bulwinkle's building goes beyond the architectural precedent set by its colorful neighbors. Cartoonishly klondike, the restaurant is a split-log lodge straight out of Frostbite Falls. Inside, children have the opportunity to play in a towering soft play structure, while Bullwinkle the Moose ("Guess I didn't know my own strength") and Rocky the Flying Squirrel ("Again? That trick never works") are as animated as ever. The play structure has slides, wobbling walkways and a club house, among many other tricks and turns for young'uns to explore. Since there is no size or age limit, parents are encouraged to accompany their mini-mounties through this rollicking obstacle course. Fortunately, after all that hard play, you won't need Mr. Peabody's Way Back Machine to find and enjoy, Rocky's Remarkable burgers, Dudley's Done Right Pizza, or some yummy Klondike Fried Chicken.

And finally the Alabama Grille, renamed "Music City Grille," (to prevent confusion with the Alabama Theatre) has re-opened at their new location also on the Highway 17 Bypass, across from Broadway at the Beach. The Grille promises as much entertainment as the Alabama Theatre at Barefoot Landing, and as many stars as Planet Hollywood and the All Star Cafe combined. The menu is suitably hearty, and special "Alabama's favorites" are marked with a musical note: bacon and cheese skins, ultimate club sandwich, southern fried chicken salad, smokehouse burger, the Alabama savory sirloin, and smoky mountain chicken. The Grille's specialty dessert is a down-home cheesecake with a luscious swirl of sweet potato. Randy, Teddy, Jeff and Mark, who make up the supergroup Alabama, got their start right here in Myrtle Beach in the '70s. Since then they have sold more records than the Beatles, a figure built on over 40 No. 1 hits. So, in one day, you can experience their beginnings at the

Bowery (near the Pavilion) have dinner amongst all their pictures, guitars, signatures, carefully framed outfits, sheet music, and favorite meals, and see them live at their theatre. Though the memorabilia posted around the restaurant (and the items in the gift store, and many of the videos played in the video walls) do concentrate on Alabama, there is a unifying country theme, bringing in the biggest country hits of the moment.

T-Bonz Gill & Grill
$$ • Barefoot Landing,
4732 U.S. Hwy. 17 S., North Myrtle Beach
• (843) 272-7111
$$ • U.S. Hwy. 17 Bypass and
21st Ave. N., Myrtle Beach
• (843) 946-7111

T-Bonz' big ole menu and spacious (if noisy) interior is fun, fun, fun. Hearty portions of beef, grilled chicken, vegetarian entrees, seafood and more are standard fare. For the Southern born 'n' bred, we think you'll be particularly fond of the shrimp-and-grits specialty—a creamier dish of the snowy stuff has never been created to our knowledge. A vast selection of imported and domestic wine and beer is offered.

We sometimes choose T-Bonz just because the folks there are so environmentally conscious. They recycle all their glass and cardboard and avoid the use of plastic foam. The atmosphere is casual, the price is affordable and kids are welcome.

Open 11 AM until late night, T-Bonz also offers light lunches and an after-hours social scene. Stop in at either location.

Tony's Italian Restaurant
$$ • 1407 Old Hwy. 17 N.,
North Myrtle Beach
• (843) 249-1314

Tony's is the oldest Italian restaurant along the Grand Strand and has been owned and operated by the Springs family since opening its doors in 1953. The recipes for Tony's dishes have been handed down from generation to generation, and the kitchen never compromises its homemade quality. Nothing on your plate at Tony's is prepackaged or frozen; even the herbs are fresh-picked from the restaurant's very own garden.

Our perfect Tony's dining experience starts with the Clams Posillipo (steamed clams draped with marinara sauce) as an appetizer followed by the Terri Lynn Veal Scallopini featuring fresh mushrooms and artichoke hearts in a brown brandy sauce.

For dessert we heartily recommend the Zuppa Inglese, a three-layer cake with alternating fillings of chocolate mousse, lemon and cannoli ... then topped with a cloud of whipped cream. Tony's is open every day of the week for dinner.

White Point Cafe
$ • 3303 U.S. Hwy. 17 S.,
North Myrtle Beach
• (843) 272-6732

White Point Cafe has successfully combined the big Calabash-style seafood house flavor with the atmosphere of the keep-it-a-secret neighborhood restaurant.

The menu offers all your favorite seafood—she-crab soup, oysters, shrimp, flounder and scallops—in plate filling combinations topped off with, what else, some of the Grand Strand's best hush puppies. Occasionally we stop in just for a hush puppy fix, lunch or dinner.

Myrtle Beach

U.S. Highway 17 Business is known as Kings Highway throughout Myrtle Beach. The Kings Highway address is used for establishments listed in this section.

Akel's House of Pancakes
$ • 6409 N. Kings Hwy., Myrtle Beach
• (843) 449-4815

For local color, don't miss Akel's; it's a Myrtle Beach landmark. In an area known for its stellar lineup of pancake houses, Akel's rates right up top. Whether for the food, the service or the all-night hours, we're not sure. The atmosphere is friendly and surprisingly familiar. Gossip, laughter and local news travels from one table to another; a meal here is as good as reading the local paper!

Open 10 PM to 2 PM, Akel's is everybody's favorite way to wrap up a night on the town. Needless to say, it's a great way to start your morning too. Come watch the locals in their element! While breakfast fare is the house speciality, Akel's offers lots of sandwiches, salads and burgers too.

Angelo's Steak & Pasta

$ • 2011 S. Kings Hwy., Myrtle Beach
• (843) 626-2800

Angelo's is the home of the all-you-can-eat Italian buffet that includes chicken cacciatore, pizza, spaghetti, stuffed shells, tortellini Alfredo, stuffed ravioli and Italian sausage. Every meal at this restaurant is accompanied with a big bowl of crisp salad served family-style and wonderful garlic rolls.

A full-service menu is available as well, and Angelo's claims to serve "the greatest steaks in the universe." If you're like us, you'll spend a good amount of time mulling over whether to head for the buffet or try a sirloin... . Both are mouth-watering.

Angelo's opens for dinner at 4 PM every day of the week. The Italian buffet closes at 8:30 PM.

The Bistro

$$$ • 5101 N. Kings Hwy., Myrtle Beach
• (843) 449-0465

The Bistro is a very quaint restaurant that serves sumptuous continental cuisine and extraordinary desserts. Indoors, about 40 people can enjoy the friendly atmosphere. If the weather cooperates, about 16 additional guests can dine on the porch. Specialties include veal, steaks, chicken and pasta dishes.

The Bistro is open for lunch and dinner, and it's the perfect choice for a romantic interlude. Dinner is served from 5:30 PM at this longtime locals' favorite.

Cagney's Old Place

$$$ • Restaurant Row,
9911 U.S. Hwy. 17 N., Myrtle Beach
• (843) 449-3824

For nearly two decades, Cagney's Old Place has been a favorite local dining and dancing spot—and tourists have discovered our secret. There's ambiance aplenty and great food too. Many of the antiques that enliven Cagney's decor came from the Ocean Forest Hotel, a fabulous oceanfront accommodation that was demolished in 1974.

Cagney's specialty has always been prime rib, but everything is perfectly delicious. A children's menu is also available. *Southern Living*, a magazine reputed for it's high standards, recommends this classic.

Only dinner is served at Cagney's.

Carolina Roadhouse

$$ • 4700 N. Kings Hwy., Myrtle Beach
• (843) 497-9911

Brought to you by Jerry Greenbaum, who created wildly successful restaurants in other cities—California Dreaming, Frank ManZetti's and Joey D's, to name a few—Carolina Roadhouse is shaping up to be another "home run."

Like her sister restaurants, Carolina Road-

Broadway at the Beach has a plethora of shops and restaurants in a breezy, bright setting.

Photo: Lisa Tomer Rentz

house displays unusually beautiful architecture and interior design. Soaring ceilings, arched windows, skillfully positioned mirrors and an abundance of recessed lighting establish a mood that is intimate without a hint of stuffiness. The sweet, spicy scent of cedar abounds, as does a medley of exquisite smells from the wide-open kitchen.

The service is outstanding; so is the food. From tender barbecue chicken to melt-in-your-mouth ribs, steaks and seafood, the portions and variety are impressive. Salads, sporting an incomparable hot bacon and honey-mustard dressing, are enormous and otherworldly. A plain ole croissant takes on a new dimension served hot, dripping with warm honey. Seafood gumbo, brimming with okra, shrimp and crawfish, is anything but ordinary. And vacating the premises without sampling a bowl of baked potato soup would be an absolute injustice. For dessert, try the brownie a la mode; served with almonds and a splash of Kahlua, it's a sophisticated, grown-up take on ordinary cake and ice cream.

Open daily for lunch and dinner (same menu), Carolina Roadhouse is one of the most happening restaurants in Myrtle Beach, so don't miss out. Dress is casual, and reservations are accepted. Go quickly.

Chestnut Hill
$$$ • **Restaurant Row,**
9922 U.S. Hwy. 17, Myrtle Beach
• **(843) 449-3984**

In an area saturated with fine dining options, Chestnut Hill distinguishes itself. Smack-dab in the heart of Restaurant Row, Chestnut Hill sits beneath age-old oaks and overlooks a small, quiet lake. Its location is worlds removed from the resort hustle-bustle and sets the stage for a dining experience that's out of the ordinary.

From the pasta sauces to the cheesecakes, absolutely everything is made from scratch, and 80 percent of the fresh seafood served here was caught on Chestnut Hill's own boat—just hours before. The menu is filled with gourmet dishes, and the service is friendly and accommodating.

Owners Chris and Greg Lee have several

INSIDERS' TIP
If you want the convenience and cost of fast food but the robust flavor of some hearty Italian, try Fazoli's at one of their two locations: 1205 U.S. Highway 17 in Surfside, (843) 477-1801, and 1561 U.S. Highway 17 in North Myrtle Beach, (843) 249-6901. They are open for lunch and dinner.

extremely popular restaurants along the Strand, and they know more than a thing or two about feeding hungry people.

Dinner is served every evening. Chestnut Hill serves an outstanding Sunday brunch.

Collectors Cafe and Gallery
$$$$ • **7726 N. Kings Hwy., Myrtle Beach**
• **(843) 449-9370**

Everybody has their own concept of a great restaurant. Some enjoy the casual, comfortable and unpretentious. Some like the blue-blood feeling they derive from the attentive service in an elegant restaurant. Still others prefer the intimacy of a neighborhood bar or coffeehouse. Amazingly, Collectors Cafe has managed to fuse all three environments, and we can't imagine anyone who wouldn't be satisfied spending an evening here.

In the dining room, columns and high ceilings exude elegance and original paintings depict Low-country seascapes as well as Parisian city scapes. Beyond the dining room, a grill room with over-size canvases and hand-tiled, bar-height tables allow you to watch Collectors' chefs chop and sizzle. In the coffeehouse room you can relax and feel a little bohemian while surrounded by more original art that includes not only hanging canvases, but artwork on every surface, table, wall and chair.

Surrounding patrons with all this art, Collectors Cafe serves up a feast for the senses as well as for the appetite. (By the way, most of the art is available to add to your own collection. Please refer to the Arts and Culture chapter for the Close-up on one of the artists, Thomas Davis.)

The restaurant bills itself as serving Mediterranean cuisine. Appetizers include a filet of beef carpaccio with extra virgin olive oil, spicy mustard, balsamic vinegar and Parmesan cheese. A favorite entree is pan-sauteed crab cakes with a white port mustard sauce, shiitake mushrooms and tomatoes. Of course, there are also pasta and salad selections as well as veal, lots of fresh seafood and grilled breast of duck.

After dinner, take time to enjoy the home-made tiramisu, or for that matter any of the desserts; you can walk an extra mile or two on the beach tomorrow.

As a gallery, Collectors Cafe opens at noon, Monday through Saturday. The restaurant is open for dinner only and reservations are highly recommended.

Dagwoods
$, no credit cards
• **400 11th Ave. N., Myrtle Beach**
• **(843) 448-0100**

Since the 1940s, the term "Dagwood" has referred to a multi-decker sandwich stuffed with anything and everything. That pretty much describes the fare here.

It takes two big hands to handle the monstrous subs at Dagwoods. There's not a lot of ambiance—Dagwoods is a frat hangout at its best—but with sandwiches and prices like these, who cares?

Baskets of homemade bread (baked fresh daily) and an authentic deli case greet you at the door—reminiscent of a New York delicatessen. Choose from a variety of hot and cold sandwiches that showcase a mile-high stack of meats and cheeses. You can feast on burgers and Philly cheese steaks too. At lunchtime, local business folk frequent the place, so it's gotta be good.

Dagwoods is open for lunch and dinner. (Suggestion: Come for lunch and eat the other half of your sub for dinner.)

Dirty Don's Oyster Bar & Grill
$$ • **408 21st Ave. N., Myrtle Beach**
• **(843) 448-4881**

Dirty Don's is small in size but big on character. Serving lunch and dinner, Dirty Don's features oyster shooters, clams on the half-shell, a variety of sandwiches, and a tasty "ragtime" fish stew. The catfish fingers are fab, especially with a Margarita. Bigger appetites are fond of the juicy steaks and king-size shrimp dinners.

Dirty Don's is the perfect place to spend an afternoon out of the sun . . . noshing on appetizers and drinking tall cool ones.

Fiesta Del Burro Loco
$$ • **960 Jason Blvd. (U.S. Hwy. 17 Bypass and 10th Ave. N.), Myrtle Beach**
• **(843) 626-1756**

Fiesta Del Burro Loco is one of the newer restaurants on the Strand, but you'd never know it by looking. The exterior of the building was created to look authentically old and straight from Mexico; its visual appeal alone is a draw.

Once inside you won't be disappointed. The interior is eclectic and every bit as extraordinary as the exterior. At the door you'll be greeted by a three-sided, 45-foot-tall mural of a bull fight. Other murals are scattered throughout. A billboard collage covers the ceiling. There's an upside-down velvet Elvis mural above the bar. And the whole place is filled with authentic artifacts . . . so filled, you'll discover something new each and every time you visit.

And you must visit. Burro Loco manages to assault your senses in a most delightful way. The smell of fajitas sizzling on a mesquite grill will make your mouth water, as will the pizzas cooking in the wood-burning oven. Once you've tasted Burro Loco's handcrafted Margaritas (the limes are squeezed by hand) and their made-from-scratch tortillas, your taste buds will be hooked.

Fiesta Del Burro Loco is open for dinner every day. Reservations are not required, but call-ahead seating is available. Don't miss the fajitas, a house specialty, or the hand-pitted, stuffed jalapenos.

Flamingo Seafood Grill
$$$ • **7100 N. Kings Hwy., Myrtle Beach**
• **(843) 449-5388**

Flamingo Grill's art-deco decor—black lacquer accented with pink and blue neon—sets the pace for a trendy evening of dining. Owned by the same folks of Cagney's fame (see this chapter's previous entry), this restaurant has become quite popular.

The menu includes lots of fresh seafood prepared in a variety of ways. The grilled fish with Cajun spices is especially tasty. Other entrees include pasta (the Pasta Flamingo is delish), chicken, prime rib and steak. As an appetizer, the filet mignon chunks are outstanding. Save room for dessert; the Outrageous Derby Pie is . . . well . . . outrageous. A children's menu is also available.

Flamingo Grill serves dinner only.

INSIDERS' TIP

Famous for their chocolates in San Francisco, Ghirardelli's (gear-ar-delly) has opened an old-timey Soda Fountain and Chocolate Shop in Barefoot Landing. One of their grandest creations is The Earthquake, made with 8 scoops of ice cream, and the traditional bananas and whipped cream (and more!) toppings. Made to share, it's $19.06. Ghirardelli's also serves single scoops, floats, hot chocolate and coffee, and the reliable chocolate bar.

Gilley's Texas Cafe
$$ • Broadway at the Beach,
U.S. Hwy. 17 Bypass, Myrtle Beach
• (843) 448-3378

Mickey Gilley, one of country music's most popular entertainers, opened this restaurant in fall 1995. As you might expect, Gilley's specializes in Southwestern cuisine served amid Southwestern decor, and the menu features several of the owner's original recipes. Examples include Gilley's chili (perfect with a salty Margarita) and the homemade salsa and barbecue sauces. The steaks here could easily qualify for consideration in a "best on the beach" competition.

One of the neatest characteristics of Gilley's is the restaurant's clever exterior; it looks as though a small airplane crashed into its side. Who can blame the pilot? It was probably worth it just for the chili.

Gilley's serves lunch and dinner daily.

Liberty Steakhouse and Brewery
$$ • Broadway at the Beach,
U.S. Hwy. 17 Bypass, Myrtle Beach
• (843) 626-4677

The idea of combining a restaurant and micro-brewery is hot these days, and Liberty Steakhouse is doing well sustaining the craze. Here guests enjoy beer that's made fresh every single day. On special holidays, such as Oktoberfest and St. Patrick's Day, seasonal brews are all the rage. Everyone who comes gets the opportunity to observe the working brewery staffed by expert brewmeisters. In itself, the beer-making lesson is worth the stop. The pleasant surprise is that the food is wonderful too.

The menu includes hearty and delicious standard fare in whopping portions: specialty cuts of beef, original-recipe burgers and unique appetizers and entrees such as buffalo shrimp.

Liberty is open for lunch and dinner.

The Library
$$$$ • 1212 N. Kings Hwy., Myrtle Beach
• (843) 448-9242

The Library is one of the most elegant restaurants in the entire South—recipient of guests' kudos as well as prestigious professional accolades. Offering consummate European cuisine and superior service, this restaurant has been quietly collecting fans since 1974. In a *Sun News* survey, locals voted The Library the "most romantic" dining spot on the Strand—with so many restaurants, that's a real coup! The menu includes veal, seafood, duck, beef and chicken . . . first-class all the way. The name come from the literary decor, of course; the walls are lined with cases of literature that accentuate the leisurely and almost genteel atmosphere. Open for dinner only.

New York Prime
$$$$ • 405 28th Ave. N., Myrtle Beach
• (843) 448-8081

New York Prime is one of the area's finest restaurants. Owners Ed Cribb and Jerry Greenbaum first envisioned the restaurant when they returned from a trip to New York, where they ate at Peter Luger's, The Palm, Spark's and Smith and Wollensky. Reminiscing, they wondered if a real New York-style steak-house would make it on the Grand Strand. In researching the concept, Ed and Jerry traveled around to see what America's best steakhouses have in common. They discovered that people will pay more for quality, but the food must be truly exemplary.

Concept confirmed, they went to Nebraska, where they established a unique supply chain, purchasing only from two slaughter houses that ship according to Ed's and Jerry's incredibly stringent specifications. Upon receipt, they age their meat for 28 to 35 days, then trim it of excess fat.

The cooking completes the technique. No spices and no tenderizers disguise inferior meat. Cuts are extra thick, and ceramic broilers cook at 1,700 degrees.

The same attention to detail in supply and preparation goes into every morsel of food at New York Prime. Expect the freshest fish, giant lobsters shipped direct and kept live (never frozen), fresh Idaho potatoes, sweet Vidalia onions and tomatoes straight from sunny California. An extensive wine cellar will complement your dining experience.

The prices are steep, but the experience is extraordinary and the quality entirely justifies the prices. Open for dinner nightly.

INSIDERS' TIP
Horry's Restaurant by the Waccamaw Rivers is a "Family Tradition Begun in 1957." Located on S.C. Highway 9, 6 miles out in the country from North Myrtle Beach, Horry's specializes in oysters and fresh catch. This is the epitome of a local's place, and going by the only true measure of culinary excellence (a full parking lot), also one of the best places in the Grand Strand for local seafood. Breaking with Grand Strand tradition, they call their hush puppies corn dodgers.

Nick's
$$$• 503 61st Ave. N., Myrtle Beach
• **(843) 449-1716**

Nick's is the brand new name with the brand new menu, at the long-standing Myrtle Beach favorite, Latif's bakery. Latif's began as a modest French bakery more than 17 years ago, and with the help of Nick's, has expanded to offer a truly delightful experience for lunch or dinner. The enclosed terrace is especially charming and will make you feel as if you ambled in for a cup of espresso somewhere on Paris' left bank.

Nick's menu takes care of your square meal: Parmesan Fried Oysters, Fried Green Tomato Na-polean (served with Louisiana crawfish, sweet corn ragout and a chipotle remoulade), plantain empanadas, potato-crusted grouper, and crispy duck breast. Do prepare your palate with the silky lobster bisque.

Latif's waits its turn to crown Nick's offerings with a treasure trove of desserts. Even *Bon Apetit* said so. We've traveled the world over and never found any we'd rate higher. The triple chocolate mocha mousse torte is beyond description. It's light as air going down, but once it hits your hips—watch out! There are scads of cheesecakes, all kinds of speciality cakes (yes, Latif's sells by the slice), brownies, cookies, pecan tassies, chocolate eclairs, baklava and so much more.

Lunch and dinner hours vary throughout the year, so please call ahead for specific hours.

River City Cafe
$ • 404 21st Ave. N., Myrtle Beach
• **(843) 448-1990**
$ • U.S. Hwy. 17 Bus., Murrells Inlet
• **(843) 651-1004**

River City Cafe is the best hamburger joint on the beach for reasons only a bona fide hamburger connoisseur would appreciate. First, it's the perfect setting: a wood-frame building that resembles an old beach house. Inside, you'll find worn wooden floors, benches and chairs. Car tags, bumper stickers and party paraphernalia adorn the ceiling and walls.

Outside at the Murrells Inlet location, you'll find a wraparound porch with swings and a sunny deck peppered with big picnic tables. Inside not a single table or chair matches. Expect a crackling fire to be burning in winter, and the music is great.

At both locations, customers serve themselves from the big bin of dry-roasted peanuts and throw the empty shells on the floor—just oozes class, huh? But this all leads to the best part: huge, 100 percent pure beef burgers topped with a variety of fixin's, such as thick slabs of cheese, jalapenos, lettuce, tomatoes, grilled onions, bacon . . . the works!

These burgers require two hands to manage, and although they can be a little messy, they're worth several napkins. Don't forget the homemade jumbo onion rings. River City also serves a variety of other sandwiches and hot dogs. It's been said that only an ice-cold longneck bottle of beer truly complements River City Cafe's burgers. We think Jimmy Buffett's *Cheeseburger in Paradise* was inspired by this savory spot. Open for lunch and dinner daily.

Rossi's
$$$ • The Galleria,
9600 U.S. Hwy. 17 N., Myrtle Beach
• **(843) 449-0481**

Rossi's bills itself as "everything a restaurant ought to be," and we have to agree. A bevy of delights awaits your arrival: overly generous servings of veal, homemade pasta, fresh seafood and Black Angus beef; fine wines; a cozy dining room featuring weathered brick, stained glass and chandeliers; a piano bar; live entertainment; and desserts that'll make you do the two-step.

Rossi's is open daily for dinner only.

Sam Snead's Tavern
$$ • Restaurant Row,
U.S. Hwy. 17 N., Myrtle Beach
• **(843) 497-0580**

In the heart of Restaurant Row, Sam Snead's Tavern offers a delicious retreat from the workaday blues—or from vacation overdrive. Not small but marvelously cozy, Sam Snead's serves up memorable food in a memorable atmosphere.

The experience begins when the dark, sweet

INSIDERS' TIP

Benito's cream sauce, House of Blues' corn bread, and Frank's crabcakes are memorable local dishes, all of which start with a fine-tuned recipe. *The Sun News* has gathered the recipes of favorite area restaurants to fill two scrumptious cookbooks: *Flavors of Myrtle Beach,* and *More Flavors of Myrtle Beach.* Reach the *Sun News* at (800) 568-1800 for more information.

smell of burning oak assaults you. Fascinating golf memorabilia from Sam Snead's renowned PGA career is richly displayed on every available surface. Soft lights spill shadows in corners and polished wood abounds. The result is casual elegance that is both fun and affordable.

As for the food, there's a lot of it—and it's remarkably good. A great many choices feature flavors fresh from the aromatic wood-burning oven. Don't miss the Deep-Fried Niblicks: delicate pastries filled with a smoky puree of chicken and peppers. The ribs—hand-rubbed, oak-smoked and served with homemade Jim Beam barbecue sauce—are a must-try item too. Desserts are wicked and well worth the mischief; save room or you'll be disappointed.

Skip lunch; you can only enjoy dinner here.

Sea Captain's House
$$$ • 3002 N. Ocean Blvd., Myrtle Beach • (843) 448-8082

Back around 1930, the Sea Captain's House was a traditional family beach cottage. Converted to an oceanfront restaurant in 1962, it has remained a family-owned and operated business to this day.

If you enjoy understated elegance, delicious food and a panoramic view of the ocean, Sea Captain's House is sure to please. Specials range from grilled salmon fillets with roasted garlic sauce to baked breast of chicken topped with Cajun-spiced shrimp. The kitchen staff is known for its culinary talents, particularly with seafood and Southern recipes.

Visit this lovely Myrtle Beach landmark—another personal favorite—for breakfast, lunch or dinner.

Sea Island, An Inn on the Beach
$$$$ • 6000 N. Ocean Blvd., Myrtle Beach • (843) 449-6406

The dining room at the Sea Island Inn is irrefutably one of the best-kept secrets in Myrtle Beach. Because this establishment caters first and foremost to its in-house guests, Sea Island doesn't do a lot of advertising to an outside market. But, on a limited basis, the restaurant is open to the public. Lucky us.

This full-service restaurant serves fine continental cuisine for breakfast and dinner with a beautiful ocean view. Dinner is a special treat—you'll need to dress up (men must wear coats).

The chef always prepares a five-course meal; you get to choose between five mouth-watering entrees. Seafood is an option, and you'll find enough chicken, beef and veal alternatives to make your decision a tough one. Everything is fresh, never frozen. The service is impeccable, the atmosphere is intimate and reservations are suggested.

Thoroughbreds
$$$$ • Restaurant Row, U.S. Hwy. 17 N., Myrtle Beach • (843) 497-2636

A favorite among locals and tourists, Thoroughbreds' popularity has grown by leaps and bounds since it opened in 1988. When the restaurant became unable to accommodate nightly reservations as well as the community's requests for public and private functions, owner and operator Scott Harrelson made the decision to overhaul. Not someone to do anything in a small way, Harrelson spent in excess of $500,000—and it shows. The new Thoroughbreds, featuring four beautifully appointed dining rooms, an elegant piano bar and a captivating garden terrace, offers an unparalleled celebration of food, spirits, music and art.

Arguably, this is the most elegant restaurant on the Strand. The wait staff is meticulously trained and very professional; harp music often is highlighted; and candlelight abounds. The menu combines gourmet seafood and continental cuisine. Caesar salads are prepared table side. In our opinion the beef is best, but you'll also enjoy chicken, veal, pork and even duck.

Lest you be fooled into thinking Thoroughbreds is too ritzy for your average vacation meal, think again. Yes, it's elegant, and you do need to dress up a bit, but the atmosphere is cozy, the staff is friendly and accommodating, and children are welcome. We think you'll be glad you donned your finery. This is one of our personal favorites.

Only dinner is served, and reservations are suggested.

Tony Roma's—A Place For Ribs
$$ • Broadway at the Beach, U.S. Hwy. 17 Bypass, Myrtle Beach • (843) 448-RIBS

It's been said that Tony Roma's offers the

> **INSIDERS' TIP**
> February 1998 was the inaugural Official All Star Cafe Myrtle Beach Marathon. Benefitting the Leukemia Society of America, the marathon is sanctioned by USA Track and Field, and the course is USATF certified, which means if you run this one in good time you might be able to qualify for the Boston Marathon!

RESTAURANTS

best ribs in America, and we believe the rumor. Conservative Republicans should choose the original baby backs. If you're a bit more adventurous, consider one of the other four flavors: Carolina Honeys are basted with a sauce made with real honey and molasses; Blue Ridge Smokies boast a hint of molasses laced with burning wood; Tony Roma's Red Hots feature a nearly electric sauce created from five types of peppers; and Bountiful Beef Ribs are big, juicy and smoky to the bone.

Tony Roma's also serves sensational salads, grilled specialities, a few seafood selections, chicken and steak. As for appetizers, don't pass up the fried jalapenos stuffed with cheese. With an ice-cold brew in hand, life doesn't get any better than this.

We'd like to point out, from personal experience, that the staff at Tony Roma's is exceptionally friendly. Obviously, they've realized that service makes the difference in a town filled with dining choices.

Villa Mare
$$ • 7819 N. Kings Hwy.
(behind Bank of America), Myrtle Beach
• (843) 449-8654

This Italian restaurant is an indisputable locals' favorite. Its simple, unassuming location in a strip mall around the corner from a grocery store is deceiving—this place has class. But, for all its class, it's not a bit pretentious. Clothing is casual; "come as you are, just come hungry," says owner Fred Fusco, in a lilting Italian accent.

You'll find everything you'd expect on an Italian menu including calzones and plenty of pastas, and the prices are pleasantly surprising. You can order veal, chicken parmigiana, shrimp piccata and fettuccine Alfredo and other pasta dishes, all made to order; absolutely everything is good. Plus everyone is friendly, and the atmosphere is light.

We think Villa Mare is a must for anyone who appreciates fine Italian cuisine. Seating is limited, so call ahead for reservations. Villa Mare is open for lunch and dinner Monday through Saturday; it's closed Sundays.

Vintage House Cafe
$$$ • 1210 N. Kings Hwy., Myrtle Beach
• (843) 626-3918

Vintage House Cafe is a gem of a restaurant in the heart of Myrtle Beach. This oasis in the midst of all the hustle and bustle is quite literally a locals' favorite. The atmosphere is cozy and unassuming, and the food is prepared with a flair that always surprises.

Plain ole salads rise to new heights thanks to Vintage House dressings such as raspberry vinaigrette and the splendid fresh herb. The grilled chicken and spinach salad, dressed in toasted pecans and Gorgonzola cheese, is a popular choice. At least one made-from-scratch soup is offered daily. Gourmet sandwiches, quiche and a host of specials round out a lunch menu that keeps business folks coming back.

The dinner menu is equally impressive. Consider these options: crisp corn waffles topped with shrimp, oysters, andouille sausage and a Cajun gumbo sauce; and local grouper dusted with Japanese bread crumbs, pan sauteed and topped with sun-dried tomatoes and fresh basil cream. Desserts change daily; all are diet-busting and wonderful.

The Vintage House Cafe is closed Sundays. Lunch is served Monday through Saturday; dinner, Tuesday through Saturday.

South Strand

Anchor Inn
$$$ • U.S. Hwy. 17 Bus.
(on the waterfront), Murrells Inlet
• (843) 651-2295

For waterfront dining along the silvery creeks of Murrells Inlet, it doesn't get better than Anchor Inn. This two-story restaurant, decorated with rich, dark wood, serves up not only great food, but also a spectacular view of the inlet. Full window walls bring the outdoors table side. The menu is varied and includes a little of everything, including fresh local seafood, aged beef and tender prime rib.

Anchor Inn is open daily for dinner only.

Anchovies Food & Spirits
$$ • U.S. Hwy. 17 Bus.
(on the waterfront), Murrells Inlet
• (843) 651-0664

Overlooking the swaying spartina grass of a beautiful marsh, Anchovies serves up a view that's as extraordinary as its food. Featuring a variety of entrees including grilled seafood dishes, juicy burgers and awesome pizzas, Anchovies' menu is eclectic enough to satisfy the most discriminating diner. Sample the raw-bar items, Italian specialties, seafood, steaks, pasta, salads, subs . . . just take care not to forego the baked mozzarella appetizer—rolled in seasoned bread crumbs, deep fried and served atop a layer of spicy marinara sauce. We guarantee it'll beat any plain mozzarella sticks you've had before.

The atmosphere at Anchovies is a bit quirky and lots of fun, sporting plenty of natural light

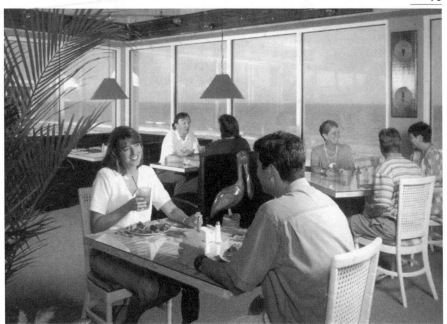

The Calypso at Litchfield Inn in Litchfield Beach delivers great food . . . with a view.

Photo: Michael Slear, courtesy of Brandon Advertising

and wooden floors and booths. Dress down, bring the kids and laugh loudly. If the weather is nice, ask to sit on the screened porch or the outside deck above the slow-moving tidal creeks. You'll see waterfowl and boats heading for the ocean.

Looking for a place to unwind? Cozy up to the big bar—one of the beach's best. Anchovies is open daily for lunch and dinner.

Bovine's
$$$ • U.S. Hwy. 17 Bus.
(on the waterfront), Murrells Inlet
• (843) 651-2888

If ever a restaurant was fun, Bovine's is the place: expansive windows overlooking Lowcountry marsh; cozy lighting spilling shadows in every corner; exquisite smells drifting from a wood-burning oven; and the low hum of happy patrons.

Bovine's decor is a tribute to the wonders of the West. Cowhide-covered seats, dark wood and the mounted head of a gargantuan bull reinforce the theme. The bar scene, separate from the main dining area, spotlights an awesome horseshoe-shaped bar as well as electronic darts, a couple of mounted TVs and bistro tables scattered about. Comfy booths offer a ringside view of swaying spartina grass and the far-away, blooming lights of Garden City. Feels a little like the summertime hangouts of lost

youth—only the patrons are seasoned and a bit more mellow. This is a great place for a beer and an individual-size, gourmet honey-crust pizza from the wood-burning oven. A see-and-be-seen crowd always gathers after work.

As for the food, Bovine's recipe for success features a few ingredients unique to the area. Nearly every selection on the titillating menu boasts a Southwestern slant. A great many choices come from the red hot, marvelously aromatic, igloo-shaped oven. The variety is quite impressive, including tender char-grilled chicken, melt-in-your-mouth steaks, seafood and pasta dishes.

Desserts are sinful but worth the mischief. The frozen vanilla-honey mousse with blackberry sauce is a sophisticated, grown-up version of an ice-cream sundae. The homemade chocolate bourbon pecan torte will make you weak in the knees.

There's a showcase full of other decadent specialities too: Italian tortes, cheesecakes and lots of chocolate.

Bovine's serves dinner only, and reservations are accepted.

The Captain's Restaurant
$$ • 3655 U.S. Hwy. 17 Bus., Murrells Inlet
• (843) 651-2416

If you've got a hankerin' for that blue-blood

feeling, head straight for The Captain's Restaurant. This beautiful old dining establishment has been in business for more than a quarter century. Only extraordinary restaurants last that long on the Grand Strand.

Good ole Southern cooks, Mattie and Ernestine, have been laboring in the kitchen since The Captain's Restaurant first opened its doors, and they prepare seafood simply, classically and complemented by from-scratch accompaniments. Everything is a treat for the palate, but if you love crab, don't pass up the jumbo lump crabmeat dish. Big tender chunks of fresh crabmeat straight from the docks of McClellanville (south of Georgetown) are pan-broiled with a little butter, then served with drawn butter for dipping. It's simple . . . and simply unbeatable. Our second choice is scallops. The Captain serves a hearty plate of the oversize deep-sea kind everyone loves but can never seem to find.

In addition to seafood, the dinner menu includes country ham, beef and chicken entrees. And nearly everything on the regular menu is also on the seniors' menu, featuring smaller portions and prices—a real hit with older folks. The desserts are to-die-for.

The Captain serves lunch too. His salads are known far and wide. The shrimp salad with capers is light and unusual. The Neptune salad, a longtime favorite, features shrimp, crabmeat and lobster. The avocado salad showcases crabmeat, the sweetest shrimp we connoisseurs have ever discovered and a tarragon-laced remoulade sauce.

This quaint Cape Cod structure overhung with centuries-old oaks is steeped in history and beauty. All the bricks, columns, beams, mahogany wainscoting, pine floors and the tabby fireplace are original and authentic. Many of the architectural elements were salvaged from the ruins of Charleston's historic buildings.

In June, July and August The Captain's Restaurant is open seven days a week for lunch and dinner. The rest of the year, the Captain takes Monday off. Reservations are not necessary.

The Charleston Café
$$$ • 815 Surfside Dr., Surfside Beach
• (843) 238-2200

Surfside Beach welcomed The Charleston Café with appropriate if inauspicious fanfare: Six hours after opening, Hurricane Hugo swept ashore and left the restaurant without power or water for 10 days. In years since, The Charleston Café has developed a fine reputation for romantic meals in an intimate setting; attentive, personable service; and creative, attractively presented food.

Specializing in certified Angus beef, local seafood and veal and chicken dishes, The Charleston Café also offers a "light eaters" menu with smaller portions of well-liked items. The dessert menu is daunting, and servers parade the choices in front of you. Who can resist?! The Charleston Café also features a large list of wines by the glass.

Lunch and dinner are served daily, and reservations are strongly suggested.

Conch Café
$$$ • 1482 N. Waccamaw Dr.,
Garden City Beach
• (843) 651-6556

Dining at the Conch Café is like inviting 100 or so good friends to your beach house for grilled tuna, baked scallops, conch fritters, tenderloin, teriyaki chicken and shrimp, mussels in garlic butter and a mess of backfin crab cakes. Throw in a Happy Hour, and it's not a shabby way to host a party, right?

Did we mention the covered outdoor deck overlooking the ocean? It's great for stargazing and drinking concoctions with tropical-sounding names.

Lunch and dinner are served daily. Come early and stay late.

Drunken Jack's Restaurant & Lounge
$$$ • U.S. Hwy. 17 Bus.
(on the waterfront), Murrells Inlet
• (843) 651-2044

As legend has it, Drunken Jack was a black-hearted pirate who patrolled Murrells Inlet incessantly, seeking treasure until his alcohol led him to a watery grave. His namesake, a time-tested restaurant and lounge, is a preferred waterfront dining establishment in the Murrells Inlet area. Take time to have cocktails in the lounge and watch the fishing boats come in. Live musical entertainment is another treat.

Seafood and steaks are the house specialties, including filet mignon; lobster Theodore (chunks of lobster and cheese in a succulent cream sauce—beware your arteries!); frog legs (a true Southern delicacy); or Robinson Crusoe Special Seafood Coquille. Lowcountry specialties abound. A children's menu is offered too. Drunken Jack's serves dinner only.

Flo's Place & Cajun Restaurant & Raw Bar
$$ • 3797 U.S. Hwy. 17 Bus., Murrells Inlet
• (843) 651-7222

Hats off to owner Flo Triska—literally! For years, she and husband Ralph have been run-

From seafood to salad, buffets offer something for everyone.

Photo: Bill Scroggins

ning this upbeat Cajun-style restaurant, and people show their gratitude by donating their chapeaus of all shapes and sizes to the area's largest hat display—right in the restaurant. This wood-framed eatery is set on the creek in Murrells Inlet and features Cajun and creole food that'll make you think you're in steamy New Orleans. In the spirit of Mardi Gras, the clientele has been known to form a Conga line through the indoor/outdoor dining room to "eat, drink and be merry."

An all-time favorite menu item is the Dunkin' Pot, a large cast-iron kettle filled with jumbo spiced shrimp, clams, mussels, oysters, corn on the cob, red potatoes and crawfish. (If you don't know how to eat crawfish, Flo will come by and demonstrate. It's really elementary: Snap off the tail and suck the head first; then, peel the tail shell away, revealing the plump meat, and pop it in your mouth.) Another time-tested favorite is the Henry the Eighth rib eye: a 20-ounce, aptly named wonder. Authentic PoBoy sandwiches, served on grilled French bread, are marvelous. There are

several sensational appetizers, two of which incorporate alligator meat. The smoked alligator ribs are prepared in a honey-mustard dressing and cooked on the grill. The alligator stew contains more than 24 ingredients!

All the food here is made from scratch. Quench your thirst with a Pitcher of Watermelons, a fruity punch with a kick of rum and vodka. "Good food, great time" says it all.

Flo's Place is open for lunch and dinner Monday through Saturday.

Frank's Restaurant & Bar
$$$ • U.S. Hwy. 17 S., Pawleys Island • (843) 237-1581

Frank's Restaurant & Bar, or just plain Frank's as locals call it, opened in 1988 and has been growing ever since. Today, many locals consider Frank's the best restaurant on the entire length of the Grand Strand. It's no wonder. The chef's creations feature an array of different influences, including Southwestern, French, Oriental and Thai.

Frank's menu changes every night, and the

selections are guaranteed to tempt the strongest dieter's resolve. Frank's solution for diners who can't choose is "small plates," portions larger than an appetizer but smaller than a full meal. This immensely popular option allows guests to sample several items in one sitting and still have room for vintage wines and dessert.

Naturally, fresh seafood is a specialty at Frank's. Selections include a delicious sauteed cornmeal-and-black-pepper-encrusted snapper entree. But seafood is only a beginning. Free-range chicken and veal are featured often, along with crispy duck and roasted lamb.

Frank's serves dinner only Monday through Saturday.

INSIDERS' TIP

North Myrtle Beach is home to the first Jackaroo Australian Steakhouse, a new branch of the infamous Hooter's chain. Jackaroo, at 1211 U.S. Highway 17 N., North Myrtle Beach, is a more family-oriented restaurant, featuring Australian flavors like the Aussie Bloom (a whole, colossal onion deep fried), coconut prawns, John Hops Chops and the Great Barrier Reef Fish of the Day. For more information call (843) 280-9800.

Orient, wows diners with tricks of his trade— knife juggling and flipping tiny shrimp tails from a spatula to a small bowl high atop his chef's hat. All entrees are served with salad (the ginger-root house dressing is the way to go) and a delicate onion soup.

The main course of chicken, beef or seafood and a variety of vegetables are diced and cooked right before your eyes. It's so satisfying, you'll literally have to push yourself away from the table.

A trip to either Kyoto's is best enjoyed with a group and is a great way to celebrate a birthday, anniversary or other special occasion. Try the sushi bar, if you dare, and spring for a glass of sweet plum wine.

Kyoto's serves dinner only, and reservations are strongly suggested; the lines can be murderous. But after all, good things are worth waiting for.

Gulfstream Cafe
$$$ • 1536 S. Waccamaw Dr.,
Garden City Beach
• (843) 651-8808

The two-story Gulf-stream Cafe sits high above the marsh and overlooks Murrells Inlet. Sunsets are spectacular and romantic. (Try to talk your host into giving you a table with a view.) Although dress is casual, the menu is upscale, and reservations are recommended.

Appetizers range from crab-stuffed mushrooms to oysters on the half-shell. A popular appetizer is the Gulfstream sampler: stuffed shrimp, bacon-wrapped scallops, oysters Rockefeller, linguine with a delicate clam sauce and blackened fish. (Hope you're hungry!)

Our No. 1 entree is Gulfstream's tenderloin medallions: beef medallions topped with a Gulfstream crab cake and bearnaise sauce, served with a baked potato and vegetables.

We've eaten at Gulfstream many times and have never had a bad night. Sounds impossible, but it's true. A children's menu is also available. Gulfstream Cafe is open for dinner only.

Kyoto Japanese Steak House
$$ • U.S. Hwy. 17 S., Murrells Inlet
• (843) 651-4616
$$ • Restaurant Row,
U.S. Hwy. 17 N., Myrtle Beach
• (843) 449-9294

Kyoto's brings the beloved Japanese tradition of hibachi cooking right to your table. The chef, usually an authentic personality from the

Tyler's Cove
$$ • The Hammock Shops,
U.S. Hwy. 17 S., Pawleys Island
• (843) 237-4848

Tyler's Cove is very elegant, very relaxed. It's the veritable hub of the Pawleys Island locals' scene. Surrounded by oaks weeping moss and a couple dozen of the famous Hammock Shops, Tyler's Cove continues to garner rave reviews from natives and tourists alike. Decidedly cozy, this restaurant somehow is simultaneously perfect for starry-eyed lovers, families with children, business meetings and informal gatherings of friends.

The menu runs the gamut, ranging from Cajun fried chicken salad with honey-jalapeno dressing (a lunchtime favorite) to elegant evening indulgences such as teriyaki-marinated tuna with angel-hair pancakes or crab-encrusted salmon with rice timbale and lobster sauce. And consider this list of appetizers for a lesson in restraint: deep-fried alligator bites with Cajun sauce and peach chutney; triple cheese French onion soup; baked brie turnovers topped with amaretto butter and toasted almonds; and melt-in-your-mouth bourbon-simmered shrimp.

Entrees—all accompanied by a fresh salad, seasonal vegetables, a starch and a basket of truly exceptional, forever-hot rolls—include every hungry soul's desire, including Black Angus prime rib, roasted duckling, pork tenderloin served with Granny Smith apple sauce and a very wicked plate of fettuccine carbonara. (There's a special "Little Friends" menu too!) For the uninitiated, the menu suggests appropriate wines for each selection. Tyler's Cove is open daily for lunch and dinner.

The Ultimate California Pizza
$ • 1502 N. Kings Hwy., Surfside
• (843) 477-8282

Listen very closely: California Pizza has more than 100 TOPPINGS! Choose from marinated mushrooms; all sorts of peppers; sun-dried tomatoes; broccoli; artichoke hearts; spinach; zucchini; dill pickles; water chestnuts; sauerkraut; smoked Gouda, Feta and Swiss cheeses; barbecue, lime and teriyaki chicken; filet mignon; roast beef; scallops; smoked oysters; Granny Smith apples; almonds; dill; cajun seasonings and . . .

As you can imagine, California Pizza has acquired quite a local following. They have the whole beach covered. For lunch or dinner delivery in Myrtle Beach, call (843) 946-6789, (843) 626-8900 or (843) 449-1160. In the Restaurant Row area call (843) 449-4985, and in North Myrtle Beach call (843) 280-2081.

RESTAURANTS

Nightlife

Like the song says, "There's no use in sitting alone in your room; come to the cabaret." With the happening nightlife this area has to offer, there is no need to entertain your own company and absolutely no excuse for lamenting that there is nothing to do. When the sun sinks below the horizon, the lights come up around the Grand Strand, alive with the buzz of animated conversation, laughter and the beat of various musical genres. Locals who can "hang" with the best of them all night long and rested vacationers congregate until the wee hours of the morning in too many nightspots to mention. Besides the places included in this chapter, many restaurants double as late-night spots, and most resort hotels provide lounges with live entertainment. And around almost every corner along the Strand you'll find a little bar or pool hall where the clientele is usually neighborhood locals.

Nightlife really picks up during the spring and summer months, so consult the Friday "kicks!" section of *The Sun News* for the most up-to-date profile on the entertainment scene.

Now, let's get into some of the rules and regulations about night stalking so you can avoid any possible trouble or surprises.

Rules and Regulations for the Night Stalker

IDs, If You Please . . .

The legal drinking age in South Carolina is 21, and that is a strict order around here. Some clubs allow underage patrons to enter with a clearly marked hand stamp—they can purchase only soft drinks at the bar. You'll find that Grand Strand club bouncers are fastidious ID checkers, so make sure you have some form of photo identification.

Make It a Double . . .

South Carolina is still a mini-bottle state when it comes to serving alcohol. You won't see a shot glass used by a bartender in these parts! Each mini-bottle contains nearly 2 ounces of liquor, so you're getting a double compared to most free-pour bars. If you prefer mixed drinks containing more than one liquor, such as Long Island iced teas or fuzzy navels, keep in mind that you must pay for each separate liquor that is opened and poured. More than one unsuspecting cocktail imbiber has nearly fainted when presented with the tab at the end of the evening!

Drinking and Driving

Local patrol officers show no mercy to drunken motorists, and if you're picked up for driving while impaired, you will spend the night in jail before facing charges. Remember: No excuse is a good excuse where drinking and driving is concerned, so use your head—and stay out of the slammer.

Dancing the Night Away

North Strand

Spanish Galleon
100 Main St., North Myrtle Beach
• **(843) 249-1047**

The Galleon has been a favorite Grand Strand dance club for years. This place houses several dance floors under one roof to appeal to a variety of musical interests, including beach music and high-energy dance music. Live beach music bands entertain Galleon customers throughout the year, and an oceanfront grill keeps everyone from going hungry. Although you can wear T-shirts and shorts, most people tend to turn a night at the Galleon into a fashion show.

Recently renovated and bigger and better than ever before.

Spanish Galleon is traditionally open nightly in the summer and several nights a week in the winter from 8 PM 'til . . . Call ahead for specific hours and admission prices.

Myrtle Beach

2001 VIP Entertainment
920 Lake Arrowhead Rd., Myrtle Beach
• **(843) 449-9434**
• **www.2001nightclub.com**

2001 is an upscale entertainment complex, complete with two separate dance floors and a private lounge.

Pulsations Dance Club features Top-40 music pumped into a high-tech sound system by DJ G. Baby and live bands. The spacious dance floor is always crowded, so watch your step. In the next room, you'll find Razzies Beach Club, where folks shag to beach music oldies and other tunes from the '50s and '60s, played nightly by house band Terry Gore & Coco Loco features DJ Crazy George who not only spins records, but also acts out skits (they seem funnier with every drink!) to songs.

The newest addition is VIP Club Sports Lounge at 2001 for those who prefer a more soothing atmosphere or want a private, classy room for a party.

Several bars are interspersed throughout the

club, and professionally trained bartenders can whip up specialty cocktails and any kind of shooter. Valet parking at 2001 adds a touch of class and convenience for patrons. The decor is finished in brass fixtures and accessories. A high ceiling provides lots of air circulation.

Casual club wear works at 2001; the dress code allows no hats or tank tops. The club is open year round Monday through Saturday from 8 PM to well after midnight. Last call is 2 AM on Saturdays. During the winter months, it often closes on Sunday and Monday. Locals are admitted free, but a cover charge applies to all others, and the exact price is contingent upon special nights and entertainment. Presently, 2001 charges $6 admission on Monday, Tuesday and Wednesday nights, $8 Thursday and $10 on weekend evenings. Call ahead for details.

The Attic
812 N. Ocean Blvd., Myrtle Beach
• **(843) 448-7477**

Above the Myrtle Beach Pavilion, The Attic is the area's only under-21 nightclub. It's well-supervised, and no alcoholic beverages are sold—just soft drinks. For decades teenagers have danced at The Attic to live bands and their favorite Top-40 hits during their summer vacations.

The Attic is open 7 PM to midnight, March through October. Admission is $7 per person.

Bahama Beach Club
1623 U.S. Hwy. 501, Myrtle Beach
• **(843) 448-4200**

Bahama is open Monday through Friday, featuring live entertainment and a DJ that spins contemporary hit tunes, including the genres of hip-hop, R&B, alternative and rock. The club describes its music selection as "nothing too avant-garde, nothing too tame." Bathing suit-clad waiters and waitresses take your orders. The standard age range for Bahama is 18 to 30, and the later it gets, the stranger this place can become.

Don't be surprised if the guy next to you is licking his pre-Tequila salt from a waitress's neck or if, suddenly, in the middle of a late-night song a "shadow show" appears on the stage.

Admission is $5 but local Grand Stranders always get in free with proper ID.

> **INSIDERS' TIP**
> If you're going out on the town, be sure to carry along some form of picture identification with you. Most establishments check all patrons to ensure they're of legal drinking age; their liquor license depends on it.

NIGHTLIFE

Beach Wagon
906 S. Kings Hwy., Myrtle Beach
• **(843) 448-5918**

Country music fans have come here for more than 18 years for live concerts and all-night two-steppin'. The club itself is a large, long dance hall with little neon but big rootin' tootin' fun. Names such as Marty Stuart, John Anderson, Sweethearts of the Rodeo, Aaron Tippin and McBride & The Ride all played the Beach Wagon just before their careers took off. It just goes to show, the performers you see at this club today might be the country music stars of tomorrow.

House band Silver plays Tuesday through Saturday nights from 9 PM to 2 AM. Ladies are admitted free Monday through Thursday and on Sunday evenings from 7 to 9 PM. Locals get in for free on Wednesday nights and are invited to take the microphone or join the band to show off their own talent. Free dance lessons are taught every Sunday, Monday and Tuesday night from 7 to 9 PM. For everyone else a cover charge of $3 each applies Sunday through Thursday, and a $5 door fee applies on Friday and Saturday nights.

Beach Wagon is open every night of the week from 7 PM to 2 AM, except during the winter when it operates Tuesday through Saturday only.

Jamaica Joe's
U.S. Hwy. 17 N.
(Restaurant Row area),
Myrtle Beach
• **(843) 449-6456**

Locals consider "J.J.'s" an after-hours spot, so it really gets shaking when most other clubs close for the night. If you're a late starter or just haven't had enough fun and dancing by about 2 AM, this is a great place to pop into. It's usually rocking until 4 or 5 AM on weeknights. The decor is classy and cozy. Top-40 hits blast into the early morning. There is no admission charge to Jamaica Joe's.

Malibu's Surf Bar
Celebrity Square,
Broadway at the Beach, Myrtle Beach
• **(843) 444-3500**

High-energy Top-40 music keeps the crowd gyrating on a dance floor that has a giant shark as its backdrop. This place is usually packed on weekends when tourists and locals wander in from a day or dinner at Broadway at the Beach.

Malibu's offers Teen Night for those 12 to 16 years of age, from March through Labor Day. Teens can bop from 6 PM to 10 PM on special nights. Call ahead for prices and the frequently changing schedule. Regular admission for patrons is $10.

Mother Fletcher's
Eighth Ave. N. and Ocean Blvd.,
Myrtle Beach
• **(843) 448-2545**

A girl could make a living just entering the contests held at Mother Fletcher's. Each night, between the sets of pumping dance tunes, girls compete in such events as the wet T-shirt contest, the skirt-flirt contest and the legs contest, cajoled by testosterone-induced howling and clapping. Wednesday night, Ladies Night, offers an especially wild night. The other breathtaking view at Mother Fletcher's is from the double oceanfront deck. The club is open daily in the summer from 8 PM until 2 AM. Cover charge is $8 per person.

Revolutions
Retro Dance Club
Celebrity Square,
Broadway at the Beach,
Myrtle Beach
• **(843) 444-8032**

Featuring songs from the '60s, '70s and '80s, Revolutions has become a surprising dance-hall hit around here. Music making alternates between DJs and bands, with performers dressed in bell bottoms, wedgies and Afro wigs. This is a happening place on weekends. Don't be afraid to don your white jacket and medallions. Get ready to bump the night away to a K.C. and the Sunshine Band tune; say "groovy" all you want. Revolutions is open seven nights a week from 9 PM, April through October. It's only open Wednesday through Saturday the rest of the year. A $5 cover charge is always the case on weekends; $7 when a live band is playing. The cover charge also entitles you to admission at Crocodile Rocks—the home of dueling pianos—across the square.

INSIDERS' TIP

A recent study by the National Restaurant Association reported that the average American spends $681 per year at restaurants. Households with annual incomes of $70,000 or more spent an average of $1,254 per person eating out; households with incomes between $20,000 and $29,000 spent an average of $581 per family member. Families composed of just a husband and wife (such as retirees) spent more: An annual average of $976 each at restaurant dining tables.

The area's abundance of theme restaurants allows lots of choices for great food and great entertainment—no matter what your interests are!

Photo: Courtesy of NASCAR Cafe

Studebaker's
2000 N. Kings Hwy., Myrtle Beach
• (843) 448-9747

The motif of Studebaker's is straight from the 1950s and, as you might already have guessed, so is the music. Actually, the music ranges from '50s to the early '70s hits. It's a real blast from the past.

Don't miss the Stude-a-boppers (bartenders and waitresses) and DJ Jumpin' Jack Flash, the self-proclaimed "oldest living brain donor," plus a floor show and line dances that are very entertaining.

Dress at Studebaker's is casual but neat, and the club is open nightly in the summer from 8 PM until 2 AM.

During the off-season, Studebaker's opens several nights a week, and the club hosts an After Work Attitude Adjustment Happy Hour for locals on Thursday nights. Studebaker's year-round hours are 5:30 PM to 2 AM on Thursdays and 8 PM to 2 AM every other night except Sunday. Locals are admitted free all year long; the cover charge for all others ranges from $5 to $10.

Yesterday's Nite Life
1901 N. Kings Hwy., Myrtle Beach
• (843) 626-CLUB

Attention to ambiance and detail is apparent everywhere at Yesterday's. The massive dance club on the main floor level has an 18-foot-tall replica of a Wurlitzer 1015 Jukebox in the middle of the dance floor from which DJs play a never-ending and ever-changing mix of the top hits from every era. Throughout the

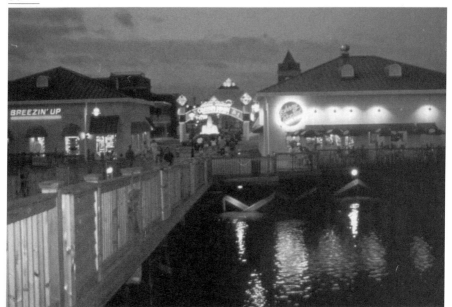

Broadway at the Beach is one of several establishments that offer shopping, dining, entertainment and more!

Photo: Courtesy of Broadway at the Beach

night, the DJs emerge onto the stage, fronting the giant jukebox to act out skits and run contests. A state-of-the-art light-and-sound system keeps the place rocking, and we have never seen so many people dancing and having such a great time!

On the other side of Yesterday's, you feel as though you've walked into a fully separate sportsbar. Virtual-reality games include Daytona Racing, QB1 Interactive Football, Full Swing Golf Simulators, Alpine Virtual Skiing and Virtual Cop for wanna-be sharpshooters. The room is filled with arcade and racing games, seven pool tables and, for the more intellectual, NTN Trivia. Hanging overhead is a life-size biplane and a replica of Richard Petty's race car. Sports memorabilia include the former scoreboard from the Charlotte Coliseum (home of the NBA's Charlotte Hornets), Michael Jordan's Final Four backboard and goal and a showcase of autographs from famous sports figures. Another separate room upstairs offers patrons five-player blackjack tables.

Two local favorites, California Pizza and River City Cafe, cater the food for Yesterday's, and the extensive selection of gourmet "pies," hamburgers and sandwiches are served all through the night.

Yesterday's is open every day of the week from 4 PM until 2 AM. The cover charge varies from season to season and mostly applies to non-locals. Locals just need to ask around as Yesterday's has stocked most area businesses with plenty of club cards for Grand Stranders. The card allows free admission for the cardholder and a guest.

The Grand Strand Band Scene

The Grand Strand has for years, enjoyed a fertile music scene that has been fostered by the overwhelming success of the nearly local group Hootie & The Blowfish and most recently by the signing of Myrtle Beach's home-grown band, The Drag, to Island Records and their release, *Satellites Beaming Back At You.*

Dozens of local bands are working hard, playing any club that will have them, building a following in a diverse and fickle market. You never know where they may turn up, but if you consult *The Sun News'* "Kicks!" insert on Friday or come across a copy of *Yikes!* (refer to our Media chapter for details about both papers), you will find a whole listing of corner bars and obscure clubs that are playing host to local talent.

Blisster is a four-guy group that evolved out of the Loris section of Horry County. They completed a demo tape in 1997 of their heavy alternative rock sound, *Retrograde*, which critics claim feature several strong original songs. Brownhouse Productionz mixes hip-hop and funk and is described as "good natured, old-school rap" with live music. In 1996 this group was the opening act for Run-DMC in Columbia and released its first CD to a packed house at the Hard Rock Cafe.

The three-man band, The Hall Monitors, plays loose, irreverent punk rock. Two of their singles appear on *Don't Attempt To Make An Effort*, a compilation CD released by King Records and *Too Much Free Time*, another compilation on Redneck Records. Always playing in Myrtle Beach and around the Carolinas is I, God, a group that refers to its brand of sound as "unusual, multilayered alternative rock that features everything from guitar fuzz to heavy percussion."

Hailing from Georgetown, Jealous Sky has been playing around town since 1992, and their melding of alternative pop and Southern rock has made them local favorites. Constantly touring the Carolinas, Jealous Sky has also independently produced their own CDs. Junction 51 is another Georgetown-based band that plays folk and acoustic-tinged alternative rock.

The Lint Puppies received strong radio airplay in Charleston and good reviews by the CMJ New Music Report for their 1996 CD release, *Tastes Like Chicken*. The group has an edgy pop-rock sound with lots of guitar and include influences from jazz and funk. Sqwearl was invited to play the Warped Tour in 1994, along with acts such as L7 and Sublime. In early 1996 Sqwearl went to New York City to record a demo for American Records. Its head pounding, hard alternative rock sound can be heard on the CD and single, *Eight Ball of Confusion*.

Other noteworthy local bands to seek out are Damn Near Alchemy (funky rock), October Chorus (Gothic-style rock), Phineas Gage (hard alternative rock), Perfect Tommy (lots of guitar, hard rock), The Speed Bumps (introspective acoustic music), Tony Blunt Project (a mix of funk and R&B), Ugly Room (rock with metal overtones), Up Spook Hill (a hybrid of metal and Gothic rock) and Velour #9 (electric guitar pop).

Sportsbars

Sometimes you just wanna hang out somewhere, have a brew, watch a game, and play a few rounds of pool or darts. If that's how you're feeling, we have a sportsbar lineup here that should satisfy. While a number of places in town hail themselves as sportsbars (apparently it's quite fashionable to do so), we have come up with some guidelines to ensure the full "sportsbar experience."

By our criteria, a bar was only given mention in this section if it had at least four televisions locked on sporting events and at least two games to play. There's never a cover charge at area sportsbars, unless a major boxing event is to be aired. Then you'll have to consult the media to find out which places will be showing the fight and what the admission cost will be.

North Strand

Mulligan's Sports Pub
1500 U.S. Hwy. 17 S., North Myrtle Beach
• (843) 249-9700, (843) 361-2999

Mulligan's relocated late in 1997 and changed its ambience to a more upscale sportsbar and steak house. The inside is impressive, with a decor of muted greens, rich woods and brass. More than 40 televisions broadcast sports all the time. Games have been moved into a separate room where you can shoot pool or play shuffleboard.

This sports pub is open every day of the week from 11:30 to 2 AM. A full dinner menu is served from opening to 11 PM every day and includes steaks, chops and pastas. Monday night is Prime Time evening, when Mulligan's offers all you can eat Prime Rib for $10.95.

Oscar's
4101 U.S. Hwy. 17 N., North Myrtle Beach
• (843) 272-0707

Oscar's is the proud owner of the only L-shaped pool table in town. This sportsbar is a

---

INSIDERS' TIP

We know that lines to use restrooms at nightclubs and amusements can be lengthy and, depending on the number of beers you've taken in, sometimes agonizing. Be forewarned: The only other offense that local police enforce as strongly as drunk driving is urinating in public. If caught, you will be arrested, fined and taken to jail.

NIGHTLIFE

continuous arena of action, with 70 TVs and an array of electronic games including air hockey and trivia. In 1996 Oscar's added pinball machines and a virtual-reality race car game, plus virtual tennis and Blitz 99.

You're likely to work up an appetite, so it's a good thing Oscar's now offers a full menu until 1 AM.

Oscar's is open from 11:30 to 2 AM Monday through Saturday and noon to 2 AM on Sunday.

Myrtle Beach

Droopy's
5201 N. Kings Hwy., Myrtle Beach
• (843) 449-2620

Droopy's stays open as late as business dictates Monday through Friday and until 2 AM on Saturday and Sunday. More than 14 TVs are scattered throughout along with two pool tables, pinball, a shuffleboard game and Foosball.

Basic grill appetizers and sandwiches are available from the kitchen, but Droopy's also takes advantage of the fish market next door, offering fresh seafood daily.

Doors open at 4 PM every day of the week. Droopy's opens earlier when the NFL season game schedule dictates.

Foster's Cafe & Bar
6307-A N. Kings Hwy., Myrtle Beach
• (843) 449-7945

Foster's just made it into the sportsbar category by one television and Foosball. The bar also sports one pool table, NTN trivia and a full menu. While this place is very small, its rough-hewn wood decor exudes a certain coziness.

Foster's is open Monday through Friday from 11:30 until 4 AM and Saturday and Sunday from noon to 2 AM. The kitchen closes two hours before the bar on weeknights and at 1 AM Saturday and Sunday.

Jimmagan's Pub Sports Bar
6003 N. Kings Hwy., Myrtle Beach
• (843) 497-5450

Jimmagan's Pub, with 11 TVs locked on sporting events, pool tables, electronic darts and Foosball is a small corner location that's cozy and down-home. Jimmagan's guarantees you can see every Sunday NFL game during football season. It is a favorite of motorcycle enthusiasts and has an additional location in Murrells Inlet, south on Business 17.

The menu is limited to sandwiches, burgers and finger foods; wings are always 25¢. Jimmagan's is open seven days a week—11:30 to 4 AM weekdays; 11 to 2 AM on weekends.

Official All Star Cafe
2925 Hollywood Dr., Myrtle Beach
• (843) 916-8326

Get prepared for a bold and total immersion dining-and-entertainment experience for the sports fan. The entire inner roof of the dining area at All Star is lined by larger-than-life video screens that play choice games and, in between games, sports highlights.

Exciting sports memorabilia is everywhere and the list of partners in this flagship cafe reads like a who's who of athletes: tennis pros Andre Agassi and Monica Seles, hockey great Wayne Gretzky, baseball star Ken Griffey Jr., former NFL quarterback Joe Montana, basketball's Shaquille O'Neal and golf phenomenon Tiger Woods (Tiger was personally on hand for All Star's grand opening). The sports motif misses not a corner of this venue—restrooms are fashioned after locker rooms and booths are designed to have you seated in the palm of a baseball glove.

Virtual-reality games pop up all through the cafe and include simulated skateboarding and car racing. The menu is pretty standard sportsbar fare. All Star's bar area is open from 11 to 1 AM daily and the restaurant operates from 11 AM to 11 PM. For more on the atmosphere, see the Close-up in the Restaurants chapter.

Magoo's Sports and Spirits
905 Oak St., Myrtle Beach
• (843) 946-6683

Magoo's is one of the only dart bars to have sprouted up along the Grand Strand. View one of 10 televisions; head to the back room, chalk up a cue stick and shoot some pool. Electronic and steel tip darts are at the front end of the bar.

Under the category of "fine food," Magoo's serves up fabulous hamburgers and fries. Every night Magoo's offers a 10-ounce prime rib dinner special for $7.99 that features a baked potato and homemade garlic bread. Ten cent

INSIDERS' TIP

Even if the romantic sunrises over the ocean make you impetuous enough to want to tie the knot while you're on vacation, Horry County maintains a 24-hour waiting period before a marriage license will be issued. The county court house in Conway takes applications; no blood test is required.

wings are the special on Sunday and Monday. Take it from us, it's absolutely delicious!

Magoo's is open Monday through Friday from 4 PM until the last sports fan leaves and Saturday and Sunday until 2 AM.

Marvin's
918 N. Ocean Blvd., Myrtle Beach
• (843) 448-4926

Marvin's has been around since 1975, evolving from a taco stand into a sportsbar, complete with pool tables and NASCAR racing simulators. Besides a vast collection of NASCAR memorabilia that owner Marvin McHone has collected over the years, this sportsbar is oceanfront with 80 feet of windows showing off the Atlantic.

The menu is basic bar fare: fried foods and appetizers, chicken wings, pizza, nachos, burgers, dogs and sandwiches. Marvin's operates from 10 until at least 2 AM, seven days a week for most of the year. Hours are 11 to 1 AM daily in January and February; the door stays open for 24 hours a day during the week of July 4th.

Murphy's Law Sports Bar
405 S. Kings Hwy., Myrtle Beach
• (843) 448-6021

Patrons of Murphy's Law enjoy two pool tables—positioned in the middle of the tables and chairs—electronic darts and golf as well as 25 television sets. Murphy's sells draft beer during Happy Hour for 50¢ a glass.

The sandwiches at Murphy's are popular fare and monstrous in their proportions. The "50-yard" steak sandwich will stuff you; the "100-yard" version requires a friend to help you. Raw bar selections include oysters, clams, steamed shrimp and crab legs.

Murphy's Law is open seven days a week from noon to 2 AM. It is closed for two weeks during the Christmas holiday season.

Phil McD's Sportsbar & Grill
2303 S. Kings Hwy., Myrtle Beach
• (843) 448-9853

Locals would know this place simply as McD's, but since the McDonald's corporation recently threatened a lawsuit over the name, the owner added his first name to the signage. Here you'll find about eight standard televisions and two big-screen TVs always tuned into sporting events from around the world. Games include NTN trivia, pool, darts, video golf and Daytona racing.

A basic selection of grill food is served. McD's . . . er . . . Phil McD's is open from 11 to 2 AM daily.

NIGHTLIFE

An assortment of venues makes Celebrity Square, located at Broadway at the Beach, a one-stop opportunity for nightlife aficionados.

Photo: Courtesy of Broadway at the Beach

South Strand

Beach Club at Fenway
118 S. Ocean Blvd., Surfside Beach
• (843) 828-1111

This upstairs sportsbar on the boulevard blasts sports (especially any NFL game that New England is playing) from one large-screen television and seven smaller tubes scattered throughout the bar area. Fenway subscribes to Direct TV and carries all NFL games as well as, of course, Red Sox games and other events. Pool tables and arcade-type games round out the sports theme, in albeit cramped quarters.

With the use of partitions, the dining room at Fenway is excluded from the bar area and serves up a full menu. This sportsbar quickly made a name for itself when it comes to baby back ribs that locals swear are "practically liquid." Lunch and dinner can be ordered from any room at Fenway Park and food ranges from steaks to chicken, pasta, soups and finger foods.

Fenway's bar is open daily from 11 until after 2 AM. On Saturday, the bar closes at 2 AM.

Sundown Restaurant & Sports Pub
810 Surfside Dr., Surfside Beach
• (843) 238-1240

Sundown offers its patrons eight televisions for viewing games, three pool tables, electronic darts, pinball and golf machines.

A full menu is available, but the staff says that appetizers and sandwiches are the usual order. A free breakfast is served every Saturday morning, whenever the cook gets to fixing the plates. You have to be there when breakfast is ready, or you're out of luck. Sundown also sells 12-ounce drafts for a dollar, all the time.

It's open all week, 24 hours a day. Sundown closes on Sundays from 2 to 10 AM.

Karaoke

We've included karaoke houses in this chapter in case you get an overwhelming urge to put to the test all of those singing lessons your mother made you take. Actually, karaoke has become serious entertainment business. The places we've included feature some tone-deaf singers who can't seem to focus on the words

to the song; but you'll be amazed at the majority of everyday Joes and Janes with incredible singing talent.

Karaoke seems to have developed a veritable cult following. Picture this: Someone gets up on stage with the microphone to belt out his or her selected tune and is met with the same audience reaction as if he or she had just blown away a panel of Broadway casting directors at a walk-on audition. The best karaoke performers pick just the right time to perform and, when finished, are met with tears, hugs and the inimitable Hollywood-style alternate cheek kissing. Hey, it's a lot of fun—and, who knows, there may be an incredible crooner hidden in those vocal chords of yours!

OK, now it's criteria time. There are a number of local clubs and restaurants that offer karaoke at one time or another. But, for our purposes, an establishment must offer this form of entertainment at least two nights per week to qualify for mention.

> **INSIDERS' TIP**
> South Carolina is the only American state that still serves liquor by the mini-bottle. Whenever you order a cocktail here, you're getting 1.7 ounces of alcohol compared to a national average of one ounce per drink. Pace yourself!

Myrtle Beach

The Original Steak House
510 N. Kings Hwy., Myrtle Beach
• (843) 445-6061

Steve Allen and Barracuda Brian haul in the karaoke equipment and alternate taking over the lounge of this steakhouse every night from 9 PM 'til closing. Sandwiches and appetizers are available until 10 PM to satisfy performers' appetites.

Warren's Restaurant & Lounge
1108 Third Ave. S., Myrtle Beach
• (843) 448-3110

Warren's Restaurant & Lounge is about as local-yokel as it gets with karaoke in full swing every night from 8:30 PM to 2 AM. This is a serious singing venue that showcases a mind-boggling number of terrific singers regularly. Warren's has added a full dinner menu that includes steaks and prime rib.

Taking In a Movie

• www.localmovies.com

The Grand Strand strip is sprinkled with class-act movie houses. All are comfortable, clean, climate-controlled and heady with the smell of fresh-made popcorn. What you won't find in this area's cinemas is an assortment of foreign or fine-arts movies. Every once in a while one pops up but not very often. This is an area where movie-going audiences eat up blockbuster hits, thrillers, adventures, love stories and comedies. To find out what's playing where, always consult the Friday edition of *The Sun News* for its "Kicks!" entertainment section. You will find descriptions of current flims, what theaters are showing them, box office figures and a theater-finder map.

As we speak, Grand Strand moviegoers enjoy selection, amenities and a range of prices. Film buffs have 39 first-run screens to choose from or have the option of waiting a few weeks after a big Hollywood release to catch it at one of the area's 24 discount houses. Viewing times vary from one cinema to the next, so it's best to call ahead for that specific information.

North Strand

Briarcliffe Cinema 10
**Colonial Mall, 10177 N. Kings Hwy.,
North Myrtle Beach**
• **(843) 272-1777**

Briarcliffe Cinema 10 is one of only two movie houses along the Grand Strand housed in a shopping mall. It's a successful marriage as Briarcliffe Mall recently cited that 85 percent of moviegoers visit the theater after a shopping spree. All matinees before 5:30 PM are $5 a seat, every day. After that, those 12 to 64 years of age will pay $7 to see a show; children 3 to 11 and seniors 65 years or older will pay $5 per ticket. A large buttered popcorn will run you $4 and large soft drink, $2.50. Briarcliffe 10 gives free refills on these large versions only.

Myrtle Beach

Broadway Cinema 16
Broadway at the Beach, Myrtle Beach
• **(843) 445-1616**

Broadway is the largest cineplex of its kind in South Carolina and sits amid the hustle and bustle of a shopping and entertainment complex. Eight of the "plexes" here are auditoriums that guarantee unsurpassed viewing and sound quality. All matinee seats are sold for $5 per person. Regular prices are $7 for adults and $5 for children aged 11 and younger and those 64 years of age or older. A large popcorn and soft drink will cost $4 and $2.50, respectively.

Dunes Cinema Eight
**44th Ave. N. and Kings Hwy.,
Myrtle Beach**
• **(843) 449-7733**

If you don't mind waiting a bit for the second run of a new release, seeing a show at the Dunes Cinema Eight is sure to be the best bang for your buck. Recently renovated to include two auditoriums plus a George Lucas (yes, of the *Star Wars* fame) sound system, you can see any movie playing at any time for just $2. The manager of this cinema described its audio system as "near perfect." Get a large buttered popcorn here for $4 and big drink for $2.50. Refills are free.

IMAX Discovery Theater
Broadway at the Beach, Myrtle Beach
• **(843) 448-IMAX**

At IMAX, you not only watch a movie, you experience it. The screen is an incredible 6-stories tall, and a six-track digital sound system surrounds you. Located at Broadway at the Beach, the Grand Strand's IMAX is one of more than 200 IMAX theaters operating in 25 countries. IMAX thrusts its guests into the action in a way no ordinary movie can. Featuring images that fill peripheral vision and 12,000 watts of sound so intense participants swear they can feel it, IMAX movies are absolutely unmatched at the art of transporting their audience to another place and time.

Join all those gone before and discover the world's greatest theater experience. IMAX features a variety of wholesome, family-friendly movies at the top of every hour. Movies vary seasonally, so there's always something to please everyone. The IMAX Cafe offers a wonderful selection of treats to enjoy during your movie experience. And afterward, do leave time for browsing among unique gifts and educational toys in the gift shop.

Adults pay $7 for a ticket. The cost for children aged three to twelve and those 65 or older is $6. Children younger than three are admitted free of charge.

Pottery Cinemas
Waccamaw Pottery off U.S. Hwy. 501
• **(843) 236-2220**

The Pottery Cinemas offers one auditorium with a digital sound system. Tickets for adults run $6.25 each. Children 3 to 12 years of age, as well as those 60 or more years old get in for the price of $4.25. All matinees prior to 6 PM cost $4.25 a seat. A large popcorn is $4; large beverages are $2.50.

South Strand

Inlet Square (Regal Cinemas)
Inlet Square Mall, Murrells Inlet
• (843) 651-5500

At Inlet Square you can enjoy twelve equipped with Digital Theater Sound (DTS). Five more theaters will become part of this movie venue in March or April of 1998. Admission for adults is $7. Those 60 years of age or older and kids 10 or younger can buy tickets for $4.75. All matinees before 6 PM are $4.25 a seat. A big bucket of popcorn runs $4 and a large beverage, $2.50. Combo specials usually apply here, giving a price break on popcorn, drinks and candy.

Cigar-Friendly Haunts

No amount of official health warnings or nose-holding whining has put a dent in the current demand for good cigars. As managing editor of *Cigar Aficionado*, Gordon Mott, said, "A cigar helps create an environment where sociability and relaxation are promoted."

Thousands of golfing enthusiasts who come to play on Grand Strand courses every year feel not fully equipped for the day without stuffing a few fine cigars in with their clubs. As a matter of fact, there's now a cigar on the market called "The 18 Hole Special" that is big enough to last a full round of golf.

It's only fitting that the Grand Strand should have a cigar-friendly atmosphere; this area has always been home to tobacco farming. Whether you want to enjoy a puff after dinner or while sipping on a good single malt Scotch, the following establishments (many of which you can read more about in our Restaurants chapter) invite you to light up to your heart's content.

North Strand

Mad Boar Restaurant & Brewhouse
Barefoot Landing, North Myrtle Beach
• (843) 272-7000

Mad Boar Brewhouse allows you to smoke

a cigar anywhere in the bar and restaurant. A Don Tomas will cost about $4.95, but Macanudos are modestly priced at $8.95 each. The Mad Boar stocks three small-batch bourbons and eight single-malt Scotches at the bar.

Dick's Last Resort
Barefoot Landing, North Myrtle Beach
• (843) 272-7794

Dick's encourages cigar puffing, albeit preferably in the bar area. In true Dick's style, a spokesperson declared, "There's something wrong with a person who can't enjoy the smell of a good cigar." Dick's sells a variety, from cheaper stogies to higher-end, hand-rolled varieties.

The Brentwood Restaurant
4269 Luck Ave., Little River
• (843) 249-2601

The Brentwood accommodates cigars in two upstairs parlor rooms plus a bar. Smokes range from $8 to $15 apiece, including the heavy Padron. Brentwood stocks a full complement of sherry, cognac and scotch; specialty coffees, desserts and appetizers can be ordered at the Brentwood—not to mention savory full course meals.

Myrtle Beach

Chuck's Steakhouse
9605 N. Kings Hwy.,
Myrtle Beach
• (843) 449-7611

Chuck's stocks the bar with brand-name cigars such as Partagas and Dunhills and keeps Cohibas on hand whenever they can get them. Chuck's joins hands with The Tinder Box several times a year to put on Cigar Dinners: One price for dinner, drinks and cigars.

Collectors Cafe and Gallery
7726 N. Kings Hwy., Myrtle Beach
• (843) 449-9370

Collectors Cafe normally carries more upscale brands including Davidoff. At Collectors you can savor a cigar in the bar and lounge areas, where they also shake or stir a list of martinis—even chocolate flavored.

Fat Tuesday's
Broadway at the Beach, Myrtle Beach
• (843) 444-3255

This is an indoor/outdoor style hangout

INSIDERS' TIP

Laws in this area require that no alcoholic beverages are to be served after 2 AM on Saturday and Sunday. Even as a customer, if you have a drink in front of you after 2 AM on the weekend, law enforcement can fine you about $200.

where a cigar will cost you anywhere from $3 to $10. Fat Tuesday's is a daiquiri bar, with 16 different mixtures to try, including a wicked "190 Octane" concoction.

Liberty Steakhouse and Brewery
Broadway at the Beach, Myrtle Beach
• (843) 626-4677

This establishment has been cigar friendly since it opened in November of 1995. Liberty brews its own beer, and a manager there claims that people who tend to drink more flavorful beverages are more likely to enjoy a cigar with drinks.

Rossi's Italian Restaurant
9600 N. Kings Hwy., Myrtle Beach
• (843) 449-0481

Puff away in the lounge and piano bar sections of Rossi's, where cigars start at $4 and range up to a $17 Porlorranaga and $25 Cohiba. Rossi's pours vintage port wines and four single malt scotches.

Neal's
10th Ave. S. next to the Pavilion,
Myrtle Beach
• (843) 448-7002

Neal's only sells the cigars that owner Neal smokes: El Producto Especionales for $2 each. Neal says he used to sell them for a buck until somebody stole one of his. The economic principle of supply and demand forced him to up the price.

Thoroughbreds Restaurant
9706 N. Kings Hwy., Myrtle Beach
• (843) 497-2636

Thoroughbreds Restaurant offers patrons either $8 or $10 fine cigars in the bar area or outdoor courtyard. It is known for mixing a mean martini and also stocks a good selection of fine cognacs.

South Strand

River Room
801 Front St., Georgetown
• (843) 527-4110

A visit to the bar of the River Room will prove cigar-friendly. Four to five cigars are always for sale—kept fresh in a humidor—for $6 to $14. River Room constantly changes brands for diversity sake.

Frank's Restaurant & Bar
10435 Ocean Hwy., Pawleys Island
• (843) 237-3030

Frank's tries to keep about 10 fine cigars on hand at all times for patrons, which can be smoked in the bar or outdoor dining area. A cigar at Frank's will run you $5 to $35.

Adult Entertainment

The Grand Strand region has its fair share of adult entertainment establishments, even though area authorities and courts seem to be constantly debating club locations and what constitutes the appropriate amount of nakedness displayed therein. A recent court battle determined that bare butts must stay outside of 6 inches from a patron's face to be within the law. However, no details were given as to how this would be enforced or whether or not it posed a health risk.

We won't list the clubs here, because all you have to do is consult the Yellow Pages or ask almost anyone—after a wink and a nod, you'll be set in the right direction. Besides, isn't half the fun just getting there? Sort of like a fleshy version of a treasure hunt? There is even one club that showcases only male dancers who strut their stuff in cages . . . things that make you go "hmmmm."

NIGHTLIFE

Shopping

LOOK FOR:
• Major Malls and Outlets
• Distinctive Shopping Stops

From the warehouse-sized to the quaint and oh-so-small . . . from grab-bag dollar stores to exclusive designer clothiers, the Grand Strand is a virtual resort destination for bargain-hunters as well as quality-seekers. It is true that many people come here for no other reason than the shopping—seemingly oblivious to sunshine, theaters, golf courses and the beach.

Belk, JCPenney, Sears and Peebles department stores all have multiple locations here. Almost every major clothing, department and dry goods store has an outlet here (the Saks store is actually part of the Off 5th chain of Saks outlets). You'll find some of the largest booth-rental flea markets in the South. Antiques stores appear in every section of the beach. And some of the very best shopping opportunities can be found in the small, privately owned stores and shops.

It goes without saying that this chapter can't even begin to detail every shop, every store or even every shopping center that comprise this 60-mile-long shopping spree. Even locals are overwhelmed by the variety; thus, we tend to migrate to the geographic part of the Strand where we live.

If you are a seasoned shopper, born to shop, then you already know as many secrets as we do for finding the best stores; at best, we can make a road map for you and highlight some of the more interesting concentrations of shops. Keep your eyes open; 'round every curve in the crowded highway there's yet another clutch of shops to browse and burrow through.

As for the basics, we've already mentioned Belk department store, which can be found at any one of three area malls. Other notable department stores with a presence on the Strand include JCPenney, Sears and Peebles. Several discount "chain" stores pepper the Strand, including Wal-Mart, Kmart and Target.

The larger supermarket chains include Food Lion, Harris Teeter, Kroger and Winn-Dixie; most are open 24 hours a day (except Sunday nights). Both Kroger and Winn-Dixie are continually opening new "superstores" with almost as much general merchandise as groceries, deli items and flowers. Meanwhile Harris Teeter has recently completed major renovations to several of their locations, increasing square footage and adding huge gourmet sections. Though A&P has closed some of its stores, it continues to be a major player on the Strand. Food Lion remains one of the most visible chains at the beach despite battling some public-relations fires.

It's impossible to take an overview of shopping without mentioning the plethora of T-shirt and souvenir stores along the Grand Strand. Stores such as Eagles, Pacific and Wings sparkle with bright lights and seemingly every-other-block locations. They specialize in swimsuits, suntan products, sun shades, beach chairs, rafts, umbrellas, souvenir items, beach toys, T-shirts and summer sportswear of the most casual sort. And believe it or not, in many of these stores you can actually negotiate with the sales staff for the very best prices.

Although Sunday hours are frequently abbreviated, most places are open seven days a week; if you shop between 1 and 6 PM, you should find most of what you're looking for.

Major Malls and Outlets

North Strand

Barefoot Landing
U.S. Hwy. 17 N., North Myrtle Beach
• (843) 272-8349

Barefoot Landing bills itself as "the East Coast's most exciting waterfront shopping, dining and entertainment destination center." While the truth of such marketing hype is disputed by other shopping areas, the fact is that Barefoot Landing plays host to an estimated 7 million visitors every year. Its restaurants, shops and attractions have been featured in magazines, newspapers and television clips throughout the nation. *Southern Living, The Wall Street Journal, USA Today, Barron's Investment, Forbes* and *Country America* are just a few of the biggest media names that have come to know and love Barefoot Landing.

Built around a 20-acre freshwater lake, fronted by U.S. Highway 17 N. and bordered in back by the Intracoastal Waterway, Barefoot has more than 1,200 feet of floating dock on the waterway as well as miles of rocking-chair-peppered boardwalks and bridges. This development, a rare marriage between commerce and preservation, prides itself on environmental sensitivity. While strolling among the more than 100 shops, 15 restaurants and an array of attractions, you can enjoy sea gulls swooping over the lakes, alligators swimming stealthily and all manner of water birds, including swans, geese, blue herons, snowy egrets, ducks and pelicans; you can even feed the fish (fish-food-filled gumball machines abound) from many of the boardwalks.

Barefoot Landing's eclectic villages of shops and restaurants are housed in quaint, cedar-shake buildings with bright green awnings. Specialty stores feature resort wear, jewelry, designer fashions, Western wear and accessories, handmade gifts and unusual collectibles.

The Boardwalk Shops, Carousel Courtyard and the Barefoot Factory Stores are separated by floating bridges and are accessible by walkways that are well worth a stroll even if you don't buy a thing. But don't think there will be no temptation—stores like Conley's House of

For years, locals have been meeting "under the clock" in the heart of Myrtle Square Mall.

Photo: Courtesy of Cotton Company

SHOPPING

Magic, River Street Sweets, Klig's Kites, Barefoot Sandals and Black Market Mineral will mesmerize you with choices of baubles and toys to take home. Brookstone specializes in gadgets and amenities. Earth, Sea & Sky, Sun Seekers Beauty Shoppe, Sweatshirt Company and the Sunglass Hut make for a lot of bags to carry home. You could even re-do your wardrobe at Club Ryno, the Geoffrey Beene and Izod Factory Stores, London Fog, Silhouettes and Tango Bay. There are a dozen factory outlet stores that sell fine apparel and designer merchandise at 20 to 50 percent savings. With this irresistible combination of atmosphere and savings, you could redecorate your life.

This breezy complex is also the home of Alligator Adventure (see our Attractions and Kidstuff chapters), the Alabama Theatre (see Entertainment) and the House of Blues (see Restaurants and Entertainment.) Throughout the year, Barefoot Landing also hosts such events as car shows and chili and rib cookoffs for charities. On top of this bounty, Barefoot is expanding— actually more than quadrupling in size, making it the Grand Strand's largest project-in-progress. Four golf courses, a swing bridge, a Main Street area with more shops, a convention center, acres and acres of horseback riding, and even homesites (eventually, over the next few years) will complete Barefoot Landing. See our Real Estate and Golf chapters for more details.

Colonial Mall
U.S. Hwy. 17 N. (north of Restaurant Row), North Myrtle Beach
• **(843) 272-4040**

Like all the area's malls, Colonial is a one-level facility. Since opening in 1986, it has been anchored by Belk, Kmart, JCPenney and a state-of-the-art cinema. Belk has recently doubled in size, replacing an earlier outlet store and actually building a few hundred additional square feet. Other Colonial stores that are recognizable from their position in malls nationwide include Lane Bryant, The Limited, Express, Lerner's, Structure, Victoria's Secret, and Waldenbooks.

Colonial is the largest of the area malls and offers an average-size food court, including

INSIDERS' TIP
If you're shopping for your pooch, or even actually traveling with your dog, be sure to visit the Bone Apetit Bakery in Barefoot Landing, (843) 361-4477. Just like any bakery where you can point to a cruller behind glass, Bone Apetit offers fresh baked goodies for dogs. Barefoot, by the way, does permit dogs on leashes to enjoy a walk around the grounds.

Chick-fil-A, Taco Bell, Great Steak and Fry and Ruby Tuesdays.

Myrtle Beach

Broadway at the Beach
U.S. Hwy. 17 N. Bypass at 21st Ave. N., Myrtle Beach
• **(843) 444-3200**

Broadway at the Beach is the centerpiece of the Burroughs & Chapin Company's plan for the future of Myrtle Beach. The complex already features more than 100 shops, a live-entertainment theater, a multi-screen IMAX theater, dozens of restaurants including the Hard Rock Cafe and a nightclub street titled Celebrity Square that features well-known musical acts and signed handprints in cement from more than 30 celebrities such as Donna Summers, Johnny Mathis, Barry Manilow and Wayne Newton.

Trying to provide an entertainment venue, a restaurant district, a complex of high-energy nightclubs and a quaint shopping village (complete with the Disney technique of ¾-scale building) seemingly would be an unobtainable mixture of tasks, but Burroughs & Chapin is pulling it off well. And despite the initial failure and closure of 30 or more stores, the crowds keep coming—and new merchants keep opening.

Do more people visit Broadway at the Beach for the shopping and the restaurants, or is it the huge attractions like Ripley's Aquarium (see our Attractions chapter) and activities like the Fourth of July and Halloween parties that the management throws? Fortunately, no one has to choose and there is enough to draw everyone, from the right jeans at the Gap to a collectible Disney print from The Fun Art Gallery. The shopping is divided up into three districts: Caribbean Village, Charleston Boardwalk and New England Village. With a range of stores from Perfumania and Autographs Plus to Kiely's Emerald Cottage and Noah and Friends, Broadway is a specialty store extravaganza, so be sure to bring your birthday and Christmas present list along.

In addition to the shopping, Broadway at the Beach has a fine selection of restaurants

The beach boasts many colorful selections.

Photo: Lisa Tomer Rentz

that in addition to the popular seafood theme, also have specialty themes such as Harley-Davidson motorcycles, sports and rock stars, movie memorabilia and, racecars. These restaurants also have some of the most popular gift shops around. (Check out the Restaurants chapter for details on the food.)

Myrtle Beach Factory Stores
**4630 U.S. Hwy. 501 (west of the
Intracoastal Waterway), Myrtle Beach
• (843) 236-5100**

Myrtle Beach Factory Stores is the latest entry in Myrtle Beach's growth as a center for outlet discount shopping. In addition to a new food court, you'll find more than 106 outlet stores, including Timberland, Cole-Haan, Ralph Lauren, Gap, Dansk, Stride-Rite, Anne Klein, Movado Company Store, Lenox, Royal Doulton, Samsonite, Coach, Off 5th (the Saks 5th Avenue outlet), Big Dogs and Tommy Hilfiger, Nike, Banana Republic, J. Crew, and many more.

Myrtle Square Mall
**2501 N. Kings Hwy., Myrtle Beach
• (843) 448-2513**

With more than 80 stores and attractions, Myrtle Square is the oldest and most centrally located mall in Myrtle Beach proper. Anchored by Sears, Peebles and Belk, it offers a nice combination of specialty shops, apparel stores, food, electronics, books, health products, music and more. This mall originally opened in the late '70s as part of the Burroughs & Chapin Company's plan to dominate the local tourism market. (Burroughs & Chapin owns the Pavilion Amusement Park, Broadway at the Beach, and more than 100,000 acres of Grand Strand real estate.)

Some of the better-known mall-esque stores include Blockbuster Music, where you can listen to music before you buy it; Things Remembered, for collectibles and gifts; and Radio Shack, for home electronics. Interestingly enough, with the opening of so many new shopping areas in the past year or so, there has been a fairly large turnover of smaller stores in the mall. Vacant stores are rare, however, because so many businesses covet this prized commercial space.

Myrtle Square boasts the area's only indoor carousel, with 20 high-steppin' horses, tigers, giraffes, spinning lights and old-fashioned music. It also claims to have the world's largest clock (though this is only a claim)—a 60-foot-diameter timepiece that combines centuries-old pendulum technology, 1960s graphics and special time-triggered fountains—in the mall's center court.

SHOPPING

Want to Cook Like a Southerner—Instantly?

Biscuits, grits and pork rinds: the foods that come to mind when someone mentions Southern cooking. And once you've been to Myrtle Beach, Calabash moves up to the top of that list. But there are some other dishes to be explored; delicious items that most visitors haven't heard of, or that restaurants won't serve because they're tired of explaining, for example, what a Lowcountry boil is.

Fortunately, quite a few gourmet shops exist along the Grand Strand, and they all rightfully place an emphasis on the down-home, wholesome flavors that abound in this region. Better still, the stores carry instant mixes so you can carry these home to relish your vacation memories for the rest of the year and maybe even share the tidbits with friends.

The Barefoot General Store, at Barefoot Landing of course, emphasizes the good old days with a penny candy counter, a roasted nut corner and a soda counter dispensing glass-bottled 6.5 ounce Coca-Colas. Amidst all the merchandise like vintage bottles and tins, speckled enamelware and antique hand tools, the Barefoot General Store also has a few aisles of savory concoctions to take home. In addition to hot sauces, you'll also find American Classic Tea in many flavors; American Classic is the only tea grown in America, just south of here in Charleston. The Carolina Kitchen line is also there, featuring a luscious Creamy Vidalia Dressing. The Bubba's brand, which you'll see all over, is a whole line of marinades, salsas and seafood seasonings out of Charleston.

The peanut, also known as the goober pea, is one of the most revered foods of the South and manifests here in many forms, from boiled to buttered. Around the turn of the century, the South's cotton crop was nearly destroyed by the boll weevil. This is when the legendary George Washington Carver saved the day by convincing farmers to plant the legume for it's many uses. Today boiled peanuts can be found at every roadside stand, and a few lucky cities have the Peanut Shop.

Also in Barefoot Landing, the Peanut Shop also successfully re-creates the old-time mercantile. The shop carries it's own line of nuts and soup mixes, and it showcases some of the finest delicacies around, all smartly packaged for you to take home. The *New Southern Cookbook* was spotted on their shelves, right along with jars of Carolina Swamp Stuff. These jars are accented with twine and hand scrawled labels that recollect road side stands hidden deep in the swamps of this state, where few people make their way. Pine Tar is a spicy salad dressing and marinade, Seaweed Splash is a tasty pesto dressing. Cafe du Monde's beignet mix is available, as is a Fiery Sweet Peach Salsa, labeled with the claim

Peanuts are a popular Southern food.

Photo: Courtesy of A & I PRoduction

that it "tastes like a hot Southern night." Try out the mix for Vidalia Onion Cheese Biscuits, or a few of the blends from Gullah Gourmet: Grandputter's Fried Oysters, Lobster Pasta with Slap Yaself Silly Cream Sauce, Hush Dem Puppies. Mixes like these are even more irresistible because of the packaging; along with the amusing descriptions, the mixes come in cotton bags with vintage illustrations and usually a tie of ribbon or twine. A similar brand, Southern Ease (the name says it all), entices you with Shrimp and Grits and She Crab Soup.

You might want to stop in at Kitchen Capers at the Hidden Village or The Extra Ingredient at Broadway at the Beach, just to make sure you are equipped to take on this new culinary adventure. The proprietors of the store have selected quite an inventory of utensils and kitchen tools, from aprons to organizers. The Extra Ingredient is filled with the aroma of gourmet coffees, which are also available to you.

While in the south end, stop by the Carolina Gourmet at the Hammock Shops. Carolina Gourmet also carries its own line of canned goods, ranging from peach preserves (from Carolina peaches, of course) to Vidalia Onion Summer Tomato Dressing to Muscadine and Scuppernong preserves. Benne wafers, which abound in nearly every gourmet shop from here to Savannah, are plentiful. Benne seeds are known to you and me as sesame seeds, but this particular recipe hails from a slave tradition of carrying benne seeds for good luck. The crispy and rich wafers come in a range of flavors from cheese to sweet. Carolina Gourmet's specialty is gift baskets, which they pack with expertise and ship anywhere.

Waccamaw Pottery and Waccamaw Factory Shoppes
U.S. Hwy. 501 (west of the Intracoastal Waterway), Myrtle Beach
• **(843) 236-6152**

If you are wondering where to find Waccamaw Factory Shoppes, just wait until a rainy day when no one is on the beach, then follow the cars. Most of them are on the way to Waccamaw Factory Shoppes.

Shoppers come literally by the bus load to the three malls that make up Waccamaw Pottery and the Factory Shoppes. In fact, this shopping experience is so popular that additional locations have been opened in Miami and central North Carolina.

Waccamaw Pottery, or "the Pottery" as locals call it, was Myrtle Beach's original attraction that brought tourists here simply for the shopping experience. Comparable to three football fields in size, its inventory of housewares and home decor is as staggering as its capacity. Everything is priced 20 to 50 percent below regular department-store prices. Waccamaw Pottery stocks name-brand china, glassware, wicker, silk flowers and trees, cookware, lamps, candles, picture frames, kitchen items, gourmet food selections, selected pieces of furniture, flower pots, delicately etched glassware and even Christmas items. Waccamaw Linen,

the Pottery's next-door neighbor, stocks an overwhelming selection of bedroom and bathroom accessories, rugs of all shapes and sizes, kitchen linens, pillows and crafts.

Waccamaw Factory Shoppes literally has grown up around Waccamaw Pottery. A quarter of a century ago the Pottery was a clay molding and firing company. Though the company primarily made bricks for building contractors, the owner started a sideline hobby of making pots for planters and other terra-cotta needs. A retail store to sell those products exploded with business, and today his original company, headed by his son, is totally out of the brick-firing business. The original brick factory was just leveled in 1996 to make way for even more expansion.

You'll find nearly 125 stores, including popular outlets such as Liz Claiborne, Bass, Oshkosh B'Gosh, Jones New York, Nautica, S&K Famous Brands, Van Heusen, Mikasa, Adidas, Geoffrey Beene, Hanes, London Fog and Rack Room Shoes. In addition you'll find stores specializing in books, jewelry, records, ribbons, rugs and silver.

With the addition of the theaters at Fantasy Harbour, a multiplex movie theater (see our Entertainment chapter) and a host of support restaurants, discount stores and hotels on adjacent property, Waccamaw Factory Shoppes has become an almost self-contained attraction.

SHOPPING

South Strand

The Hammock Shops
U.S. Hwy. 17, Pawleys Island
• (843) 237-8448

Once you've been to The Hammock Shops, you'll understand what many of the other outdoor shopping complexes on the Strand attempting to imitate. This was the first . . . arguably 70 years old and possibly 100 years old. Just to see it is an experience; we even considered including it in our Attractions chapter, but its function as a shopping destination cements its place here.

In 1889 John Joshua Ward, a young riverboat captain who shipped supplies up and down the Waccamaw River from Pawleys Island to Georgetown and Charleston, created the first Pawleys Island hammock. In an attempt to find relief from the scratchy straw mattresses then used on river barges, he first tried working with canvas, then knotted string; but both were as uncomfortable as the straw. What finally evolved was a hammock of soft cotton rope—woven, rather than knotted, and held open by use of a curved "spreader bar." The new design allowed air to circulate, making the hammock far cooler and more comfortable than the scratchy straw beds. And the spreader bar lent a gentle curve, keeping the soft weave from collapsing inward.

This concept behind the famous Pawleys Island hammock spawned a design faithfully retained for more than 100 years. Ward taught the intricacies of the pattern to his brother-in-law, A.H. "Cap't Doc" Lachicotte, and soon the Lachicottes and Wards were busy making hammocks for family members and friends. In the late 1930s, "Doc" set up a small shop on U.S. Highway 17 to sell the hammocks to travelers. And that modest business became the nucleus around which today's famed Hammock Shops at Pawleys Island sprang up. The Lachicottes remain one of the most prominent families on the South Strand and head a real estate conglomerate on Pawleys Island.

"Quaint" might be an overused adjective, but it is truly appropriate when applied to The

INSIDERS' TIP

As you drive through the beachfront neighborhoods, you'll notice that many of the houses have colorful names and professionally carved signs to match. If you'd like a decorative, personalized plaque for your home (or office, or garden), Grand Strand craftspeople are ready. Check out, among others, the Sign Man at 1811 U.S. Highway 17 S. in North Myrtle Beach.

Hammock Shops. This clutch of retail establishments is the kind of place you can return to again and again, finding something new and unique each time. Two dozen shops, many offering the work of Carolina artists and craftspeople, are now clustered beneath moss-draped trees on the edge of a beautiful salt marsh. Some occupy historic Lowcountry buildings that include an original post office and schoolhouse. The newer shops are careful not to compromise the mood of the original architecture; they feature old beams, used timber and ballast brick. Clearly this complex is a welcome complement to the razzle and dazzle of Myrtle Beach.

But this little complex features much more than beautiful nature scenes and great hammocks. You also will find gourmet foods at The Carolina Gourmet, wildlife prints at The Audubon Shopping Gallery, hand-crafted jewelry and contemporary clothing at Three Feathers Gallery, toys and gifts for the "child in all of us" at Hollipops and a host of other distinctive and unusual items. If you want a genuine taste of local color without the neon, glitter and paved parking lots with numbered rows, then you must visit The Hammock Shops. Springtime visits offer the extraordinary beauty of blooming azaleas, dogwoods and tulip trees. Around Christmas, the trees sparkle with tiny white lights, and all the stores don holiday finery, making the holiday season a particularly enjoyable time to visit.

Inlet Square Mall
U.S. Hwys. 17 Bus. and Bypass, Murrells Inlet
• (843) 651-3499

Anchored by Belk, Kmart and JCPenney, Inlet Square offers most of what you'd expect from a typical midsize mall: apparel shops, a bookstore, electronics, jewelry, shoes, a cinema and more. Foxy Lady, a women's boutique, stocks some of the local trend of sequins, hand-beading, scarves, fitted silhouettes and flashy accessories.

The Oasis Food Court (currently undergoing expansion) at Inlet Square offers a rare (for

Shopping is almost as popular as beachcombing on the Grand Strand.

Photo: Courtesy of Myrtle Beach Factory Stores

Barefoot Landing has many fine specialty and retail shops, factory direct stores and mouthwatering restaurants.

Photo: Michael Slear, courtesy of Brandon Advertising

SHOPPING

malls) wide selection of choices. Chick-fil-A is a fast-food staple of almost every mall in America. Glen's Hot Dogs serves up a favorite treat, Prosser's BBQ is a local finger-licker and Mandarine Express makes a mean egg roll.

The mall recently changed ownership for a third time in its short history and manager Joe Pearl is a genius when it comes to promotions and little extras that entice customers. Whether it's free Saturday morning movies for kids at the theaters, the most elaborate Christmas centerpiece on the Strand or live elephants and a real circus, promotions at Inlet Square Mall provide vacationers special diversions that they likely couldn't find at malls back home.

Distinctive Shopping Stops

North Strand

The Town of Calabash

Calabash is one of those sleepy little towns that is just now beginning to awake to the alarm of Myrtle Beach's growth. Even though it's in North Carolina, Calabash can't escape

progress; it's only 15 minutes across the border from North Myrtle Beach. A series of small shops has sprung up, creating an atmosphere akin to Barefoot Landing or The Hammock Shops (see previous entries), featuring antiques, flowers, fashions and curiosities. This is also where all the Calabash-style restaurants you see in North Myrtle Beach and Myrtle Beach get their cue from, so you might want to stay and try out the originals like the Docksider, Ella's and Captain Nance's. Most of the restaurants are waterfront with scenic views.

Calabash Nautical Gifts
9973 Beach Dr., Calabash, N.C.
• (910) 579-1708

Aside from the seashell roadside stands that clustered around the restaurants of Calabash, the Nautical Gift Shop was one of the first stores in the area and it has been growing every year for the past 20 years. The long arm of this L-shaped store has a fudge counter, a clothing section, weather vanes and a whole review of items from a $1 harmonica to $3,500 brass and leather telescopes, stand included.

St. Nick Nack's completes the other arm of the L, and probably has the most, if not the best, selection of Christmas decorations around. The displays of St. Nick Nack's are breathtaking. Glass ornaments from teeny to colossal surround you, oversized reindeer vault down from the ceiling, thick garlands trim everything and Christmas trees are tucked in every corner. There is also a Halloween and an Easter room.

Calabash Low Country Stores
8550 Beach Dr., Calabash, N.C.
• **No central phone**

The facade of this grouping of boutiques is a successful blend of colorful Charlestonian and the laid-back Hammock Shops (see previous entry in this chapter). The yellow, blue, pink and brick shops include the Calabash Art Gallery, Shells & Candy (the essentials of a beach vacation!) and Granny's Cream, a delightful little parlor serving up your favorite flavors of ice cream. Calabash Antiques, a store many locals keep their eye on, takes up four separate storefronts, so be sure to visit them all. Nearby are also the Bagel Cafe and the Book Nook.

Ragpatch Row
10195-3 Beach Dr., Calabash, N.C.
• **No central phone**

Nestled against a backdrop of live oaks, this row of shops gets its name from Victoria's Ragpatch, a fashion standby for many locals. Victoria's is heavily stocked with everything from casual wear to evening gowns to perfumes. The whole store drips with style and creative displays. The Mole Hole is next door, one of five in this successful chain that is the epitome of a gift store; you will be delighted at every turn.

Just across the way is one of the cutest post offices we've ever seen; the little cottage has scalloped trim and an old fashioned life-preserver ring for a sign. Across the pathway from the post office is the Art Plus Gallery, featuring quite a few pieces of pottery amongst all the paintings and prints. Tucked behind all of this is Caffe Latte, a casual restaurant whose menu includes homemade soups and the popular fried shrimp platter.

The Town of Little River

Little River looks like the rest of Myrtle Beach as you drive through on U.S. Highway 17. However, its distinction lies in its waterfront: Little River has a working coastline. Instead of children building sandcastles, when you see the ocean from Little River, you will find shrimp boats pulling up to dock, happy fishermen back from the Gulf Stream, and well-fed pelicans roosting on the piers. Instead of lifeguards, the fresh seafood restaurants (with inlet views) await you. The waterfront of Little River is canopied by resplendent live oak and Spanish moss, creating a setting that looks as good as the local hushpuppies taste. To find the waterfront, and the heart of Little River, turn at Mineola Avenue from U.S. Highway 17.

Toby's Old World
1530 U.S. Hwy. 17,
Little River
• **(843) 249-2174**

Toby's Old World is another one of the original shops in the North Strand. Anchoring the growing restaurant section of Little River (refer to our Restaurant chapter for more details), Toby's takes up decorative two-story house right on U.S. Highway 17. The owners have filled every room, including the porch, with local craft items, souvenirs, jewelry, handmade dolls and candies. The setting is an antique atmosphere with a massive wooden counter in the center and old glass display boxes. Authentic and reproduction signs decorate the walls and are for sale; there are also shelves and shelves of vintage hand tools and kitchen gadgets, quite a few pieces of furniture and a good selection of old books.

North Myrtle Beach

Main Street
Ocean Dr. Section, North Myrtle Beach
• **No central phone**

Shag shops and ice cream are the phrases that sum up this small town-style Main Street. Ocean Drive is quintessential North Myrtle Beach and set the mold for a summertime, seaside community. The mom and pop shops here make for great window shopping and browsing; they also serve to break up the shag clubs that line Main Street. Windows are filled with shag record albums, bathing suits, hand-painted

> ## INSIDERS' TIP
> Jammin' Leather, (843) 903-3603, and Easy Rider Motorcycle Sales and Service, (843) 236-2453, have set up shop on U.S. Highway 501, just inland from Waccamaw Pottery. If you are vrooming in on your Harley (or just wish you were) stop and check out the merchandise, and all the other customers' impressive rides. If you're in the southend Myrtle Beach, stop at Myrtle Beach Harley Davidson in their new location, right on U.S. Highway 17 as you get to Surfside, or call them at (843) 651-5555.

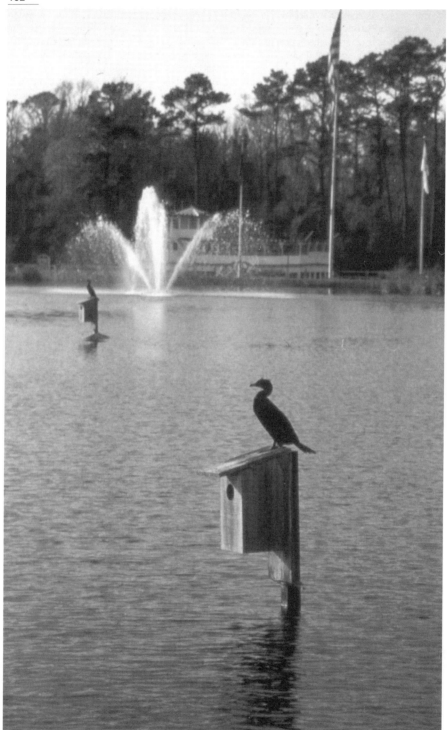

The natural beauty of Barefoot Landing, built around a 20-acre freshwater lake, enhances the unique shopping village.

Photo: Michael Slear, courtesy of Brandon Advertising

rocking chairs and historic O.D. (as Ocean Drive is referred to by the locals) memorabilia. If you claim to be a Myrtle Beach fan, you don't want to miss the place where it all started.

Cameron Diego
3303 U.S. Hwy. 17, North Myrtle Beach
• (843) 272-7699

This is one of those boutiques that make you sigh with relief that finally you've found a place that combines style and comfort. You could happily find your entire traveling and entertaining wardrobe behind these stained-glass doors. With all the accent pieces also available, this breezy flair could run over into your home too. Owned and managed by local Frankie Jones, this boutique shows off the best of Myrtle Beach's casual style. Be sure to stop in next door at the neighborhood's favorite seafood eatery, the White Point Cafe (see our Restaurants chapter).

Myrtle Beach

Christmas Elegance
4301 N. Kings Hwy., Myrtle Beach
• (843) 626-3100

Christmas decorations in the middle of July? No, really. The complex features seven stores in a natural setting. This wonderland features a seemingly endless variety of holiday decorations in addition to items such as music boxes, collector-quality dolls, electric trains—even a cutlery shop. White Heron showcases an incredible collection of wind chimes. Other stores carry yard ornaments, fine handmade jewelry, candles, cards and Native American crafts. While most of the shops carry lots of Christmas merchandise, you'll find gifts for all occasions.

The Galleria
9600 U.S. Hwy. 17 and
Lake Arrowhead Rd. (Restaurant Row),
Myrtle Beach
• No central phone

If you're looking for convenience, The Galleria is a place to keep in mind. Its location in central and visible Restaurant Row makes it easy to find, and the stores there thrive by providing you with the essentials—and the conveniences—you might need on your vacation. The Kroger grocery stores dominates the highway front, and offers everything from produce to a full pharmacy to beach chairs. From Kroger a long line of storefronts ensue: Kligs Kites, Jerry's Ice Cream Shop, Heavenly Hams and Fudge Nut. You can also drop off your dry clean-

ing at Sunny Cleaners, get your hair done at McQuaigs, send a fax from Mail Boxes Etc., and pick up breakfast at Manhattan Bagels. At New Life Natural Foods you can get your vitamins in pill form, or fresh squeezed out of your choice of fresh fruits.

Gay Dolphin
Ocean Blvd. at Ninth Ave. N.,
Myrtle Beach
• (843) 448-6550

No chapter on Grand Strand shopping worth its salt could overlook Gay Dolphin, a world-famous shopping attraction and Myrtle Beach institution for more than four decades. Even if you're not interested in shopping, you'll be wowed by an inventory of more than 60,000 items, ranging from postcards to collectibles. You've got to see this place to believe it.

This gift shop actually has "coves," small shops within the larger store, extending from the boulevard to the oceanfront. Collector's Cove features Hummel figurines, Sebastian and Norman Rockwell items, clowns, gnomes, bells and more. In the Pearl Booth, you can actually pick your own pearl from genuine South Sea oysters, then watch while experienced staff mount it in jewelry made just for you. More than 50 coves include merchandise such as stuffed animals, souvenirs, golf memorabilia, shark's teeth, nautical items, toys, swimwear, ceramics and shells.

We can remember shopping here with family in the early 1960s, and when we visited them recently we noticed that little had changed. Definitely check out the shark's-teeth cove!

Hidden Village Shops
9902 U.S. Hwy. 17 N.
(Restaurant Row area), Myrtle Beach
• No central phone

On the east side of U.S. Highway 17, look for this interesting strip of specialty stores. Kitchen Capers has everything any cook could dream up. Expect typical stuff, such as cookbooks, aprons, oven mitts, pot holders and cookie cutters as well as unusual items, such as bacon presses, expandable trivets, odd kitchen gadgetry you didn't know you needed and decorative ceramics for your counter tops. Diva's has recently expanded to take up two full store fronts, offering colorful clothing and gifts. The Wild Bird Marketplace and Derrick Collector Baskets and Accessories have also found their niche at the Hidden Village. If you can turn your gaze from the colorful facades of Hidden Village, immediately across U.S. Highway 17 is the busy and useful Corning Revere Outlet, which, we have noticed, is constantly being restocked.

King's Highway
Kings Hwy. at 79th Ave. N., Myrtle Beach
• No central phone

Two impressive shopping centers face each other across King's Highway (also called U.S. Highway 17), forming a busy intersection. On the inland side is Northwood, where a brand-new and extensive SteinMart offers clothes for everyone. A Food Lion Grocery Store, a GNC (in case you need some protein powder), and the soothing Michael and Company Salon and Spa also occupy Northwood, as does the Atlanta Bread Company, serving a medley of sandwiches on their own fresh baked breads. A Bank of America and Blockbuster form the outparcels. Across King's Highway, at the Professional Plaza, the Jolly Roger is a time-tested Myrtle Beach favorite, and features fine home furnishings. The Wacky Rabbit is a whimsical gift shop featuring bunnies and samples of chocolate fudge.

INSIDERS' TIP

The Myrtle Beach Convention Center is host to a few shopping extravaganzas throughout the year. The Carolina Women's Show has endless tables of accessories and fashions, J. Crew held an open house here last year and, of course, the perennial Gun and Knife show makes the circuit. Contact the convention center at (843) 918-1225 to find out what events are going on while you're in town.

At the tail end of this same shopping center, at the corner of 77th Avenue, is Studio 77, a colorful and contemporary gift shop, while at the opposite end of the parking lot, back at 79th Avenue, a produce stand sets up during the summertime under a big umbrella, offering some of the best local watermelon around.

A few worthwhile shops radiate south on Highway 17 from these two centers.

One block down at 75th Avenue N., on the same side of U.S. 17, is Joan Crosby's. This women's-wear store is a 40-year-old Myrtle Beach institution and is a particularly nice find for older women seeking traditional clothing styles in sizes that leave Kate Moss out in the cold. Again on your left, two blocks south at 73rd Avenue N., is Country Vogue. This elegant shop features scads of popular, high-quality apparel from Lanz, Liz Sport, Liz Claiborne and J.H. Collectibles. Styles lean toward classic more than trendy, and Country Vogue has a good selection of petite sizes too. The clothing here is top-quality—the kind of stuff you wear around your country club buddies who recognize designer names.

Rainbow Harbor
Kings Hwy. at 49th Ave. N., Myrtle Beach
• (843) 449-7476

This group of retail options is clearly designed for people who cherish the finer things in life. Cheryl Newby Gallery, for example, is in its 15th year of specializing in antique prints, engravings and fine art. Browse through more than 3,000 natural-history prints, including collections by John James Audubon. Also featured is an extensive collection of rare and decorative antique maps and charts. This gallery can restore fine art and old documents as well. The real treat at Rainbow Harbor is Diane Kirkpatrick Ramsay's Femme Fatal. At first glance you might think that this is just a clothing and accessory store for large-size women. But after examining the inventory, you will see why women travel from surrounding states and even large cities such as Charlotte and Atlanta just to shop at Femme Fatal. Diane flies to New York twice a year to handpick the latest designer fashions in large sizes. Her attention to cutting-edge style and the most minute detail has led her to begin a catalog and consider opening other stores in several cities. Her store alone is worth the visit to Rainbow Harbor.

In 1996 The Melting Pot joined Rainbow Harbor as the only fondue restaurant along the Grand Strand. Dining tables are furnished with their own hot plates to keep oil, broth, cheese or chocolate bubbling as you cook your food on skewers. The Motor City Market next door wraps up homemade pierogies to go, among other imported delicacies.

South Strand

Antiqueing in Murrells Inlet
U.S. Hwys. 17 Bus. and Bypass,
Murrells Inlet

With a deep history, Murrells Inlet is a great find for antiques collectors. Both U.S. 17 Business and Bypass here are peppered with a number of antiques shops. This strip of the Grand Strand is less developed and more relaxed in atmosphere, brimming with history and full of Lowcountry color. The drive itself is pleasant

SHOPPING

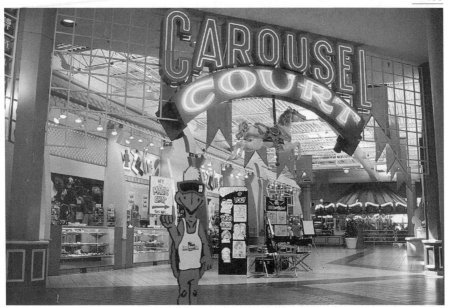

Carousel Court at Myrtle Square Mall serves as an eating place, and meeting place, for many mall patrons.

Photo: Courtesy of Cotton Company

and pretty. Begin at Wachesaw Row Antique Mall, just south of Inlet Square Mall on U.S. 17 Business, where you can pick up a brochure that will list all the antique shops. Here you'll find A & G Furniture, a 9,000-square-foot outlet of antiques, furniture, glassware, clocks, books and a staggering amount of collectibles. Also in Murrells Inlet is Legacy Antique Mall, where you'll find estate jewelry, silver and paintings.

The Island Shops
U.S. Hwy. 17, Pawleys Island
• No central phone

Just south and across the highway from The Hammock Shops are The Island Shops. Nestled beneath gnarled, weathered oaks, these shops are filled with one-of-a-kind finds. A ribbon of wooden walkways and bridges amid a series of small ponds unites the different shops and boutiques. Be sure to pause and enjoy the antics of the friendly population of ducks. Happily splashing in and out of their Lowcountry "swimming hole," they graciously accept tasty tidbits from shoppers. And if the web-footed friends can't calm your shopping frenzy, cozy benches, oversize rockers and well-placed hammocks surely will do the trick.

If you're curious about what you'll find, here's a few of the shopping selections: Locals "in-the-know" travel from miles around to visit

The Cricket Shop. Featuring fine swimwear from leading designers, this fun shop also boasts sportswear and dresses. Meander through the door of Love, Pawleys and relish a symphony of smells. Dried flowers and herbs, lavish floral arrangements and oodles of handcrafts make it tough to tuck away the credit card.

If the kitchen is your favorite place, head to Pawleys Pantry for an absolutely unmatched selection of great gadgets and gourmet cookware. The Mole Hole is an infinitely intriguing little gift shop that's become a Pawleys Island landmark. There's no telling what delightful trinket you might discover. Before you stash the cash, peruse hand-carved birds, whimsical characters, collectibles and framed and unframed prints at The Wooden Duck.

Harrington Altman Ltd.
10729 Ocean Hwy., Pawleys Island
• (843) 237-2056

Just north of The Island Shops is Harrington Altman Ltd., an extraordinary gift shop on the west side of the highway (look for the big digital clock). The inventory here leans toward elegant—with more than a touch of "cozy" tossed in for spice. This shop features a rotating selection of tastefully striking furniture: coffee tables, sideboards, china cabinets, bookshelves and dining tables. Many items are hand-painted and one-of-a-kind. It also stocks a medley of

SHOPPING

what your mom might call "knickknacks" or "whatnots"—lovely collectible pieces of table-top decor that could add a touch of whim or an element of class to an existing display. Harrington Altman showcases some art, flower arrangements, fancy pillows, lots of handmade heirlooms and an impressive collection of up-holstery fabrics.

Pawleys Town Square
2634 U.S. Hwy. 17 N., Pawleys Island
• (843) 237-4886

Across the street from Harrington Altman, in Pawleys Town Square, you'll find George Pawley Company Inc. Since 1990, owner Michael York has provided his customers with the finest in outdoor furnishings, decorative accessories and practical pieces for the serious birder or gardener.

Check out the handmade items of heirloom quality: fountains, furniture, planters, statuary, weather vanes, mailboxes and so much more. All those garden catalogs you covet in the spring come to life at George Pawleys. A growing reputation has prompted the store to expand and offer even more choices.

And ask Mike (or his mom) to tell you the history of George Pawley and why they chose that name for their store.

Bookstores

Out of all the attractions in Myrtle Beach, sitting in front of the ocean with your toes in the sand and a good book on your lap ranks in the top five, at least. Stroll down the beach and you will see quite a few people relaxing with their favorite classic or the latest bestseller. Most of these places even carry the Insiders' Guide® series!

North Strand

The Bookstall
10497 U.S. Hwy. 17 N.,
North Myrtle Beach
• (843) 272-2607

Sandwiched between Colonial Mall and

Barefoot Landing, The Bookstall is a book lover's dream; it's an entire house covered with books and book shelves. Here you can buy, sell or trade your books. We recently were shopping for a hard-to-find book and this was the place we found it. The selection includes comics, collectibles and rare books.

Waldenbooks
4720 B Barefoot Landing,
North Myrtle Beach
• (843) 361-8756
Myrtle Square Mall, Myrtle Beach
• (843) 448-4534

In addition to the usual lists of classics and bestsellers, Waldenbooks sets out quite a few tables of discount books, racks of magazines and many regional newspapers.

> **INSIDERS' TIP**
> It's Christmas all year round in quite a few shops in the area. Fantastic decorations are always available at stores like the Christmas Mouse at Barefoot Landing, the Christmas Elegance village in Myrtle Beach and St. Nick Nack's in Calabash, N.C.

Myrtle Beach

Barnes & Noble
1145 Seaboard St.,
Myrtle Beach
• (843) 444-4046

One of America's oldest bookstores, Barnes and Noble's large freestanding building can be seen from the U.S. Highway 17 Bypass, just south of Broadway at the Beach. The store is a more than complete source of reading materials that include a tremendous selection of newspapers and magazines, software and a Starbucks Cafe. Additionally, Barnes and Noble offers more interactive happenings: local artists exhibit in the cafe, regular children's story times are held, the Sherlock Holmes Society meets every third Monday. Barnes and Noble maintains an active calendar, including open poetry readings (usually the last Thursday each month) and book signings by current authors, so be sure to stop by and pick up their flyer to fill in your idle or rainy-day time.

Book Warehouse
3301 Outlet Blvd., Myrtle Beach
• (843) 236-0800

Book Warehouse is part of the Factory Shoppes at Waccamaw, therefore you have a tempting selection of literature and pulp at a discount prices. Bestsellers are 20 percent off and the rest of the inventory up to 50 percent less than usual.

Entertainment

It all started in 1986 with Calvin Gilmore's Carolina Opry, a family-style opry house in Surfside Beach. Locals clearly remember that the buzz around town was, "It'll never make it. . . . There are not enough people to support it year round. . . . This Gilmore guy is crazy." But before long, shows were sold out in advance as throngs of residents, bus tours and visitors vied for tickets to see the countrified, musical/comedy production that was whispered to be "better than anything in Nashville or Branson." If you didn't have your tickets to the Christmas show by June, you were certainly out of luck.

Gilmore was crazy . . . crazy like a fox, that is. The former timeshare salesman opened Carolina Opry only after conducting extensive marketing research that indicated the Myrtle Beach area was fertile ground for such grand entertainment. Regardless of most locals' patronage, estimates showed the opry house could survive on ticket sales from tourists and the ever-growing retirement community. The rest is a history lesson in success.

Up until 1995 Gilmore owned and operated three entertainment palaces along the Grand Strand. Fierce competition from a bombardment of new shows and attractions forced him to lease out two of his Grand Strand theaters, and he opened another in Charleston, South Carolina. Paving the way for live productions, Gilmore and the Carolina Opry are the forerunners of the area's entertainment explosion that now includes Dolly Parton's Dixie Stampede, and Alabama Theatre. And the list of entertainment options doesn't stop there. As you read on, you'll discover the full extent of live performances here. As a rule, the variety shows are wholesome and entertaining for the entire family. Tickets are sold by reservation, so call ahead to secure seats. Keep in mind that prices are subject to change, we've listed what we knew at press time. Refreshments are sold before each show and during intermission; only a few venues serve alcohol on site.

LOOK FOR:
• North Strand
• Myrtle Beach
• South Strand

North Strand

Alabama Theatre
Barefoot Landing,
U.S. Hwy. 17 N.,
North Myrtle Beach
• (843) 272-1111,
   (800) 342-BAMA

With a spectacular red, white and blue grand-opening gala on the Fourth of July 1993, the supergroup Alabama unveiled its $7 million, 2,000-seat theater.

Their latest, greatest house production is truly a must-see show. Featuring the vision and skill of Supergroup Alabama and Opryland USA, two of the biggest and best-respected names in the entertainment industry, this production delivers a rich musical mix spiced with side-splitting comedy and dynamic dance numbers. Music runs the gamut from the smooth sounds of the '40s to Broadway show tunes; from classic country to exhilarating swing; from lively Gospel to upbeat rock 'n' roll.

Boasting access to the nation's brightest new stars, Opryland USA conducts an annual audition that reaches more than thirty U.S. cities—and abroad too. Handpicked from more than 10,000 contenders, the Alabama Theater troupe represents the *creme de la creme* of promising performers. Little wonder the theatre was recently awarded the coveted honor of being named the Palmetto State's top-attended theatre—for the fourth year in a row! The Alabama Theatre's 2000 show was also named the Tourism Event of the Year by the South Carolina Tourism Board.

The Theatre also boasts a Celebrity Concert Series featuring such stars as Patty Loveless, Diamond Rio, Kenny Chesney, Tim Conway, Don Knotts, Billy Ray Cyrus, Ricky Van Shelton, the Oak Ridge Boys, Jim Nabors, Charlie Pride, Sammy Kershaw, Roy Clark, Lou Rawls, and—of course, the theatre's namesake supergroup Alabama.

For value, the $69 season pass can't be beat. This pass entitles the holder not only admission to Alabama Theatre's house show, but also the customer's pick of one guest-artist performance, plus unlimited admission to the Christmas in Dixie Show.

Showmanship, eclectic music, lavish costumes and dazzling special effects . . . Alabama Theatre has it all. You'll wonder why you didn't visit sooner.

House of Blues
4640 U.S. Hwy. 17 S. at Barefoot Landing, North Myrtle Beach
- **(843) 272-3000**

It was an exciting time for Grand Stranders when the House of Blues officially opened to the public with a gala ceremony that featured The Blues Brothers—Dan Aykroyd and John Goodman—and the Godfather of Soul himself, James Brown. Even South Carolina's then-Governor, David Beasley, roared in on a Harley for the event.

The House of Blues now stands as the area's only true music hall, a massive space that can hold 2,200 people at one time. Sellout crowds have come to the House of Blues to see ZZ Top, Steve Winward, INXS, K.C. and the Sunshine Band, Gregg Allman, Collective Soul and The Wallflowers. Acts are booked all year round depending on artist availability. Each performance commands its own ticket price, but it's safe to say you'll pay $5 and up for admission to any of the shows. Except for low seating and scattered barstools, the music hall is a stand-up, dancing venue.

In its trail-blazing style, The House of Blues also brought Gospel brunches to the Grand Strand. At 9 AM and 2 PM on Sundays, the House is spiritually inspired by gospel choirs singing praises while the audience dines on a South-ern-style all-you-can-eat buffet meal. Gospel show and buffet is $16.95 per adult and $8.50 for those 6 to 12 years of age. Children 6 and younger need not pay.

For more on the House of Blues, which also has a restaurant, see the Close-up in the Restaurants chapter.

Myrtle Beach

Carolina Opry
N. Kings Hwy. (at U.S. Hwy. 17 Bypass), Myrtle Beach
- **(843) 238-8888, (800) 843-6779**
- **www.thecarolinaopry.com**

Since 1986 when Calvin Gilmore opened The Carolina Opry and launched the entertainment industry in Myrtle Beach, South Carolina, the Grand Strand has taken its place among the nation's most popular centers for live entertainment. Taking in at least one show is an absolute must and The Carolina Opry, the area's original show, is one great choice. Need proof? *USA Today* called it "a big hit." *New York Post* said it was "a hot ticket." *The Saturday Evening Post* wrote, " . . . tourists can't beat the two-hour show at The Carolina Opry." And, *Southern Living* magazine delivered this accolade: "Music, comedy and glitter . . . an entertainment phenomenon."

Offering something for everyone, this ultimate variety show is a mix of Nashville, Vegas and Broadway and showcases stellar performances by world-class singers, musicians, comedians and dancers. Set in a 2,200-seat show palace with premier sound and lighting systems and three giant screens, every guest sees every performer "up close and personal."

The Carolina Opry has remained the only show that has won every major South Carolina tourism award, including the Governor's Cup and Most Outstanding Attraction. Readers of the Myrtle Beach Knight-Ridder newspaper, *The Sun News*, has voted this live music and comedy variety show the Best of the Beach year after year. These accolades only reinforce what people who see the show already know: The Carolina Opry entertains with America's best-loved music and is widely acclaimed as Myrtle Beach's best show. Visit their website for show photos and videos, as well as to purchase tickets on-line.

Shows begin at 8 PM except during Novem-

> **INSIDERS' TIP**
> The Grand Strand's own Long Bay Symphony orchestra has made quite a name for itself by offering this area outstanding performances.

ber and December when the curtain rises at 7 PM. Ticket prices for the regular season are $28.95 for adults, $18 for students and $13 for children. During the November and December Holiday Shows, tickets for adults are $28.95 to $29.95 and children are $19. Reservations for all shows are strongly recommended.

Comedy Cabana
9588 N. Kings Hwy., Myrtle Beach
• **(843) 449-HAHA**

If you're in the mood for a good belly laugh, the Comedy Cabana is the only comic emporium on the Grand Strand. The Cabana features three new comedians each week and the 2000 lineup included Tim Wilson, James Gregory and Killer Beaz.

Comedy Cabana is divided into two rooms. The Good Humor Bar and Grill is open before and after shows for food and drink. The menu offers appetizers, burgers, sandwiches and pizza. Showtime is in another theater room where members of the audience comfortably sit at round tables.

As is the norm with most comedy clubs, guests must buy at least two items during the evening. The Cabana stocks a full bar plus a good selection of coffee drinks, non-alcoholic elixirs, soft drinks and sparkling waters.

Performances are two hours long and begin at 8 PM, Wednesday through Saturday during the spring and fall seasons, with an additional show at 10:15 PM on Friday and Saturday nights. From mid-May through Labor Day, you can go to this comedy house every night of the week.

Children thirteen and younger are not encouraged to attend. There is a $3 cover charge on Mondays, Tuesdays and Wednesdays. Thursday through Saturday, admission is $5. The Comedy Cabana is closed on Sunday.

Crocodile Rocks Dueling Pianos Saloon
1320 Celebrity Cir.,
Broadway at the Beach, Myrtle Beach
• **(843) 444-2096**

Crocodile Rocks is a unique show that features nonstop dueling pianos. Two grand pianos face one another on stage and alternating players ensure high-energy tinkling of the ivories all night long.

Usually packed on weekends, audiences are normally clapping and screaming with laughter at bawdy renditions of songs. Patrons are brought up on stage during the show to become the brunt of a joke or to participate in enacting the lyrics of a tune. The singer-musicians at Crocodile Rocks are incredibly talented. Requests (with a little cash) for songs are taken throughout the evening.

Use caution if escorting an ultraconservative relative or child; some of the skits could make even your drunken cousin blush. Admission to Crocodile Rocks is $5 per person and allows you entry into Revolutions Retro Dance Club across the square.

Dixie Stampede
N. Kings Hwy. at U.S. Hwy. 17 Bypass, Myrtle Beach
• **(843) 497-9700, (800) 433-4401**

Dixie Stampede, a Dollywood Production, is a dinner attraction that combines country cookin' with a rodeo-style show for a rompin', stompin', finger-lickin' good time. And we're not just whistling Dixie about the finger-lickin' part: Don't expect silverware for your four-course dinner of creamy vegetable soup, whole roasted chicken, hickory-smoked pork, corn on the cob, herb-basted potato, homemade bread, dessert and beverage. And just in case you're wondering, the soup is served in a drinking cup. Thankfully, you can wash your hands with warm, wet towels provided by the singing waiters and waitresses.

Before dinner, everyone is corralled into the Dixie Belle Saloon (no alcohol served) for live musical entertainment, specialty drinks served in boot mugs, popcorn and peanuts. Then, the audience is seated in stadium fashion above the arena where the action is held. Country-music artist and icon Dolly Parton had a hand in developing this $5 million dinner attraction, so expect Southern belles, glitzy costumes that light up in the dark, cowboys who perform trick riding with some 30 trained horses and audience participation that's downright neighborly. The show's theme is created from the romance of the Old South and the rivalry of the Civil War. Let's face it, a pig race between Ulysses S. Grunt and Robert E. Lean is pushing the cornball, but it sets the pace for a knee-slapping good time. The Dixie Stampede spent $2 million to update their show recently, adding more segments that command audience interaction as well as spectacular new illusions.

INSIDERS' TIP
Check ahead with theaters before bringing your camera or camcorder along to any performances. Most have strict policies about shutterbugging or filming during showtime or even within the building itself.

Featuring the vision and skill of Supergroup Alabama and Opryland USA, two of the biggest and best-respected names in entertainment, Alabama Theatre delivers a rich musical mix spiced with side-splitting comedy and dynamic dance numbers.

Photo: Courtesy of Alabama Theatre

ENTERTAINMENT

The vocal talent—and costumes—will "wow" you all night long.

Photo: Courtesy of Alabama Theatre

As if outstanding vocals and dancing are not enough, the costuming showcased by many of the area's first-rate shows is also spectacular.

Photo: Courtesy of Carolina Opry

World-class dancers move Myrtle Beach to the "Big-League."

Photo: Courtesy of Lesnik Himmelsbach Wilson Hearl & Hirsch

ENTERTAINMENT

Dixie Stampede was responsible for bringing ostriches to the Grand Strand to step up the show's North-South conflict. Two riders, one in Union blue, the other in a Confederate uniform, jockey their big birds around the arena. These feathered racers are between 3 and 6 years old, already 7 feet tall and weigh in at about 350 pounds.

Tickets are $32.99 plus tax for adults and teens and $16.99 plus tax for children ages 4 to 11; kids younger than 4 are admitted free. The theater seats about 1,000, but call ahead for reservations. Regular shows are held 6 PM daily from March through May. Two shows, at 6 and 8 PM, are performed nightly from June through August. You can catch one show per evening at 6 PM during September and October, and performances are scheduled for every Tuesday, Wednesday, Friday and Saturday night at 6 PM in November and December.

The holiday *Christmas at Dixie* show is performed from mid-November up until New Year's Eve. The yuletide season finds the trick horse rider dressed as a toy soldier and the sassy girls bantering about who (the North or the South) celebrates Christmas with the most style. *Christmas at Dixie* costs adults $32.99 and children 17 and younger $16.99.

Medieval Times Dinner & Tournament
• (800) 436-4386, (843) 236-8080

There's nothing on the Grand Strand quite like Medieval Times. This 60-mile stretch of vacation paradise offers plenty of great places to dine, but none features the awe-inspiring thunder of rare Andalusian stallions. There are theatres, more than a few, but not one has a more fantastic (and authentic!) story line. There are world-class performers, but none more committed to excellence. Dinner at Medieval Times is anything but a typical night on the town. Dinner at Medieval Times is a journey into the past . . . a journey into fun . . . and a truly unique vacation experience.

Medieval Times is family entertainment from the Middle Ages, when the Lord of the castle would invite a thousand friends, neighbors and foes to a feast and royal tournament. Guests should expect to eat without utensils and experience horsemanship, swordplay, falconry, sorcery and romance created by the cast of 75 actors and 20 horses.

INSIDERS' TIP

Book your tickets for special holiday shows at least six months in advance. By June of any given year, a waiting list for available seats is already being compiled at most of the area's entertainment venues.

As a member of the royal audience, you'll boo and cheer as six Knights of the Realm compete to become Champion of the Evening. The champion knight is bestowed the pleasure of choosing his Queen of Love and Beauty from the audience and crowning her as such. For the 1996 season, Medieval Times added the Knight Club, where guests may adjourn after the show is over to dance the rest of the night away. A cash bar is available.

A 12-year-old relative adamantly swears that Medieval Times is the best place to go out for an evening—that the entertainment and food are second to none!

Tickets are $34.75 plus tax for folks over the age of 12 and $18 plus tax for children ages 3 to 12. Kids younger than 3 are admitted free of charge. Prices do not include gratuity.

Medieval Times is closed from January 1 to mid-February. It's best to call ahead to secure reservations. (See our Kidstuff chapter for more information.)

The Palace Theatre
Broadway at the Beach,
From 21st to 29th Aves. N.
(off U.S. Hwy. 17 Bypass), Myrtle Beach
• (843) 448-0588, (800) 905-4228

The Palace Theater, located at Broadway at the Beach, is best known for its ever-changing line-up of world-class entertainment. From legendary performers like Kenny Rogers, Bill Cosby, Martina McBride, LeAnn Rimes, B.B. King, Willie Nelson, George Carlin and The Righteous Brothers, to a parade of Broadway productions and the Radio City Christmas Spectacular, The Palace consistently showcases big-name performances that can accurately be described as "only the best."

Characterized by the style of theaters built in the 1950s, The Palace is one of the most elegant venues of its kind. Crowned with a striking cupola dome easily visible for miles, the theater makes a memorable first impression—even before guests pass through the doors. In true ante-bellum style, the luxurious foyer showcases a winding staircase, enormous marble columns and grandiose chandeliers.

The 2700-seat auditorium is equally impressive. A magnificent Austrian curtain—fashioned from rich, wine-colored velvet—graces the area's largest stage. The electrically oper-

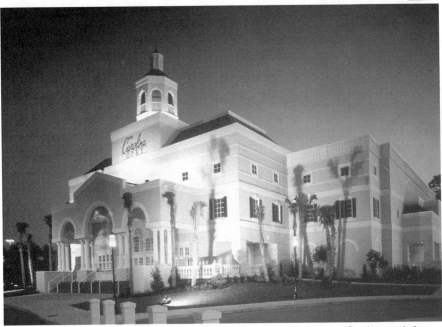

The Carolina Opry's elegant, 2,200-seat theatre, reminiscent of an opulent Southern-styled plantation mansion, is home to a show USA Today referred to as "A Big Hit."

Photo: Courtesy of Carolina Opry

ated curtain measures an awe-inspiring 30 by 75 feet and weighs in excess of 7,000 pounds! Equipped with a state-of-the-art lighting system that can handle more than 275,000 watts of lighting, the auditorium is also noted for an advanced sound system (with capacity for upwards of 80 microphones!) that delivers true stereo separation to every seat in the theater. The seating arrangement bespeaks elegance, too. Every row is set 40 inches apart—which allows ample room for guests to enter and exit from any seat without inconveniencing other patrons.

A wonderful and easy way to check out The Palace Theater's schedule is to visit their website. In addition to a current schedule, you'll find special offers, detailed show information, group sales information and much more.

South Strand

Legends in Concert
301 U.S. Hwy. 17 S., Surfside Beach
• (843) 238-7827, (800) 960-7469

Words alone cannot describe the music and magic of Legends in Concert. A live, on-stage recreation of performances from the world's best-loved entertainers, Legends showcases as-tounding impersonations of stars that include Tom Jones, Dolly Parton, The Blues Brothers, Rod Stewart, Roy Orbison, the inimitable Elvis and more! Legends' stars deliver much more than uncanny resemblances to the stars they portray. Their acts are not lip-synched; this line-up of performers actually sing the memorable tunes you remember. Close your eyes and you'll swear Dolly is on stage. Rod Stewart swings his microphone precisely as the "real" Rod always has. Elvis has mastered "the King's" legendary moves. And, if it is at all possible, the Blue's Brothers may actually bring even more vim and vigor to their act than the original Brothers did!

In addition to the Superstars' glittering recreations, this world-famous show showcases an accomplished line-up of singers and dancers, as well as the smooth sounds of the live Legends Orchestra. State-of-the-art sound, lighting and multi-media special effects round out a spectacular full-stage production that's anything but ordinary. Legends in Concert has been awarded the titles "Show of the Year," "Entertainers of the Year" and "Show of Shows" by the International Press Association. The annual Christmas show is a particular delight.

Tickets are priced at $26 for adults and $13 for children aged three to sixteen.

ENTERTAINMENT

Attractions

LOOK FOR:
- Amusement Parks
- Water Parks
- Nature Centers
- Museums and Educational Activities
- Historic Churches

The Grand Strand is an attraction; every aspect of a visit here involves one or more attractions. And, if you try to hit them all ... well, you might as well move here like us!

Of course, in a more broad sense, there are many attractions here beyond the beach, restaurants, theaters, shopping destinations and golf courses. You'll also find amusement parks, water parks, nature centers, historic gardens, museums, zoos, racecar tracks, bumper boats, arcades, hundreds of miniature golf courses, driving ranges and par 3 courses (see our Golf chapter for details) ... more attractions than you can possibly imagine. If you have kids, or just want to feel like a kid, be sure to peruse the Kidstuff chapter; it's filled with neat stuff we don't list in this chapter. This chapter culminates with a special Historic Churches section featuring some architectural treasures.

Here are a few suggestions to get you started. In many instances, prices and hours vary seasonally. We provide peak-season rates and times; call ahead during the off-season.

Amusement Parks

North Strand

Alligator Adventure
U.S. Hwy. 17 N.,
North Myrtle Beach
• (843) 361-0789

Alligator Adventure, an alligator park and reptile research institute that adjoins Barefoot Landing, has differentiated itself from any other attraction along the Grand Strand over the last two years. One of the largest facilities for reptile life in the world, the natural 15-acre setting of this unique facility is home to a variety of exotic birds, frogs, snakes, tortoises and lizards as well as a huge collection of alligators and crocodiles.

Here are a few examples of the fascinating things you and your family will see: the world's only known collection of rare, snow-white albino American alligators; giant Galapagos tortoises; West African dwarf crocodiles (they're often referred to as "ferocity in a 4-foot package"); a serpentarium that holds enormous pythons, boas and anacondas (the largest species of

snake on earth); beautiful but deadly King cobras (some more than 13 feet long); and hundreds of American alligators, from newly hatched to 13-foot-long adults that weigh nearly a half-ton. In 1999 they also hosted a tour of giraffes.

Alligator Adventure's 5,000 feet of boardwalk weave in and out of natural surroundings that emulate the beautiful wetland habitats to which these animals are accustomed. Thanks to unusual plants, colorful birds, rare species, giant snakes and 'gators galore, photo opportunities abound 'round every bend in the boardwalk. To help visitors understand the wildlife of the wetlands, a rotating collection of exciting and informative exhibits are displayed throughout the park, and demonstrations are scheduled. For example, an on-site amphitheater with 700 seats hosts a "show" of sorts every hour. Often, but not always, these shows feature hands-on interaction with the audience. But don't waste time worrying about safety; Alligator Adventure is supervised by a safety-minded, world-renowned staff that's dedicated to protecting guests and animals alike.

Alligator Adventure is handicapped accessible. The park is designed for self-guided tours; guests can wander the entire 15 acres or choose only the exhibits and demonstrations they find interesting.

During the summer, general admission for folks 15 and older is $10.95; kids ages 4 through 14 get in for $7.95; and little ones 3 and younger get in free. Rates drop slightly during slower seasons.

Alligator Adventure is open year round. Hours vary from season to season, but generally the park opens at 10 AM. Closing time depends on the time of year, so please call ahead. Tickets are sold until an hour before closing. For more information on Alligator Adventure, see the Close-up in our Kidstuff chapter.

Barefoot Landing
U.S. Highway 17 N.
• (843) 272-8349, (800) 272-8349

Barefoot Landing is a scenic attraction; the wood boutiques blend with the lake setting comfortably (see our Shopping chapter), and the intracoastal waterway as a backdrop makes Barefoot quite unique. Barefoot highlights this with firework displays all summer long, the *Barefoot Princess River Boat*, plenty of wildlife to ooh and ahh at, Jet Ski rentals and Carousel Courtyard for the kids. Additionally, Barefoot has gathered a superior selection of restaurants (see the Restaurant chapter for more information) that is an attraction in itself.

Myrtle Beach

Broadway at the Beach
21st to 29th Aves. S. and Hwy. 17 Bypass
• (843) 444-3200

Broadway at the Beach deserves mention in this chapter because it has gone way past the whole nine yards it takes to lure tourists to its facility. In addition to all the shopping, kidstuff and restaurants (see the pertinent chapters for more details) Broadway also has some delightful attractions and activities—beyond the simple fact that there is all ready so much to do in one place. Broadway's attractions can be summed up in one word: spectacular. From Memorial Day to Labor Day there is a firework display every Tuesday. The lake in the center of it all isn't just for the ducks; you can take a water taxi or get yourself around in a paddle boat. There are even a few specially padded spots just for kids, including Carousel Park, so see the Kidstuff chapter for more details.

Family Kingdom
Third Ave. S. and Ocean Blvd., Myrtle Beach
• (843) 626-3447

We remember back in the 1960s when the Swamp Fox roller coaster was being built in a (then) newly paved marsh. It was planned to be the largest old-style wooden roller coaster (with a 62-foot drop) in the South. It wasn't until some years later that the South's largest Ferris wheel—nearly 100 feet in diameter—was added to the complex.

Owned today by the Sea Mist hotel, Family Kingdom is open to one and all. Kids of all ages love the miniature locomotive that tours the perimeter of the park. An antique carousel is also a favorite of those who might not be daring enough for the roller coaster or Ferris wheel. There is even an indoor arcade in the center of the park.

This home of family fun takes a great deal of pride in its reputation as a family-friendly park. Little kids are the focus here; in fact, there's a special separate area called Kiddie Land that's just for toddlers and tots. In Kiddie Land, you'll find lots of "small" rides for the small fry, including a miniature Ferris wheel and kid-sized roller coaster.

If hunger strikes, enjoy pizza, hamburgers, ice cream and lemonade. There are a number of ticket-pricing plans that vary depending on the time of year and the options taken; it is best to call ahead. In peak season, however, day passes are $14.95 per person; individual tickets are 50¢ each.

Family Kingdom is open from late March to late November. Operating hours vary, depending on the season. Peak-season hours are 4 PM to midnight Monday through Friday and 1 PM to midnight on weekends.

NASCAR SpeedPark
Hwy. 17 Bypass at Broadway at the Beach
• (843) 626-8725

Not only is the SpeedPark new to Myrtle Beach, but it is the first SpeedPark in the world! You, Myrtle Beach, Rusty Wallace, Dale Jarrette and Dale Earnhardt (who all serve as spokespersons) get to set the standards and the records for the ten additional SpeedParks scheduled to open nation-wide. The SpeedPark is designed to bridge family entertainment and the professional NASCAR stock racing circuit. The 26-acre park is an authentic replica of the NASCAR experience: 151 downsized NASCAR race cars, 4,000 Goodyear Racing Eagle tires, 17 NASCAR show cars on display, a scoring system measuring the lap speed of each car with a 1/1000 of a second margin of error.

There are seven tracks to test your driving skills and courage. "The Qualifier" is specially designed for the younger driver; children at least 40 inches tall can take on this 220 foot track. For the "Young Champions" 725 foot track, add eight inches to that minimum.

With the "France Family 500" things get serious; you must be at least 60 inches tall to compete with 23 other drivers. However, passengers of at least 40 inches are allowed on this 1200 foot track featuring both a tunnel and a bridge. The "Slidewayz" track is an indoor, tough, challenge for anyone over 60 inches tall.

"The Intimidator" is so tough that it is named for NASCAR champion Dale "Intimidator" Earnhardt, and is for drivers at least 54 inches tall. "The Intimidator" features an 800 foot slick track and 12 open wheeled cards in each race. "The Competitor" is considered high performance, which raises the height minimum to 64 inches. This is a chance to race half-scale NASCAR style cards side by side on a 36-foot wide, D-shaped oval with high-banked curves.

Finally, "Thunder Road" is the largest rack with the most realistic cars—just what you've been looking for. The half mile twisting, turning road is also the fastest experience at the SpeedPark. The 5/8-scale NASCAR Winston Cup style cars were custom built for this wind-in-your-face experience. Anyone 16 years or older, with a valid state-issued driver's license and a height of at least 64 inches can race.

When you get too dizzy from racing around, the SpeedPark also offers the "Speed Dome", a state of the art arcade, a souvenir shop, an indoor/outdoor restaurant, the NASCAR Challenge miniature golf course, and free parking for you and 1,000 competitors. Racers, start your engines!

North Myrtle Beach Grand Prix
3900 U.S. Hwy. 17 S., North Myrtle Beach
• (843) 272-6010

We were at an amusement parks trade show in New Orleans recently when we were pleased to learn that the North Myrtle Beach Grand Prix was being pointed out as an example of excellence in park operation. And we have to agree with that assessment.

North Myrtle Beach Grand Prix offers a total of more than 50 acres of family entertain-

ment. From kiddie rides to Formula 1 racecars, speed racers and go-carts, Grand Prix is a must-see-every-visit destination on the itinerary for most of the Strand's experienced vacationers.

The impressive Grand Prix array of vehicles includes go-carts, mini Ferraris, Jeeps and professional-style racecars that can be maneuvered on any one of numerous tracks for high-performance fun. A few of the most challenging tracks are accessible only to licensed drivers; however, you'll find plenty of racing excitement for all ages and abilities.

INSIDERS' TIP

Avoid unnecessary accidents from pushing the boundaries of safety. Make sure that kids are regulation size and height for any amusement rides or go-carts.

The park also offers a miniature golf course and water-race park with bumper boats. There is a complete Kiddie Park with rides that include Dinosaurs, a Car Carousel and a merry-go-round.

We tested the Grand Prix out on a group of 13 little girls from Russia. After trying every track, every ride and playing every game in the arcade, they wanted to start all over again. As one of the girls jumped out of a bumper boat, she gleefully shrieked, "This is best of America!"

Tickets range from $3.59 to $6 per ride. Parking is free of charge. In summer, the gates are open from 10 AM until about 11 PM or midnight. Hours vary during other seasons, so call ahead for details.

Pavilion Amusement Park
812 N. Ocean Blvd., Myrtle Beach
• (843) 448-6456

The granddaddy of all Grand Strand attractions is the world-famous Myrtle Beach Pavilion Amusement Park. In the very heart of downtown Myrtle Beach, the Pavilion has been the area's No. 1 family attraction for more than four decades.

Covering 11 acres, the Pavilion offers 40 rides. Many of these rides have become annual favorites for return visitors. Lines never stop for the Hydro Surge, an 1,100-foot-long whitewater experience that re-creates the excitement of rafting down a wild river in an eight-person raft. Another hair-raiser, the Typhoon Plunge, sends you plummeting down 40 feet of hairpin twists, fast turns and heart-in-your-throat drops.

But there are more than get-your-clothes-wet rides here. The Pavilion Grand Prix Road Course, a 900-foot-long go-cart course, allows the young and the young-at-heart to test their driving skills on sharp turns and straightaways. There are two separate kiddie areas, one of which showcases the gentle beasts of a lovely, turn-of-the-century merry-go-round. Food booths abound at every corner, tempting you with soft drinks, snow cones, hot dogs, corn dogs, ice cream and cotton candy.

The Pavilion area includes the amusement park, a much-loved boardwalk along the ocean, a shopping area and an alcohol-free, teenagers' dance club called The Attic (see our Nightlife chapter).

All-day passes are $21.95 plus tax for those ages 7 and up. Children ages 3 to 6 enter for $10.95, and anyone under 3 gets in free. Individual tickets cost 65¢, and each ride requires from two to seven tickets. The Pavilion is open from early March through mid-October. The park is open only on weekends until April and then every day through mid-September; it's open on weekends in October. Peak-season hours are 1 to 11 PM. Operating hours do vary, so please call ahead.

Wet and wild rides abound at area parks.

Photo: Courtesy of Cotton Company

South Strand

Garden City Pavilion Arcade
103 Atlantic Ave., Garden City Beach
• (843) 651-2770

This attraction is one of those classic finds that really sets the Grand Strand apart as a unique vacation spot. In this relatively quiet section of the South Strand known as Garden City, you'll find the incongruously flashy Garden City Pavilion Arcade. Featuring the neon and clamor of more than 200 arcade games, this little gem feels exactly like the Myrtle Beach of 35 years ago. In fact, if you want to know what it was like to visit the Strand in the early 1960s, stop by here; though, we have to admit that the arcade games are a lot more high-tech than we remember from those black-and-white television days.

Within walking distance are lots of carnival-type games and a batting cage as well as several souvenir shops. In addition, Ice cream, snow cones, popcorn and hot dog booths make a showing to appease both your appetite and your sweet tooth. Visit this little Garden City street—welcome to the real Grand Strand. Peak-season hours are 9 to 2 AM daily.

Water Parks

All tourist areas seem to have a water park or parks. But like many things on the Grand Strand, we've outdone them all with a wild and wicked collection of water-park rides and slides. Food concessions are available at all parks, as are lockers and clean restrooms. Get ready for some really serious water splashing.

Myrtle Beach

Myrtle Waves
3000 10th Ave. N.
(off U.S. Hwy. 17 Bypass),
Myrtle Beach
• (843) 448-1026

This 20-acre park of water slides and rides is the Strand's largest water park, with more

Brookgreen Gardens, built on the ground of four former plantations, fills every space with plantings and sculpture.

Photo: Courtesy of Brookgreen Gardens

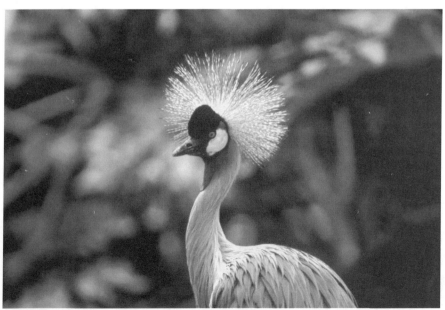

A wide variety of exotic birds can be found in the outdoor sanctuaries at Alligator Adventure.

Photo: Courtesy of Brandon Advertising

ATTRACTIONS

The South Carolina Hall of Fame is one of the Grand Strand's best kept secrets. History buffs will love this free attraction.

Photo: Courtesy of Myrtle Beach Area Chamber of Commerce

Coasters, Ferris wheels, and more make for a classic vacation experience at the Myrtle Beach Pavilion.

Photo: Courtesy of Cotton Campany

ATTRACTIONS

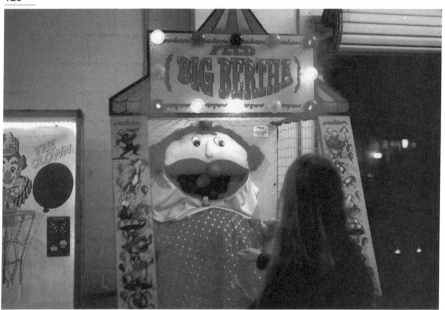

The Grand Strand has many arcades to throw balls, clobber moles and spend some quarters.

Photo: W. Irby Rentz

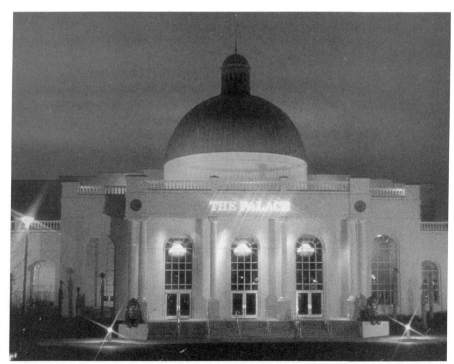

The Palace at Broadway at the Beach is known for its always impressive lineup of "star power."

Photo: Courtesy of Cotton Company

ATTRACTIONS

than 30 rides and attractions. It is anchored by a 10-story "Turbo Twister" that plunges through a dark tunnel. Myrtle Waves is staffed by certified lifeguards.

The just-for-kids Tadpool, only 18 inches deep, includes a Little Dipper Slide and the Magic Mushroom water fountain. The Lazy River is a leisure soak-and-float pool. Then there are a host of water slides: Snake Mountain, Pipeline Plunge and Ricochet Rapids. Of course, there is a flume ride . . . in fact, Myrtle Waves has two body flumes. Finally, Myrtle Waves even has a wave pool; Ocean In Motion uses wave-making machines to create an effect that many amusement parks in other parts of the country use as their central attraction. In spring 1996 Myrtle Waves introduced Splash Zone, with a 256-foot Racin' River that swirls riders around at nearly 10 mph and the Bubble Bay leisure pool with bubbler jets.

Food concessions and a picnic area are available. Footwear, such as aqua booties or sandals, is suggested but not required. Admission is $19.95 for those 7 and older. Kids ages 3 to 6 enter for $12.95, as do senior citizens; children under 3 enter free.

The park is open weekends from April through May and throughout September, and daily from late May through August. Operating hours are 10 AM to 5 PM, with extended hours until 7 PM during peak season.

South Strand

Wild Water Water & Race Theme Park
910 U.S. Hwy. 17 S., Surfside Beach
• (843) 238-WILD

This popular park takes two of the Strand's most popular attractions—water parks and go-carts—and combines them into a day-long adventure.

This 16-acre park features a tremendous variety of water rides and slides. The Dark Hole is a fully enclosed tube ride filled with dramatic dips and twists. The 16-foot-wide Lazy River takes you through a rainforest and waterfalls and traverses the entire length of the park. You'll also find the Sidewinder and Serpentine body flumes. The 65-foot-high Free Fall Cliff Dive and the 65-foot-high Triple Dip Speed

INSIDERS' TIP

Do you have the rainy day blues? Kids driving you nuts in the hotel room with nothing to do? Take them to one of the discount movie theaters in town listed in our Nightlife chapter. They can watch movies for hours for about $2 each.

Slide remind you that these parks can be as exciting as they are massive.

Wild Water also offers a kids' park with a pool, a simulated shipwreck, slides and more.

More than a waterpark, this park also features six race tracks. Since the tracks are age-scaled, everyone from toddlers to adults can participate. An arcade, bumper boats, and 18-hole miniature golf course round out the recreational opportunities.

Admission is $18.95 per adult, $13.95 for children shorter than 48 inches and for seniors 55 and older; children younger than 3 are admitted free. The park opens for the season in early May and closes in mid-September. Operating hours vary until after the Memorial Day weekend; then the park is open daily from 10 AM to 7 PM.

Nature Centers

Myrtle Beach

Waccatee Zoological Farm
8500 Enterprise Rd.
(in the Socastee Community),
Myrtle Beach
• (843) 650-8500

For kids and animal lovers, this is a not-to-be-missed opportunity to view myriad unusual animals. This is a real off-the-beaten-path surprise! For more information, please see our Kidstuff chapter.

South Strand

Brookgreen Gardens
U.S. Hwy. 17 S., Murrells Inlet
• (843) 235-6000

One of North America's most renowned sculpture gardens is on the Strand. If you see no other natural beauty here, do visit Brookgreen. Less than 20 miles south of Myrtle Beach you will find more than 500 classics of American sculpture showcased amid botanical wonders. In addition to its sculpture and plant collections, Brookgreen is also home to a 23-acre wildlife park that protects the habitats of indigenous animals.

ATTRACTIONS

The property that is today Brookgreen Gardens once flourished as four rice plantations. A designated National Historic Landmark, Brookgreen's history is awash in famous faces. "Swamp Fox" Francis Marion, the South's much-loved and legendary guerilla leader, plied its waterways during the American Revolution. Washington Allston, celebrated painter of the Romantic period, was born on Brookgreen Plantation in 1779. In April of 1791, George Washington enjoyed an overnight stay at Brookgreen. Theodosia Alston, daughter of Aaron Burr and wife of former South Carolina Gov. Joseph Alston, made her home at The Oaks Plantation, one of the four aforementioned rice plantations, until her tragic disappearance at sea in 1813. Carolina golden big-grain rice, which played a central role in the Old South's economy, was discovered and cultivated at Brookgreen. And Pulitzer Prize-winning author Julia Peterkin used the plantations as a backdrop for several of her novels published in the 1920s about the descendants of the slaves who worked this land.

The acrylic tunnel at Ripleys Aquarium at Broadway at the Beach brings the undersea world "up close and personal."

Photo: W. Irby Rentz

It was through the extraordinary vision and generosity of railroad magnate Archer Milton Huntington and his wife, sculptress Anna Hyatt Huntington, that this magnificent site was dedicated to the preservation of nature and art. In 1930, when the Huntingtons purchased the four colonial plantations that make up the Brookgreen property, their plan was to establish a winter home. But the beauty and history of the land quickly transformed their simple vision into something far more grand. In 1931 they organized a nonprofit institution with a dual mission: to preserve habitats for native plants and animals while providing an outdoor showcase for American figurative sculpture.

Under the directorship of only one curator from the day it opened until recently, Brookgreen became world-famous for its sculpture collection. In 1995 the original director retired, and a professional museum administrator from Williamsburg, Virginia, was brought in.

Brookgreen Gardens has maintained world renown to this day for its skillful integration of superb art with the complementary beauty of nature. What began with a small number of art works from the Huntington's personal collection as well as Anna's own creations has grown into the world's largest and finest outdoor collection of American figurative sculpture. You'll find works from the country's premier contemporary figurative sculptors, such as Marshall Fredericks and Charles Parks, as well as many of the greatest sculptors in American history, including Augustus Saint-Gaudens and Carl Milles. And, with each passing year, the sculpture collection continues to grow in size and stature.

Brookgreen's botanical gardens feature more than 2,000 species and subspecies of plants. The collection includes moss-laden oaks, magnolias and wildflowers as well as numerous naturalized and exotic species, including propagated azaleas and camellias. Beneath the stately oaks and nestled around murmuring fountains, the beautifully orchestrated plant collection provides a breathtaking backdrop for the diverse sculpture. The simple beauty of green foliage against cool, white marble or the visual excitement of brightly colored blooms in contrast with bronze exemplifies the cooperative interplay of the plant and sculpture collections. While each of the gardens has its special emphasis, all mesh into a delightful medley of landscapes and walkways.

Brookgreen is also home to a 23-acre wildlife park that exhibits indigenous animals in their natural environment. The young and young-at-heart always enjoy the Cypress Bird Sanctuary, Otter Pond, Alligator Swamp, Fox and Raccoon Glade, Raptor Aviary, and the Whitetailed Deer Savannah.

Free walking tours (included in the admission price) are offered every day at Brookgreen Gardens. For an additional fee, tour guides are available. Light refreshments and lunchtime fare are available in the Terrace Cafe. Picnic areas are available. Brookgreen Gardens is completely accessible to handicapped individuals, and wheelchairs are provided.

Brookgreen has launched a slew of ecological and educational programs to enable people to interact more with our unique Lowcountry environment. Every weekend from September 13 to November 23, Brookgreen offers the following activities (even more reasons to come here in the off season): a two-hour guided horseback trail ride, a guided two-hour hike through the wildlife sanctuary, a kayak trip down Springfield Creek, a 5-mile bicycle back-roads trek, even an overnight camping trip at the historic Laurel Hill Plantation complete with a wild game dinner.

The latest project is a Southern Living Showcase Home. The home is the product of a partnership between Brookgreen and *Southern Living* magazine to showcase the Lowcountry lifestyle in a 2,100-square-foot floor plan (which is of course for sale). The house was built and landscaped with the help of South Carolina companies, including interior design by Harrington Altman, also in Pawleys Island, and furnished by Gregory Douglas and Co. in Charleston. It was featured in the September/October 2000 issue of *Southern Living*.

One of the most popular tours Brookgreen provides is the 50-minute exploration of the waterways around Brookgreen Gardens on the 48-foot pontoon boat, *The Springfield*. View the scenic cypress swamps, remains of irrigation systems, Spanish moss-covered trees and abandoned rice fields.

Brookgreen Gardens is open daily (except Christmas Day) year round, 9:30 AM to 4:45 PM. Admission is $7.50 for folks 13 and older and $3 for children ages 6 through 12. Children 5 and younger are admitted free of charge.

INSIDERS' TIP

Get the most out of a trip to one of our amusement parks: get an all-day pass, go early and stay late. Day passes even allow you to leave the park and come back later.

Hobcaw Nature Center
U.S. Hwy. 17, south of Pawleys Island
• **(843) 546-4623**

The Hobcaw Nature Center is part of Hobcaw Barony, the former home of stockbroker and 1940s powerbroker Bernard Baruch.

The Hobcaw Nature Center features displays and audiovisual programs on Hobcaw's history, local wildlife, coastal environments, and the teaching and research programs of the Baruch Institutes. If you want to get a real "feel" for the animals that call our area home, stop by the center and visit the saltwater touch tank and snake displays. Audiovisual programs are also shown daily. There are no walking trails or self-guided tours, and advanced reservations are required for guided tours and special programs.

Hobcaw Nature Center is open year round, and admission is free. Operating hours are 10 AM to 5 PM Monday through Friday and 1 to 5 PM on Saturday. From April 1 throughout summer, it's open Saturdays only.

Museums and Educational Activities

Myrtle Beach

Carolina Safari Jeep Tours
• **(843) 497-5330**

This unique attraction is brought to you by the team of Virgil Graham, photographer and naturalist, and Valerie Graham, nature and history writer, who guide passengers through the history and natural beauty of the Lowcountry. Covered Jeeps take you on a tour, complete with binoculars. Turn to our Kidstuff chapter to get all the details of this safari experience.

The Children's Museum of South Carolina
2501 N. Kings Hwy., Myrtle Beach
• **(843) 946-9469**

A visit to this museum guarantees a fun-filled day for adults and children of any age, while sneaking in a little education. Exhibits include "Starlab" and "Bubble Play," among others; a hospital room was recently added so kids can experience the fun and science side of a hospital. See our Kidstuff chapter for information about hours and admission fees.

IMAX Discovery Theater
Broadway at the Beach,
1195 Celebrity Cir., Myrtle Beach
• (843) 448-4629

With its six-story screen and state-of-the-art sound technology, this John Q. Hammons theater makes you feel involved in every picture. History and breathtaking nature was the thrust of *The Great American West*. Members of the audience gasped as they traveled across canyons and mountain ranges, experiencing the perils of the featured pioneers. Please refer to the Kidstuff and Nightlife chapters for more information.

Ripley's Believe It or Not! Museum
901 N. Ocean Blvd., Myrtle Beach
• (843) 448-2331

Explorer and cartoonist Robert Ripley has put together a bizarre collection of human oddities, amazing artifacts and displays of the unbelievable, including a two-headed calf, shrunken heads from Ecuador and a man who could put three golf balls in his mouth and whistle at the same time. Check out the replica of Cleopatra's barge made entirely out of confectioner's sugar—the ship's detailing is incredibly "delicious." Take a self-guided tour of the more than 500 exhibits displayed throughout the two-story museum. By the way, don't let this building's "cracked" exterior fool you; though it looks as if an earthquake has wreaked havoc, it's just part of the decor.

Don't expect a museum in the traditional sense. This is more of an attraction than a museum; most displays are either reproductions or pure fantasy. But that doesn't take away any of the fun.

Tickets cost $8.95 for adults and $5.95 for children ages 6 to 12; children 5 and younger are admitted free of charge. Ripley's is open year round. Summer hours are 10 AM to 'round midnight; off-season hours vary, so call ahead for specifics.

Ripley's Sea Aquarium
Broadway at the Beach,
between 21st and 29th Aves. N.,
Myrtle Beach
• (843) 916-0888

Opened in spring 1997, this 74,000-square-foot aquarium, in the middle of Broadway at the Beach, is a stunning fish-behind-glass ex-

hibit. Five major portions of the aquarium feature different sea habitats: Seas of Danger, Ray Bay, The Amazon Rainforest, Rainbow Reef and The Gallery. Expect to tour on a moving pathway, get up-close and personal with sharks and moray eels and experience the glorious beauty of a living coral garden. This is an attraction that everyone has been talking about. Please refer to our Kidstuff chapter for further information.

South Carolina Hall of Fame
Myrtle Beach Convention Center
21st Ave. N. and Oak St., Myrtle Beach
• (843) 918-1225

Regional history buffs will find the South Carolina Hall of Fame provides interesting insight into the growth of the state. Set as a display inside the Myrtle Beach Convention Center, this designated area honors native South Carolinians who achieved fame as well as people who were born elsewhere but made significant contributions to the Palmetto state. Portraits of each inductee are accompanied by a written biography.

Admission is free. The convention center is open 8 AM to 5 PM Monday through Friday all year long.

South Strand

Hopsewee Plantation
U.S. Hwy. 17 S.,
12 mi. south of Georgetown
• (843) 546-7891

Yes, this is South Carolina, and you can visit a Tara-like mansion here.

The house at Hopsewee Plantation, a National Historic Landmark, is an early Georgian-style mansion—a typical example of a Lowcountry rice plantation dwelling of the early 18th century. Although it was built nearly 40 years before the Revolutionary War, only four families have owned it. Surprisingly, it is not a publicly owned tourist attraction, rather a privately owned plantation.

Built of black cypress, the history-steeped residence features four rooms opening into a wide central hall on each floor. In particular, note the charming attic rooms as well as the full brick cellar, lovely staircase, hand-carved molding in every room and beautiful heart pine floors.

Hopsewee was the home of Thomas Lynch Sr. and Thomas Jr. Both men were distinguished political figures, and they were the only father and son who served in the Continental Congress. Unfortunately, the elder Lynch suffered a stroke and could not sign the Declaration of Independence. A space remains on the document where his signature was supposed to appear.

Featuring a beautiful vista of the North Santee River, Hopsewee is open to the public 10 AM to 4 PM Tuesday through Friday from early March through early November. Other times are available by appointment. The gracious Mrs. Maynard, current owner of Hopsewee, serves as your tour guide.

Admission is $6 for adults and $2 for children ages 5 through 17. Visitors may view the grounds and cabins year round at any time for $2 per carload.

Mansfield Plantation
S.C. Hwy. 701 N., Georgetown
• **(843) 546-6961, (800) 355-3223**

Mansfield really isn't a museum per se, but it sure is filled with history. To experience this rarity, a reservation is required, as are groups of 12 or more. This authentic antebellum plantation stands as a poignant reminder of the Old South. It was once owned by Dr. Francis and Mrs. Mary Parker; the gentleman was one of the signers of the Ordinance of Secession. Approximately 100 slaves once lived and worked at Mansfield. Today, visitors can tour the former slave village and even the chapel. Visitors can also see the old rice fields, serene marshlands and the only winnowing building (where rice chaff was separated from rice kernels) that still stands in these parts.

Three separate tours are offered. The first tour, which lasts about an hour and costs $6 per person, leads through the slave village and across the plantation landscape. If you opt for the second tour ($9 per person), you get not only the slave village tour, but also a tour of the plantation house filled with mid-19th century American paintings and furnishings.

You'll also enjoy a tour of the residence's special features: double parlors, a grand dining room, beautifully carved woodwork, elaborate mantelpieces and genuine antique furnishings. The third tour includes all of the above and is capped off with tea and sweets served in the dining room of the big house. The tea is poured from antique silver tea pots into china cups,

and the homemade sweets are created from 19th-century recipes adapted for 20th-century tastes. (Both the original recipes and the adapted versions are available to visitors.) Mansfield is also a bed and breakfast.

Rice Museum
Front St., Georgetown
• **(843) 546-7423**

The Rice Museum, in the beautifully renovated heart of Georgetown, offers a concise and fascinating overview of the society that flourished around rice cultivation. Old maps, dioramas, artifacts and a 17-minute-long video give the visitor an intriguing glimpse into the past . . . into a history that literally changed the face of this country. A changing exhibit gallery provides revolving exhibits—contemporary as well as historic.

The building itself was erected as a two-story structure in 1842 and is known locally as the Town Clock because it has clock faces on all four sides of its bell tower and, presumably, can be seen from all directions. Originally a hardware store, this building has evolved from two to three stories over the past 150 years.

In 1878 a rear addition was added and the facade remodeled. In 1989 a renovation to the first floor earned the Rice Museum the coveted Superior Renovation Award, presented by the American Institute of Architects. And the evolution continues. Currently, renovations are under way on the second and third floors. When complete, the second floor will include a small theater, rice exhibits and an area dedicated to African-American history. The actual frame of the Browns Ferry Vessel, a ship built in the early 1700s, will be displayed on the third floor.

Tickets are $3 for adults; students and children are admitted free. The Rice Museum is open year round Monday through Saturday from 9:30 AM to 4:30 PM and is closed on major holidays.

Beyond the Strand

Horry County Museum
438 Main St., Conway
• **(843) 248-1282, (843) 626-1282**

This place is actually off the Strand, just west

of Myrtle Beach. The name of the Horry County Museum is a bit misleading in that it showcases not only Horry County history, but also much of the surrounding area's history. You'll find a variety of informative displays, interesting artifacts, old photographs, life-size animal specimens, scale models and memorabilia galore.

Originally a post office, the building stands on what was formerly the grounds of a historic home. Just outside the museum, the twisted arms of the stately old Wade Hampton oak tree welcomes visitors. A plaque on the oak commemorates the day in 1876 when Confederate General Wade Hampton brought his campaign for the governorship to Conway and addressed the residents from beneath the tree. Many years later, when construction of a railroad threatened the historic oak, a spirited local lady named Mary Beaty brandished a loaded shotgun and ordered workers, "Touch not a single bough." Her defiance inspired other residents to actively protect the town's magnificent live oaks.

In a recent *The Sun News* article on the Grand Strand's "strangest" attractions, the Horry County Museum was highlighted for its odd collection of road-kill animals.

Start your self-guided museum tour by ambling among display cases filled with wildlife specimens. One fascinating display—a favorite of visitors both young and old—features a black bear family. Papa bear, tipping the scale at 300 pounds, was actually hit by a car on U.S. Highway 501 many years ago. Papa represents an estimated population of 400 black bears that still call the less-developed areas of Horry County home.

Other exhibits feature birds of prey such as owls, hawks, ospreys and herons as well as a 400-pound, 11-foot-long alligator. A *Bats of South Carolina* display showcases striking color photographs, informative write-ups and lots of interesting trivia.

Resources of the Land, a three-dimensional exhibit, brims with photos and scale models of naval stores produced in the area in the 1700s. *Loggers and Locomotives* boasts nearly life-size images of loggers, wagons and other lumber-related subjects. Antiquated logging equipment is also on display. It's truly fascinating to see how much life has changed.

For another surprise, be sure to peruse the exhibit on *Native Americans of the Coastal Plains*. Displays feature tools, arrowheads and other artifacts, along with models that re-create the intricacies of the Indians' daily existence.

Admission is free. Open from 9 AM to 5 PM Monday through Saturday year round.

Historic Churches

Some fine examples of historic churches are still in operation, if you'd like either a soul-saving or a historic peek. See our Worship chapter for an overview of the Grand Strand's spiritual scene.

South Strand

Prince George Winyah Episcopal Church
Highmarket St., Georgetown
• (843) 546-4358

Prince George Winyah is one of the town's most fascinating examples of historic meeting places. Its story begins in the early 18th century.

The Parish of Prince George, formed in 1721, was named for the man who eventually became King George II of England. The first sanctuary was situated in a bend on the Black River, roughly 12 miles north of the current Georgetown location. Due to the area's growth, the parish divided in 1734. Since the original church fell within the boundaries of the newly established Prince Frederick's Parish, commissioners were appointed to build a new sanctuary for the Parish of Prince George. The first rector, sent by the English Society for the Propagation of the Gospel in Foreign Parts, held the initial service in Prince George on August 16, 1747.

The church building was ravaged by enemy troops in both the Revolutionary War and the War Between the States. In 1809, following the American Revolution, the existing gallery and chancel were added. The steeple that overlooks the shady streets of Georgetown was added in 1824.

The box pews still used today were a customary feature in colonial churches. Heating systems were nonexistent, so pew owners usually brought charcoal burners to their own "boxes" in winter. The design of the box pews helped to retain some of the heat lost to the beautiful building's high ceilings.

The stained-glass window that graces the back of the altar is English stained glass and was originally in St. Mary's Chapel at Hagley Plantation on the Waccamaw River. St. Mary's was a lovely little sanctuary built by Plowden C.J. Weston for his slaves. (Colonial churches did not have stained-glass windows.) The windows on either side of the church were installed early this century. Four of the original clear windows remain. Prince George is one of South Carolina's few original colonial church buildings still in use.

All Saints Episcopal Church
River Rd., Pawleys Island
• **(843) 237-4223**

All Saints, in Pawleys Island, is a not-to-be-missed historic site. The church was established by an act of the Colonial Assembly of South Carolina on May 23, 1767, primarily because it was very difficult for worshipers to get from the Waccamaw Neck area to Georgetown for services at Prince George Winyah. The first chapel was built on land donated by George Pawley II. In 1997 the church celebrated its 230th anniversary.

After the War Between the States, All Saints came close to perishing due to a lack of funds. The church's only income came from the rental of a house built in 1854 as the rector's summer home. By 1876 the Rev. William Habersham Barnwell was hired at a salary of $700 a year. From that point, All Saints began its journey down the road to recovery.

It is an understatement to say that the original All Saints is a lovely church. Overhung with enormous oaks, its historic setting is peaceful and genuinely captivating. The cemetery offers a fascinating history lesson in itself.

Beyond the Strand

Kingston Presbyterian Church
800 Third Ave., Conway
• **(843) 248-4200**

West of Myrtle Beach, the city of Conway boasts its own taste of history. Kingston Presbyterian is on the National Register of Historic Places and is designated as an American Presbyterian and Reformed Historical Site. No one knows exactly when Presbyterians started meeting in Conway, but local historians believe it was before 1754. The church was assigned its first preacher, the Rev. William Donaldson, in 1756.

One of the first churches on the site overlooking Kingston Lake was destroyed in 1798 in a storm (probably a hurricane) and wasn't rebuilt until the 1830s. In fact, one local historian, Catherine Lewis, said Conway survived for about 40 years without any churches at all. However, Conwayites didn't neglect their worship during those years; they simply met in private homes and at a campground outside the town. In 1858, the present building was erected. Since then, it has been extensively renovated.

The Kingston Presbyterian Church yard is undoubtedly one of the most serene spots in the Grand Strand area. The lake, huge oaks, dogwoods, camellias and azaleas add to the sense of history and beauty. A community burial ground that dates to the 1700s makes for a fascinating afternoon excursion.

First United Methodist Church
1001 Fifth Ave., Conway
• **(843) 488-4251**

Organized in 1828, First United Methodist is also on the National Register of Historic Places and on the Register of United Methodist Historic Sites. The original church, now home to the Hut Bible Class, was built in 1844 and was replaced by a Gothic building in 1898. The mission-style church, now a fellowship hall, was built in 1910. The present Georgian-style sanctuary was built in 1961. Of special interest is the cemetery, with graves dating back to the 1830s.

Kidstuff

LOOK FOR:
• North Strand
• Myrtle Beach
• South Strand

Kidstuff. It's a trick word. If you cruise the "kids" attractions along the Grand Strand, you are going to discover that the term "kid" has very little to do with age and refers more to fun. While, clearly, there are scores of Grand Strand adventures that anywhere else in the world would be loved by kids only, here at the beach Kidstuff fun overtakes everyone, regardless of age.

Just recently one of us in our 40s spent three hours in a video arcade blasting away at aliens in a match with a 38-year-old and five 12-year-olds, all of whom met for the first time at this kidstuff attraction.

Accepting the premise that in the magic world of the Grand Strand we are all kids, let's explore some attractions and activities that specifically cater to younger kids (ages 6 to 16).

We'd be absolutely nuts if we didn't tell you that the beach itself is the biggest kids' attraction. But step away from the ocean; the Strand offers outdoor playgrounds, water parks, arcades, adventures, candy makers, amusement parks, racetracks, adventure theaters (not recommended for some so-called "adults"), skating, splashing, oversize playpens and even a supervised overnight lockup inside a giant playground/mall. In fact, the only thing lacking here is time; there is just not enough in one vacation to hit all the Kidstuff and the beach.

Be sure to scan our Watersports, Fishing, Attractions and Parks and Recreation chapters for rad stuff we didn't list or detail here because, like we said, it is all kidstuff!

North Strand

Alligator Adventure
U.S. Hwy. 17 N.,
North Myrtle Beach
• (843) 361-0789

Alligator Adventure, an alligator park and reptile research institute that adjoins Barefoot Landing in North Myrtle Beach, is completely different from any attraction along the Grand Strand. It's a must-see for children.

Alligator Adventure is handicapped-accessible. The park is designed for self-guided tours; guests can wander through the 15 acres or choose only the exhibits and demonstrations they find interesting.

Hours and rates are seasonal, so definitely call before you go. At press time, general admission for folks 15 and older is $10.95; kids ages 4 through 14 get in for $7.95; and little ones 3 and younger get in free. Refer to the Attractions chapter for more details.

Barefoot Landing
U.S. Hwy. 17 N.,
North Myrtle Beach
• (843) 272-8349

Despite the more grown-up venues of nightclubs, bars and boutiques, Barefoot thoughtfully includes distractions for kids. You can start with the above listed Alligator Adventure, then walk the planks over the lake to check out the enormous fish, take a ride on the carousel in Carousel Court and, finally, round off the whole afternoon at Johnny Rockets where the chirpy wait staff will serve you a sizzling burger and milk shake while singing and dancing to favorite, bouncy '50s tunes. Just don't step on their blue suede shoes. For more on Barefoot Landing, please see the Attractions chapter.

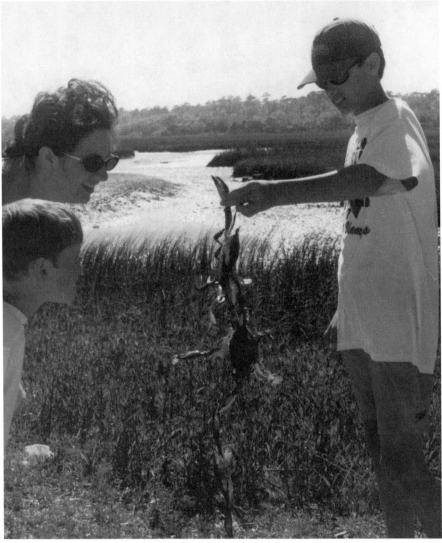

Blue crabs are fun to catch and delicious to eat on the South Carolina coast.

Photo: Lisa Tomer Rentz

Jenet's Make Your Own Sundae
4019 Highway 17 S.
• (843) 272-7578

What would make your kid's vacation more complete than a gooey, handmade ice cream sundae. Your imaginative child could end up inventing a never-tasted-before recipe with the choice of toppings Jenet puts out for customers of all sizes. Fruit, cookie crumbles, chopped candy bars, sprinkles, syrups and more are all at your disposal. Jenet also serves frozen yogurt, for the more calorie conscious, and sand-wiches for lunch. Your eyes are bigger than your stomach when you walk through Jenet's door.

Peachtree Farms
N.C. Hwy. 57, Calabash
• (910) 287-4790

Horseback beach and trail rides, carriage rides and a horse-lover's adventure on a private island all highlight this attraction for kids of all ages.

Ride through hundreds of acres of fields and forests, over high rolling terrain, past salt marshes and along miles and miles of uninhab-

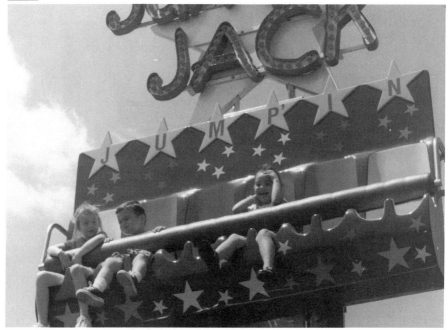

Kiddie rides at Broadway at the Beach provide big fun for your little ones.

Photo: Lisa Tomer Rentz

ited barrier island beaches. This family-fun adventure offers a genuine alternative to the glitter and ping of the high-tech arcades and all-inclusive amusement park rides.

Reservations are highly recommended because prices and hours vary greatly. One-hour trail rides begin at $30 per person, and you must be 9 or older.

Myrtle Beach

Butterfly Pavilion
Broadway at the Beach, Myrtle Beach
• **(843) 839-4446**

Discover the world of entomology! Or, just get to know some bugs. The Butterfly Pavilion is a welcome addition to the beach's growing emphasis on nature. This creepy crawly pavilion features native North American butterflies, and includes a discovery center, a lorikeet aviary, a gift shop and a restaurant. Once within the magnificent butterfly pavilion, you will be surrounded by thousands of butterflies. The pavilion is a glass structure towering to a height of 40 feet, encompassing 9000 square feet of lush landscape. Over 2000 native North American butterflies and moths make their home in the carefully reproduced natural habitats. The

Butterfly Pavilion is truly a pathway to discovery for kids: Enter the Nature Zone to be immediately transported to the mountainous jungles of Mexico, the winter home of thousands of Monarch butterflies. Step back into time into the Carboniferous Era to see giant dragonflies whose wing is span 2½ feet across. Enter the English beehive and come face-to-face with thousands of honeybees as they make their golden sweet concoction. Crawl into a giant ant mound alongside thousands of leaf-cutter ants. All this creepy crawly information could actually come in handy someday in your future travels— or in your own back yard.

Broadway at the Beach
U.S. Hwy. 17 N. Bypass at 21st Ave. N., Myrtle Beach
• **(843) 444-3200**

Broadway successfully strives to cater to everyone's vacation dreams—and that includes kids. On-site, permanent attractions include the fenced-in, padded, jungle-gym-filled Family Play Park to let your little ones run around in and work off some of that energy; the Carousel Park & Kiddie Rides section that is a deal at four rides for $3; and, finally, an activity that will really wear anyone out, pedal boats to get around the whole Broadway lake by your very own leg power. Additionally, Broadway has street performers sparking laughter everywhere, hands-on dinosaur statues and an arcade. For more on Broadway, see the Attractions chapter.

Build A Bear Workshop
Broadway at the Beach, Myrtle Beach
• (843) 839-4446

"Choose me, stuff me, stitch me, fluff me, name me, dress me, take me home!" The Build A Bear Workshop is an activities-oriented, stuffed animal store where cuddliness abounds. As quoted above, you choose your teddy bear from almost 20 forms: from the classic brown teddy ($12) to a 17-inch-long floppy bear ($18) to the sumptuous white Polar bear ($25). When we visited, a frog, a cow and a few bunnies were also waiting for homes. The store is set up like a factory, which is where the stuffing and stitching and fluffing and naming come in. The end of the production line is at a wall full of clothes and accessories for your new found friend (all at an extra charge). This is definitely the place for kids who like hands-on activities and handmade souvenirs.

Carolina Safari Jeep Tours
• (843) 497-5330

These tours are the first of their kind in the Lowcountry. Tour directors Virgil and Valerie Graham, a magazine photographer-naturalist and a nature and history writer respectively, have a professional knowledge of the area so you can look forward to more than a few unique and beautiful sites. Each specially designed tour vehicle seats 10 to 13 passengers and a tour guide "safari-style," allowing for an extensive and personalized overview of area history and local lore as well as tons of narrative information.

The itinerary includes natural coastal attractions, historic areas, old plantation homes, two islands and an unexpected abundance of natural beauty; until you've seen the natural side of the Grand Strand, you're missing something extraordinary. You'll see Atalaya, an imposing Spanish-style castle; the lovely old homes of Pawleys Island, the oldest resort area in the United States; a maritime forest; mystery-shrouded marshes; historic grave sites; nesting bald eagles and more.

Binoculars are provided, and you're welcome to bring cameras; you'll likely encounter lots of photo opportunities for the vacation scrapbook. Don't worry about inclement weather; the tour Jeeps have covers and heat and are winterized. Carolina Safari will even pick you up!

Tours take place twice daily during the summer; other seasons, once a day. Ask about tours

Golf can get complicated at the Beach!

Photo: Lisa Tomer Rentz

Alligator Adventure

Except for the sun-bleached wooden outpost behind you, the 15 acres of Alligator Adventure that lay before you are a veritable jungle of scaly, slimy reptiles and a Louisiana-esque swamp full of 'gators and crocs. Around the grass huts, throughout the tropical vegetation and to the beat of deep drums thumping in the background, more than 800 alligators and crocodiles seethe in the water and bask on the sand around you. They appear to be companionable, resting their long chins on each other, but be glad they can't climb the short fences that separate the little pathway from their impressive habitat. As you walk around Alligator Adventure, you will be surrounded by monstrous, fascinating animals of a hundred varieties. At one point you might have a puny-looking cayman crocodile (don't let its size fool you) on your left; a Capybara, the world's largest rodent (the only mammal in the place), on your right; a large macaw squawking up ahead; and approaching stealthily behind you, a safari-clad staff member with a boa constrictor wrapped around her and a friend—and they want you to wear it too!

Adamm Smith is director of Alligator Adventure, and he obligingly answered questions for us—the most important being how they keep that many reptiles contained. "Around the perimeter of the park there are three fences; a wooden fence, a 12-foot steel fence with half of it underground and another wooden fence."

"What do you do with all these cold-blooded creatures in the wintertime?" we asked.

"Some animals are brought inside," Smith says, "the birds on a daily basis. Many of the pools and cages are heated, so all animals can be seen all year round. In fact, most of the animals are more active and more visible when it is cooler—they come out of the water for sun."

We wondered how someone would get involved in the alligator business and end up in Smith's job.

A baby albino alligator at Alligator Adventure. The albino alligators at Alligator Adventure are part of a small group of true albinos known to exist.

Photo: Courtesy of Brandon Advertising

"I'm originally from Florida and I grew up around environmentalist types. I have a have a conservation background," Smith says. "Since I was 11, I've been working with snakes as a hobby. For a while I was a firefighter and medic, so I've always been involved in very active, hands-on jobs. Most careers here are based on hands-on experience. While I was in Florida I worked for an alligator breeder."

He uses that breeding experience at Alligator Adventure too, with several species reproducing each year. Smith says, "Last year we got babies from alligators, Siamese crocodiles, Morlet crocs, Yacare Caiman crocs, snakes, lizards and turtles. . . .Most go to other zoos."

Feeding the animals requires lots of other animals, we learned.

"The snakes eat mice, rabbits and rats," Smith says. "The crocodiles eat chicken and nutria, which is a rodent bred for fur coats. Nutria carcasses are normally wasted otherwise. These animals go through 50,000 pounds of meat per year, tons of vegetables—Kroger supplies us the veggies at a discount.

"Consumption goes down in the winter because the big alligators that can stay out unheated don't eat. They can't digest in the cold, because the food will rot in their stomachs."

So, of all the beasts in Alligator Adventure, who's the biggest of them all, we asked.

"That would be Tommy, a False Gharial Crocodile from Thailand and Malaysia. He weighs 1,200 pounds, and is over 14 feet long," Smith says. Tommy's tail is as wide as his body. He is kept alone in his own pond, testament to his power.

Though Alligator Adventure is mostly about getting to know the usual but scary reptiles, the park does have a few unusual animals.

Casper is Alligator Adventure's albino alligator and heralded as the Ghost of the Swamp. He was collected from the wilds of Louisiana and, unlike all the other gators and crocs, he is enclosed by a roof in his own pool, though fellow reptiles are brought in to keep him company. The roof is to protect him from the sun—without all the pigments that would normally make him green, he'd get a bad sunburn if left outside.

In the snake house we spotted a beautiful albino Burmese python about a foot in diameter. Its skin was a creamy white with bright yellow markings.

Charlie is another of the park's characters. He is a mammoth tortoise weighing, for the moment, 550 pounds. He's only in his mid-30s, and since these tortoises live to be older than 100, he could reach more than 800 pounds.

Smith loves his job, as do other Alligator Adventure employees. "It's great to be able to do something you've always loved, make a living at something you enjoy. Staff members often come in on their day off—we're excited to get things done."

Smith sees various reactions to the animals from visitors young and old.

"We get lots of kids of course, but surprisingly also a lot of adults," he says. "I see people who haven't been exposed to reptiles before, and it's fun to watch them. At first they won't go into the snake house, but after a while they get curious and go in or even bring themselves to touch one. They convert to understanding because they become interested."

Alligator Adventure has alternating snake and alligator shows each hour. The snake show is hands-on, everybody gets a chance to feel the cool smooth skin of these reptiles that are usually considered a dangerous enemy.

"Why are people afraid of snakes?" the handler calls out to the crowd seated on the bleachers around him.

"Because they bite!" many people yell out.

"No," he carefully explains, "because people don't know enough about snakes."

Throughout the 20-minute show the staff takes great pains to educate people about snakes, how to identify them and how to handle them. For example, how

(Continued on next page)

can you tell the difference between a poisonous and a non-poisonous snake? In what way is a snake more useful than a cat? How many teeth do snakes have? Why is a snake not a legless lizard? How does a snake smell with its tongue? You can find all the answers here.

Alligator Adventure is probably most people's only chance to see a Tomato Frog or a Komodo Dragon. This combination of adventure and education is wonderful for all but the most squeamish. The safari setting with big ferns, rushes and reeds makes for an exotic stroll if you don't actually want to get personal with a reptile. The park is entirely dependent on weather so call ahead, but the staff graciously provides free umbrellas to use while you're in the park when it is raining.

"Alligator Adventure has been visited by zoo directors from all over the world," Smith explains. "This is an advanced environment. Previously reptiles were an afterthought, but public interest is growing now. If you have a good time, you learn."

to additional locations. Rates are $22 for adults and $15 for kids 12 and younger. Coupons are available. Call for reservations.

The Children's Museum of South Carolina
2501 N. Kings Hwy., Myrtle Beach
• (843) 946-9469

Adjacent to Myrtle Square Mall and next door to Office Depot, The Children's Museum features exhibits with good kid names: *Calling All Colors Gallery, Bubble Play, Fairway Physics, Fossil Safari, Boating* and *Starlab*. Ideal for children of all ages, this place sneaks a little education into a fun-filled adventure, and the kids are none the wiser (yet all the more informed!).

The Children's Museum is open Tuesday through Saturday from 10 AM to 4 PM. Admission is $4 for anyone over 3. Annual Family Memberships are $45, and Annual Grandparents' Memberships run $35.

Dixie Stampede
N. Kings Hwy. at U.S. Hwy. 17 Bypass, Myrtle Beach
• (843) 497-9700

It's always a fun addition to pencil-in Dixie Stampede (see our Entertainment chapter) on your vacation agenda. Created by a league of talented planners, performers and all-star dreamers, Dixie Stampede is brought to you by the Dollywood Theme Park Association and is the same famous show as the ones in Pigeon

INSIDERS' TIP

Broadway at the Beach often has unannounced, free kids activities. Check any of the sandwich-board directory signs there. Recent freebies included a Hollywood dinosaur adventure and a petting session with live tigers.

Forge, Tennessee, and Branson, Missouri. For one all-inclusive admission ($35.47 plus tax for adults and $18.27 plus tax for children ages 4 to 11 at press time; prices might change midseason, so please call ahead), this unique dinner attraction serves up heaps of Southern food, unlimited beverages and as much rib-ticklin' horse-filled show as a body can stand. Even if they're too young to understand the context, kids will love the thrilling reenactment of the North/South rivalry, complete with prancing horses, handsome heroes and fair maidens. The spectacular finale showcases no fewer than 15,000 sparkling lights. Little ones 3 and younger can enjoy the fun for free if they sit on an adult's lap and share the grown-up's meal.

You can't just walk in like a traditional restaurant; there are specific show and dinner times, and generally there is only one sitting (two during peak season). You will need reservations because the place is always packed. (See our Entertainment chapter for specific prices and showtimes.)

IMAX Discovery Theater
Broadway at the Beach, Celebrity Cir., Myrtle Beach
• (843) 448-IMAX

More than 400 million people have viewed giant-screen productions in more than 100 permanent IMAX theaters around the world. This amazing high-tech filming and projection process puts you in the middle of movie action in

Water, water everywhere. There are several water parks to choose from; choose at least one.

Photo: Courtesy of Cotton Company

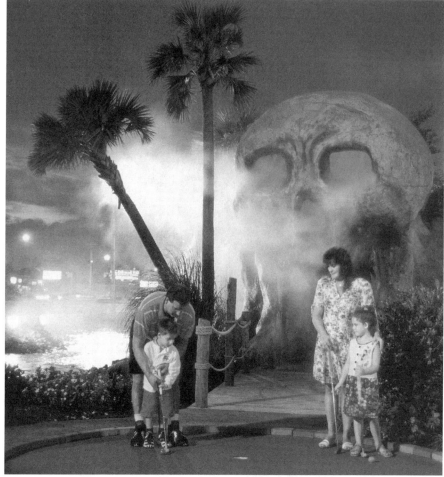

The Grand Strand area has been called the "Miniature Golf Capital of the World."

Photo: Courtesy of Cotton Company

*Pencil in NASCAR Speedpark on
your vacation itinerary.
Your family will thank you for it.*

Photo: Courtesy of Cotton Company

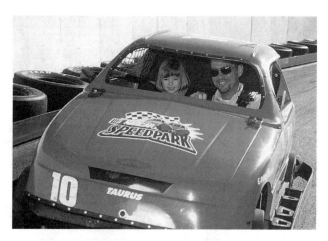

a way no ordinary screen presentation can. At this theater you don't just watch a movie; you'll actually feel propelled into the scene as you view six-story-tall images and listen to digital surround-sound. With titles such as *Cosmic Void, Thrill Ride, Elephant Kingdom* and *Into the Deep*, it should be quite a show.

There are shows every hour of every day, though operating hours vary from month to month. The theater is open 364 days every year (it's closed Thanksgiving day), and prices are $5.25 for kids ages 3 through 12, $7 for teens and adults and $6.25 for seniors. See our Attractions and Nightlife chapters for more details.

Medieval Times
Fantasy Harbour,
2904 Fantasy Way, Myrtle Beach
• (843) 236-8080

Imagine the year is 1093 A.D., and you are a noble guest of the Spanish kingdom's Royal Family. The Lord of the Castle has invited more than 1,000 of his friends, neighbors and foes to enjoy the sport and splendor of a royal tournament. As you step back in time nearly a millennium, you will feast on a hearty four-course meal. You'll marvel as spirited stallions perform intricate equestrian drills, and you'll gaze in awe as fearless knights compete in daring tournament games, jousting matches and sword fights. Sound intriguing? You bet it is!

In North America there are currently seven Medieval Times castles in locations from Florida to Ontario to California; all operate within the same program format, and all have been tremendously successful. A Spanish-owned company, the spectacle is based on an actual event in the family history of one of the company's founders. (You can guess which side is his family after you see the show.)

At Medieval Times (see our Entertainment chapter), the evening of quality family entertainment begins as you cross a drawbridge into the 11th-century castle.

Once inside, you are personally greeted by the Count and Countess of Perelada, who invite you to share in a sumptuous banquet while cheering for brave knights on horseback.

Festivities begin as trumpeters herald the guests into the Grand Ceremonial Arena. Gracious serfs and wenches scurry to fill glasses and attend to the Count's honored guests who feast on succulent roasted chicken, tasty spare ribs and castle pastries. An awe-inspiring thunder of hooves fills the arena as the Master of Ceremonies leads a talented cast through a truly spectacular array of medieval pageantry. Sitting proudly astride colorfully attired Andalusian horses, the valiant knights of yore face their competitors in breathtaking and authentic tournament games, including the ring pierce, the flag toss and the javelin throw.

The one-price admission includes the show, dinner and two rounds of beverages (and adults can order alcohol). Sales tax and gratuity are extra. Adult and teen admission is $34.75. Children ages 2 to 12 get in for $18.95. Reservations are suggested.

Motion Master Moving Theater
917 N. Ocean Blvd., Myrtle Beach
• (843) 448-2331

As implied by its name, Motion Master is a theater that literally thrusts participants into film adventures, with seats that move in eight different directions. Seats are motion-synchronized with the giant-screen action for realism that's heart-pounding, nonstop fun. Brought to you by the folks of Ripley's Believe It or Not! fame, you can be sure this pastime will keep your attention from start to finish. This adventure is really for kid-age kids the able-bodied . . . management describes the ride as "aggressive" and doesn't want anyone with any type of health condition to take any chances.

The cost is $6.50 for one ride or $9.75 for two rides, with several discount packages available if you also go to the Ripley's museum up the street. Take note: Your little one must be 43 inches tall to climb aboard.

Hours are 10 AM until 8 PM, depending on the volume of business . . . sometimes until midnight during midsummer.

Ripley's Sea Aquarium
Broadway at the Beach,
between 21st and 29th Aves. N.,
Myrtle Beach
• (843) 916-0888

This 74,000-square-foot aquarium, right in the middle of Broadway at the Beach, is a stunning fish-behind-glass exhibit.

Expect to tour on a moving pathway, get up-close and personal with sharks, eels and stin-

INSIDERS' TIP

In the open boardwalk area between Mad Boar and the General Store, Barefoot Landing in North Myrtle Beach has added a jungle gym for kids.

grays and experience the glorious beauty of a living coral garden.

Five major portions of the aquarium explore different sea habitats. Dangerous Reef is centered around a shipwreck swarming with large sharks, poisonous predators, Caribbean reef fish and green moray eels. Rainbow Rock recreates the Pacific Ocean to be home to more than 1,000 fish, which dazzles with a swimming kaleidoscope of colors. To take it all in, the aquarium is viewed through two movie-screen sized windows. The Living Gallery is also a Pacific environment. The inhabitants are unusual, even mythic, and include the Pacific giant octopus, jellyfish and sea anemones. Rio Amazon highlights the threatening piranha. Finally, at the Sea-For-Yourself Discovery Center, the experience is "hands on" as you actually get to touch some of these creatures.

Ripley's Aquarium is open from 9 AM to 8 PM Sunday through Thursday, 9 AM to 9 PM Friday and Saturday. Admission is $12.95 for adults, $6.95 for ages 5 through 11; kids 4 and younger are admitted free.

Waccatee Zoological Farm
8500 Enterprise Rd.
(in the Socastee Community),
Myrtle Beach
• (843) 650-8500

For kids and animal lovers, this is a not-to-be-missed opportunity to view a myriad of unusual animals including Bengal tigers. It's a real off-the-beaten-path surprise. Waccatee covers 500 acres that include pasture and woodlands for the zebras, buffalo and deer. In the zoo itself you can see the traditional lions, tigers, bears and monkeys—more than 100 species of animals. In the zoo the walk is about a mile

long and makes for a casual, relaxed, educational afternoon.

Admission is $5 for those 13 years and older, $3 for kids 12 and younger; hours are 10 AM to 6 PM every day, year round, excluding holidays.

South Strand

Brookgreen Gardens
U.S. Hwy. 17 Bypass, Murrells Inlet
• (843) 237-4218

This Grand Strand landmark melds nature and history in an incomparable way. An absolute must for families with kids (and without), Brookgreen Gardens is an unequalled picnic spot. See our Attractions chapter for full details.

Captain Dick's Educational Cruises
4123 U.S. Hwy. 17 Bus., Murrells Inlet
• (843) 651-3676

If you're looking for a fun and unusual activity add "educational cruises" to your calendar. These anything-but-boring boat trips offer firsthand exposure to the vast array of plants and animals that make the salt marshes of Murrells Inlet their home. Narrated by a marine biologist, these cruises last up to two hours and are restricted to the calm waters of the inlet. Using crab traps, bottom dredges, plankton nets and rods and reels, a collection of marsh plants and animals is produced for up-close looks and touches. During the last portion of the trip, participants can fish for samples of inlet dwellers like spot, croaker and pinfish.

Cruises operate from late spring through early fall. Please call Captain Dick's Marina for current rates, which vary, and schedules, which are sporadic.

Annual Events

With all of the entertainment options available along the Grand Strand, you will probably be amazed at this lineup of annual events, festivals, tournaments and shows. And you can well believe that even though there are 101 things for you to see and do here, these events are well-received and attended. Myrtle Beach Convention Center hosts a number of annual events and, although we don't provide the center's address in respective listings, we won't leave you in the dark as to its whereabouts—Oak Street and 21st Avenue N. in Myrtle Beach. Since plans can vary at any given time when coordinating such large programs, we cannot guarantee that dates, places, times and prices won't change. Keep your eyes and ears tuned to the news for current information or call the number listed to verify details.

Now, let's get in the game and join in the fun!

LOOK FOR:
• Event schedules January through December

The Sun Fun Festival Parade showcases local talent.

Photo: courtesy of the Myrtle Beach Area Chamber of Commerce

January

North Strand

North Myrtle Beach Winter Run
Throughout North Myrtle Beach
• (843) 280-5570

This event includes the 5K and 15K road races for the Southeastern Region. Sponsored by the North Myrtle Beach Recreation Department, this competition, which takes place each year on the last Saturday in January, attracts 400 to 500 entrants. Following the grueling race, an awards ceremony is held to recognize the top-five overall runners and the best in each age category—including those older than 60! Registration costs $12 to $15 and is open until the day of the race.

Myrtle Beach

Lifestyles Expo Myrtle Beach
Convention Center
• (800) 62-SHOWS

Dedicated to our senior citizens, this mid-January, two-day expo usually attracts more than 6,000 people each year. Continuous entertainment and speakers fill the agenda.

The two-day extravaganza marks its 15th consecutive year in 2001. Offerings include cooking demonstrations, blood-pressure screenings and floral design displays. Nearly 140 exhibitors are on hand and the entertainment—which is always commendable—is continuous throughout the two-day show. Previously featured acts have included the famous Dancin' Grannies, lots of big band groups, the Myrtle Beach Barbershop Quartet and many others.

The Lifestyles Expo is sponsored by Media Services Inc., a South Carolina-based publishing and consumer show enterprise based in Charleston, South Carolina. The admission fee is $2 per person.

February

Myrtle Beach

Burroughs & Chapin KidsFest
Myrtle Beach Convention Center
• (843) 626-6385

The Kid's Festival, generally held towards the end of February, is a fun-filled weekend of educational, cultural and safety-related presentations and exhibits for children and their families. More than 120 booths provide interactive presentations in the fields of science, art or health. Continuous entertainment includes dancers, tumbling acts, magicians, singers and storytellers. Children are given the opportunity to take part in various contests on stage.

Admission is $3 for adults and the cost for children is $6.

South Carolina Hall of Fame Induction Ceremony
Myrtle Beach Convention Center
• (843) 626-7444

Two notable South Carolinians are inducted into this hall of fame each year, representing a gallant procession of statesmen, scientists, artists, soldiers and teachers. Inductees include President Andrew Jackson, jazz legend Dizzy Gillespie, painter Jasper Johns, Gen. William C. Westmoreland, author Elizabeth Boatwright Coker and more than 30 others. The South Carolina flag that was taken to the moon by NASA astronaut Charles M. Duke Jr. is also on display.

As of this writing, induction ceremony dates remain undecided, and upcoming recipients have yet to be named. However, here's a sampling of previous recipients you may enjoy reading about:

Bobby Richardson joined the New York Yankees at the age of 19 and played more than 1400 games while the Yankees were winning American League pennants. Named the Most Valuable Player in the 1960 World Series (still the only player from a losing team to be so named), Bobby holds numerous World Series records, including runs-batted-in in a game, runs-batted-in in a series and hits in a series. He also holds the record for having played in 30 consecutive World Series games.

Josephy Cardinal Bernadin was ordained to the priesthood in 1952 and served fourteen years in the Diocese of Charleston before being named a papal chamberlain in 1959 and a domestic prelate in 1962 by Pope John XXIII. He was appointed Auxiliary Bishop of Atlanta by Pope Paul VI, which made him the youngest bishop in the country. In 1982, Archbishop Bernadin was appointed by Pope John Paul II as Archbishop of Chicago and was elevated to the Sacred College of Cardinals in early 1983. He died in 1996.

In 1980, Charles F. Bolden, Jr. was selected as an astronaut candidate by NASA, qualified as a shuttle pilot in 1981 and subsequently flew four missions logging more than 690 hours in space. In 1986, he helped deploy the SARCOM KU satellite; in 1990, he piloted the shuttle *Discovery*, which launched the Hubble telescope. In 1992, he commanded the shuttle *Atlantis* on NASA's

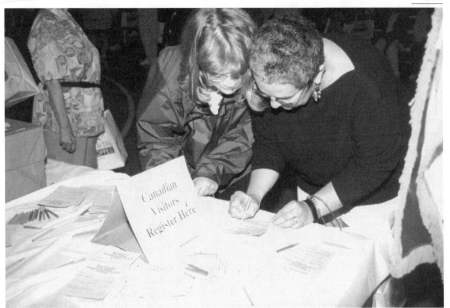

The Canadian-American Days Festival attracts tens of thousands of Canadian and American visitors for mid-March sporting events, concerts, a parade, and other special activities.

Photo: Courtesy of Myrtle Beach Area Chamber of Commerce

Mission to Planet Earth; and in 1994, commanded STA-60, the first joint US/Russian mission. After leaving NASA, he was promoted to major general and assumed duties as Deputy Commander, United States Forces, Japan.

The hall is open from 8:30 AM to 5 PM Monday through Friday, and admission is free.

Grand Strand Boat Show and Sale
Myrtle Beach Convention Center
- **(843) 238-0485**

This mid-January/ early February show attracts up to 10,000 boating enthusiasts and more than 90 exhibitors displaying motor boats, fishing equipment, pontoon boats, sailboats, one-person kayaks, watersports gear including scuba-diving equipment and a host of accessories. Safety instruction is offered, and the U.S. Coast Guard is represented. Recent seminars have included Flounder Fishing, Live Bait Fishing and Speckled Trout and Drum Fishing. Admission is $5.50 for adults; children younger than 16 are admitted free of charge.

Myrtle Beach Stamp Show
Holiday Inn West
(next to Waccamaw Pottery)
101 Outlet Blvd., Myrtle Beach
- **(843) 347-0087**

Children receive a free pack of stamps and an album to begin their stamp-collecting careers at this mid-February event. Ten dealers participate from the Southeastern region and display goods from beginner status to advanced. The United States Postal Service is on hand to sell current stamps. Collections are appraised free of charge. About 600 philatelists and other enthusiasts join the fun every year.

National Shag Dance Championships
To Be Announced, Myrtle Beach
- **(843) 497-7369**
- **www.shagnationals.com**

For enthusiasts of the shag, the vintage dance born and bred in the Carolinas, this is nothing short of stupendous! (For an in-depth look at this dance, refer to the related Close-up in our Nightlife chapter).

The National Shag Dance Championships originated in March 1984 and celebrated its 17th year during CanAm days in March of 2000. This mid-March competition, where shaggers dance for placement in four divisions—juniors, non-professional, professional and masters—is often called the longest-running shag contest in the USA. The Nationals contest is the winner of two Feather Awards as Best Swing Event in the USA. National winners have appeared on *Good Morning America*, *CBS This Morning*, *The Crook & Chase Show*, *The Gatlin Brothers*, and *From Nashville to*

Broadway in Myrtle Beach. They have also performed exhibitions at the Charlotte Hornets games, The Beach Ball Classic, the P.G.A. annual banquet, The Cammy and more.

In 1998, the Myrtle Beach–based National Shag Dance Championships Dance Team beat nine teams from across the United States at the U.S. Open Swing Dance Championships in the team division. This represented the third award in the Triple Crown of team championships in the U.S. In 1997, the team won the American Swing Classic in New York and the S.O.S. Grand Nationals in Atlanta.

As of this writing, lots of locations and events remain to be announced. For late-breaking details, please visit the Championships' website.

Home Show
Myrtle Beach Convention Center
• **(843) 448-7166**

This annual event held in late February or early March is literally 100,000 square feet of displays concerning home building, design and decorating. Sponsored by the Horry-Georgetown Home Builders Association, a recent show offered designer furniture, floor covering, wallpaper, window treatments, whirlpool tubs, doors, stained glass and mirror ideas.

For the yard and garden, plants, flowers, shrubs, trees, pools, spas and statuary exhibits were on hand. The three-day event featured a list of seminars and workshops that ranged from learning to make garden stepping stones using recycled materials to orchid care to the Plant Doctor Booth where participants could take a sick plant for care.

A one-day ticket for adults is $4. A three-day ticket can be purchased for $6, and children under the age of 14 are admitted free.

March

North Strand

St. Patrick's Day Parade and Celebration
Main St. and Ocean Blvd.,
North Myrtle Beach
• **(843) 361-0038**

Not only do most of the area's nightclubs and restaurants host themed parties for this much-lauded party weekend, the North Myrtle Beach Parade and town square party has become the biggest thing to hit the North Strand

since that shimmy-in-your-shoes state dance known as the shag.

A Saturday parade kicks off this mid-March event (look up St. Patrick's day on your calendar and plan accordingly). The parade begins at 9:30 AM at the Surfwood Shopping Center (look for Lowe's) and continues down Main Street. There are dozens of bands, floats and beauty queens, as well as Irish musicians, cloggers, and more. Plenty of food and entertainment, kids activities and a fine display of arts and crafts make this the ideal family outing. After the parade, an all-day "Irish Publick Square" commences. Best of all, admission is free of charge!

Myrtle Beach

Annual Canadian-American Days Festival
Throughout Horry County
• **(843) 626-7444, ext. 7239**

The Canadian-American Days Festival is the Myrtle Beach area's premier kickoff to the spring season. The 2000 event attracted more than 100,000 Canadian and American visitors who came to see the sporting events, concerts, parade and other special activities. The festival, which celebrated its 39th year in 2000, has been chosen as one of the region's top 20 events during March for the past 12 years by the Southeast Tourism Society.

Can-Am, which happens in the middle of the month, traditionally coincides with Ontario's school holiday, so many families attend. The 2000 event included a special celebration of the seventh anniversary of Myrtle Beach and Burlington, Ontario, as sister cities. The festival, as always, culminated with a St. Patrick's Day celebration and parade in North Myrtle Beach.

The festival includes a wide variety of indoor and outdoor activities, with a ever-growing line-up of new events each year. Highlights of the 2000 festival included the National Shag Dancing Competition, a Can-Am fishing tournament, an antique car show, celebrity look-a-like contests, an International Kitefest, Can-Am Little Olympics, and the Can-Am Cup YMCA Soccer Invitational.

During this much-anticipated week, local radio stations feature Canadian news and weather broadcasts. For more information call the number above or visit myrtlebeachlive.com and follow the links to the Myrtle Beach Chamber of Commerce's Calendar of Events.

North Myrtle Beach's ever-popular St. Patrick's Day Parade grows bigger every year!

Photo: Courtesy of Myrtle Beach Area Chamber of Commerce

Annual Doll Show & Sale
Myrtle Beach Convention Center
• (843) 248-5643, (843) 448-7166

You'll find doll dealers from 15 states and more than 200 tables of goods at this show which is usually held the first weekend in March. Items include antique dolls, collectibles, modern artists' dolls, accessories, doll-making supplies, miniature furniture, replacement parts and molds. Special exhibits and demonstrations are scheduled, and a raffle is held to raise money for a number of area charities. Tickets for adults are $4. Children ages 6 to 12 can enter for a minimal fee of $1.

April

North Strand

S.O.S. Spring Safari
Throughout North Myrtle Beach
• (888) SOS-3113

This is the world's largest spring break for mature adults. More than 15,000 shaggers, members of the Society of Stranders and lovers of the beach gather in North Myrtle Beach in mid-April for an annual rite of spring. Ten full days and nights of beach music and activities

are all part of this riotous ritual. There's a parade along Main Street in North Myrtle Beach. At one point during the 1996 festivities, 3,000 of the crowd danced in unison, completely unconcerned about traffic. Admission to the dance clubs (Ducks and Ducks Too, 229 Main Street, Fat Harold's Beach Club, 212 Main Street and Spanish Galleon, 100 Main Street) is free for card-holding S.O.S. members. The S.O.S. card costs $35.

Myrtle Beach

Grand Strand Fishing Rodeo
April 1 through October 31
• (843) 626-7444

The Grand Strand Fishing Rodeo, sponsored by the Myrtle Beach Area Chamber of Commerce, was created nearly fifty years ago in an effort to enhance recreational fishing along the Grand Strand. It has succeeded admirably. The seven-month long tournament awards more than $12,000 in cash and merchandise to recreational fishermen entering qualified catches from April 1 to October 31.

The event includes four divisions: pier, surf and inlet, deep-sea catches and tag and release. The tag and release program has been instituted to award special certificates for marlin, sailfish, swordfish and tarpon to fishermen submitting documentation of their participation. Entrants receive an official Grand Strand Fishing Rodeo decal. An official shoulder patch is awarded to anglers entering the three heaviest fish of each species in each division for that month. Additionally, Fish-of-the-Month awards consisting of various donated prizes are given to the anglers entering the four heaviest fish out of all eligible entries for the month's designated species.

Entry forms are available at any one of the official weigh stations: Harbourgate Marina, Cherry Grove Pier, Apache Pier, Pier 14, 2nd Ave. Pier, Springmaid Beach Pier, Myrtle Beach State Park, Pier at Garden City, Marlin Quay Marina, Capt. Dick's Marina Voyager's View Marina, Surfside Pier, Chapin's All Sporting Goods, and Garden City Bait & Tackle.

For additional information regarding locations, rules, regulations and other details, please contact the Myrtle Beach Area Chamber of Commerce at the number given above.

Annual Spring Games
Kite Flying Contest
Broadway at the Beach, between 21st and 29th Aves. N., Myrtle Beach
• **(843) 449-2856, (843) 448-7261**

This is a great mid-April event for veteran kite flyers and novices alike. Professional flyers will take to the breezes for stunt and single-line flying for a points only competition. Professor Kite will be on hand to give out free kites to participating children and to give demonstrations and lessons.

Look to the empty fields beside Broadway at the Beach for this event, which is usually held on a Saturday and Sunday. Admission is free. A donation can be given that benefits a local charity.

South Strand

Annual Georgetown Plantation Tours
Throughout Georgetown
• **(843) 546-2292**

Sponsored by the women of Prince George Winyah Parish, one of the oldest and most beautiful churches in Georgetown, this much-loved annual event is more than 50 years old! The tour, usually held early in April, allows an up-close look at a wide variety of plantations and Colonial town houses. Most of the homes are privately owned and are graciously "loaned" to this worthy cause once each year. Many are

listed on the National Register of Historic Places. A different selection of homes is featured each day.

A one-day ticket for Friday or Saturday costs $30. A two-day ticket costs $50. Histories and maps are provided with the tickets. Tickets are sold at the Prince George Winyah Parish Hall on Highmarket Street in Georgetown on each day of the event. Visitors must arrange their own transportation. At each location, trained hostesses are available to answer questions. Box lunches will be available at the Parish Hall and may be reserved in advance. Call ahead for information on advance purchase of tickets.

May

North Strand

Blue Crab Festival
On the waterfront, Little River
• **(843) 249-6604**

In 2000 more than 30,000 people flocked to the waterfront streets of this historic fishing village to attend the Blue Crab Festival. Held late in May, this much loved festival features more than 150 arts-and-crafts booths with everything from paintings to brass and copper sculptures, wearable art, jewelry, woodcarvings and children's goods. Food booths boast yummies including steamed crabs, grilled tenderloin and pizza. The children's area includes a petting zoo, pony rides, face painting and puppets. Entertainment promises widespread appeal; enjoy a variety of live musical performances including jazz, country, bluegrass and gospel. Admission is $4. Children 5 years of age and younger enter free.

Myrtle Beach

The Carolina Harley-Davidson Dealers Association and Harley-Davidson Motor Company Spring Rally
Throughout the Grand Strand
• **(843) 651-5555**

As a Grand Strand Insider, you can always tell when "bike week" is fast approaching. Makeshift trading posts (mostly hocking metal and leather goods) spring up all along U.S. Highway 501, the roads begin to rumble and roar, tattoos cease to seem out of the ordinary and bar owners are smiling ear to ear as they stock up on beer. Rated as one of the top-five motor-demonstrations. Admission was free; service tents and technicians were on hand, and sponsors held a factory closeout sale of clothing, parts and accessories.

Fees are charged only to attend organized races; expect to pay around $15 per spectator. This nonprofit event recycles monetary proceeds into the next rally.

Omar Shrine Temple Parade
Culminating at Chapin Park, Kings Hwy. at 16th Ave. N., Myrtle Beach
• **(843) 651-5675**

This is your chance to see grown men ride around in miniature cars! Yes, the ceremonial mid-May parade includes 50 to 60 Shrine units that delight the annual crowds with go-carts, clowns, floats and motorcycles. The parade gets started between 10 and 10:30 AM at Fifth Avenue N. in Myrtle Beach, travels to Ocean Boulevard and then moves north to Chapin Park.

June

Annual Sun Fun Festival
Throughout the Grand Strand
• **(843) 626-7444**

The Myrtle Beach Area's well-known Sun Fun Festival will celebrate its 50th birthday in 2001. This fun-filled four-day festival kicks off the summer season along South Carolina's Grand Strand with a host of events featuring national celebrities and fun for all ages. The largest annual event of its kind in either of the Carolinas, Sun Fun attracts more than 300,000 visitors of all ages and interests. The dazzling sights and sounds of a typical summer vacation combine with dozens and dozens of exciting festival events—from celebrity concerts to high-flying air shows—making Sun Fun a tradition with thousands of teenagers and families alike.

During Sun Fun, visitors participate in such beachfront activities as beauty contests, sandcastle-building competitions, watermelon eating and bubblegum blowing contests, beach

The South Carolina's Hall of Fame, located inside the Myrtle Beach Convention Center, pays homage to famous South Carolinians.

Photo: Courtesy of Myrtle Beach Area Chamber of Commerce

cycle events in the nation—and the oldest dealer-sponsored motorcycle event in the country—the 2000 rally marked its 60th year on the Grand Strand.

An estimated 200,000 cyclists roar into town for four days in mid-May. A race is usually held on the Friday of the event at the Myrtle Beach Speedway.

In 2000 motorcyclists held demonstration rides at the Myrtle Beach Convention Center and sponsored a drag race featuring riding skills and games. The rally made use of the convention center to present the Harley-Davidson traveling museum, featuring Harley as well as Buell games and volleyball games galore. A huge kick-off parade always features some favorite big-name celebrity, as well as high school and military bands, pageant queens, and all manner of roving entertainment.

Extensive event listings are available at all Chamber offices and on myrtlebeachlive.com. Follow the link to the Myrtle Beach Area Chamber of Commerce; you will find the full calendar of events under "Chamber Festivals."

South Strand

LPGA Golf Tournament
Wachesaw East Golf Club, Hwy. 17,
Murrells Inlet
• **(843) 357-7454**

Wachesaw Plantation East, formerly the site of a thriving rice plantation, has taken off as one of the Grand Strand's best-known centers of golfing. Directly adjacent to the PGA-owned Tournament Players Club, this course is home to the official LPGA Golf Tournament, which is generally scheduled for a week in June. Thousands of spectators attend to witness big-name female golfers like Dottie Pepper, Kelly Robbins, Michelle McGann and Julie Ingster.

Competitors vie for a $750,000 purse. Little wonder some 60,000 fans flood the South Strand for a glimpse! Ticket prices generally range from about $15 per day at the gate to $35 for a weeklong pass.

July

North Strand

Fourth of July Fireworks Display
Various Locations
• **(843) 280-5555**

Fireworks let loose on the north end of the strand at 9 PM from just south of the runway at Grand Strand Airport. Since the airport is adjacent to Barefoot Landing, the complex offers some parking at the Alligator Adventure entrance. Besides Barefoot Landing as a vantage point to watch the show, try a spot any-

where along U.S. Highway 17 N. from 33rd Avenue S. in North Myrtle Beach to Barefoot Landing.

Myrtle Beach

Fourth of July Concert Series
Myrtle Beach Memorial Stadium,
Oak St. at 33rd Ave. N., Myrtle Beach
• **(843) 448-3189**

The concert, a dazzling fireworks display and plenty of food attract more than 8,000 people to the stadium every Fourth of July weekend. The local Long Bay Symphony orchestra is always the lead act for the celebration. Bring your own lawn chair or blanket if you want to be close to the stage; bleacher seating is available farther back. Admission is free, and spectators are allowed to bring their own coolers.

Fourth of July Fireworks Displays
Various Myrtle Beach Locations
• **(843) 444-3200,**
  (843) 448-2331

The only venue in the Myrtle Beach area that shoots off fireworks on Independence Day is Broadway at the Beach.

Broadway at the Beach usually begins its display at 10 PM and included a light and music fountain show.

On the following evening, Second Avenue Pier (second phone number) holds its Beach Bang with a 25-minute fireworks display that can be seen along the beach and in the downtown area.

South Strand

Murrells Inlet
Fourth of July Boat Parade
Murrells Inlet
• **(843) 651-0900**

For 14 or so years, more than 100 boats have gussied up for the Fourth of July and entertained multitudes who watch from and picnic on the shores. From 14-foot fishing boats to 40-foot yachts, participating watercraft start the aquatic caravan at high tide at the jetties of

---

INSIDERS' TIP

When in town, mix interest with fun and learning by attending one of the history-flavored annual events such as the Annual Georgetown Plantation Tours in April or the Atalaya Arts & Crafts Festival in September. Besides being just plain enjoyable, these events will give you a satisfying taste of the Old South and antebellum life as it was once gracefully lived.

Garden City Beach and proceed to Murrells Inlet. Public points of view to watch the flotilla are Captain Dick's Marina, the newly completed Marsh-walk, Belin United Methodist Church and the Murrells Inlet boat landing, all on U.S. Highway 17 Business in Murrells Inlet. Launch time is 5:30 PM. Trophies are given out to the three best-decorated boats and to the three most-adorned docks along the route.

INSIDERS' TIP

If there's an annual event that particularly interests you, give the coordinators a call to see how you can be of assistance. Most annual events are put on by community volunteers and need lots of people to help run the project. What better way to gain free admission to your favorite event, get the scoop on the inner workings and, most likely, meet a whole new group of friends?

largest amateur golf championship in the world. The competition, which began with 680 golfers in 1984, has attracted more than 45,000 golfers of all ages and abilities. Last year's event drew 4,888 participants from all 50 states and 25 foreign countries.

Appropriately referred to as The Everyman Open, neither skill level, age, height, weight, nor gender affects an individual's ability to participate in the event. Thanks to the golf handicap system absolutely anyone and everyone can compete. Over the years, players with handicaps ranging from 3 to 35 have been crowned World Champions in this four-day, 72-hole event.

The fun begins on Sunday when participating golfers pick up registration information and a gift bag at the Myrtle Beach Convention Center. The next four days are filled with spirited competition, score viewing, long drive contests, putting equipment demos, lots of food and drink and—if you're lucky—bragging rights, too.

Fourth of July Fireworks Displays
Various South Strand Locations
- **(843) 651-5850**

The Murrells Inlet Fireworks Display blasts off at 10 PM and can easily be seen from just about anywhere in Murrells Inlet and Garden City Beach. Best viewing points cited are Belin Memorial United Methodist Church parking lot, Captain Dick's Marina, the newly completed Marsh-walk and the public boat landing in Murrells Inlet.

Another south end display begins at 9 PM as the City of Georgetown puts on its firecracker show. The display is visible all along the Harborwalk in Georgetown on Front Street.

August

Myrtle Beach

Annual DuPont World Amateur Handicap Championship
Various Grand Strand golf courses
- **(800) 833-8798**
- **www.worldamateur.com**

Generally held at the end of August, The DuPont World Amateur Handicap Championship is the world's largest amateur golf tournament. With nearly 5,000 participants, ten major sponsors, 60-plus exhibitors, and more than $400,000 in prizes, there's nothing amateur about the fun at this eagerly anticipated annual event. It's a week most people never forget, leading many to make the annual trek an opportunity to visit with old friends—and make new ones.

Now in its 17th year, the World Amateur has firmly established itself as the premier and

Craftsmen's Summer Arts & Crafts Featival
Myrtle Beach Convention Center
- **(336) 274-5550**

Collectors and unique gift-givers alike are surrounded by a smorgasbord of authentic, hand-crafted items at this arts and crafts show in early August. More than 250 exhibitors from 20 states bring in original designs that include pottery, wood, fine art, toys, jewelry, baskets, stained glass, leather, tin, weaving, sculpture, musical instruments and furniture.

Prices are $5 for adults and $1 for children from 6 to 12 years of age. Please call in advance for specifics on group rates.

South Strand

Pawleys Island Festival of Music and Art
Various South Strand Locations
- **(843) 237-1700**

The hugely successful Pawleys Island Festival of Music and Art usually opens in late September and runs for four weeks. Now in its

The watermelon-eating contest is popular during the annual Sun Fun Festival.

Photo: Courtesy of Myrtle Beach Area Chamber of Commerce

Nearly fifty years old, the Myrtle Beach Area's Sun Fun Festival
kicks off the Strand's busy summer season.

Photo: Courtesy of Myrtle Beach Area Chamber of Commerce

No matter what the event, there's always something to entertain the younger set.

Photo: Courtesy of Myrtle Beach Area Chamber of Commerce

tenth year, each new season brings a new theme and a veritable plethora of music and art performances at venues throughout the South Strand all the way to the historic port of Georgetown. There are far too many events to list separately and the schedule changes dramatically from one year to another, but if you are the "artsy" type rest assured you will not want to miss this. Call ahead for specifics.

and area restaurants who specialize in Italian cuisine bring in the goodies that range from New York-style pizza to pastas. Musical entertainment usually features the smooth sound of the Big Band Era, while strolling accordionists provided a little taste of Italy. The event runs from 10 AM to 6 PM in the park, and admission is free.

September

North Strand

S.O.S. Fall Migration
Various locations in North Myrtle Beach
• **(888) SOS-3113**

The Society of Stranders calls its thousands of active members to return to North Myrtle Beach in mid-September for one last big party before winter sets in. Days and nights are filled with activities, shagging and sight-seeing. Eight clubs around the Ocean Drive section pitch in to make sure that every evening resounds with nonstop beach music.

Myrtle Beach

South Carolina's Largest Garage Sale
Myrtle Beach Pavilion Parking Garage, Kings Hwy. and Ninth Ave. N., Myrtle Beach
• **(843) 918-1242**

For one whole Saturday in mid-September, the Pavilion's parking garage is filled with the hubbub of hagglers hawking wares. Hundreds of booths set up on every parking level feature household goods, clothing, toiletries, sporting goods, furniture, toys, food and just plain junk. The sale runs from 8 AM to 1 PM, and admission is free.

Italian Festival
Chapin Park, Kings Hwy. at 16th Ave. N., Myrtle Beach
• **(843) 650-3466**

Mid-September of 2000 will mark this event's sixth year. It's a day of food, music and arts and crafts—Italian-style. The Sons of Italy

South Atlantic Shrine Parade
Along Ocean Blvd., Myrtle Beach
• **(843) 651-5675**

This 4-hour procession in late September features Shrine Temple representatives from six states: West Virginia, Virginia, North and South Carolina, Tennessee and Kentucky. Expect to see a proliferation of wacky go-carts, clowns and floats traveling along Ocean Boulevard from Sixth Avenue S. to 11th Avenue N. in Myrtle Beach. The parade usually starts at 9:30 AM.

Those little motorized units competed in the parking lot of Waccamaw Pottery; title challenges for the legion-of-honor band, Highlander Concert and Chanters were held at the Myrtle Beach Convention Center; and the clown units out-mugged one another at a meet at the Sea Mist Resort.

The 1999 event brought approximately 4,000 Shrine families to the area. The South Atlantic Shrine Association supports 22 Shriners hospitals and three burn institutes.

South Strand

Annual Atalaya Arts and Crafts Festival
Huntington Beach State Park, U.S. Hwy. 17 S., Murrells Inlet
• **(843) 734-0156, (843) 237-4440**

For the Atalaya Arts and Crafts Festival, one of the largest art shows in the Southeast, the food and fun with a view formula has proved successful for 25 years. Scheduled in mid-to-late September at Huntington Beach State Park, this festival has earned a reputation for attracting some of the region's—even the nation's—finest artisans. Because the show is juried—meaning participating artisans are screened for merit and appropriateness—you can be assured the maze of artwork is top-of-the-line in quality. It is, in fact, quite an honor to be accepted as an exhibitor. Consequently, the festival has become a not-to-be-missed pilgrimage for knowledgeable art collectors and plain-ol' admirers.

Not only does the Atalaya Arts and Crafts Festival give you an opportunity to peruse the wares of talented artists and craftsmen, it offers you a delicious taste of authentic history. Atalaya (pronounced At-a-lie-a not At-a-lay-a), after which the festival is named, is a majestic Moorish inspired structure located in the park. Construction was launched on Atalaya in 1931. Archer and Anna Hyatt Huntington, new owners of a vast track of land that included four Colonial plantations, orchestrated plans for the castle which was to be their winter home. Mr. Huntington was a scholar of Spanish history and culture, so it is not surprising his new home was fashioned after the eighth-century Moorish fortresses along the Mediterranean coast of Spain. Mrs. Huntington was a brilliant sculptress and her creative influence can also be detected in Atalaya.

This year, as always, the breezy courtyard and rooms of this beautiful old building will serve as a breathtaking and mystical backdrop for the eclectic works of over a hundred artists and craftsmen. There will be lots of area food vendors offering delicious Lowcountry cuisine (With the exception of special tours, Atalaya is typically closed to the public. So, just seeing the interior of the old castle is reason enough to attend!)

INSIDERS' TIP

If you're hungry and planning to attend an annual event that features food, be sure to go early! Organizers can never be absolutely sure of attendance numbers, and food vendors often miscalculate the crowd. More than once we've found ourselves at a festival in late afternoon with nothing to eat.

Miles, the popular Elvis Presley tribute artist and Jimmy Diamon & The Skylarks, who played a repertoire of upbeat jazz numbers.

The Indian Summer Festival, quickly approaching its 10th birthday, has evolved into an eagerly anticipated event for both locals and tourists alike. It is a truly enjoyable way to commemorate the end of a busy summer season and to welcome the beginning of autumn. Free admission makes the Indian Summer Festival a particularly great way to spend the day with the entire family!

Trick or Treating
Various North Strand Locations
• (843) 272-8349, (843) 272-4040, (843) 280-5570

If you're looking for tried and true trick-or-treating opportunities for kids on Halloween night, one option is to take the little gremlins to Barefoot Landing. Kids can trick-or-treat through the stores from 5 to 7 PM.

Colonial Mall, located at 10177 N. Kings Highway, (843) 272-4040, hosts a Boo Bash on All Saints' Hallow night with a costume contest at 6 PM and trick-or-treating throughout the mall at 7 PM.

The annual Halloween Carnival is held at the North Myrtle Beach Recreation Center on Possum Trot Road, from 6:30 to 8:30 PM. The carnival typically features lots of games for the kids, a haunted house and costume contest. Call (843) 280-5570.

October

North Strand

Indian Summer Festival
Downtown Main St., North Myrtle Beach
• (843) 249-6921

Usually held in mid-October, the Indian Summer Festival is sponsored by Downtown Organizations Interacting Together, a revitalization group in North Myrtle Beach. It's a day of arts and crafts, food, entertainment and special activities for the kids.

Previous performers have included Eddie

Myrtle Beach

Oktoberfest
Baseball stadium at the former
Myrtle Beach Air Force Base, Myrtle Beach
• (843) 918-1242

Beer and bratwurst are the favorites at this early October celebration of the harvest season. Authentic oom-pah music is played and arts and crafts are on display. Visitors show up to consume German brown bread, sauerkraut and sausages in addition to the usual festival fare of hamburgers, pizza and funnel cakes. Some hot-selling items that you are likely to find are homemade dolls, clothing and Christmas and Halloween decorations.

Oktoberfest admission is $2 for adults 21 and older and $1 for those under the age of 21; kids 6 and younger are admitted free.

Ride-A-Thon
29th Ave. S. to 45th Ave. N., Myrtle Beach
• (843) 626-3939

Hundreds of horses trot along the Grand Strand shoreline for this annual event that raises money to fight heart disease and stroke. More than $60,000 was raised for the American Heart Association by more than 500 riders and their equines in late October 1999.

Each adult participant contributes a minimum of $75 and teenage and child riders must kick in at least $50. After the 20-mile hike on horseback, entrants are treated to a barbecue lunch, awards ceremony and a raffle. The horses are led along the beach by a police escort and the public is invited to watch from the sidelines.

Trick or Treating
Various Myrtle Beach Locations
• (843) 448-2513,
(843) 444-3200

For trick-or-treating, the Scare Fair held at Myrtle Square Mall, 2501 N. Kings Highway, is always a good bet. Free Halloween bags are given out in the Food Court and children can beg candy from stores from 5 to 7 PM. Games and prizes, entertainment, and caricature drawing are all part of the Scare Fair.

Broadway at the Beach, (843) 444-3200, also invites kids to come trick-or-treat with them from 5 to 7 PM. Free bags are given to children at the visitors center and a costume contest is held at 8 PM.

South Strand

Surfside Beach Family Festival
One block off Surfside Dr., Surfside Beach
• (843) 238-4131, Ext. 333

What started out as a little ole family picnic in 1985 has now grown into a full-fledged festival attended by more than 10,000 people each year! It's a day-long affair in early October, with plenty of food and arts and crafts for sale plus information booths if you need directions. Even during a downpour in 1999, an estimated

9,000 people came out to enjoy homespun crafts, games and performers under a covered bandstand.

Several bands perform, and more than 90 vendors offer everything from hot dogs to rides on an oversized stuffed panda and tiger. This event always coordinates lots of games for children. There is no admission fee.

Pawleys Island Tour of Homes
• (843) 237-8454

The Pawleys Island Tour of Homes, scheduled for mid-October, benefits the Georgetown Chapter of Habitat for Humanity. The five-year-old-tour is comprised of a dozen or more Pawleys Island beach homes—ranging from 19th century summer cottages to contemporary year-round residences. Unusual artifacts, windswept landscaping and porches perched on the edge of the Atlantic combine to make this house tour uniquely enjoyable. Tickets are $20 per person and can be ordered in advance. Even the locals come, so don't miss this.

INSIDERS' TIP

During the hotter months of May, June, July and August, it would be prudent planning to attend an outdoor annual event in the morning. Especially if you have children in tow, the heat of the day coupled with the gathering of hundreds of people can turn your pleasant outing into a nightmare.

Annual Wooden Boat Exhibit and Challenge
Front St.
(on the waterfront),
Georgetown
• (843) 546-0064

Here's an exciting twist to the usual boat shows and races: You make your own boat from scratch before sailing! At the Annual Wooden Boat Exhibit and Challenge, two-person teams are given a four-hour time limit in which to construct a functioning 12-foot rowing dory. Each team starts off with the same raw materials and equipment, marine-quality plywood, nails, and oar locks.

The overall competition takes into account speed, quality, and the results of a short relay race in the dory to Goat Island and back. After being awed by the pace of building, onlookers usually get a real kick out of watching the rowers trying to steer the rudderless, awkward boats in a straight line.

The event also includes all the trappings of maritime life: displays of handmade oars, intricate models of shrimp boats, pillows decorated with nautical themes, knot-tying demonstrations, and simmering pots of spicy, delicious gumbo.

There is no admission fee to the exhibit;

Atalaya (pronounced At-a-lie-a not At-a-lay-a), after which the Atalaya Arts & Crafts Festival is named, is a majestic Moorish-inspired structure located in Huntington Beach State Park.

Photo: Courtesy of Myrtle Beach Area Chamber of Commerce

spectators are allowed to watch from outside the working tents of the competing teams.

Trick or Treating
Various South Strand Locations
• **(843) 651-6990, (843) 546-6317**

Trick or Treat at Inlet Square Mall in Murrells Inlet allows children to collect candies from store to store from 6 to 8 PM on Halloween night. The mall also hosts a costume contest at Center Staff at 6:30 PM. For more information, call (843) 651-6990.

The Georgetown County United Way and the Downtown Business Association work together to assist kids in their Trick-or-Treating ventures along downtown Front Street in Georgetown. Call (843) 546-6317.

November

North Strand

Intracoastal Christmas Regatta
Little River to North Myrtle Beach
• **(843) 280-6354**

On the Saturday after Thanksgiving, dozens of vessels get decked out for the holidays. Beginning at 5:30 PM, boats launch from Little River Inlet and travel down the waterway for an estimated 7:30 PM arrival at Dock Holiday's Marina at 13th Avenue N. in North Myrtle Beach. Viewing sites encompass the restaurants along the Little River waterfront, the Riverboat Restaurant at North Myrtle Beach Marina, the Blue Marlin Yacht and Fishing Club at Anchor Marina and Marker 350 at Harbourgate Marina (See our Boating chapter for extensive information on each of these marinas).

The regatta benefits local children's charities and spurs an annual toy collection for needy kids. Participating boaters pay a $25 entry fee or donate new, unwrapped toys. The event offers a $1,000 grand prize.

Myrtle Beach

Taste of the Town
Myrtle Beach Convention Center
• **(843) 249-4885**

If you would like to sample foods from a variety of Grand Strand restaurants, make sure you do not miss this early November event. More than 40 restaurants participate each year, serving up the best they have to offer. Taste of the Town has become so popular that it began to take over two rooms of the convention center. Attendance has risen to more than 7,000 people.

The competitive part of the show is watched closely by residents and other restaurants. While the event is always good-natured, a positive showing can mean an increase in business for the coming year; for smaller restaurants that must close to send their staff to Taste of the Town, winning or placing is everything. In fact, some popular mainstay establishments had to bow out because of the tremendous amount of work involved to participate in Taste of the Town. To give you an idea of the pace, one restaurant served 2,000 portions of food by 8 PM!

Awards are bestowed for the best overall food, the best entree, the best dessert and the People's Choice.

This event is a fund-raising project for St. Andrews Catholic School. Taste of the Town is held from 4 to 9:30 PM. Admission is $8 for a family and $4 for individuals; food tickets are $1 each. Food tidbits cost from one to three tickets each.

ACBL Sectiona Bridge Tournament
Sites to be announced
• (843) 449-3279

This tournament in early November draws 1,200 duplicate bridge players to compete for three days. Eighty tables are set up per day, and entrants pay a nominal fee to compete. A championship match of the Myrtle Beach Bridge Association is played during Can-Am Days in mid-March (see previous entry in the "March" section).

Senior Tour Championship
Tournament Players Club
•(843) 357-3399, (888) 742-8721

Since 1994, the first week of November has been an unusually exciting time along the Grand Strand because The Senior Tour Championship chose to call the Myrtle Beach Area home. For the past five years, the tournament has been held at the Dunes Golf and Beach Club. In 2000, this much-anticipated event moved to the Strand's 100th golf course—the Tournament Player's Club. Designed by premiere golf architect Tom Fazio, in collaboration with PGA Tour player consultant Lanny Wadkins, this beautiful course showcases spir-

INSIDERS' TIP

Be sure to check out the whole schedule of events added to the Dickens Christmas Show & Festival in November. Besides a labyrinth of Yuletide gifts and decorations, the festival adds new activities each and every year.

ited competition among the Senior Tour's finest players.

This 72-hole stroke-play event culminates an exciting season of golf, and world-famous players compete for a $2 million purse, as well as many of the season's top honors. The competition hosts the Top 31 Senior Tour players; you'll thrill to watch golf legends vie for the highest purse awarded on the Senior Tour.

This internationally televised event donates all profits to charity and has generated more than $800,000 for area charities since its inception in 1994.

Tickets are limited. Daily and weekly passes are available. To purchase tickets by phone or just to ask questions, the Tournament Office can be reached at 444-4782 or 800/868-7563.

Annual Dickens Christmas Show & Festival
Myrtle Beach Convention Center
• (843) 448-9483

You know that Christmas is just around the corner when the Dickens Show gears up at the convention center in mid-November. And what a charming way to get in the holiday spirit. Grand Stranders spend hours decorating the trees and wreaths on display, and the adornments are a sight to behold. The beautifully trimmed tannenbaums and handsome wreaths are usually auctioned off by the end of the festival, and hundreds of holiday gifts and ornaments are available for show and sale. Money collected from the silent auction of the Festival of Trees, decorated by area businesses, benefits Citizens Against Spouse Abuse. The Myrtle Beach Jaycees are the charity of choice for the proceeds from the Festival of Wreaths. In 1996 a Festival of Holiday Tables (featuring centerpieces) was added; proceeds were donated to Habitat for Humanity of Horry County.

The 2000 admission price to the show and festival was $7 a head for adults, $3 for children ages 1 to 12; a multiple-day pass was $9.

Charles Dickens' great-great-grandson, Gerald Charles Dickens, travels from Kent, England, to join the festivities. Sharing a strikingly similar look and expression as his famous ancestor, Gerald Dickens delights audiences with his readings of Dickens' material at two high-noon teas.

The Beggars Ball, featuring costumed street characters and a dance band, represents yet another eagerly anticipated part of the show.

Annual South Carolina State Bluegrass Festival
Myrtle Beach Convention Center
• **(706) 864-3721**

This festival is touted as "the Palmetto state's oldest, largest and best bluegrass event."

Drawing fans from throughout the eastern United States and Canada, promoters are proud to say that the late November festival will always be a "who's who" of traditional bluegrass performers. The festival has played host to such performers as the Grand Ole Opry's Osborne Brothers, the Lewis Family, Doyle Lawson & Quicksilver, Jim & Jesse and the Virginia Boys, IIIrd Tyme Out, Ralph Stanley & the Clinch Mtn. Boys, Raymond Fairchild, the Bass Mountain Boys, Mike Stevens, Chubby Wise, J.D. Crowe and the New South, Country Gentlemen Reunion, Mac Wiseman, the Larry Stephenson Band, the Mayor and Buford, Lou Reid, Terry Baucom and Carolina, Bob Paisley & the Southern Grass, the Del McCoury Band, the Sand Mountain Boys and the Lonesome River Band.

This music festival differs from most, since jam sessions are prevalent and a good number of audience members join in with the bands at any given time. As bluegrass lovers admit, this music represents a way of life.

In addition to an almost seamless stream of performances, the Bluegrass Festival offers arts and crafts booths, food and beverages and CDs from all of the scheduled artists for sale before and after their shows.

Tickets are available at the gate and are sold at the convention center box office during the festival. Prices are undetermined as of this writing but vary as they are based on age, seating, number of days you are interested in attending, etc. Please call ahead for details.

December

North Strand

Christmas Tour of Homes
Throughout the North Strand
• **(843) 249-6449**

Like its Georgetown cousin, this Christmas Tour of Homes gives one the chance to see stately homes dressed up for the Yuletide season. Sponsored by the North Myrtle Beach Women's Club, six abodes are opened to the public for one afternoon in December. Proceeds from the event help a mix of charities like Children's Hospice, the North Myrtle Beach Rescue Squad, the North Myrtle Beach Animal Shelter and various scholarship funds.

Myrtle Beach

Springmaid Beach Craft Show
3200 S. Ocean Blvd., Myrtle Beach
• **(843) 238-5189**

This early December event includes more than 300 booths, representing craftspeople and artists alike. Some 20,000 show-goers were treated to an incredible array of quilts, jewelry, clothing, woodcrafts, baskets, stained-glass doll houses, and collectibles plus wreaths and decorations for the holiday season. The Springmaid Beach Craft Show is open to the public, with booths found both indoors and outdoors. Admission is free.

SCADA
North-South All-Star Football Game
Doug Shaw Memorial Stadium,
33rd Ave. N. and Oak St., Myrtle Beach
• **(843) 448-2214**

As the name implies, this mid-December game showcases the best young players from the northern and southern portions of South Carolina. The teams battle it out on the field, while college scouts get a good look at potential recruits. In the past, head coaches and representatives from Clemson University, the University of North Carolina and Wake Forest University were on hand to assess the skills of 88 hopeful high schoolers. Tickets for the event cost $5 in advance; $7 at the gate.

Beach Ball Classic
Myrtle Beach Convention Center
• **(843) 650-7222**

Sponsored by Belk department store and McDonald's, the Beach Ball Classic in late December is always an exciting showcase of this country's best high school basketball talent. Teams are rated and selected to play in this tournament before standing-room-only crowds of cheering fans, basketball enthusiasts and college scouts. To give you an idea of the kind of talent to expect at the classic, check out this impressive list of former Beach Ball stars that wound up in the NBA: Kenny Anderson, Grant Hill, Jimmy Jackson, Don MacLean, Jerrod

Mustaf, Billy Owens, Cherokee Parks, Rasheed Wallace and Dontonio Wingfield.

The 20th Beach Ball Classic was played in 2000.

Games start each day at 3:30 PM and culminate around 10 PM. An admission fee is announced close to tournament time.

South Strand

Christmas Tour of Homes
Throughout Georgetown County
• (843) 546-8101

This early December tour will get you in the Christmas spirit while providing some of the most beautiful Yuletide decorating ideas. Varying numbers of gracious historic homes and bed and breakfast inns in Georgetown and Pawleys Island, resplendent with holiday adornments, are open to the public for this program. This annual event has become one of the most popular, piquing interests in architecture, history, decorating and antiques.

Tour prices vary from one year to another and are announced close to tour time. Please call for details.

Georgetown County Festival of Trees
Litchfield Beach and Golf Resort
• (843) 546-3410

Delight in the true spirit of Christmas by attending the Hospice of Georgetown County's Festival of Trees. Breakfast with Santa kicks off festivities on a Saturday morning in early December, and attractions include a breathtaking display of uniquely decorated Fraser firs and a variety of music and entertainment. The Christmas Shop, Country Kitchen and Santa's Shop offers lots of opportunities for shortening your shopping list, too. Call for a complete schedule.

Wacca Wache Marina
Christmas Boat Parade
Murrells Inlet
• (843) 651-2994

This event is usually held on a Saturday evening in early December to give special effect to the light displays on these Yuletide decorated boats. The parade begins at the marina at 6 PM, 2 miles west of U.S. Highway 17 on the Waccamaw River and Intracoastal Waterway. Boats must register to enter the parade, but there is no fee. The marina provides dockage for the event, and admission is free.

Arts and Culture

LOOK FOR:
- Arts Councils
- Auditoriums and Theaters
- Music and Song
- Performing Arts
- Visual Arts

In an area replete with state-of-the-art theaters built to showcase international headline stars, you would think that the Grand Strand's community arts scene would head for the beach to bury its proverbial head in the sand. Instead, our native artists seem to have absorbed this main-stage professional energy and talent, launching more ambitious programs than ever before.

The loose Latin translation of the word amateur is "for the love of it." Never underestimate the momentum and power created by amateur talent that performs and presents out of pure joy, without pay for the hours invested.

The Grand Strand boasts a nationally recognized symphony orchestra, a row of art galleries, a true cafe society, resident artists whose works are being shown worldwide, legitimate entrance to the museum community, a Broadway-class method actor and much more.

Not too surprisingly, when summer has packed the beach with tourists, the Grand Strand's arts and cultural organizations taper or curtail their activities. In fact, most of these organizations' seasons run from September to March or April. Traditionally, tourists have not provided large audiences for cultural offerings, and many of the organizations' volunteers are too busy working at their "real jobs" during the summer months to devote more than minimal time to their favorite artistic endeavors. VIVACE! in October (described at the end of this chapter) is one way many local artists get to showcase their talents and many locals get to show their appreciation.

Arts Councils

Horry Cultural Arts Council
1001 Second Ave., Conway
- **(843) 248-7200,**
  (800) 868-ARTS

The Strand's first organized arts effort actually started in 1989 with the formation of the Horry Cultural Arts Council (HCAC). As an umbrella organization for the arts, HCAC offers information and assistance to artists, arts-related organizations and Horry County's residents and visitors. HCAC coordinates an arts and cultural events calendar and funds grants for various organizations to help them present arts productions. It also funds an Arts Education Initiative Program that places professional artists in public schools to instruct students in various media.

Horry County organizations that offer opportunities in the arts are too numerous for us to provide a comprehensive listing here. We suggest you check out HCAC's *Arts & Cultural Directory*; call the council at (800) 868-ARTS for additional information.

Waccamaw Arts and Crafts Guild
- **(843) 497-4294**

The Waccamaw Arts and Crafts Guild, with about 300 members, is dedicated to promoting interest and creativity in the visual arts. Approximately half the members are artists, the other half being patrons or fans. Monthly meetings include demonstrations, slide presentations, social gatherings to exhibit members' recent works and panel discussions on topics such as copyrighting. The guild is adding a second show this year; in June they will host an exhibit at the new art museum and in October they will return to the 30th Annual Judged Show at the Myrtle Beach Convention Center. Call Millie Doud at the number listed if you are interested in joining the guild.

Wheelwright Council for the Arts
Coastal Carolina University, Conway
• **(843) 347-3161**

This organization, composed of community members and Coastal Carolina University faculty and staff, supervises the use of Wheelwright Auditorium. The Wheelwright group coordinates the univer-sity's arts program, including a cultural arts series and student plays. The Wheelwright Council's stated function is to bring to the area high-caliber art performances that other groups are unable to secure. The council presents a Passport Series that offers experiences in film, dance and the performing arts. David Millard is the contact to call.

Wheelwright's upcoming playbill is ambitious, with performances of *In the Woods, The Complete Works of Shakespeare, Fabulas,* Broadway musical medleys and more. Tickets at the door for student productions are $10 for adults and $5 for students, touring productions are about $15; ticket prices vary for other events.

South Strand

Georgetown County Cultural Council
1001 Front St. Ste. 220, Georgetown
• **(843) 527-2822**

In Georgetown County, the Georgetown County Cultural Council serves as a catalyst to promote, coordinate and stimulate the cultural, social and economic climate of the arts in the county. The council is a true grass-roots movement, because in 1997 Georgetown City Council terminated funding. Most of the members are artists and provide hours of volunteer support to keep the council active. The Cultural Council is housed in the renovated Customs House Post Office with the Georgetown Chamber and Visitors Bureau.

Auditoriums and Theaters

Myrtle Beach

Myrtle Beach High School Auditorium
3300 Central Pkwy., Myrtle Beach
• **(843) 448-7149**

The Myrtle Beach High School Auditorium is the area's largest auditorium, seating 2,000 people. The school district had planned to build a 1,000-seat venue, but Myrtle Beach residents convinced them to enlarge it so their city could attract bigger and better productions. Community-raised funds helped pay for the increased cost of the exceptionally well-equipped if not particularly elegant auditorium.

South Strand

Strand Theatre
710 Front St., Georgetown
• **(843) 527-2924**

The Strand Theatre seats 160 people. Home to Georgetown's Swamp Fox Players (see subsequent entry), it's often called the Swamp Fox Theatre.

Beyond the Strand

McCown Auditorium
Corner of Ninth Ave. and Main St., Conway
• **(843) 626-1211**

This old auditorium was defunct for many years until Horry County bought it and transformed the entire building. Seating about 350 people, the auditorium is used for many community functions including elementary school plays, the Theater of the Republic with performances such as *A Funny Thing Happened on the Way to the Forum,* county board meetings, the museum's quilt gala and a children's theater workshop.

Wheelwright Auditorium
Coastal Carolina University,
U.S. Hwy. 501 E., Conway
• **(843) 347-3161**

Wheelwright Auditorium, on the campus of Coastal Carolina University, roughly 10 miles west of Myrtle Beach off U.S. Highway 501, is an elegant facility that seats about 800 people. Among many performances (see the previous entry about the Wheelwright Council for the arts,) *Songwriter in the Round* is an extraordinary event. Organized by George McCorkle of the Marshall Tucker Band (of Greenville, S.C.), the event allows songwriters, who usually turn their work over to more famous performers, to explore their music with the audience. Local blues woman Jaynie Trudell has been invited back for the 1998 show.

Music and Song

Church Concert Series

Several churches along the Strand now offer quality concert series. They include North Myrtle Beach's Ocean Drive Presbyterian Church, (843) 249-2312, Myrtle Beach's Trinity Episcopal Church, (843) 448-8426, and First Presbyterian Church, (843) 448-4496. The concert series concept was brought here by Brown Bradley, minister of music at First Presbyterian, who participated in a successful series in New York before relocating to Myrtle Beach.

Trinity Episcopal Church's Performing Arts Series entertains the community with five quality performances each year. Events include choral concerts, recitals, instrumental ensembles, musical revues, comedies, complete Broadway musical productions and periodic art displays. One series opened with the internationally ac-claimed Vienna Boys Choir; subsequent events included Peter Schickele of PDQ Bach fame, Moscow's Russian Men's Choir, the musical *Godspell* and *The Fantasticks*. The Argentine pianist Martha Felcman has performed here and the Mikado played recently. For dates and specific information on upcoming events and season memberships, contact the series director at (843) 448-8426.

At the First Presbyterian Church, ticket holders are treated to a variety of featured vocalists and instrumentalists performing classical, pop and Broadway selections. A popular past event featured the remarkable Dutch classic quartet Quink. Each year, sellout performances of *The Best of Broadway* are presented. The FPC Players Drama Troupe spotlights local talent in family-friendly shows like *Dogs*, and in timeless Broadway hits like *Bells Are Ringing*. Season memberships are encouraged.

Since 1991 the Ocean Drive Presbyterian Church Concert Series has provided programming such as the Wheaton College Men's Choir, The Palmetto Brass, Frederico Hayler and the Furman Singers. The North Myrtle Beach Christmas Cantata, featuring members of the Long Bay Symphony (see entry below), is a part of the series that has become a community favorite during the holiday season. Although series memberships are sold for $50 and $100, donations of $5 or more are accepted at the door.

Myrtle Beach's first art museum delights visitors with local and international exhibits.

Photo: Lisa Tomer Rentz

Thomas Davis

"I want to express worldwide that South Carolina is beautiful," artist and third-generation Grand Strander Thomas Davis explained. "The Lowcountry lifestyle and culture is not what is usually expected. I stayed in the South of France to paint, in the Rhone Delta, and it's almost the same there—they also have rice fields and the intense light we have here."

"In the 1770s Lafayette landed right here at North Island." Thomas poked the table we sat at as if it were sand on the beach. "He came here. Now I'm doing the reverse, to bring our cultures full circle. While I traveled, people asked me all about South Carolina, they wanted to know what Lowcountry is." His plans, for both his paintings and our beautiful Carolina seascape, seem to culminate in a Paris exhibit. Just imagine Myrtle Beach in Paris, sand in the Louvre, shag at the Centre Pompidou!

"My goal is to show expressions of this land by blending color with culture on canvas. The viewer needs to look beyond the modern era to view and relive lifestyles of a simpler time. Despite changing times and cultures, the wetlands have survived; today the struggle between development and conservation continues this cycle. My paintings are an attempt to preserve the history, romance and adventurous soul of South Carolina's beloved wetlands."

Excluding his French scenes, Thomas' paintings are filled with Lowcountry life. *Creek Critters* is a relaxing afternoon drifting down the river. *Prontopup* is taken from a ride at the historic Pavilion. *No Fake Smiles in Pawleys Today* enjoys the rigors of paddling. *Creekpeople*, which is from a shrimping expedition, won first round people's choice at the 1997 VIVACE! fine arts festival.

"You have to make it elsewhere to be appreciated here," Thomas remarked about the Myrtle Beach art scene. "But Myrtle Beach is growing, there's so much opportunity now," he said happily. "The beach is good at being a community. The Waccamaw Arts Guild is active, but it needs more youth. You don't have to be experienced or fancy—just send in some slides."

Davis' work is displayed in homes along the East Coast.

Photo: Robert Clark

In return for the inspiration and success the Grand Strand community has allowed him thus far, Thomas is busy reinvesting his energies into the community, like so many permanent residents here do.

Thomas has also been asked to be a part of the Community Appearance Board to help monitor and enforce new codes that have to do with the appearance of new buildings and signage. "The main guideline is knowing that the committee is there," he stated, confident that as Myrtle Beach grows as a city, it will show more of its natural beauty.

Thomas' work can be viewed, along with other local artists', at the Collectors Cafe and Gallery in Myrtle Beach (see the Restaurant chapter for more details). His art is also working its way into homes up and down the East Coast. Who knows, maybe after a spicy Mediterranean dinner at Collectors Cafe, you could end up taking home a painting that might be known someday as "a Davis."

Now that he is back from his travels, "I think I'm going to paint some landscapes, get back to my roots," Thomas told us with satisfaction, sounding like he'd already started in on his favorite subject again.

Myrtle Beach

Coastal Concert Association
• (843) 449-7546

This group has been bringing wonderful traveling troupes to Horry County since 1971. From the North Carolina Symphony to the San Francisco Pops, diverse performances and cultural events have included the award-winning Broadway musical *Brigadoon*, the off-Broadway hit *Nunsense*, the River City Brass Band and the original orchestration of the Glenn Miller Band. Concerts are usually held in October, November, January, February and March or April in the Myrtle Beach High School Auditorium. Tickets are available at the door ($20 for adults and $5 for students), but annual memberships ($45 to $60 for adults and $20 for students) are encouraged. Please call for a current schedule.

Community Choral Society
• (843) 444-5774

Anyone who enjoys singing is welcome to join the Community Choral Society. This avid group of harmonizers, about 80 strong, offers concert performances for residents and visitors throughout the year. Classical choral arrangements have included Rutter's *Magnificat*. The group's year culminates in the Festival by the Sea, a two-day event in February. The associa-

tion invites a guest conductor and choirs from three states and Canada to attend area workshops, producing a tremendous performance for the community. For a recent show, Norman Scrivener, conductor of the Choral Arts Society of Washington D.C. lead the aural undertaking. Expect an inspired performance from this enthusiastic amateur group. Ticket prices vary but usually range from $8 to $15 per seat.

The Long Bay Symphony
Long Bay Youth Orchestra
1811 Oak St., Myrtle Beach
• (843) 448-8379

The Long Bay Symphony performs a full season of classical, chamber and POPS concerts, including playing the original scores during a silent film.

Many of the Long Bay Symphony members have performed with such respected organizations as the Metropolitan Opera in New York and the pop-infused Radio City Music Hall Orchestra. With this array of influences, the Long Bay group melds a variety of musical backgrounds, performing selections from classical to pop as well as full stage productions. It presents 12 concerts each season and performs at the City of Myrtle Beach's annual Fourth of July Celebration (see our Annual Events chapter for details), thus claiming the unofficial "official" orchestra position in the community.

INSIDERS' TIP

If you get the urge to paint or otherwise artistically express yourself while at the beach, visit Broadway Street near the Pavilion. This small shopping district includes artists supply stores, upscale salons, galleries and a Cajun restaurant.

The Long Bay Symphony performs a variety of classical, chamber and POPS concerts each year.

Photo: Danny Chamblee, The Long Bay Symphony

Musicians range from high school students to retirees, from points all along the Grand Strand. For concert information or season memberships call the number listed.

The Long Bay Symphony promotes its approximately 50-member youth orchestra to spark youngsters' interest in "serious music" and to train older members for the symphony orchestra.

Adults who haven't played in years as well as those who are just learning to play can hone their skills with the youth symphony; the addition of adults has prompted some people to call the group the "Long Bay Orchestra for the Young and Youthful." Members of the youth orchestra also have a chance to be awarded scholarships for private lessons.

Under the direction of Dr. Charles Evans, the youth orchestra performs two or three times a year, once with the symphony and the symphony offers master classes for interested musicians.

INSIDERS' TIP

Many communities publish weekly events in an independent newspaper that is free to the public. Look for one in your area for information on local entertainment.

Performing Arts

Myrtle Beach

**Grand Strand
Seniors for the Performing Arts
1268 21st Ave. N., Myrtle Beach**
• **(843) 626-3991**

In 1991 several Horryites 50 and older started playing with the idea of forming their own theater group. They decided to give it a try. And when *Send Me No Flowers* attracted 2,000 people over six performances, they figured they were onto something good.

With an influx of retiring talent from the North, this thespian group produces at least five shows a year. Tickets are $5 each. *Send Me No Flowers, Arsenic and Old Lace* and *Fiddler on the Roof* are examples of the group's scope. Auditions for each play are publicized, and the cast is selected from the general public and the membership. Volunteers from the general membership handle scenery, publicity, lighting, costuming, makeup, sound and stage work. Please call for a current schedule.

The South Carolina Syndicate Theatre Company
• (843) 272-4019

The South Carolina Syndicate Theatre Company, with Sean Pierce as artistic director, offers an alternative to typical Grand Strand theater. This group performs plays not often presented in this area (or many other areas of the South, for that matter)—plays that are decidedly more bold than the standard local fare. Examples include *True West, Four Dogs and a Bone* and a performance of *Sylvia* at VIVACE!

This company has a core group of talented local actors who strive to present quality shows at a reasonable cost—around $5 per ticket. The group is part community "little theater," part street theater, part crazy and lots of fun. Performance venues change—so it's best to call ahead—and are often in alternative "stages" such as The Algonquin Cafe. And at $5 per ticket (kids are usally free with an adult), the performances are worth seeing.

Tricycle Players Inc.
313C S.C. Hwy. 15, Myrtle Beach
• (843) 448-8221

Tricycle Players Inc. is another nonprofit, amateur theater group on the Grand Strand. The group's specialties are musicals featuring large casts, especially those including children. Since 1989, this group has entertained audiences with productions such as *Pump Boys and Dinettes, Peter Pan, Alice in Wonderland* and *Nunsense. Pump Boys and Dinettes,* their first production, was so successful, the cast was invited to perform in Charleston's Dock Street Theatre. Please call for current information.

South Strand

Bill Oberst and
His Experience Theatre
• (843) 237-7681, (800) 239-7681

When Broadway and Hollywood actor Hal Holbrook took time off from his world-famous Mark Twain stage show, his manager called Pawleys Island to find Oberst as a replacement. The Grand Strand actor's own one-man Twain show has become truly legendary. His 1996 addition of *Jesus of Nazareth* and *The Senator* as well as his 1997 *John Kennedy* are all remarkable presentations.

Once the youngest chamber of commerce executive director in America, a former candidate for the United States Congress and the marketing director who guided Calvin Gilmore's Carolina Opry empire, Oberst is a complex man who brings his vast experiences to the stage in a unique presentation he calls "Experience Theatre."

Experience Theatre is a concept that takes the audience into a personal, interactive encounter with an individual historical figure. In *Jesus of Nazareth,* the messiah walks among the audience members, responds to their questions (handed out on cards as they enter the theater), shares bread with them and even washes the feet of unsuspecting audience members. For each Experience Theatre performance, the room is sprayed with scents of the epoch to complement its respective show (e.g. heavy leathers for Twain's study; damp linens for Jesus).

It is not uncommon to see audience members weeping as they leave an Oberst performance, feeling deeply touched by the historical character; it really is an experience.

Unfortunately Oberst spends most of the year on the road, performing or lecturing university students worldwide. When on the Strand, however, he does many shows—mainly for local charities. Call the number listed for a schedule and ticket prices.

Swamp Fox Players Inc.
710 Front St., Georgetown
• (843) 527-2924

Established in the early 1970s, this amateur theatrical group coordinates at least four productions per year. Since the community seems to be particularly fond of musicals and comedy, many of the Swamp Fox productions are flavored accordingly. Recent shows included *Second Samuel, Vanities, Murder in the Magnolias* and the musical *Working.*

This group calls the Strand Theatre, on Front Street in Georgetown, "home." Tickets are $10 each; a season pass is $37.50.

INSIDERS' TIP

If you are a student, make sure to travel with your student ID. Many venues offer a student discount when you show your card.

ARTS AND CULTURE

ARTS AND CULTURE

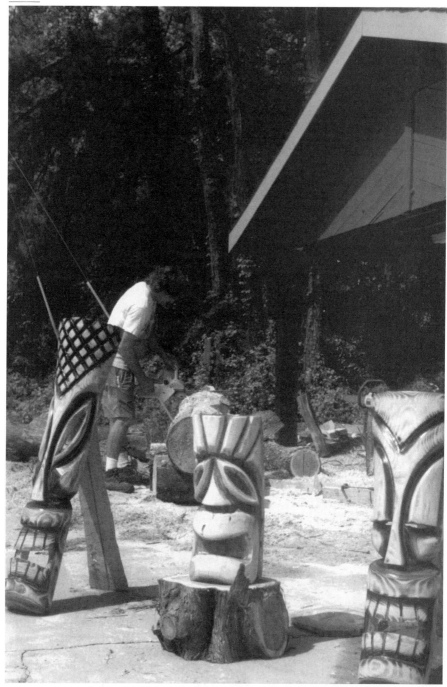

Artists of all kinds make their homes all along the Grand Strand.

Photo: Lisa Tomer Rentz

Visual Arts

Myrtle Beach

Franklin G. Burroughs and Simeon B.
Chapin Art Museum
3200 S. Kings Hwy., Myrtle Beach
• **(843) 238-2510**

The Franklin G. Burroughs and Simeon B. Chapin Art Museum, a former two-story Spring-maid Beach home donated by Cox Construction Co., is Horry County's first art museum. "A New Home for the Visual Arts" unveiled in June of 1997, the museum features an art gallery, a gift shop, and an art education center.

The art gallery building is housed in the former Springmaid Villa, a 1920s beach house that was saved from demolition. Renovations created 10 galleries with a total 3,600 square feet of exhibition space, a tea room and a large seminar room. Exhibits in the gallery showcase local and regional artists and national art exhibits. The permanent exhibit is the Waccamaw Arts and Craft Guild Purchase Award Collection 1970-1983.

The new art education center building, which is attached to the art gallery building, provides ample space for an art library, studio classrooms, a gift shop and storage space for the museum collection. Recent activities have included corporate functions, watercolor classes and a Christmas ornament-making class.

INSIDERS' TIP
Be sure to give your age when you make reservations for shows. Many area theatres offer student and senior discounts.

Admission is $4 for adults, $3 for students and $2 for children under 12. The hours are Tuesday through Saturday 10 AM to 4 PM and on Sunday, 1 to 4 PM.

VIVACE!
• **(843) 248-7200, (800) 868-2787**

This 10-day fine-arts festival in mid-October began in 1996 and delivered a lineup of vocal, theatrical, instrumental, visual and literary arts groups. Sponsored by the HCAC, the festival includes activities all over the Strand. Knockout performances included Double Exposure, a piano and violin duo featuring Jamaican pianist/composer Eleanor Alberga and British violinist Thomas Bowes; the comic opera *Don Pasquale* (in English), featuring Josef Gustern and Melody Johnson from Broadway's *Phantom of the Opera*; The Long Bay Symphony's *American Delight*, a tribute to American composers; *Sounds for the Soul* by the Coastal Carolina University Gospel Choir; a performance by internationally acclaimed organist Diane Bish; and a production of the Broadway musical *42nd Street*.

More interactive events included literary evenings, visual arts demonstrations and a gallery crawl along West Broadway in Myrtle Beach. VIVACE! highlights just for children showcased the senior members of The Strand Ballet Theater presenting *The Enchanted Toy Shop* and *Soirees, Matinees & Musicales*, a morning with noted storyteller Suzette Hawkins and a participation play *The Mirrorman*. Ticket prices range from free to $3 to $30 each.

Parks and Recreation

There is no debate about it: Some of the most abundant natural beauty in all the world is right here along the Grand Strand. And thanks to the Work Projects Administration (WPA) and the Civilian Conservation Corps (CCC)—federal agencies that were created as part of President Franklin Delano Roosevelt's New Deal program, which was enacted during the Great Depression to create employment by establishing and building parks— these natural resources are preserved today in their original splendor, even surviving hurricanes and booms of real estate development.

During the summertime, sunshine is hot and plentiful in the Carolina-blue sky. The water is cool and equally plentiful. Autumn is brilliant . . . crisp mornings and breezy afternoons are perfect for beach walks and surf fishing. Winter comes in bite-size pieces: a string of brisk, snappy days, with long warm stretches in between. And when spring quickly arrives bearing wisteria, daffodils and bright-faced college kids, it's hard to believe another year has passed. This deliciously temperate climate enables tourists and residents to enjoy the great outdoors for most of the year. So, head for the parks and take advantage of our enviable climate. While you're here, choose from the myriad parks; this overview should set you in a direction that's perfect for you.

If you're looking for something a little more strenuous than stretching your legs, look to the Recreation portion of this chapter for an exhausting array of physically active ways to stay busy. Whether you enjoy biking, beach volleyball or working out at fitness clubs, you'll find a recreational outlet for any age and fitness level. And we do mean any age. One of the

Protected dunes forming on the beach.

Photo: Lisa Tomer Rentz

biggest annual events along the Grand Strand is the Senior Games, sponsored and coordinated by the Myrtle Beach Recreation Department and held each April (see our Annual Events chapter). Participants must be 50 or older. Watching the Senior Games marathon run gives you a whole different perspective on what the word "older" means. Many people half the age of these senior runners would have a difficult time keeping up.

We've also included a Spectator Sports section for those times when you want to sit in the bleachers and root for the home team.

Parks

State Parks

Myrtle Beach

Myrtle Beach State Park
U.S. Hwy. 17 S.,
between Myrtle and Surfside Beaches
• (843) 238-5325

Situated in the heart of the Grand Strand, Myrtle Beach State Park boasts one of the most popular public beaches along the Carolina coast. This 312-acre oceanfront park is one of the last remaining natural areas along the northern shores of South Carolina. Natural beauty reigns here and gives visitors a glimpse of the way the entire Strand looked long ago before its development as a glittery resort mecca.

Myrtle Beach State Park was developed by the Civilian Conservation Corps. During World War II, the U.S. military took over the park as a coastal defense staging area. In March 1945, the park was returned to the citizens of the state. It was the first state park opened to the public in South Carolina, and it also holds the distinction of having the first campground and fishing pier on the Grand Strand.

Park facilities include 350 camping sites, rented on a first-come, first-served basis; 40 additional sites are available by reservation up to 14 days in advance. (See our Accommodations chapter.) The park also offers five cabins, two apartments and picnic areas with shelters. In addition to the 730-foot pier, there's a nature trail and nature center. A park naturalist conducts activities year round and interprets the natural history of the coast. Surf fishing and pier fishing are allowed. Swimmers can splash about in the ocean or in the park's pool. The park also provides a snack bar and playground equipment.

Park hours are 6 AM to 10 PM year round. Office hours are 8 AM to 5 PM daily. In summer, admission to the park is $3 per carload.

South Strand

Huntington Beach State Park
U.S. Hwy. 17 S. (across from
Brookgreen Gardens), Murrells Inlet
• (843) 237-4440

Huntington Beach State Park, worth a visit even if you see nothing else on the Strand, offers the best-preserved beach on the Grand Strand and one of the best we have seen anywhere in the world. Observe the diverse coastal environment at the freshwater lagoon, salt marsh, nature trail and along the wide, beautiful beach.

The park is also the site of the imposing Spanish-style castle Atalaya, the former winter home and studio of American sculptress Anna Hyatt Huntington. Mrs. Huntington and her husband, Archer, were the visionary founders of Brookgreen Gardens. Seasonal tours of Atalaya are available.

Park facilities include about 186 camping sites, picnic areas with shelters, a boardwalk and a general store. Activities such as surf fishing, swimming and crabbing are encouraged, and the park offers one of the finest bird-watching sites on the East Coast. Nature programs and playground equipment are available for the young and young-at-heart. Atalaya Arts & Crafts Festival, a prestigious juried arts-and-crafts show, attracts thousands of visitors to the park every fall (see our Annual Events chapter for details).

Park hours are 6 AM to 10 PM daily from April through September and 6 AM to 6 PM daily from October through March. Office hours are 9 AM to 5 PM Monday through Friday and 11 AM to noon on Saturday and Sunday year round. Admission to the park is $4 for adults, $2 for kids under 12 and free for children under 6.

Hampton Plantation State Park
1950 Rutledge Rd., McClellanville
• (843) 546-9361

Southwest of Georgetown, Hampton Plantation is not technically a part of the stretch of real estate we call the Grand Strand. However, Hampton offers a peek at one of the most impressive restored plantation homes in South Carolina and, therefore, is well worth the short drive.

Adjacent to the Santee River, this 322-acre property was once a coastal rice plantation and

Chapin Memorial Park is an oasis of green in the center of Myrtle Beach.

Photo: Lisa Tomer Rentz

last served as the home of Archibald Rutledge, noted writer and South Carolina poet laureate. The state purchased the property from Mr. Rutledge in 1971.

A National Historic Landmark, the Hampton mansion stands as the centerpiece of the park and is a monument to the state's glorious rice empire. The mansion's colossal Adam-style portico is one of the finest and earliest examples of its kind in all of North America, while its interior—purposely unfurnished—highlights the structure's design and construction. Cutaway sections of walls and ceilings exhibit the building's evolution from a simple farmhouse to a grand mansion. Exposed timber framing, hand-carved mantels and delicately wrought hinges and hardware reveal the 18th-century builder's craft.

The grounds surrounding the mansion offer a unique opportunity to examine the wildlife of the Carolina Lowcountry. Cypress swamps, abandoned rice fields and pine and hardwood forests are home to a staggering variety of flora and fauna. From the massive live oaks to the wildflowers and shrubs, Hampton Plantation is a naturalist's and photographer's delight in every season.

In addition to the beautiful home, the park includes a picnic area and marked nature trails.

The park is open year round from 9 AM to 6 PM Thursday through Monday, and office hours are 11 AM to noon Thursday through Monday. The mansion is also open year round from 1 to 4 PM Thursday through Monday. Admission to the grounds is free of charge. Mansion tours cost $2 for adults and teens and $1 for kids 12 and younger.

City Parks

City parks pepper the Strand and are perfect for a little rest and relaxation. Several parks provide playground equipment, basketball courts, and running tracks for your use and enjoyment; others offer serene picnic areas complete with tables and restrooms.

North Strand

For more information about the parks in North Myrtle Beach, call the recreation department at (843) 280-5570. There is no admission fee and the city parks are open 24 hours.

Central Park
1030 Possum Trot Rd., North Myrtle Beach

This park is a kind of athlete's track and field course. It features four tennis courts, four baseball/softball fields, a soccer field, a quarter-mile running track, a paved basketball court, two playground areas and a picnic area.

Hill Street Park
Hill St., North Myrtle Beach

The 1-acre spread showcases what might be the North Strand's best lighted tennis court and a complex of playground equipment in addition to the standard swings.

McLean Park
Second Ave. S., North Myrtle Beach

McLean Park is a couple of blocks from the ocean and is sometimes used for outdoor concerts, Easter egg hunts, and small local festivals. In addition to two tennis courts, a paved basketball court, and playground equipment, the park also features a picnic area, a small lake, and a baseball field. Restroom facilities are available as well.

Oceanfront Park
First Avenue S. and S. Ocean Blvd., North Myrtle Beach

This cartoon-colored park serves as a convenient ingress and egress to the beach in the Ocean Drive section of North Myrtle Beach. Matching the pavement of nearby Main Street, the small park is constructed of brightly tinted concrete; the restroom facilities and concession stand are in a modern art-deco style suited to the beach, accented with palm trees, of course. The delightful design won national recognition from the National Recreation and Park Society in 1989. Amenities also include beach wheelchairs, boardwalks onto the sand, a parking lot and an outdoor shower. The concession stand is only open in the summer from 9 AM to 5 PM and the restrooms are locked for the night at 9 PM and "when it gets cold," explained city maintenance.

Yow Park
Windy Hill Rd., North Myrtle Beach

This quaint neighborhood park features a basketball court, playground, picnic area, restroom facilities and a charming decorative archway made from branches. The parking lot for this park is hidden; drive around the corner to Eyerly Road then walk through the archway and trees to get to the playground.

Myrtle Beach

For more information about the parks in Myrtle Beach, call the recreation department at (843) 918-1188. There is no admission fee, and the city parks are open 24 hours.

Chapin Park
16th Ave. N. and Kings Hwy., Myrtle Beach

In the very hub of downtown traffic, everybody's favorite park offers an unbelievably tranquil setting featuring a beautiful arbor area, picnic tables and garden swings. Local business folk seeking to escape the rat race frequent the calm of Chapin during lunch, especially in the spring and fall. The swings are ideal for reading the paper, eating a homemade sandwich, or simply for taking in the sights that surround you.

Political candidates, outdoor festivals, and a host of city functions favor the atmosphere and location of Chapin Park. Weekends bring a variety of activities including art shows, outdoor concerts and small festivals. Also, more than a few couples have exchanged wedding vows in the two-story gazebo that sits in the heart of this pretty green space. The playground, favored by local parents, features wooden equipment and lots of sand.

Hurl Rock Park
20th Ave. S. and Ocean Blvd., Myrtle Beach

Wooden decks create a lovely trail through Hurl Rock Park, which features a spectacular view of the beach. This park is great for photo opportunities, hand-holding and people watching.

Midway Park
19th Ave. S. and Kings Hwy., Myrtle Beach

Tennis is the name of the game at Midway, with six lighted courts. But that's not all. You'll also find a lighted basketball court here complete with two goals as well as a rest area and bathroom facilities.

South Strand

For more information about the parks in the South Strand, call the recreation department at (843) 650-4131. There is no admission fee and the city parks are open 24 hours.

> ## INSIDERS' TIP
> Murrells Inlet is a small and scenic section of the South Strand crowded with big trees, marsh grasses, and restaurants. As you drive through on U.S. Business 17, keep an eye out for a few "parks." Since the inlets and the salt marsh take up most of Murrells Inlet, the city has provided a few spots immediately along the road to invite you to stretch your legs, watch the beautiful egrets and smell all that good seafood cooking.

PARKS AND RECREATION

Fuller Park
Surfside and Myrtle Drs., Surfside Beach

Fuller Park is an ideal family destination, with two lighted tennis courts, two basketball courts, a playground and a picnic area with bathroom facilities. The Horry County Memorial Library is immediately adjacent, so make time to stop there too.

W.O. (Bill) Martin Park
Lakeside Dr. and Eighth Ave. S., Surfside Beach

A great place for a family reunion, the W.O. (Bill) Martin Park—formerly Lakeside Park—features a large picnic area and the Floral Clubhouse that can be rented by contacting the Town of Surfside Recreation Department, (843) 650-4131. A large, open area adjacent to the park is perfect for Frisbee tossing, kite flying and informal baseball and football games.

All Children's Park
10th Ave. S. and Hollywood Dr., Surfside Beach

This innovative playground, designed and equipped to accommodate both able-bodied and handicapped children—hence its name—has set a nationwide example.

All Children's Park features "standard" equipment modified to suit the singular needs of challenged youngsters—without separating them from their peers. Specially designed equipment includes a slide with tiered ramp along its side, mesh-net swings and an elevated tic-tac-toe board and sandbox. A landscaped, shaded area with picnic tables and an adult swing adjoins the park.

Residential Parks

The following parks are public residential facilities maintained by the City of Myrtle Beach.

Carefully manicured landscapes and multicolored blooms create a delightful series of green sanctuaries—retreats from the hustle and bustle of resort living. Read a book; take a nap; ponder the mysteries of life. For more information, call (843) 918-2280.

Pinner Place Park is at Pinner Place and

Pridgen Road. You'll find Withers Park at Second Avenue S. and Myrtle Street. Loblolly Park is on Loblolly Circle in the prestigious Dunes section. A personal favorite, Gray Park is a pretty little space on 45th Avenue N. and Burchap Drive. Memorial Park, at Porcher Avenue and Haskell Circle, is a gem. Right around the corner, McMillan Park is on Haskell Circle and Ocean Boulevard. Another Boulevard park is Cameron Park at 28th Avenue N. You'll find Springs Park at Springs Avenue and Hampton Circle, and McLeod Park is on 61st Avenue N.

Recreation

Myrtle Beach offers visitors opportunities to participate in lots of healthy sports such as bicycling, kayaking and beach volleyball as well as "thrill sports" such as parasailing, bungee jumping and sky diving. Health and fitness clubs abound; recreation centers and leagues provide organized activities for kids and adults alike. Of course, you'll find plenty of tennis and golf opportunities at nearly every turn as well. Golf is so popular, in fact, we've devoted an entire chapter to it in lieu of discussing it here.

Beach Volleyball

Setting and spiking on the inviting sands of the beach is a favored activity during the summer season. The level of competition ranges from that found at family picnics to competitive tournaments with skilled professionals.

In the summertime, pickup games abound all along the beach from Surfside to North Myrtle. Public volleyball nets in Myrtle Beach are set up at Downwind Sails, 29th Avenue S. (adjacent to Damon's restaurant), and at Kingston Plantation (see our Accommodations chapter), located on the beach near Restaurant Row.

Biking

Bicycle paths in Myrtle Beach are clearly marked along the beach and Ocean Boulevard, and the residential area north of 54th Avenue N. features an outdoor fitness trail with exer-

INSIDERS' TIP

Skateboarding and in-line skating are prohibited in downtown Myrtle Beach, where the prime flat property is full of railings and curbs to hop but also, unfortunately, lots of people on the sidewalks to avoid. The city has come up with a solution: a skate park. The city built the park for the many enthusiasts the sport is attracting. It's built behind the Pepper Geddings Recreation Center, (843) 918-2280, and has all sorts of demanding obstacles and ramps for skaters and, of course, no pedestrians.

PARKS AND RECREATION

cise equipment along the beach. Bicycles and adult-size, laid-back tricycles can be rented from a variety of locations along the beach including the following vendors.

North Myrtle Beach

The Bike Doctor
800 Sea Mountain Hwy.,
North Myrtle Beach
• (843) 249-8152

This shop is a full-service and fully stocked bicycle outlet, just two blocks from the beach. Parking is provided, so you can leave your car and ride your new or rented bike. Rentals include beach cruisers, standard two-wheel bikes, three-wheelers, "funcycles," tandems and four-wheel, four-passenger bikes. Fees start at $4 per hour per bike. Gear such as helmets and pads is not included in the rental rate.

The Bike Doctor is in seven days a week from 9:30 AM to 6 PM.

Myrtle Beach

Bicycles-N-Gear
515 U.S. Hwy. 501, Myrtle Beach
• (843) 626-2453

Beach-cruiser bikes can be rented for $10 a day and you can rent in-line skates from this store for $15 per day. Both rentals include helmets and protective gear.

This bike outfitter is open every day from 9 AM to 9 PM.

The Bike Shop
715 Broadway, Myrtle Beach
• (843) 448-5335

Open 8 AM to 6 PM Monday through Saturday, The Bike Shop loans customers complimentary helmets, locks and baskets with every rental. Beach cruisers cost $5 for a half-day rental and $10 for the whole day, and a whole day of mountain biking is $15.

Fitness Clubs

Fitness is a thriving industry along the Grand Strand, which probably stands to reason if you take into consideration the premium locally on firm bodies, male and female.

All of the area's gyms and fitness clubs welcome visitors at any time of the year. It's not unusual to see packed aerobic classes during peak tourist times when visitors pop in to get their exercise high while on vacation. That most of these clubs are so affordable might pleasantly surprise you. To join an aerobics class for an hour or so, rates usually run $4 to $6. Annual memberships to fitness centers average $35 to $60 per month, although some might charge an up-front initiation fee.

North Strand

The Little River Swim & Fitness Club
103 U.S. Hwy. 17 S., Little River
• (843) 399-2582

Little River has lined up a gamut of programs from step aerobics to karate. The Next Generation Nautilus machines fill the weight room, along with treadmills, steppers, a Skywalker, Lifecycles and recumbent bikes. To accommodate the wetter side of a workout, Little River has indoor and outdoor pools (aqua-aerobics classes are available), a whirlpool, steam room and sauna. If your workout leaves your muscles sore, massage therapy is available. Little River also holds certified arthritis-therapy classes.

Little River is open Monday through Friday from 6 AM to 10 PM, Saturday from 8 AM to 6 PM and Sunday from 1 to 5 PM. The club offers a variety of rates and fees.

Myrtle Beach

American Health and Racquet
S.C. Hwy. 544 (Socastee area),
Myrtle Beach
• (843) 650-0271

This 20,000-square-foot club keeps expanding and seems to answer just about any fitness need you might have. Here you'll discover a fully equipped weight room, private aerobics studio, two racquetball courts, an indoor swimming pool, dry-heat saunas plus a juice bar and nutrition center. Aerobics classes in water or on the floor and Spinning run from 6 in the morning to 7 in the evening each day. American Health and Racquet is open Monday through Friday from 6 AM to 9 PM, Saturday from 9 AM to 7 PM and Sunday from 1 to 7 PM.

Gold's Gym
951 Jason Blvd. (10th Ave. N. and
U.S. Hwy. 17 Bypass), Myrtle Beach
• (843) 448-3939

Probably the longest-standing fitness outlet in the area, Gold's has been locally owned and operated by Ted and Nancy Capp since 1982.

This is a venue for serious workouts as evidenced by folks Olympic and power lifting in the weight room, where many competitive body builders come to pump up and shape their muscles. Besides free weights, complete

StairMaster and BodyMaster systems are available. Warm up on treadmills, bikes, steppers or a stair climber. The gym also has a full aerobics schedule and a boxing class. Operating schedules change seasonally, as do rates; but for the most part, Gold's is open from 6 AM to about 9 PM Monday through Thursday, Friday from 6 AM to 7 PM, Saturday from 7 AM to 7 PM and Sunday from 4 to 7 PM.

Ocean Dunes/Sand Dunes Fitness Center
74th Ave. N. (on the oceanfront), Myrtle Beach
• **(843) 449-7441**

As you might guess from its name and address, this health club is housed in one of the Grand Strand's largest oceanview resort properties. Ocean Dunes is open seven days a week from 6 AM to 9 PM, with the pool staying open until 10 PM.

There are no aerobic classes offered here, but a fully equipped workout room sports Nautilus, treadmills, Lifecycles and Universal bikes, stair climbers, rowing machines and a heated indoor pool. To wind down apres workout, Ocean Dunes has three Jacuzzis, a steam room and dry sauna. Call ahead for rates; daily, weekly, monthly and yearly memberships are available.

Sweat Express
Village Square Shopping Center, 38th Ave. N., Myrtle Beach
• **(843) 946-0073**

Sweat Express opened during the summer of 1995, introducing a new concept to the area: the workout studio. There are no amenities attached to the Express; you go there to work out for an hour, choosing from a great variety of aerobics classes. A professional sound system pumps out high-energy tunes for all the sessions, whether it's power step, Circuit Challenge or The Bottom Line. Classes are led by licensed instructors, cost $4 each or $30 per month and, above all, are fun. No membership is required.

Sweat Express has six instructors who maintain a busy schedule; the first class starts at 9 AM; the last, at 6:30 PM. Phone ahead for the complete daily lineup.

The Sport & Health Club at Kingston Plantation
9760 Kings Rd., Myrtle Beach
• **(843) 497-2444**

This $4-million facility is perhaps the prettiest club along the Grand Strand, nestled amid the beautiful setting of Kingston Plantation. It has a complete cardiovascular center with Life Fitness Circuit (a computerized system) equipment for strength training. Aerobics and "aquacise" programs are scheduled daily.

On the grounds you'll find clay and hard-surface tennis courts as well as racquetball and volleyball courts. Other features of this club include indoor and outdoor pools, a whirlpool, sauna, tanning beds and massage therapy. The Sport & Health Club is open from 6:30 AM to 10 PM Monday through Thursday, 6:30 AM to 9 PM on Friday, 7:30 AM to 9 PM on Saturday and 7:30 AM to 6 PM on Sunday.

Fitness One-On-One
Galleria Shopping Center, 9600 N. Kings Hwy., Myrtle Beach
• **(843) 449-6486**

Whether you're a neophyte or seasoned in bodybuilding regimes, and no matter what your age, Fitness One-On-One promises to take you to the height of your fitness potential. This is the only one-on-one, personalized-training facility on the Grand Strand. All individually tailored programs combine a personal workout plan with nutrition advice, cardiovascular exercise and weight training. Owner Herb MacDonald offers clients weight-loss programs, body toning, beginner and advanced bodybuilding and spot training. And, to make sure you're feeling and looking your best, One-On-One offers massage therapy and tanning facilities.

South Strand

Grand Strand Fitness & Racquet
671 JamesTowne Dr., Garden City Beach
• **(843) 651-8428**

Grand Strand boasts a complete Life Fitness cardiovascular-conditioning system that incorporates treadmills, bikes, life steppers and rowers. You can pump it up with weight-training machines or free weights and dumbbells. The fitness center is open Monday through Thursday from 6 AM to 10 PM; Friday from 6 AM to 8 PM; Saturday, 7 AM to 7 PM; and Sunday, 1 to 6 PM.

The club has four racquetball courts and volleyball under its roof plus a large aerobics studio with a custom-built floor to reduce impact. Aerobics classes use steps, slides and weights in the programs and are offered every day of the week. The aerobics sessions are scheduled at various times between 7:30 AM and 6:30 PM. For beginners, Grand Strand can help you determine your initial fitness level with body-composition and pre-exercise analyses. Personalized training is also an option here.

Amenities include steam rooms and

Oceanfront Park on Ocean Drive offers beautiful ocean front vistas.

Photo: Lisa Tomer Rentz

Jacuzzis, supervised child care, tanning beds and a video security system in the parking lot. Membership rates are just too complicated to list here; Grand Strand Fitness has a roster of different membership packages, depending on what part of the facility you want to use. It's best to call ahead or drop by.

Plantation Resort
Health & Swim Club
1250 U.S. Hwy. 17 N., Surfside Beach
• (843) 238-4885

This fitness club is as comprehensive as it gets—even offering programs for those who suffer from arthritis. It's no surprise that Plantation Resort has a full Aqua Aerobics program, as the club sports a 70-foot-long heated pool and giant whirlpool. Amenities include men's and women's saunas and steam rooms, a children's playground, a fully equipped weight room and an aerobic space with Exerflex floor, where aerobics, yoga and karate classes are held.

Plantation Resort is open 6 AM to 10 PM Monday through Friday, 7:30 AM to 10 PM on Saturday and 9:30 AM to 10 PM on Sunday. Membership fees vary, based on particular programs or full use of club facilities.

Horseback Riding

Horseback riding is another popular pastime, but not many Grand Strand stables have horses for rent. Please note: Horses are prohibited from the beach during the busy summer tourist season. See our Beach Information chapter for details.

Best View Farm
6129 Best Western Tr., Myrtle Beach
• (843) 650-7522

Just call and ask for Caroline; she'll set up boarding, riding lessons or a ride. Best Western Ranch is nestled on 45 densely wooded acres, and Caroline revels in taking guests on a guided trail ride. The one-hour ride costs $25 a person. Full-service boarding is available for $250 a month.

Peachtree Farms
N.C. Hwy. 57 (just off U.S. 17),
Calabash, N.C.
• (910) 287-4790

Peachtree Farms is strictly a riding stable; boarding is not available. One-hour trail rides can be booked for $30 per person. The hour-long beach ride takes you to a private, sandy island for $50 per person. Call Gloria or any of her staff to reserve a horse. (See our Kidstuff chapter for additional information.)

Kayaking

Kayaking has grown in popularity, both along the beach and in local rivers and swamps.

The following places (see our Watersports chapter for details) are worth investigating if you're interested in this up-and-coming sport.

Myrtle Beach

Sailing & Ski Connection
515 U.S. Hwy. 501, Myrtle Beach
• (843) 626-SAIL

This outfitter bills its kayak tours as "the adventure of a lifetime." New tours are scheduled weekly, and some are customized to suit group interest. Safety is a top priority: Complete supervision is provided (if desired), and the rules of boating are stressed every step of the way. See the entry in our Watersports chapter for rates and schedules.

Downwind Sails
29th Ave. S.,
Myrtle Beach
• (843) 448-7245

Downwind Sails rents ocean kayaks for fun and frolic in the surf. This shop is open between April and September. Rates vary with the time of year and availability of equipment. See the entry in our Watersports chapter for details.

South Strand

Black River Expeditions
U.S. Hwy. 701,
Georgetown
• (843) 546-4840

Black River Expeditions offers half-, full- and multi-day tours on the area's abundant marshes, rivers, and creeks. Explore the aptly named waters of the Black River, the tidal creeks leading to the secluded beaches of Huntington Beach State Park and the deserted and mysterious Drunken Jack Island—reputed to hold treasures of the pirate Blackbeard. See the entry in our Watersports chapter for details.

Miniature Golf

Serious golfers, forget about tee times, golf cart fees and buckets of lost balls! By playing any one of dozens of miniature golf courses along the Grand Strand, you can enjoy spirited competition with the kids (your own as well

as those you might wander upon) and the joy of sinking a hole-in-one—without breaking the budget. Actually, miniature golf might be even more challenging than a professional course. After all, how many long-necked llamas, bearded pirates or spooky caves have you tripped over on a fairway lately?

Several miniature courses are part of amusement parks as complete properties. Most courses are open from 9 AM to midnight and have snack bars or cold drink machines. Admission ranges from $2 to $8 per putter. Special prices are offered for all-day play, which means you can play for a while and then come back later to play some more.

INSIDERS' TIP

Myrtle Beach and North Myrtle Beach both have a beach-going wheelchair program to ensure that wheelchair-bound people get to enjoy the ocean too. There is no charge, but there is a time limit of one hour to ensure that everybody gets a turn. The wheelchairs are sturdy, have large balloon tires that allow the chair to be pushed through the soft sand and come quipped with umbrellas. Beach-going wheelchairs and handicapped parking are available at the following locations: First Avenue S., North Myrtle Beach, and in Myrtle Beach at 77th Avenue N., 72nd Avenue N., 54th Avenue N., 24th Avenue N., 5th Avenue N., 8th Avenue N. and 8th Avenue S.

North Strand

Hawaiian Rumble
Miniature Golf
33rd Ave. S.,
U.S. Hwy. 17,
North Myrtle Beach
• (843) 272-7812

Ranked by *GOLF Magazine* as the No. 1 miniature golf course in the United States, Hawaiian Rumble offers a challenging gambit of shots in a lush and expertly landscaped setting of tropical palms, hibiscus and other plants. The course circles and climbs up around a rumbling volcano, leis in almost every color are handed out to the players, and gentle Hawaiian music plays in the background. Hawaiian Rumble also sponsors the Masters Putting Championship, with a purse of $20,000—definitely worth a shot!

Mayday Miniature Golf
U.S. Hwy. 17, North Myrtle Beach
• (843) 280-3535

Two 18-hole courses make up this extravaganza. The centerpiece of the course is an actual plane crash-landed in the jungle. It is your mission to herd your ball around the 18-hole Mayday Mountain Course and then, if you have the fortitude, escape the thundering waterfall and wild animal calls of the Roaring River Falls Course. The Roaring River course features 18 holes, is handicapped-accessible and uses premium putting carpet that's as fast as a pool table, the owners claim. Mayday does have all-day play until 5 PM.

Myrtle Beach

Captain Hook's Adventure Golf
2205 N. Kings Hwy., Myrtle Beach
• **(843) 626-1430**
Marked by a haunting Skull Cave, water-falls, lagoons and swinging bridges, this 36-hole course is one of the newest additions to the area's minigolf lineup. Players can choose the Lost Boys' Course or the more challenging Hook's Course, which has uphill shots and includes water holes and sand traps.

Dragon's Lair Fantasy Golf
Broadway at the Beach,
1197 Celebrity Cir., Myrtle Beach
• **(843) 444-3215**
A favorite attraction at the huge Broadway at the Beach complex is the fire-breathing volcanic mountain for you to putt around, through and inside. You'll also putt over water, through castle doors and up hills. This huge multi-course indoor complex is touted by its owners as employing cutting-edge minigolf technology. Whether or not this is true, we can assure you that it is the only miniature complex amid the shopping, theater and dining action of the Broadway at the Beach complex.

Jungle Lagoon
Fifth Ave. S. and Kings Hwy., Myrtle Beach
• **(843) 626-7894**
In this tropical jungle setting you might wish you had a machete instead of a putter. You'll have to contend with lots of uphill shots, fast downhill curves and angles on both courses (18 holes each). Special rates are offered for children 5 and younger. All-day play is available.

Jurassic Golf
29th Ave. S. and Kings Hwy., Myrtle Beach
• **(843) 448-2116**
You guessed it—ferocious dinosaurs threaten your score. Choose from two 18-hole courses. Discounts are offered to children 5 and younger. All-day play ends at 5 PM.

Pirates Watch
1500 S. Kings Hwy., Myrtle Beach
• **(843) 448-8600**
Enjoy 36 holes brimming with action-packed waterfalls, daunting pirates, water traps and lagoons. All-day play is offered until 5 PM, 9 PM in fall.

Rainbow Falls
Restaurant Row,
9850 U.S. Hwy. 17, Myrtle Beach
• **(843) 497-2557**
Tricky corners, animal caves and fairy-tale castles make up 36 holes of these two courses. One or two uphill holes could throw your game. Special rates are offered to groups and children 4 and younger. All-day play is available until 5 in the evening.

SpyGlass
3800 N. Kings Hwy., Myrtle Beach
• **(843) 626-9309**
This 18-hole course has a fun degree of difficulty and offers discounts to senior citizens, children and groups. Waterfalls, uphill holes and those bloody pirates are the main obstacles. All-day play ends at 6 PM.

Treasure Island
48th Ave. N., Myrtle Beach
• **(843) 449-4754**
A hole-in-one is not easy to come by on this 18-hole course, but the play at Treasure Island is definitely worth the challenge. Discounts are available for senior citizens, children and groups. All-day play ends at 6 PM.

South Strand

Adventure Falls
735 U.S. Hwy. 17, Surfside Beach
• **(843) 238-0168**
Animals and castles overlook the 36 holes of two courses. Groups and children are offered discounts, and all-day play ends at 5 PM.

Buccaneer Bay
6001 U.S. Hwy. 17 S., Surfside Beach
• **(843) 238-3811**
Two courses filled with pirates and big boats—36 holes between them—will make you ache to walk the plank. Several holes feature difficult angles and tricky obstacles. All-day play ends at 5 PM.

Parasailing

Parasailing has become a popular activity along the beach. Participants wear a parachute and are pulled by a towrope behind a speed boat. The parachute fills with air and lifts the parasailor to heights around 300 feet. Parasailing adventures are offered through the following businesses: Wind N Sea Outfitters, 803 28th Avenue S., North Myrtle Beach, (843) 272-4420; Capt. Dick's Marina, 4123 U.S. Highway 17

Business, (843) 651-3676, Murrells Inlet; and Marlin Quay Marina, 1398 S. Waccamaw Drive, Garden City Beach, (843) 651-4444. See our Watersports chapter for more details on each establishment.

Recreation Centers/ Leagues

The recreation centers we've included in this section offer a smattering of leagues for kids. Call each respective center to find out about sign-up dates; parents often get upset if they miss a registration deadline.

North Strand

North Myrtle Beach Community Center
Possum Trot Rd., North Myrtle Beach
• **(843) 280-5570**

Serving the community for decades, the North Myrtle Beach Community Center offers four meeting rooms and a gymnasium/ auditorium. Activities include classes for the young and young-at-heart. Just a few of the offerings include arts and crafts, clogging, sign language, karate, drama and creative dance. Team sports include basketball, T-ball, softball, baseball and volleyball. Other activities offered at the center are aerobics, seniors' toning classes, introduction to bridge and bridge games. Nominal fees are set by each individual instructor or coach. You might pay $5 for a yoga class or $35 for six weeks of line-dancing.

The center is open Monday through Friday. Operating hours hinge on activities, so please call for details.

Myrtle Beach

Grand Strand YMCA
904 65th Ave. N., Myrtle Beach
• **(843) 449-9622**

Our local YMCA actively sponsors community events, many geared toward children. Kids enjoy T-ball, baseball, soccer and swim classes, after-school day care and day camps. Adults can enjoy coed volleyball, basketball, shag and ballroom dancing, softball and health enhancement workshops. The center features a Nautilus and free-weights center, a selection of cardiovascular equipment and aerobics classes. Fees are competitive, ranging from a $5 one-day fee to $186 per year for an adult, $120 per year for seniors and $264 per year for a family.

Pepper Geddings Recreation Center
3205 Oak St., Myrtle Beach
• **(843) 918-2280**

Otherwise known as the Frank M. Beckham Complex, Pepper Geddings Recreation Center is the most complete recreation center in the area. This facility features a 25-yard heated indoor swimming pool that is fully accessible to the physically challenged. Programs include American Red Cross swimming lessons for all ages and abilities, a variety of water-exercise programs and a swim team as well as lifeguard-certification and water-safety classes. You can pump up in the weight room with free weights and Nautilus equipment under the supervision of a professional trainer. Instructional classes include arts and crafts, a variety of dances such as ballroom, shag and tap, and bridge and other card games. The Parks and Recreation Department also offers after-school care and a summer day camp.

City-sponsored aerobics, swimming and team sports including basketball are coordinated through this center. In addition to meeting rooms and a game room, the complex is surrounded by softball, baseball and football fields, three lighted tennis courts and a picnic shelter with a grill and tables.

Fees for most classes are nominal, and annual passes for the weight room and swimming pool are available. The center is open six days a week: Monday through Thursday from 6 AM to 9 PM; Friday, 6 AM to 6:30 PM; and Saturday, 10 AM to 5 PM.

South Strand

Surfside Beach Recreation Department
H. Blue Huckabee Recreation Complex, Spanish Oak Dr. and Glenns Bay Rd., Surfside Beach
• **(843) 650-4131**
Dick M. Johnson Civic Center, Pine Dr., Surfside Beach
• **(843) 650-4131**

The Surfside Beach Recreation Department provides year-round recreational programs for all ages. Many of the sports activities are held at the H. Blue Huckabee complex, which boasts three ball fields. Instructional courses and seminars, held at the Johnson Civic Center, include arts and crafts, dance, aerobics and more. Special events include Easter egg hunts, Sun Fun Volleyball competitions (see our Annual Events chapter), an Old-fashioned Family Festival in October, a Christmas Tree Lighting Ceremony and a Santa Hotline.

PARKS AND RECREATION

*Professional baseball came to the Grand Strand with Coastal Federal Field and the Pelicans,
offering something fun to do away from the water.*

Photo: Robert Gurganies

Tennis

If spirited competition on the courts is what you love, you can slam an ace or volley for fun on any one of numerous tennis courts that span the length of the Grand Strand. We'll start with the freebies, available on a first-come, first-served (pardon the pun) basis. Pay-as-you-play courts require reservations, so call in advance.

North Strand

Central Park
1030 Possum Trot Rd.
(between 13th and 15th Aves. S.),
North Myrtle Beach
• (843) 280-5570
Central Park offers four outdoor, lighted asphalt courts. Lights-out is 11 PM.

Hill Street Park
Hill St. (off Sea Mountain Hwy.),
North Myrtle Beach
• (843) 280-5570
Be the first to grab the one lighted asphalt court. The lights go out at 11 PM.

McLean Park
First Ave. S., North Myrtle Beach
• (843) 280-5570
McLean offers two outdoor, lighted asphalt courts. Lights-out is 11 PM.

Ocean Creek Tennis Center
U.S. Hwy. 17 (Windy Hill section),
North Myrtle Beach
• (843) 272-7724 Ext. 1011
The center offers seven Tru-Flex courts, one practice court and two lighted courts at $12 per hour, per court. Lessons are available through the United States Professional Tennis Registry (USPTR).

Myrtle Beach

Kingston Plantation Sport
& Health Club
9760 Kings Rd., Myrtle Beach
• (843) 497-2444
Past host of the GTE Tennis Festival, which featured pro players such as Pete Sampras, Michael Chang, Andre Agassi and Jimmy Connors, this $4 million health club offers four outdoor clay courts and five Har-tru courts. All courts are lighted and the cost is $17.75 per hour.

During the late fall and winter months, people can frequently be seen riding horses on the beaches.

Photo: Virgil Graham

Myrtle Beach Public Courts
3200 Oak St., Myrtle Beach
• (843) 918-2280
U.S. Hwy. 17 and 20th Ave. S.,
Myrtle Beach
• No phone
The two outdoor, asphalt-surfaced courts on Oak Street are next door to the Myrtle Beach Recreation Center. Lights allow you to play all night; however, when the center closes at 9 PM, so do the restroom facilities.

The 20th Avenue S. complex has six lighted courts, along with restrooms and outdoor water fountains. All courts are asphalt-covered.

Myrtle Beach Tennis & Swim Club
U.S. Hwy. 17 Bypass (across from
Dixie Stampede), Myrtle Beach
• (843) 449-4486
Two of the 10 composition courts are

lighted. You can practice with the ball machines or at the free backboard area. Full-time tennis professionals offer adult and junior programs year round. Courts cost $15 per player per hour for singles and $5 per player per hour for doubles. A match setup service and racquet stringing are available. There's also a pro shop.

Pan-American Resort
5300 N. Ocean Blvd., Myrtle Beach
• (843) 449-7411

Guests of the Pan-American can play any of the three outdoor Cushion-tex courts for free. Others pay $8 per hour for singles or $10 per hour for doubles.

Prestwick Health & Tennis Club
1375 McMaster Dr., Myrtle Beach
• (843) 828-1000

Prestwick offers 11 clay courts, three lighted courts and two lighted hard-surface courts. Non-members pay $15 an hour per court. Private lessons are available for $40 an hour from the head pro. If you're really in top form—or want to get there—you can have a video tape made of your match, to see just what needs improvement.

South Strand

Litchfield Racquet Club
Hawthorn Dr., Litchfield Beach
• (843) 237-3411

The club maintains 17 Har-tru clay courts and one outdoor Rubico stadium court. Three lighted courts are available; hourly fees are $15, and instruction is available from two full-time professionals. Ball machines are also available. Litchfield also offers a year-round tennis school.

Surfside Beach Public Courts
Surfside Dr., Surfside Beach
• (843) 650-4131

All three of these outdoor lighted courts are treated with asphalt. Restroom facilities and water fountains are nearby.

Spectator Sports

Auto Racing

Myrtle Beach Speedway
4300 U.S. Hwy. 501, Myrtle Beach
• (843) 236-0500

Amateur and professional drivers thrill racing fans as the roar of engines ricochets off the asphalt of the Myrtle Beach Speedway. With each wave of the checkered flag, this spectator sport draws increasingly larger crowds.

Races are held on Saturday nights from March to September and feature four divisions: ministock, late-model stock, street stock and chargers.

The local racing season is highlighted by The Winston Racing Series and also includes the All-Pro, NASCAR Dash, Open Wheel Modified and Busch Grand National touring series.

The roots of stock-car racing in this area can be traced back more than three decades, when dirt tracks were carved out of remote forests near modern-day downtown. The present speedway facility was built in 1958 and was known as the Racing Association of Myrtle Beach Inc. (RAMBI) Raceway. At that time, racing fans were following the budding careers of Richard Petty, Ralph Earnhardt, Ned Jarrett and David Pearson. After a decade of dirt-track racing, the speedway was paved in 1969.

The popularity of auto racing fell during the '70s but produced a name to be reckoned with—Dale Earnhardt. In 1978, Earnhardt won the late-model sportsman championship at Myrtle Beach Speedway. A year later he joined the Winston Cup roster and won Rookie of the Year honors.

Since the mid-'80s, auto racing has gained momentum. It's not unusual that hot racers at Myrtle Beach Speedway become stars later.

Gates open at 4 PM, and drivers take practice laps before the green flag drops on the first of five heats at 7:30 PM.

Concession items are available including beer, soft drinks and snack food such as hot dogs, chips and candy. Spectators are permitted to bring small hand-held coolers.

Seating is stadium-style, so you might want to bring a blanket or a cushioned seat for comfort. Admission varies widely per race.

Baseball

Myrtle Beach Pelicans
Coastal Federal Field1251,
21st Avenue N. Myrtle Beach
• (843) 918-6000

The Pelicans are an Atlanta Braves Class-A affiliate, managed by Brian Snitker. Snitker was Atlanta Braves Minor Manager of the year in 1998 and has twenty-two years of experience with the Atlanta Braves.

The $12 million Coastal Federal Field provides a suitable nest for the Pelicans, and brings fans right into the fast paced action of the game while providing a load of amenities. There are

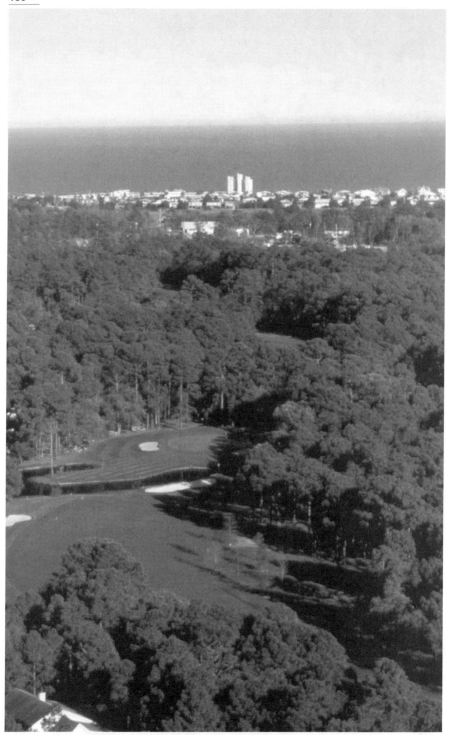

*From golf courses to shoreline to everything in between, you'll never suffer
from lack of things to do when you visit the Myrtle Beach Area.*

Photo: courtesy of the Litchfield Country Club

2,676 box seats, and 1,481 reserved seats, originally from Fulton county Stadium, former home of the Atlanta Braves. There are lounges, suites, patio boxes, picnic areas with views of the field, and a handicap-accessible children's playground. Parking is free. Specials, such as dollar drafts, are often announced, and entertainment such as the "Steel In Time" steel drum band plays during half time. Dinger the Home Run Dog also scores with some impressive maneuvers. Dinger, a sleek, yellow retriever, runs bases, shags fly balls and retrieves bats. And of course, hot dogs and popcorn, in addition to a few Myrtle Beach specialities, are available, with plenty of napkins on hand.

The Pelicans are part of the Carolina League, which over the past 54 years has turned out Muscle Shoals, Willie Duke, Woody Fair, Harvey Haddix, Crash Davis, Earl Weaver, Wade Boggs, Rod Carew, Dwight Evans and Barry Bonds.

The current Pelicans team is composed of professional athletes playing hard for the chance to wear the A and the tomahawk of the Atlanta Braves. Besides the players mentioned earlier, the roster of future all-stars includes outfielder Jayson Bass of Alabama; center Scott Bronowicz of Pennsylvania; right hand pitcher Jacob Shumate of Florence, South Carolina (just an hour and a half from the Strand) and center Steve Torrealba of Venezuela.

The home team has the advantage of a clubhouse designed to assist them in their strenuous struggle to the major leagues. To complement the Brave's modified strength and conditioning program, the workout room has Cybex weight equipment, a training room, whirlpools and batting cages.

Box seating is $7.50, reserved seating $6.50 and grass seating $3.00.

Coastal Carolina University Sports

Sports fans may be interested in checking out events at Coastal Carolina University, about 14 miles west of Myrtle Beach on U.S. Highway 501.

During the academic year, Coastal Carolina University fields men's and women's teams that compete in 15 sporting events, all of which are open to the general public at the campus. As members of the NCAA's Division I Big South Conference, the Chanticleers play soccer and tennis in autumn and spring, basketball and volleyball during the winter months and golf and baseball in spring. For specific details, the

sports section of *The Sun News* is a comprehensive resource. For complete schedules contact the athletic department at Coastal Carolina University, (843) 448-1481.

Coastal's latest athletic endeavor is women's cross-country running; in 1997 the women finished 24th in the nation after ranking 19th in the interim, which is the highest ranking ever of any team at Coastal. The team won three consecutive championships and five altogether in the 1997 conference, and finished second in the 1999 Big South Conference.

Coastal Carolina's men's basketball team won four Big South championships from 1987 to 1991 and advanced to the NCAA tournament in 1991 and 1993. The team plays in Kimbel Gymnasium, two blocks east of campus on an unnamed dead-end road between U.S. Highways 501 and 544. Tickets are $5 for adults and $3 for students.

The men's baseball team won five conference championships between 1986 and 1992, and won the 1999 Big South regular season. The collegiate baseball season lasts from mid-February to May, and the team plays at the Coastal Carolina Baseball Stadium. The event is free, but donations benefit the Coastal Carolina Baseball Scholarship Fund and the Tara Hall Home for Boys.

The men's tennis team won conference championships in 1988, 1989, 1993 and 1994.

The men's soccer team won five conference championships from 1986 to 1995 and has participated in two NCAA tournaments. The soccer season lasts from September to November.

The baseball, tennis and soccer venues are on the Coastal Carolina campus.

Golf

The Grand Strand has established itself as a veritable golfing mecca.

A number of golf tournaments are played around the Grand Strand, mostly for charity. The Omar Shrine Clowns "One Club" Golf Tournament tees off every February at Whispering Pines Golf Club; contact Bob Cape, (843) 650-2800. Myrtle Beach National golf course (see our Golf chapter) hosts the Retired Military Golf Classic every May; call Jerry Cox, (843) 448-2308. The Mark Sloan Memorial Golf Tournament is played in August at Myrtlewood Golf Club, (843) 626-3638. And the Charles Tilghman Junior Tournament is set for December at The Surf Club; call Bill Campbell, (843) 249-1524.

For more information on tournaments and myriad golfing opportunities—regulation, par 3 and mini-golf courses—see our Golf chapter.

Golf

"Fore."

"Five. Six. Seven. . . . " The old golf joke gets seriously out of hand on the Grand Strand, especially if you are counting golf courses instead of strokes. During the past 10 years, the course count has expanded to more than 100, stretching Myrtle Beach's tradition of summer vacationers into the spring and fall, when the climate in the Carolinas yields the most enjoyable temperatures for golfing.

In 1999 golfers played nearly 4.3 million rounds here, making the Myrtle Beach area the No. 2-ranked golf destination in America (behind Florida but ahead of Arizona). Though no one keeps a central count of how many actual golfers come here every year, it is projected—comparing those 4 million rounds with hotel occupancy figures—that approximately 1.4 million golfers come to the Grand Strand every year.

The average golfer comes to the Grand Strand with three other golfers, spends three days here and is a 39.8-year-old male with a household income of about $52,000. Golf has ranked as the No. 2 generator of tourism revenues here since 1996, pulling players primarily in spring and fall.

Yes, golf is a big deal here. It's so big, in fact, that golfing legend Gary Player has commented, "If you do not have a high-profile presence in Myrtle Beach, you are not considered a serious player in the golf industry."

For 2000, greens fees have risen a few dollars at almost every course. Most courses market either through hotel package deals or through an advertising co-op association; package deals usually include a welcome

Long Bay & Clubhouse—a Jack Nicklaus Signature Course—is ranked by Golf Digest as one of the "Top Ten Courses" in the entire state of South Carolina.

Photo: Michael Slear, courtesy of Brandon Advertising

gift, breakfast, greens fees and a cart. Recently, heavy discounts in the off-season (summer for golf) have begun to bleed over into the once-inflated fall fees.

Although the sheer abundance of courses is staggering, perhaps more impressive than the quantity is the quality. This 60-mile stretch of real estate boasts a collection of the country's finest course layouts. Creations of golf-great architects such as Jones, Player, Nicklaus, Fazio, Palmer, Maples and Dye, these courses offer a lot more than what you might expect—they're everything golf fantasies are made of.

Something you might not know about the Grand Strand is that the topography of our countryside is delightfully diverse. If you're a beach-goer, you might know and love our salt-scrubbed beaches, sandcastles, sailboats, sea oats and little else. But wander inland just a bit; you'll discover bountiful secrets in the corners of our counties. You'll find undulating river bluffs and panoramic river vistas, shadowy swamp lands, stately old oaks weeping silver moss, sandy pine forests and seemingly unchanging marshlands. The assortment of ecosystems continues to provide golf course architects with some of the richest natural resources in the world.

Mother Nature not only has given us an abundance of beautiful real estate, but also has blessed us with a subtropical climate that makes the outdoors pleasant almost every day of the year. Crisp days and aqua-blue skies make autumn and spring the favored seasons of many golfers. Still, lots of folks are learning the local secret that outrageous bargains abound during the summer and winter months. Since our weather is governed by cool Gulf Stream breezes when temperatures rise and warm Gulf Stream breezes when temperatures dip, golfing is a year-round delight.

Like everything else in our neck of the woods, golf offerings are eclectic, electric and just plain fun. Provocative and dazzling new courses flourish, along with the vintage, time-tested tracks graced with history and tradition. Pine Lakes International Country Club, a semiprivate layout designed by Robert White in 1927, launched golf's popularity in this area and today is appropriately known as "The Granddaddy." Myrtle Beach's highly regarded Dunes Golf and Beach Club, designed in 1948 by Robert Trent Jones, carried on the tradition. In decades following, a parade of splendid designs have come to maturation along the Strand. As the number of courses spirals well past 100, the area's reputation blossoms accordingly.

With so many courses, the Grand Strand is naturally host to many tournaments for any and every kind of golfer. One of the oldest and biggest golfing events along South Carolina's Grand Strand is the DuPont World Amateur Handicap Championship, billed as the world's largest onsite championship. Golf Digest dubbed the August event the "Everyman Open," and Golf World crowned it the "mother of all golf tournaments." Little wonder. Over the past 14 years, well more than 35,000 golfers from all over the world have participated in the four-day, matched handicap competition. In 2000 (a banner year) . . . participation was limited to 5,000. For information regarding participation, call (800) 833-8798.

The DuPont tournament is held at various courses, as are the tournaments hosted by Myrtle Beach Golf Holiday: the International Summer Family Golf Tournaments, the PING Myrtle Beach Junior Classic and the Annual Golf Writers Association of America Tournament.

Two organizations in the Grand Strand sort out and smooth out this universe of golf. Myrtle Beach Golf Holiday, founded in 1967, is a nonprofit association of accommodations and golf courses along "The Carolinas' Golden Golf Coast," from Georgetown, South Carolina, to Southport, North Carolina. The organization's mission is to increase consumer awareness of the advantages of a Myrtle Beach-area golf vacation and make it as easy as possible for a golfer to reserve accommodations of a preferred level of luxury or economy. Devised as an advertising co-op program and originally put together by the head of a local ad agency, the tax-exempt status of the organization has allowed hotels and golf courses to advertise at rates and in media that they could never initially afford; it is a brilliant promotional tool for Myrtle Beach golf.

Prospective vacationing golfers and travel agents can call (800) 845-4653 to receive a free vacation planner complete with golf package rates for 96 different accommodations, details on 87 golf courses, travel tips and information on how to directly book a golf vacation with a

INSIDERS' TIP

The LPGA, the oldest, longest-running women's sports association in the world, is celebrating its 50th anniversary in 2000. The LPGA tour in 2000 alone features 40 events, and total prize money in excess of $36.5 million. Throughout its history of tournaments, the LPGA has generated more than $110 million for charity.

GOLF

The ruins on the Love Course (designed by Davis Love III) at Barefoot Resort.

Photo: Michael Slear, courtesy of Brandon Advertising

member accommodation. There are also toll-free numbers to call from the UK, Finland, France, Germany, Ireland, Japan, The Netherlands, Norway, Sweden and Switzerland.

The Links Group represents 10 select golf courses: Burning Ridge East and West, Cypress Bay, Colonial Charters, Indigo Creek, Indian Wells, Island Green, Quail Creek, International Club, the Links at Lost Plantation and Sea Gull. Membership with the Links Group includes guest privileges and discount rates, VIP merchandise discount at clubs, advanced tee time privileges, member newsletter to keep you up to date, a centralized reservation and membership services, and member discounts at more than 15 sister courses throughout the eastern United States. The Group often offers specials on a weekly basis, such as multi-round discounts and summer passes. Additionally, the Links Group offers a Locals' Appreciation card. The Locals' card is $55 per year and admits card holders to member courses at less than $30 per round. Advance booking is limited according to various seasons. Another bonus is 10% off in the proshops. The Links Group seems to specialize in the esoteric ins-and-outs of the local golf scene, so please contact them at (843) 449-5665 and (800) 833-6337 for more information.

Service-oriented Myrtle Beach caters to a golfer's every need; there are also more than a dozen golf schools in town, many with PGA instructors, great student-teacher ratios and programs keyed to all levels of play. For a listing of these schools as well as more details on the entire golf scene, check out *The Insiders' Guide® to Golf in the Carolinas,* by far the best guide to Grand Strand golfing, available where you bought this guide and anywhere that quality books are sold.

For the inside scoop regarding golf on the Strand, refer to *The Sun News'* monthly magazine, *Myrtle Beach Golf.* You'll discover scads of interesting editorial, dining and entertainment tips, a directory of courses, maps and much more. A subscription costs $12 per 12 issues or $24 for 24 issues. Write Myrtle Beach Golf, P.O. Box 406, Myrtle Beach, SC 29578, or call (800) 568-1800, to start your subscription.

Tournaments

With so many courses, the Grand Strand naturally hosts many tournaments—local, national and international—for any and every kind of golfer, not just the pros. For instance, one of the oldest and biggest golfing events along South Carolina's Grand Strand, the DuPont World Amateur Handicap Championship (see subsequent entry), is billed as the world's largest on-site championship. The DuPont tournament is held at various courses as are the tournaments hosted by Myrtle Beach Golf Holiday: the International Summer Family Golf Tournaments, the PING Myrtle Beach Junior Classic and the Annual Golf Writers Association of America Tournament; call (800) 845-4653 for information about MBGH-hosted events.

Of course, many tournaments carry large cash purses, including sizable sums awarded to the winners. Spectators also win, as they are treated to some of the best golf played by some of the best golfers on the planet. But the real winners of all PGA (and Nike) tour events are charitable organizations. In 1997 the United Way of Horry County, Disabled American Veterans, Make-A-Wish Foundation, Mobile Meals in Myrtle Beach, Hook-A-Kid-On-Golf and the Elizabeth Chapin Patterson Community Assistance Center shared $200,000. In 1999 the SENIOR PGA TOUR tournaments combined raised a record $11,050,000 in charitable donations. This is the ninth time in the last 11 years that a record level has been achieved, and brings the SENIOR TOUR's all-time charity total to more than $74 million. Even if some of the best-played golf were not on display here, the best reasons for viewing it certainly are.

DuPont CoolMax World Amateur Handicap Championship
• (800) 833-8798

The venerable DuPont CoolMax World Amateur Handicap Championship, one of the oldest and biggest golfing events on the Strand, is billed as the world's largest on-site championship. *Golf Digest* magazine dubbed the August event the "Everyman Open," and *Golf World* magazine crowned it the "mother of all golf tournaments." Little wonder. During the past 14 years, well more than 35,000 golfers from all over the world have participated in the four-day, matched handicap competition. In 2000 (a banner year) participation was limited to 5,000.

Jimmy D'Angelo Senior Golf Classic
• (843) 236-8888, (800) 340-0072

Belle Terre hosts the Jimmy D'Angelo Senior Golf Classic for players who have reached their 50th birthday by November 4 of the present year. The entry fee is $150, which includes three rounds of golf, a luncheon, prizes and an awards banquet at the Dunes Club (see subsequent entry).

Grand Strand Golf Courses

With literally 100 courses on the Grand Strand, there are far and away too many for us to tell you about more than a fraction. Nonetheless, here's a representative assortment featuring different styles, prices and locales. You should also take into account that, for the full picture of Grand Strand golfing, we extend the Grand Strand beyond the state line to include the southern tip of North Carolina, as it touches the traditional Grand Strand. This "extension" of the Strand applies only to our look at golfing, and we do so because those North Carolina courses really are part of the local golfing community.

Area golf courses reserve the right to alter greens fees at any given time. It's almost a sure bet that rates will be higher from March 1 to May 1 and during September and October; these times of year feature prime golfing weather and golf course conditions. Morning greens fees are usually highest, with rates dropping beginning around noon and continuing to fall as the day gets warmer. To give you a proper perspective on greens fees on Grand Strand courses, we include the highest greens fees (including a cart unless otherwise noted) during peak season (March to May) for each entry. We also state each course's policy on walking.

Yardage from the men's white tees and par are provide in the course description. Remember, although there are oodles of courses to choose from, tee times are precious, especially during prime seasons. Call well in advance—three months or more—to book reservations.

North Strand

Angels Trace Golf Links
1215 Angels Club Dr. S.W.,
Sunset Beach, N.C.
• (910) 579-2277, (800) 718-5733

Angels Trace opened two 18-hole courses, the North Course and the South Course, in November 1995. Tees, fairways and rough are

INSIDERS' TIP

The view from Greg Norman's Australian Grille in Barefoot Landing is Greg Norman's Golf Course (the "Norman Course") in Barefoot Resort. Only the intracoastal waterway separates the bentgrass greens from your salad bowl.

419 bermudagrass, and greens are bentgrass. Gently rolling fairways, moderate mounding and shallow bunkers lead to large greens. The course designs each submit to the natural lay of the land and feature natural streams and lakes bordered by oyster shells.

The North Course has designated No. 5 as its signature hole. The par 4 dogleg left requires a placement shot, then a carry over water. Each side of the fairway is lined with two sand traps, and the green is elevated and surrounded by oyster shells. This premier course was designed by Clyde Johnston, measures 6216 yards and plays par 72. The 6442-yard, par 72 South Course, also designed by Johnston, incorporates features similar to those of the North Course. Greens fees at Angels Trace are $74; no walking.

Brunswick Plantation and Gold Links
U.S. Highway 17, NC
• **(800) 848-0290**

Brunswick Plantation inhabits a convenient, central point between Myrtle Beach, S.C., and Wilmington, N.C., (which is an hour north of Myrtle Beach) and lies just minutes from beautiful Carolina beaches.

The 27 holes of this course measure 6200 yards and plays par 72 as they emphasize the natural beauty of the terrain by integrating quick bent grass greens and beautiful lush fairways with the wooded Carolina Pines.

The first nine holes of the Magnolia Course draw from the historic links of Scotland. The extensive mounds and large sand and grass bunkers present the challenge of this nine. The second nine, the Azalea Course, is carved from thick Carolina Woodlands. Water is the dominant theme on many of the holes, demanding thought and strategy on every shot. The 4th hole is an island green accessible by bridge and surrounded by beautiful oyster shells. The Dogwood Course, which composes the final nine and opened February 1998, meanders along the historic Caw Caw Run among the dense hardwood trees. The #6 hole will provide you with another challenging island green and you can look forward to the #7 hole where you'll discover a 300-year-old Cypress tree over 10 ft. in diameter!

Greens fees are $75; no walking.

Carolina Shores Golf & Country Club
99 Carolina Shores Dr., Calabash, N.C.
• **(910) 579-2181, (800) 579-8292**

Not for the faint-of-heart, Carolina Shores has earned a reputation as a hazardous layout that absolutely demands accuracy. Little won-

der, since there are (count 'em) 96 diabolically placed bunkers, a dozen natural crater lakes, tree-lined fairways reminiscent of roller-coaster layouts and perhaps the most dramatic starting hole in Grand Strand golf.

Although Carolina Shores demands precision play, brute strength is not necessary. Bring your best game and put yourself to the test. What's the joy of life without a few genuine challenges? Greens fees for this 6231-yard, par 72 layout are $70; no walking.

The Gauntlet
St. James Plantation, N.C. Hwy. 211, Southport, N.C.
• **(910) 253-3008, (800) 247-4806**

Although relatively young (The Gauntlet opened in 1991), this course is already widely known as one of the most formidable challenges on the Grand Strand. Set on a 200-acre tract characterized by marsh, maritime woodlands, lakes and the ever-beautiful Intracoastal Waterway, the 6448-yard, par 72 Gauntlet provides a magnificent arena that pits a golfer against one of P.B. Dye's finest and most challenging courses.

A stunning clubhouse and a tennis and swimming center hint at The Gauntlet's cherished old-fashioned Southern flair. Greens fees are $93; no walking.

Glen Dornoch Waterway Golf Links
U.S. Hwy. 17 N., Little River
• **(843) 249-2541, (800) 717-8784**

This 260-acre site along the Intracoastal Waterway was created as a tribute to Dornoch, Scotland, the birthplace of golf legend Donald Ross. The 18-hole, 6035-yard, par 72 Clyde Johnston design, which opened in September 1996, is set amid pines, oaks, lakes, a river, marsh and the Intracoastal. At least four holes flank the waterway, and dramatic elevation changes—you'll find some 35-foot drops to the water—are nothing short of spectacular. Bring your most accurate game—there are no wide-open fairways here.

Greens fees are $123; no walking. Glen Dornoch includes a self-contained resort with a hotel, condominiums and an array of related facilities.

Heather Glen
2111 U.S. Hwy. 17 N., Little River
• **(843) 249-9000, (800) 868-4536**

Timeless oaks and stately pines stud the 400-acre historic setting of Heather Glen, a course reminiscent of the best Scotland has to offer. Designed by Willard Byrd and Clyde Johnston, this course was pegged a masterpiece as quickly as it opened for play. *Golf Digest* named it 1987's "Best New Public Course in America" and one of the "50 Best Public Courses in America" in 1990.

Heather Glen made a great thing even better when it expanded from 18 to 27 holes. This allows golfers to personally design their rounds by picking two of three stellar sets of nine holes from among the Red (3127 yards), White (3198 yards) and Blue (3183 yards) courses, all par 72. Greens fees are $101; no walking.

Back at the 18th-century–style clubhouse, cap off your round in an authentic-style pub serving Bass Ale and grilled sandwiches.

Lion's Paw Golf Links
Ocean Ridge Plantation,
351 Ocean Ridge Pkwy. S.W.,
Sunset Beach, N.C.
• **(843) 448-5566, (800) 233-1801**

Since opening in 1991, the untamed Lion has often been described as Willard Byrd's finest work. Given Byrd's résumé, that description heartily endorses Lion's Paw as a course worth considering. This masterful layout is simultaneously wild and peaceful.

Perhaps the most striking feature of Lion's Paw is the contrast between the front nine holes and the back nine. The front nine features a traditional layout, with natural elevation changes and features such as Carolina pine trees. The back nine, however, is links-style after the great courses of Great Britain, with low-lying, mounded farmland and no trees.

No. 3 is a par 3 requiring a carry over water. Oyster shells flank each side of the fairway. No. 18 has a water hazard in the second-shot landing area, and the green is a peninsula surrounded by water. In all, this par 72 course measures 6457 yards.

The scenery is breathtaking, and your game will be memorable. Greens fees are $75; no walking.

The Long Bay Club
S.C. Hwy. 9, Longs
• **(843) 399-2222, (800) 344-5590**

The fact that The Long Bay Club is a Jack Nicklaus "signature course" is reason enough to pen it in on your golfing schedule. Open since 1988, the course continually has ranked among the top courses in the country.

A typical Nicklaus design, the 6565-yard, par 72 layout showcases deep pot bunkers and vast waste areas; challenges abound. If the definition of a great layout is "a course with holes that become etched in memory," then Long Bay is indisputably great. In fact, the 10th hole, which features a scalloped, horseshoe-shaped sand trap, is one of the most recognizable holes in the entire golf world.

Greens fees are $115; no walking.

Marsh Harbour
Marsh Harbour Rd., Calabash, N.C.
• **(843) 236-9318, (800) 552-2660**

This Dan Maples course has an interesting claim to fame—some holes are in South Carolina and some are in North Carolina. Marsh Harbour covers wetland along an inlet and the Intracoastal Waterway, making the course every bit as enjoyable to look at as it is to play. The combination of manicured turf and sparkling water creates a green and blue backdrop that's nothing shy of spectacular. Upon opening in 1980, the 6000-yard, par 71 Marsh Harbour was rated among *Golf Digest's* "Top 25 Public Courses in America."

The course's signature hole is the 570-yard 17th. Marvelously terrifying, this par 5 has three landing areas, two of which sport water on three sides. No one leaves Marsh Harbour without talking about No. 17.

Greens fees are $100; no walking.

Meadowlands
350 Calabash Rd., Calabash, N.C.
• **(888) 287-7529**

Meadowlands threw open the barn doors in September 1997 and ever since has been befriending golfers. The grounds that once were farmland have been carefully and patiently sculpted by Willard Byrd and have been compared to Dan Maples' Man O' War Course (see subsequent entry). Meadowlands is wide open for your grazing pleasure, cultivates tidewater greens, and welcomes you with a 6,000-square-foot, two-story clubhouse in a turn-of-the-century-style farmhouse setting. Meadowlands has a few memorable spots, from the alligator sanctuary located behind the 17th green to the 5-foot vertical drop lurking beyond the 13th.

INSIDERS' TIP
Rain policies vary from one course to another. In most cases, some form of rain check is available. Contact the individual course for specifics.

GOLF

Caledonia Golf & Fish Club—The original plantation was named by its founder, Dr. Robert Nesbit, a Scottish immigrant who named it Caldonia, the ancient Roman name for Scotland.

Photo: Michael Slear, courtesy of Brandon Advertising

GOLF

Metal spikes are not permitted, nor is walking. This 6000-yard, par 72 course costs $67 to play.

Ocean Harbour Golf Links
Ocean Harbour Golf Dr.,
off N.C. Hwy. 179, Calabash, N.C.
• (910) 579-3588

This breathtaking 18-hole layout was created on a spectacular tract of land that straddles North and South Carolina's border. Clyde Johnston, the course's architect, used the tract's outstanding topographical details—the Intracoastal Waterway, tidal marshes, an inlet and the Calabash River—to create a showcase of dramatic holes. Word has it you'll need to sharpen your accuracy, since several holes force players to shoot across the expansive marsh. In fact, No. 7, with a sharp dogleg left, forces all but monster hitters to play over marsh three times. When 6591-yard, par 72 Ocean Harbor opened in 1989, GOLF Magazine rated it among the top 10 new courses. Greens fees are $85; no walking.

Oyster Bay
Lakeshore Dr., Sunset Beach, N.C.
• (843) 236-9318, (800) 552-2660

Yet another Dan Maples design, Oyster Bay really does have it all—6305 yards set amid pretty lakes, sweeping marshes, the Intracoastal Waterway and teeming with wildlife. Expect to see all sorts of shore birds, and don't be surprised if you glimpse an alligator basking in the Carolina sunshine. This par 70 course was rated the "Best New Resort Course in America" in 1983 by Golf Digest. In 1990 the magazine sang its praises again, rating it one of the "Best 50 Public Courses in America."

A lake flanks the entire right side of the 13th fairway, and the green is guarded by a cavernous bunker. The 15th and 17th holes are par 3s with island greens, the latter of which is built on a mountain of oyster shells.

Greens fees are $110; no walking.

Panther's Run Golf Links
Ocean Ridge Plantation,
351 Ocean Ridge Pkwy. S.W.,
Sunset Beach, N.C.
• (843) 448-5566, (800) 233-1801

The 18-hole, 6267-yard, par 72 Panther's Run was created to deliver a different kind of challenge—one some call a "wild breed of golf." You'd be hard pressed to find a more incredible variety of elevation in one location. Add twisting fairways and the classic beauty of a nature preserve and marshlands, and you've got a course that's as memorable for its scenery as for its challenge. A signature hole at Panther's Run is No. 15, which flanks a lake for the length of its right side. Avid golfers swear this is one of the finest driving holes to play.

Wildlife abounds here, so you might want to bring your binoculars. Panther's Run golf shop was rated in the top 100 in 1997 by *Golf Digest*, so bring your wallet too.

Greens fees are $85; no walking March through May.

The Pearl Golf Links
1300 Pearl Blvd. S.W., Sunset Beach, N.C.
• (910) 579-8132

The omnipresent and magnificent Dan Maples strikes again with The Pearl's two courses. Both the East and West courses easily qualify as some of the finest in all the nation. Both are ranked among the top courses in the Carolinas and have been nominated "Best New Public Courses in America" by *Golf Digest*.

The par 72 East Course, encompassing 6543 yards, is the more traditional of the two. Carved from pristine maritime forest, it boasts a dramatic finishing hole along the Calabash River—a mid-length par 4, uphill off the tee and downhill to the green, with the river and salt marsh on the left.

The Pearl's 6738-yard, par 72 West Course is links-style; lots of wide-open stretches complemented by thick displays of pampas grass. The 18th hole alone is worth the greens fee; it features a finishing hole—in 1997, it was voted best finishing hole by *GOLF Magazine*—along bluffs that overlook the blue ribbon of Intracoastal Waterway. Attention to detail and meticulous grooming characterize this course, which has hosted a number of major tournaments.

Greens fees are $76; no walking.

Possum Trot Golf Club
U.S. Hwy. 17 N., North Myrtle Beach
• (843) 272-5341, (800) 626-8768

Open since 1968, Possum Trot bills itself as "the friendliest course down South, where the guest is number one." Noted among locals and returning tourists for consistently excellent playing conditions, this 6388-yard, par 72 course features wide fairways that make for a low-maintenance round whether you're an average golfer or a low handicapper.

Possum Trot also offers a unique 16-acre practice facility, a driving range complete with chipping, pitching and putting greens and a practice bunker. Greens fees are $71, and walking is allowed at times; call ahead.

River Hills Golf & Country Club
U.S. Hwy. 17 N., Little River
• (843) 399-2100, (800) 264-3810

Just one year after opening, River Hills was nominated by *Golf Digest* as its "Best New Course for 1989." Also in '89, *Golf Week* named the course one of the Southeast's "Top 50."

A public resort facility in an impressive country club setting, River Hills remains an outstanding course that offers a pleasing blend of old and new design features, frequent elevation changes (more than any course in the area!) and championship conditioning. This 6285-yard, par 72 course is definitely worth adding to your playing schedule. Greens fees are $70; no walking.

> # INSIDERS' TIP
>
> The Official All Star Cafe, which opened in 1997 at Broadway At The Beach, is owned in part by Tiger Woods. Inside the stadium-like structure—the ceiling is molded like a golf course—Tiger has his own Club House decorated with memorabilia from his career. A semiprivate room holds about 50 people and is available for private parties.

Sandpiper Bay
800 Sandpiper Bay Dr., Sunset Beach, N.C.
• (910) 579-9120, (800) 356-5827

With some of the best bentgrass greens on the Strand, Sandpiper Bay has been a local's favorite for nearly a decade. A Dan Maples design, players consistently find this 6020-yard, par 71 course in great shape. With six par 3s and five par 5s, it's a challenge for players of all skill levels. A magnificent clubhouse, set among wind-whispering pines and glassy lakes, reflects Sandpiper Bay's commitment to quality and exceptional service.

Greens fees are $75; no walking.

Sea Trail Plantation
211 Clubhouse Rd., Sunset Beach, N.C.
• (843) 272-2185, (800) 624-6601

Sea Trail Plantation has three courses, designed by notable architects Dan Maples, Rees Jones and Willard Byrd. (With those names, how could you go wrong?!) Each course is manageable—not too easy, not too tough—the kind you'll remember fondly once you've returned home. Even so, the traditional design of the Rees Jones course stands out to golf aficionados. Wide fairways, elevated greens, large mounds, swales, pot bunkers and freshwater lakes add to its aes-

GOLF

thetic beauty. But, rest assured, its good looks haven't softened its challenge.

All three courses are par 72. The 6251-yard Byrd Course costs $84 to play; the 6334-yard Jones Course is $94; and the 6332-yard Maples Course, $84. Walking is not permitted, and golfers must wear spikeless shoes on all three courses.

Surf Club
1701 Springland Ln., North Myrtle Beach
• (843) 249-1524, (800) 765-SURF

This club opened in 1960 and has been a popular golfing destination for nearly four decades. Recently, all the greens were rebuilt to enhance this George Cobb classic. Those who knew and loved the Surf before the renovation will appreciate the way architect John LaFoy retained the course's classic appeal while adding new challenges for golfers of all abilities. One avid local golfer described the Surf simply: "Traditional design without gimmicks. Strong par 4s merit playing."

The 6360-yard, par 72 Surf Club course costs $93 to play; no walking.

Tidewater Golf Club & Plantation
4901 Little River Neck Rd.,
North Myrtle Beach
• (843) 249-3829, (800) 446-5363

If scenic vistas showcasing water suit your taste, you'll fall in love with Tidewater in a hurry. Truly incredible views of the Intracoastal Waterway, saltwater marshes and the Atlantic Ocean abound. At least one hole plays alongside Hogg Inlet (a popular fishing area for Cherry Grove residents), so you can watch anglers reel in a few as you plan your next shot. This fabulous course was named one of the best new public courses by both *Golf Digest* and *GOLF Magazine* in 1990.

Situated on 560 acres of seaside peninsula, Tidewater gives you plenty of elbow room and privacy. The only hole you can see at any given time is the one you're playing, which creates the feeling of absolute solitude. The course has five sets of tees, so golfers can select those that best suit their games. Depending on tee selection, you can stretch this par 72 course from 4765 to 7020 yards.

Tidewater is one of the Grand Strand's most expensive golf courses (greens fees are $145), but when you see it, you'll understand why. Hale Irwin, three-time U.S. Open champion, called Tidewater "one of the finest and most spectacular courses on the East Coast." This course is definitely not to be missed. Walking is permitted.

Myrtle Beach

Arcadian Shores
701 Hilton Rd., Myrtle Beach
• (843) 449-5217

Rees Jones designed this course that opened in 1974. It features standard bermuda grass fairways and lush bentgrass greens. Surrounding the greens and sprinkled along the fairways, you'll find no fewer than 64 sand bunkers amid this 6446-yard, par 72 track—just so you'll remember you're at the beach! A variety of picturesque natural lakes adds to the challenge. In 1993 the course was listed among *Golf Digest's* "Top 50 Resort Courses." *GOLF Magazine*, too, has noted Arcadian Shores's outstanding design.

Greens fees are $83; no walking.

Arrowhead Country Club
1201 Burcale Rd., Myrtle Beach
• (843) 236-3243, (800) 236-3243

This Raymond Floyd-designed course continually garners rave reviews. Twenty-seven holes currently are open for play; each nine-hole course has its own name. The appropriately named Lakes Course meanders 3119 yards through a pristine pine forest and features striking undulations in the fairways, numerous white sand bunkers and abundant lakes. The 3123-yard Cypress Course, in contrast, is set amid a beautiful stand of hardwoods, unique to the Myrtle Beach area. The Waterway Course, which opened in November 1995, stretches 3060 yards through hardwoods to the Intracoastal Waterway and includes a liberal mix of mounds and lakes. The feel is similar to the Lakes and Cypress courses but is enhanced by the waterway view. All three courses are par 72.

Arrowhead's design, masterminded in collaboration with Tom Jackson, offers the feeling of playing golf in the Carolina foothills. A beautiful clubhouse, large practice facility and a well-stocked pro shop add to the quality of this course. Greens fees are $96; no walking.

Belle Terre Golf Course
4073 U.S. Hwy. 501, Myrtle Beach
• (843) 236-8888, (800) 340-0072

"Belle Terre" is French for "beautiful earth." The 701-acre golf complex was named from architect Rees Jones's description of the land when he called it, "the most beautiful earth I have ever seen." The 54-hole complex features a Championship Course and an Executive Course, which is a par 58 course.

As for the Championship Course, expect

no gimmicks and no housing developments—just pure, unadulterated golf. This traditional par 72 layout measures 7013 yards from the championship tees.

Belle Terre's 3200-yard, 18-hole Executive Course is distinctive in that it offers the opportunity to either walk the course or ride along state-of-the-art concrete cart paths. Complete with four par 4s and 14 par 3s, this jewel packs a lot of great golf holes, including water hazards and bunkers, into its classic layout. Designed to be fast and fun—and to make golfers use every club in the bag—this course allows busy executives to squeeze in a game of golf even when schedules seem unyielding.

The greens fees for Executive Course are $35 to walk, $42 including cart; for the Championship Course, $92, and walking is not allowed. The clubhouse features an outstanding pro shop and restaurant as well as complete dressing rooms with eight showers and lockers. Belle Terre hosts the Jimmy D'Angelo Senior Golf Classic (see the previous "Tournaments" section).

The Dunes Golf and Beach Club
9000 N. Ocean Blvd., Myrtle Beach
• (843) 449-5914

The Dunes Club is one of the area's oldest and best-loved courses. A par 72 Robert Trent Jones design, Dunes was only the second course built in Myrtle Beach—back in 1949. Recent renovations make it one of a handful of courses with PennLink bentgrass greens.

Through the years, the 6174-yard course has achieved worldwide renown. The 13th hole, rated one of the best 18 holes in America as rated by *Sports Illustrated*, is particularly popular. *GOLF Magazine* included the 13th hole in its "100 Best Holes in America," and *Southern Living* named it one of the "18 Ultimate Golf Holes of the South," proclaiming:

If a single golf hole can be given credit for popularizing Myrtle Beach golf, this is it. Its crescent-shaped fairway winds around the former Singleton Swash, now a lake. A monstrous drive is advised, to be followed by a monstrous 3-wood, and you're still a strong iron from a round green. It's a par 6 for most of us.

So few people have reached the 13th green in two shots that those who have are noted in The Dunes Club's history. The hole is known as Waterloo; don't let it be yours.

The rest of the course is fairly traditional, with wide-open fairways, deep bunkers and elevated greens. The course's beauty is any-thing but ordinary. The Atlantic Ocean is the backdrop for several holes, while others wind around and through the marsh. Understandably, this course has a maturity that other Grand Strand courses envy.

Rest assured, when you wrap up at No. 18, you will have used every club in your bag. And you may be hungry. If so, drop by the grill for a quick bite or the elegant dining room for a formal dinner with a panoramic view of the beach.

The Dunes remains one of the Strand's most exclusive private clubs and is available to the guests of a few select member hotels: The Breakers, The Caravelle, The Caribbean, The Driftwood, The Dunes Village and The South Wind. Tee times are scheduled through the hotels; greens fees are $160 if booked that way.

The Legends Complex
U.S. Hwy. 501, Myrtle Beach
• (843) 236-9318, (800) 552-2660

Since 1990, the Legends Complex has offered three distinctive courses along the Grand Strand: Parkland, Heathland and Moorland. The newest, and arguably the best, of the three is Parkland. When members of the Carolinas PGA held a championship here, the pros pointed out similarities to New Jersey's highly acclaimed Pine Valley course. Parkland requires the ability to draw or fade the ball, and accuracy is an absolute must. This complex is not a place for beginners. Don't try this par 72, 6425-yard course unless you're up to the challenge; you'll only get frustrated and slow down play.

Heathland is one of the most unusual courses along the Grand Strand. It would seem more at home in the Scottish landscape, given its lack of trees, menacing winds and rolling fairways. Pot bunkers appear more ominous than they are, so don't be intimidated. One of the more interesting holes requires golfers playing from the men's tees to drive straight over a grove of trees; the ladies' tees are positioned on the other side to bypass the grove. Upon opening, this Tom Doak design was immediately selected as one of *GOLF Magazine's* "Top 10 New Courses for 1990." Par 72 Heathland measures 6190 yards.

Rounding out The Legends Complex is Moorland, which features some of the most-feared holes in Myrtle Beach; you'll either love or hate this 6125-yard, par 72 P.B. Dye course. When Legends's owner Larry Young hired the renowned Dye to design the course, his instruction was simple: "Make it as hard as you can." And Dye did! It can be downright difficult in places, especially the short par 4 called "Hell's Half-Acre," although when the tees are placed

GOLF

forward, it isn't an impossible challenge even for average golfers. Ironically, the higher a player's handicap, the more the individual seems to enjoy Moorland.

The Legends has one of the most impressive clubhouses we've ever seen. It climbs skyward from the undulating green terrain like a Scottish castle. Inside, the tradition of elegance continues with an upscale pro shop, comfortable pub and dining room. There is also a state-of-the-art driving range with greens and flags as targets, instead of the usual wide-open space with distance markers.

Greens fees are $105; no walking. You can also book tee times at The Heritage, Marsh Harbor and Oyster Bay by calling the listed telephone numbers.

Man O' War
U.S. Hwy. 501, Myrtle Beach
• **(843) 236-8000**

World-famous architect Dan Maples definitely won the battle with this legendary new layout, created from the depths of—believe it or not—a 100-acre lake. This long-awaited 6402-yard, par 72 course, which opened in January 1996, features a pair of back-to-back island greens (remember when one island green was impressive?) plus an awesome island 9th hole that's surrounded by water from tee to green. Distinctive wide fairways, bentgrass greens, a practice range and a unique marina clubhouse add intrigue to an already marvelous course. Greens fees are $94; no walking.

Myrtle Beach National
U.S. Hwy. 501, Myrtle Beach
• **(843) 448-2308, (800) 344-5590**

You'll find an outstanding trio of impeccably conditioned courses at Myrtle Beach National, each bearing Arnold Palmer's special touch. (All three par 72 courses were designed by Frank Duane with input from the master himself.)

If you can take your pick, choose the North Course. One of the oldest and most requested on the beach, this course reopened in December 1995 following extensive renovations.

Enhancements to the 6413-yard layout include reshaped and enlarged greens sodded with the new hybrid Crenshaw bentgrass. Trees have been removed to open the course. Several of the bermudagrass fairways feature increased undulation, and bunkers and lakes have been dramatically reshaped. The famous par 3 No. 12, which includes sand traps shaped like the letters "SC," has bulkheads and a foot bridge. This is one of the most recognizable holes on the Strand.

If you can't get on the Kings North Course (greens fees are $147), don't despair; you'll enjoy playing the SouthCreek (6089 yards; $72) or West (6113 yards; $72) courses too. West is probably the easiest of the trio. All three offer gently rolling fairways, towering pines and a few perilous lakes. Myrtle Beach National serves up the perfect opportunity for a multi-round day. Walking is not allowed on any of the three courses here.

Pine Lakes International Country Club
Woodside Dr., Myrtle Beach
• **(843) 449-6459, (800) 446-6817**

Affectionately hailed as "The Granddaddy," this is quite literally where Myrtle Beach golf began. This course, the oldest in the area, was constructed in 1927 and was originally called the Ocean Forest Club. Course architect Robert White, first PGA president and a native of St. Andrews, Scotland, endowed the 6176-yard, par 71 layout with a unique Scottish flair.

Today, as always, golfers are greeted by starters donning kilts, welcomed with hot chocolate or a cool mimosa on the 1st tee, refreshed with a cup of Lowcountry clam chowder near the turn and comforted with a "crying towel" at the finish. The par 3 No. 7 is a favorite during the springtime when an ambrosia of azaleas are in full bloom. The effect is nothing short of breathtaking. "Granddaddy" can be tough, with bunkers flanking both sides of numerous fairways, but being a part of the legend is worth the heartache.

Greens fees are $105; no walking.

River Oaks Golf Plantation
831 River Oaks Dr., Myrtle Beach
• **(843) 236-2222, (800) 762-8813**

Rated in the top 5 on the Grand Strand by Golf Course Rankings of America in 1994, this course has something for everyone. You can't help but enjoy the 27 holes of undulating greens, mounded fairways, large lakes and finger-shaped bunkers among the Bear (6314 yards), Fox (6345) and Otter (6425) courses, each of which is par 72. Greens fees are $64; no walking.

INSIDERS' TIP
A mulligan is a second shot, which mysteriously leaves no mark on a scorecard.

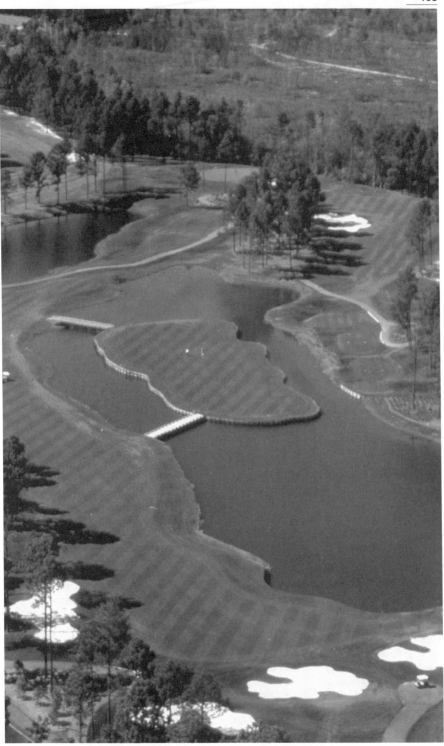

King's North—designed by the "king of golf" Arnold Palmer.

Photo: Michael Slear, courtesy of Brandon Advertising

In addition, the natural beauty and abundance of wildlife makes every golf experience a mini-adventure. A professional staff, excellent practice areas and beautifully manicured fairways, greens and tees have made River Oaks a popular choice. River Oaks offers the American Golf Academy to help you improve your game. The course's convenient location across from Wac-camaw Factory Shoppes is also appealing.

Kingfishers Shrine Unit held their Second Annual Golf Tournament for Crippled and Burned Children's Hospital at River Oaks in 1997. This captain's choice event—$150 per three-player team—is a day well spent. Please call Elmer Stone at (843) 650-6672 for detailed information.

Waterway Hills
U.S. Hwy. 17 N., near Restaurant Row, Myrtle Beach
• **(843) 449-6488, (800) 344-5590**

Robert Trent Jones, sometimes called the "Dean of Golf Architecture" (Donald Ross fans likely would argue that distinction), designed this gem of a course.

When you emerge from the enclosed tram that ferries you across the Intracoastal Waterway, you'll find 27 superbly maintained holes set amid woodland seclusion, with more than a few lakes for spice.

Traditional in design, Waterway Hills offers rolling terrain and a variety of strategically placed bunkers. The three beautiful courses—Oaks (3080 yards), Lakes (3001 yards) and Ravine (2927 yards), which are all par 72 in pairs—are characterized by landscape challenges that make each course suitably named. The Oaks' 27 holes wind through trees, and its fairways are lined with large oaks. The Lakes features four holes with water hazards and meanders around five substantial bodies of water. And No. 3 at The Ravine is a par 5 with a harrowing hazard: a 60-foot chasm.

Greens fees are $72 for any 18-hole combination; walking is permitted in the afternoon.

Wild Wing Plantation
1000 Wild Wing Blvd., off U.S. Hwy. 501, Myrtle Beach
• **(843) 347-9464, (800) 736-WING**

Wild Wing Plantation is a highly acclaimed, multi-course facility that delivers world-class golf in a world-class setting. With four award-winning courses that cover more than 1,000 acres, Wild Wing has gone to great lengths to preserve the property's natural beauty.

A special distinction at Wild Wing is computerized golf carts. These computers give exact yardages from the ball, wherever it lies, to the center of the green. The computers also offer helpful hints like "bunker on left" and "green slopes to the right." (Sounds a little like cheating, but ya gotta live with your conscience.)

The par 72 Falcon Course, a favorite among locals, was designed by Rees Jones. Measuring 6697 yards and featuring mounding, narrow fairways and small greens, the Falcon specializes in diversity and visual excitement. There are two lakes, each 20 acres or more, on this 18-hole course plus a 500-yard bunker that'll haunt your memory for a long time to come. In 1994 *The Sun News* named the Falcon the best new course in Myrtle Beach.

The Sun News named the Avocet "Best New Course in Myrtle Beach" in 1993. Designed as a signature course by Jeff Brauer and two-time PGA Champion Larry Nelson, the Avocet will keep you seeing double; creative contouring presents a host of elevated tees and greens, double fairways, grass bunkers . . . even a double green. The par 72 course covers 6614 yards. *Golf Digest* named it one of the "Top 10 New Courses in America" in 1994.

The Wood Stork, Wild Wing's first course, has been open for play since 1991 and has had time to garner even more praise than her sister courses. *Southern Links* magazine called it "Best in the South" for course conditioning and presentation. *Golf Digest* listed Wood Stork in its "Top 100 Great Value Courses in America" and in its "Top 3 Value Courses in Myrtle Beach." Willard Byrd preserved the lay of the land, the natural vegetation and water resources on this 6598-yard, par 72 track. The first eight holes play through pristine wetlands; the remaining 10 holes wind through the shade of a stately pine forest.

Byrd also designed the 6310-yard, par 72 Hummingbird Course. Stands of love grass and other native grasses form the course's wetland perimeter. Lush bermudagrass fairways, strategically placed lakes and an array of pot bunkers and waste areas create excitement and an undeniable challenge. It's little wonder the Hummingbird has racked up the same awards as her sister, the Wood Stork.

Greens fees are $122 for the Avocet, $104 for the Falcon and $99.65 for Hummingbird and Wood Stork. Walking occasionally is allowed on the Falcon Course; call the number listed for details.

Don't miss WishBones, Wild Wing's restaurant, in the 33,000-square-foot clubhouse. ("Wows" are in order.) It's a favorite hangout for golfing and non-golfing locals alike. A 45,000-square-foot putting green, a practice green with a 138-yard practice hole and a huge pro shop round out the amenities at this outstanding development.

The Witch
1900 S.C. Hwy. 544, East Conway
• (843) 448-1300

Just off the Strand, outside Myrtle Beach, The Witch serves up a spectacular 6011-yard, 18-hole course that seems to rise from the earth like some kind of inexplicable magic; it's nothing short of beautiful. Dan Maples molded this par 71 course—complete with nearly 4,000 feet of bridges—from woodlands and mystery-shrouded wetlands without disturbing the enchanted nature of the setting.

Playing The Witch is like taking a nature walk through swamps, marshes and forests, with pine, cypress and live oak trees, deer, foxes and ospreys. The par 4 No. 15 requires an uphill drive followed by a placement shot to a landing area surrounded by wetlands. The 9th green is an island surrounded by wetlands.

Deceptively beautiful, the hundreds of acres of wetlands are Mother Nature's perfect hazards. Challenge lurks 'round every bend of this unforgettable course. Greens fees are $94; walking is not permitted.

The Wizard
U.S. Hwy. 501 N., Myrtle Beach
• (843) 236-9393

This Dan Maples design, which opened in fall 1996, replicates an old-world Scottish course, complete with a Celtic castle-like clubhouse that actually looks worn from age and battle.

Maples moved an astounding 800,000 cubic yards of earth to bring the flavor of mountain golf (complete with rock bridges) to our seaside paradise of Myrtle Beach. This miraculous transformation of landscape has delivered unto the Grand Strand a premier Scottish-links course. Players always comment on No. 13; its rolling hills on both sides of the fairway give the impression of the Scottish countryside. The par 71 Wizard measures 6206 yards of old-world charm and challenge.

Greens fees at The Wizard are $92; walking is not permitted.

South Strand

Blackmoor
S.C. Hwy. 707, Murrells Inlet
• (843) 650-5555

Trite as it sounds, Blackmoor Golf Club at Longwood Plantation is truly unique. This beautiful design is Gary Player's first in the Myrtle Beach area. And what a debut! Player's experience as the world's most traveled golfer is evident in every hole.

Flanking the tea-colored waters of the Waccamaw River, Blackmoor's design takes full advantage of the naturally lovely terrain. No. 14 is a dogleg right with water on one side and sand traps lurking on either side of the fairway; gamblers go for the green, which is 285 yards from the tee. The 8th hole sports a split fairway, and thickets of trees flank both sides.

INSIDERS' TIP

Barefoot Resort and Golf Club boasts a "folio system" which implements barcodes and bypasses the obligatory check-in prior to tee time.

If you play from the left, you'll need a 347-yard drive; from the right side it's a straight-away (if you miss the trees!) 270 yards. *Golf for Women* magazine rated this course in the top 100 women-friendly courses in America. At 6533 yards and par 72, Blackmoor is a challenge for everyone.

Greens fees are $93; no walking. This course is one of our favorites.

Caledonia Golf & Fish Club
King River Rd., Pawleys Island
• (843) 237-3675, (800) 483-6800

Caledonia, constructed on the site of a former rice plantation along the black ribbon of the Waccamaw River, is dazzling. The oak-lined drive to the antebellum-style clubhouse sets the tone for the experience. It won't take you long to realize that no expense has been spared here. Even the bridges that connect one hole to another feature old Charleston brick. *Golf Digest* ranked Caledonia 31st of the top 75 upscale courses to play in 1997.

Designed by up-and-coming architect Mike Strantz, this course is highlighted by huge oaks, shimmering natural lakes, broad expanses of long-abandoned rice fields and more than an occasional glimpse of the area's rich wildlife. *Golf Digest* voted Caledonia "5th Best Public Course in America" in 1994, and *GOLF Magazine* voted it one of the 10 best public courses in 1994. (What a debut, Mike!) And in 1995 *Golf*

GOLF

Digest rated Caledonia as one of the top five courses on the Grand Strand. In 1996 the course continued its excellent reputation as *Golf Digest* awarded it four stars (out of a possible five) in its "places to play" ratings.

Caledonia measures 6104 yards and plays par 72. Greens fees are $130; walking is permitted. When you've finished your round, take some time to hang around the clubhouse, a replica of an 18th-century Colonial plantation home. With its rocking chair-studded wraparound porch, old brick fireplace, soaring ceilings and delicious food, it's a great place to reflect on your game . . . and watch the sun set. Don't miss this one.

Deer Track Golf Resort
U.S. Hwy. 17, Surfside Beach
• (843) 650-2146, (800) 548-9186

Deer Track, a time-tested favorite, offers two 18-hole championship courses. The carefully crafted Toski Links—a 6511-yard, par 72 layout—offers wide, tree-lined bermudagrass fairways, elevated bentgrass greens and picturesque landscaping. The more modern par 71, 6143-yard South Course features sculpted sand bunkers, dramatic bentgrass greens, and spectacular lakes and ponds. Greens fees at each course are $74, and walking is permitted in the afternoon.

Home of the Classic Swing Golf School, Deer Track has a natural turf driving range and putting greens. A bit of trivia for golf fanatics: Deer Track is owned and operated by Gary Schaal, former president of the PGA of America.

The Heritage Club
King River Rd., Pawleys Island
• (843) 237-3424, (800) 552-2660

The Heritage Club's 6565-yard, par 71 course, designed by Dan Maples, is built on the site of not one but two historic rice plantations. Here, overlooking the Waccamaw River, you'll feel a little like you've stepped onto the set of *Gone with the Wind*. The majestic tree-lined approach to the plantation-style clubhouse sets the stage. This grand avenue of 300-year-old oaks would impress even Rhett and Scarlett. In contrast to the historic atmosphere of the course, the Heritage also has a technological angle; a computerized yardage system accompanies all carts.

While you play, enjoy not only the captivating hole designs but also the breathtaking views of the scenic Waccamaw River, endless marshes, freshwater lakes and towering oaks and magnolias. But take heed: The Heritage demands accuracy off the tee.

Greens fees are $110; no walking.

The pro shop, bar and dining room are exquisitely appointed with rich wood paneling. Before your round, loosen up at the driving range or the practice putting green. Lessons are available.

Litchfield Country Club
U.S. Hwy. 17 S., Pawleys Island
• (843) 448-3331, (800) 845-1897

Litchfield, sculpted by Willard Byrd from yet another former rice plantation, was one of the first dozen courses built along the Grand

True Blue Golf Club—the name True Blue was inspired by the local cultivation of indigo from the 1740s to 1777. The vivid dye made from indigo plants was in great demand by the British textile mills during those years.

Photo: Michael Slear, courtesy of Brandon Advertising

GOLF

Strand. Time has given the course a seldom-found maturity. Litchfield meanders lazily around an upscale neighborhood, and though technically private, the club allows a limited number of visiting golfers. The signature hole is No. 14, a straightaway par 4 with a stream to the right. Add two large traps and a preponderant tree to the left, and you have a murderously narrow hole.

For the most part, however, the 6342-yard, par 72 course isn't noted for its difficulty, so your round here should provide a pleasant memory. Greens fees are $95; no walking.

The antebellum-style clubhouse, the tree- and flower-lined approach—the entire ambiance of the club, in fact—will make you feel like you're "walking in high cotton." Actually, you are. So why not continue the self-indulgence after your round? Stay for "supper" and sample the fare that locals love.

Pawley's Plantation
70 Tanglewood Drive, Pawleys Island
• (843) 237-6200, (800) 367-9959

Pawleys Plantation is an upscale residential community of one to three bedroom villas surrounding a lush par 72 golf course. 6127 yards set amongst coastal tidal plains, golden rice fields, and moss-draped oaks. It was the exquisite setting that ultimately drew Jack Nicklaus to Pawleys Plantation. "I have a particular fondness for the Lowcountry," says Nicklaus. "We used what's there without forcing or changing what Mother nature provided."

A few of the course highlights include: the par 3, third hole requiring a forced carry over water from tee to green; the par 5, fourteenth hole where you must negotiate the marsh off the tee shot to a split fairway just before the green; or the tremendous par 4, eighteenth hole that permits only a well-placed drive down a narrow fairway bordered by marsh, sprawling oaks and pines. There's an elegant clubhouse with a grill room that's ideal for a little 19th-hole rlaxation.

Greens fees are $126; no walking.

Prestwick Country Club
S.C. Hwy. 544, Surfside Beach
• (843) 293-4100

Prestwick, a semiprivate course, is another jewel designed by Pete and P.B. Dye. A 20-acre lake created for the course separates the 9th and 18th holes in dramatic fashion and highlights the natural beauty of this masterful 6347-yard, par 72 layout. An assortment of winding streams and ponds bring water directly into play on eight of the course's 18 holes. Each hole has six different sets of tees to challenge any skill level. Dye-inspired features abound: undulating greens, seemingly bottomless pot bunkers and railroad ties galore. Prestwick's current clubhouse opened in fall 1995.

Greens fees are $105. Only members can walk this course during late afternoon.

TPC Myrtle Beach
U.S. Hwy. 17 Bypass, Murrells Inlet
• (843) 357-3399

The opening of this course in the fall of 1998 has significant impact in the world of Myrtle Beach and of golf everywhere. The course is number 100 for the Grand Strand, reinforcing our position as the "Golf Capital of the World." Additionally, the course is a Tournament Players Club (TPC) endeavor, which means it was designed with PGA players in mind. The design incorporates easy spectator movement and stadium style seating at key holes for the thousands of golf enthusiasts who will flock to the Strand each year to view the sport's most significant tournament, the Ingersoll-Rand Senior Tour Championship.

In November, top senior Professionals will come together to compete for purses totaling $2,760,000. The tournament lasts a luxurious week, with ESPN broadcasting live over the weekend. A variety of tickets are available, from $20 to $1,400. Childen under twelve are admitted free with a ticketed adult.

The tournament covers the 7,014 yard, par 72, 18-hole course. Tom Fazio and Tom Marzolf, of Fazio Golf Designers, created the course, complete with a grand clubhouse, nine lakes (one on the driving range) and L-39 bent grass greens (some as large as 6,500 feet.) The culmination of all their work is softly sculpted ridges that create unobtrusive promontories. Peripheral areas around the greens have been "feathered up" to blend in the spectator locations. The finishing hole is a par 5 with a winding "Wadkin's Creek" and a large lake, culminating at a two-tiered green near the 20,000 square foot clubhouse. The course has five sets of tees with yardages ranging from just under 7,000 to around 5,100.

On days when the pros aren't playing (at least not in such big groups), the greens fees are $175 including cart, and metal spike alternatives are encouraged.

The Tradition Club
U.S. Hwy. 17 S., Pawleys Island
• (843) 237-5041

The Tradition Club opened to accolades in fall 1995. Adjacent to the upscale Willbrook community, The Tradition Club boasts a legendary, time-tested course (6508 yards, par 72) with the requisite classic features: large tees, wide fairways and huge, well-placed greens. Five sets of tees serve golfers of all skill levels.

Course architect Ron Garl has designed courses that have hosted PGA tour events and have been honored by *Golf Digest* and *GOLF Magazine* as tops in their class. More of Garl's courses have been named to Florida's top-50 list than any other architect's. In addition, The Tradition is rated in the top 75 women-friendly courses by *Golf for Women*. Every indication is that The Tradition lives up to—even surpasses—Garl's own standard of excellence. Greens fees are $99; no walking.

The Tradition features the most elaborate practice area anywhere along the Strand. It includes a 43,000-square-foot, clover-shaped putting green with four practice locations. The 18th green is guarded by an 8,000-square-foot clubhouse decorated with Italian marble, leather upholstery, imported designer furniture and original European artwork. The Tradition is a must-see—certainly among the area's finest courses.

True Blue Golf Club
King River Rd., Pawleys Island
• **(843) 235-0900, (888) 483-6801**

True Blue is Caledonia's sister course, strategically located across the street. Built on the acreage of a 19th-century indigo and rice plantation by the same name, this course features bentgrass greens and an 18-acre practice facility with a learning center.

All the appeal of True Blue comes from the preservation of the abundant nature in the Lowcountry: native grasses such as field rye, natural elevations, and sandy areas including waste bunkers. On the 14th hole, the tee box is nearly 50 feet above the green.

Greens fees are $130 for True Blue's 6958 yards at a par 72. Walking is permitted.

Wachesaw Plantation East
U.S. Hwy. 17 Bypass, Murrells Inlet
• **(843) 357-2090, (888) 922-0027**

This former rice plantation is about to take off as one of the centers of golfing on the Strand; it is directly adjacent to the new PGA TPC course that will open in November 1998.

Architect Clyde Johnston accented the course's traditional Scottish-links design with wetlands and lakes amid rolling woods. This 6297-yard, par 72 course features five sets of tees for golfers of all abilities.

Greens fees are $102; no walking.

Wedgefield Plantation
100 Manor Dr., Georgetown
• **(843) 448-2124**

Another once-upon-a-time rice plantation, this beautiful course is on the very southern tip of the Grand Strand in historic Georgetown. Cited by *Golf Week* magazine as one of the top 50 golf courses in South Carolina, this course features fairways winding through live oaks and patches of wildflowers; keep an eye out for the abundant wildlife. Practice up for the 14th hole, where two precise shots are required to carry the lakes. Wedgefield's course measures 6325 yards (par 72).

Greens fees are $55; no walking. This is a South Carolina golfing experience that you really should take in on your southern leg of Strand play.

Wicked Stick
U.S. Hwy. 17 Bypass, Surfside Beach
• **(843) 215-2500, (800) 79-STICK**

With his first-ever signature course in the area, John Daly has brought his "grip it, rip it" style to the Grand Strand. Along with architect Clyde Johnston, Daly has created a stunning links-style course patterned after famed Scottish designs. Wide-open spaces feature expansive "dune fields," large sand waste areas with gorse-like vegetation, deep (read bottomless) pot bunkers and strategically placed water hazards. This par 72 course measures 6080 yards (more than 7000 yards from the championship tees!).

"Our main goal was to design and build a course that is fun for the average golfer to play," said Gary Schaal, former PGA president and a member of the partnership that owns the course. "Together, John and Clyde have mapped out a course that looks intimidating but encourages golfers to 'grip it and rip it.'"

Greens fees are $82. Golfers can walk in late afternoon if the course isn't too busy.

Willbrook Plantation Golf Club
U.S. Hwy. 17 S., Pawleys Island
• **(843) 237-4900, (800) 344-5590**

Dan Maples carved Willbrook Plantation from the fertile forests and wetlands of two historic rice plantations. He calls the course "one of my best"...quite a statement considering his résumé. The course's scenery, design and inherent challenge are as captivating as its history. In fact, flora and fauna are so abundant here, the course is registered with the Audubon Society to preserve its wetlands and wildlife.

The ruins of an old plantation home are visible from No. 5, and historic markers along the course signify a slave cemetery near the 8th hole as well as an old slave settlement near the 4th green. You don't have to play great to score well; Willbrook is easy in some spots and tough in others, making it an ideal 6124 yard, par 72 course for golfers of mixed abilities.

Greens fees are $108; no walking.

Willbrook hosts the Carolina Couples Classic each November (see "Tournaments").

Miniature Golf

Driving to and from the more "serious" courses in the Grand Strand, you'll be sure to notice the abundance of colorful, special-effect filled miniature golf courses. Although most of them are better suited to children, Spring Breakers and those who haven't developed their power drive yet, there are a few that are worth the traditional golf enthusiast's attention, either to test your skill or to give you another shot at the elusive purse.

North Strand

Hawaiian Rumble Miniature Golf
33rd Ave. S., U.S. Hwy. 17,
North Myrtle Beach
• (843) 272-7812

Ranked by *GOLF Magazine* as the No. 1 miniature golf course in the United States, Hawaiian Rumble offers a challenging gambit of shots in a lush and expertly landscaped setting of tropical palms, hibiscus and other plants. The course circles and climbs up around a rumbling volcano, leis in almost every color are handed out to the players, and gentle Hawaiian music plays in the background. Hawaiian Rumble also sponsors the Masters Putting Championship, with a purse of $20,000—definitely worth a shot!

Golf Driving Ranges

Myrtle Beach

Cane Patch
72nd Ave. N., Myrtle Beach
• (843) 449-2732

Practice your swing year round starting at 8 AM. The range is lighted for nighttime prac-

tice during summer. All you need is a club and putter, both of which are furnished. Buckets are $4.50 for 45 golf balls, $5.50 for 75 and $8.50 for 115.

Midway
29th Ave. S. and Ocean Blvd.,
Myrtle Beach
• (843) 448-6137

Buckets cost $4.50 for 45 golf balls, $5.50 for 75 and $8.50 for 115. The range is also lighted for nighttime practice. Hours are 8 AM until . . . depending on the season.

South Strand

Harbor Light
701 U.S. Hwy. 17 N., Surfside Beach
• (843) 238-8978

Half the tees at Harbor Light are covered. Buckets are $5 for about 75 golf balls. In springtime the range is lighted for night practice. During the summer season the range is open 8 AM to 11 PM; it closes earlier in the winter.

Par 3 Courses

Myrtle Beach

Cane Patch
72nd Ave. N., Myrtle Beach
• (843) 449-6085

From March through Labor Day, nine holes cost $8 and 18 holes, $12. Those prices fall to $6.50 and $9.50, respectively, off-season. The yardages at the three nine-hole courses are 698, 672 and 653. Locals are always privy to discount passes at Cane Patch. This course also organizes leagues that play members of other Par 3 courses in town.

Midway
29th Ave. S. and Ocean Blvd.,
Myrtle Beach
• (843) 448-4713

Midway offers three nine-hole courses— 759, 743 and 715 yards—that are lighted from March 7 to the start of Daylight Savings Time. It opens at 8 AM daily. It costs $12 a person to play 18 holes and $8 for nine-hole play.

GOLF

Fishing

We could have named this chapter "Everything you always wanted to know about fishing but didn't know who to ask." The first attempt at this subject got us as snarled up as fishing line gone haywire. Luckily, one of us had just the father-in-law to set us straight.

He loves to fish. In fact, at least one day of his annual Myrtle Beach vacation is devoted to wetting a line. According to him, most anglers want to know what species they can expect to find in which waters, what tackle to bring along and where to find the fish at different times of the year.

We took his advice seriously. As a result, we think this chapter should answer the who, what, where, when and, often, the why questions about fishing along the Grand Strand. If you don't find the answers to your questions here, the South Carolina Department of Natural Resources, Marine Resources Division, in Charleston, is a wonderful resource; call (843) 762-5000.

Surf Fishing

Surf fishing is the most "friendly" form of the sport, since you only need to bring a rod and reel to the edge of the Atlantic Ocean. With year-round access to the beach, common catches from the surf—which can be plentiful—include bluefish, flounder, whiting, spot, pompano and channel bass. With a simple tackle rig and a bucket for bait and catch in hand, surf anglers can be spotted along the coastline at just about any time of the year. But, if you're serious about snagging dinner for the family, the less humid fall months are best for this type of fishing, especially when the sea is relatively calm.

Experienced surfcasters suggest using fresh shrimp, minnows or whiting (not more than 3 inches long) as bait. For best results, consult tide tables and hit the beach at low tide. Look along the shoreline for washed-out areas that resemble creek beds in the sand leading out to the ocean's breakers. If you can discern a slough, pool or drop-off, cast into that area; it's often 2 feet or more deeper than the surrounding water. Now comes the fun part. . . . Just sit back, watch and wait for the big bite.

Surfcasting for Pompano and Whiting

The delicate, fine-tasting pompano is relatively abundant during late summer. But to catch them you must be accurate in your fishing technique. Pompano frequent the surf zone, right where the waves break in "suds" on the beach. There they feast on tiny mole crabs before the crustaceans have time to burrow into the sand. Pompano anglers use a small #1 or #2 hook tied directly to the line (8-pound–test is recommended)—no leader necessary. Flip the baited hook into the breakwater and allow it to drift with the current. A split shot ($1/16$- or $1/32$-ounce) attached about 12 to 18 inches above the hook will keep it slightly down in the water column as it drifts.

Whiting, which feed on small worms, crabs and shrimp, can be caught from the surf during the summer. Fish the areas around groins, sloughs

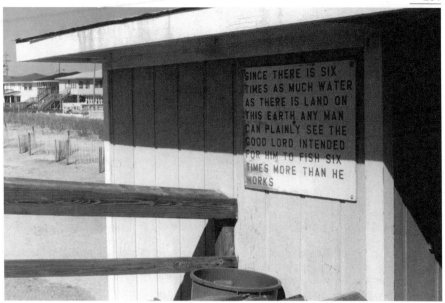

SINCE THERE IS SIX TIMES AS MUCH WATER AS THERE IS LAND ON THIS EARTH ANY MAN CAN PLAINLY SEE THE GOOD LORD INTENDED FOR HIM TO FISH SIX TIMES MORE THAN HE WORKS

Grand Stranders have spent many years developing the right attitude for fishing.

Photo: Lisa Tomer Rentz

and cuts along open beaches. A two-leader rig with #1 or 1/0 hooks, baited with cut shrimp and fished on the incoming tide, frequently yields good results.

Both pompano and whiting generally weigh less than a pound and don't put up much of a fight, but they are certainly excellent table fare.

Inshore Fishing

Nothing will acquaint you as graciously with the pulse, sounds and smells of Lowcountry life along the Grand Strand as fishing its coastal waters, estuaries and salt marshes. The slow-moving, dark, acrid waters offer up sweet mysteries of lively marine life for the avid angler. At the mercy of tidal change, inland waters can cover everything at high tide, then unmask an incredibly bustling sea-life community at low ebb.

Fishing inland waters provides an opportunity to snag crevalle jack, Florida pompano, sheeps-head, Southern flounder, black drum, spotted sea trout, king mackerel, Spanish mackerel, red drum and whiting. Inshore fishing action usually slows with the heat and mosquitoes of summer—especially compared with spring and fall. But, if you're so inclined, summer fishing can be thrilling too, as coastal waters teem with bait fish and shrimp—favorite meals for game fish.

Making the Most of Inshore Fishing

If spotted sea trout is your catch of choice, look for them in lower parts of estuaries during the summer and around oyster bars, rocks and pilings in spring and fall, when tidal currents are running strong. Cooler periods of the year will be your best bet, though, as the fish form larger schools. When luring the sea trout around areas with a structure, fish your bait either on the bottom, with a slip sinker placed above a 20-pound–test monofilament leader attached to a 1/0 or 2/0 hook, or from a float rig. The recreational size limit for the sea trout is 13 inches, and only 10 can be kept per day in aggregate.

During July juvenile red drum leave shallow creeks and form schools in the main estuaries. They're easy to catch en masse at this time of year but are often smaller than the allowable minimum size in South Carolina—14 inches. Late summer is the time to catch adult drum (often between 20 and 30 pounds) around jetties and at the mouths of bays and sounds. Their favorite bait seems to be live menhaden and finger mullet bottom-fished with fish-finder rigs. Use a smaller (4/0) hook for live bait so it can swim more naturally in the current. Five red drum a day is the legal aggregate keeper limit.

South Carolina fishing laws dictate that gigging red drum or spotted sea trout is prohibited from December through February. However, on a calm, hot summer's eve, while estuary waters are clear on an early incoming tide, flounder gigging can yield a hearty harvest. Shallow-draft boats are the best for the this type of flounder hunting; one person polls the boat while another stands on the bow and spears any flounder seen on the bottom.

> ## INSIDERS' TIP
>
> When buying waders or boots, always buy them one and one-half sizes larger than your shoe size. The larger size will enable you to slip them off in the event that you fall overboard. Boots or waders filled with water will make you sink like a stone.

Summer trolling for flounder around inlets is a favorite Grand Strand sport. Troll live bait, such as mud minnows, slowly along the bottom or adjacent to rock jetties. Flounder must be at least 12 inches long to keep, and 20 per day is an angler's aggregate limit.

Sheepshead like to hang out around jetties, piers and bridge pilings during summer months. They're very fussy eaters and usually will not bite anything other than the favored fiddler crab or live shrimp. Successful sheepshead anglers suggest a 1/4- or 3/8-ounce split shot crimped to a 20-pound–test monofilament leader. Appropriate hook sizes for sheepshead are #1, 1/0 or 2/0.

Black drum are the bottom-feeding cousins of the red drum; they do not consume other fish and prefer to be around rocks, pilings and piers. Whether 5 pounds or 40, the black drum cannot resist a large piece of blue crab. A tried-and-true method of luring this fish is to pull the top shell from the crab and cut the meat into quarters. Thread a large piece onto a 5/0 to 9/0 hook tied onto a swivel with a 50-pound–test monofilament leader. Above the leader, which should be 18- to 24-inches long, attach a 2- to 3-ounce slip sinker to get the bait to the bottom. Black drum connoisseurs insist that a fish heavier than 15 pounds will have coarse flesh and be less tasty.

Although they don't make spectacular runs like a king mackerel or perform graceful jumps like the tarpon, the crevalle jack is considered one of the toughest fish you'll encounter around these parts. At night or at dusk, jacks lurk around rips during ebb tide, feeding on their favorite fish. Experienced anglers use a 20-pound–test line on a large-capacity reel and a moderately stout rod. Best baits for jacks are surface popping plugs, such as the Striper Swiper, or swimming plugs by Redfin, Rebel or Rapala. Sought after mostly for sport, jacks are not good eating and should be released.

Offshore Fishing

From sea bass hugging underwater reefs to blue marlin racing through the Gulf Stream, the Grand Strand is a point of departure for a variety of offshore fishing opportunities.

During the summer, sometimes following four or five consecutive days of flat, calm conditions, many of the area's blue-water fish move to within 15 miles of the coast. Of course, in early spring you'll have to travel by boat about 50 miles offshore to catch the same fish.

Offshore marine fishes in these waters include the blue marlin, yellowfin tuna, great barracuda, crevalle jack, wahoo, dolphin (the fish, not "Flipper"), king mackerel, little tunny, Spanish mackerel, white marlin, amberjack and sailfish. Downriggers and planers are key elements to a successful offshore trip during the summer, especially during the steamy days of July and August. Summer heat polarizes much of the feeding activity of these fish into early morning and late afternoon, as they keep to deeper, cooler waters.

Avid offshore anglers continually argue the question of what bait is best for these fish. Natural baits offer real food—so if the fish strikes short, it will more than likely return for another nibble. On the other hand, artificial lures can be trolled faster, allowing more area to be fished, and don't require extra time to rig the bait.

Making the Most of Offshore Fishing

Blue and white marlin fishing is most productive in ocean depths of 300 to 1,200 feet during summer months and around 80 feet in cooler weather. Successful fishing for marlin usually calls for large bait—mullet, ballyhoo, ladyfish, and Spanish mackerel—rigged to skip across the surface or to swim. The bait often is dressed with brightly colored plastic skirts or attached to artificial lures.

Many blue marlin in local waters are in the 125- to 200-pound range—typically below the 99-inch minimum fork length for this species.

Sailfish reach peak abundance during July and August and may be caught only 10 miles off the beach, but many are below the legal minimum 63-inch fork length. Weed lines, current rips and natural reefs in 120 to 300 feet of water are the best areas for these prized game fish. Averaging 35 to 45 pounds, sails prefer smaller baits than their larger marlin cousins. Effective trolling for sails requires small- to medium-size ballyhoo and mullet with a small artificial lure or colored skirt placed ahead of the bait. Sails have even been caught on spoons and plugs intended for king mackerel.

As summer progresses, the size of both dolphin and wahoo gradually declines. Dolphin, for instance, start summer at 10 to 20 pounds and drop to about 8 pounds, while wahoo start at 35 to 50 pounds and weigh in around 20 pounds by season's end. The best concentrations of these species can be found at 180- to 600-foot depths.

The same typically holds true for the yellowfin tuna, though unlike the dolphin and wahoo, tuna increase in size during the summer to an average of 45 pounds.

Effective live bait for dolphin, wahoo or tuna includes ballyhoo or mullet rigged with a small- to medium-size artificial lure or colored skirt. Although all baits are usually fished on the surface from outriggers, it is wise to run at least one line 60 to 70 feet deep via a downrigger.

For an action-packed day of offshore fishing, try trolling for amberjack and barracuda along artificial reefs and coastal shipwrecks. Tenacious fighters, these fish go out of their way to test an angler's equipment and skills.

Most anglers fish for amberjack with a 50-pound–class outfit, but for the ultimate experience, challenge the 'jack with 20- or 30-pound–test line. Wire leader is mandatory for barracuda (whose teeth are razor sharp), while heavy, 100- to 150-pound–test monofilament works well for the 'jacks. Large live baits, such as mullet up to 14 inches and menhaden, floated or free-lined down current, often are successful. Depending on the test line you use, a 5/0 to 8/0 extra-strength hook is recommended—stainless steel, please, since most of these fish are released, not eaten. Artificial lures have also proven effective: The 'jack and 'cuda are partial to surgical rubber

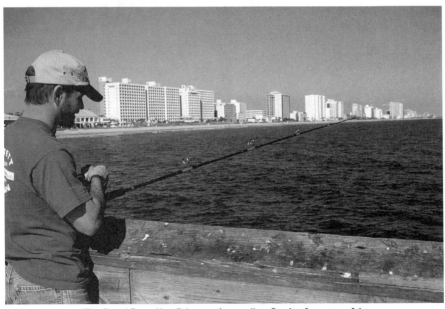

The Grand Strand is a fisherman's paradise. Casting from one of the area's piers is a special vacation treat.

Photo: Courtesy of Myrtle Beach Area Chamber of Commerce

FISHING

tubing colored dark green, chartreuse and hot pink. They have also been known to get excited enough to strike at noisy surface lures.

Artificial and natural reefs are focal points for schools of king mackerel. These fish are very unpredictable and finicky during the summer months and frustrate anglers into wild goose chases with every bait and lure known. The only agreed-upon technique for summer king mackerel fishing is to pull in the rod and reel by 10 AM, when macks seem to disappear. The larger female mackerel prefers nearshore waters just outside bays and sounds, while the males frequent depths of 60 to 120 feet.

Considered great game fish, but not esteemed as food fish, little tunny (locally known as bonito), crevalle jack and Spanish mackerel are abundant in summer 15 miles from shore. One to 5 miles outside bays and sounds and around artificial reefs are prime areas for schooling fish. To determine prime casting areas, just locate the wheeling and diving terns feeding on the bait fish pushed to the surface by these voracious feeders. Small silver or gold spoons such as Hopkins, Clark, Captain Action and Tony Accetta are the most productive; try fishing

Busy shrimpboats in Little River.

Photo: Lisa Tomer Rentz

them on a 20-inch, 60-pound–test wire leader to prevent cutoffs. These fish are extremely fast, so you must retrieve your lure as quickly as possible or troll at a rapid pace.

The Lowcountry Tradition of Shellfishing

Oysters and Clams

Harvesting oysters and clams has been part of the Lowcountry culture for generations. From Hogg Inlet behind Cherry Grove Beach to the salt marshes of Murrells Inlet and Pawleys Creek, many Horry County families fed themselves with the natural bounty of shellfish. That all came to an end in 1987 when nearly all the marshes were closed to the public due to pollution from a bacteria linked to human and animal waste.

Today, portions of Murrells Inlet and North Inlet are open in Georgetown County, and only one location, on the north end of Huntington Beach State Park (U.S. Highway 17), is accessible without a boat. Oyster and clam gathering is limited to South Carolina residents who have a bona fide saltwater fishing license.

FISHING

South Carolinians can only harvest a reasonable amount of the shellfish—enough for personal consumption. In these authorized harvesting areas, no one can disturb oyster or clam beds between May 15 and September 1 of any year. The harvest limit is two bushels of oysters, a half-bushel while wading in the water. The lawful harvest of shrimp by cast net is limited to 60 days—between September 1 and November 15.

Drop nets can be fished from bridges, docks or seawalls and are almost exclusively used at night. Unlike the other meshed methods, drop nets require bait—and the best, we're told, is smoked herring. Drop netting typically doesn't yield large quantities of shrimp, but it sure is enjoyable and relaxing.

The legal daily limit for shrimp is 48 quarts (heads on) or 29 quarts (heads off) per boat or seining party.

For specific questions and current shellfish bed closings, the local Department of Health and Environmental Control is a great resource; call 843-448-1902.

Shrimping

If you like working with nets, you can try your hand at snaring shrimp, America's most popular seafood. The coastal marsh creeks are home to two penaeid shrimp species brown shrimp *(Penaeus aztecus)* and white shrimp *(Penaeus setiferus)*. As shrimp become larger, they leave the brackish waters and move gradually toward the higher salinity of the ocean. Once they've reached about 4 inches in length, they inhabit coastal rivers, spend some time maturing then move into the lower reaches of sounds, bays and river mouths.

Recreational harvest of brown shrimp by cast nets and seines usually starts in early June in the tidal creeks. White shrimp initially are caught in these same creeks in late July or early August but disappear completely by late October. Harvesting by drop nets from docks and seawalls is most popular during the fall when larger white shrimp are moving seaward

Seines for shrimping cannot exceed 40 feet in length, and webbing must be a half-inch square mesh or larger for nylon nets. Law also prohibits the blockage of more than one-half the width of any slough, creek or other waterway on any tidal stage. Seines must be pulled by hand, not by any engine-powered boat or staked to poles. The most effective way to pull a seine is with the falling tide and along banks or sandbars, which provide areas to haul nets ashore and remove the shrimp. Less expensive and cumbersome than seines, cast nets are used more often for shrimping. Cast nets are also devoid of restrictions on lengths or mesh sizes. Casting is popular in creeks with a mud bottom during low tide. Deeper areas of 3 or 4 feet or more often produce larger shrimp during the day since the shrimp avoid light. A cast net can be used from a boat, creek bank, pier or even while wading in the water. The lawful harvest of shrimp by cast net is limited to 60 days between September 1 and November 15.

Drop nets can be fished from bridges, docks or seawalls and are almost exclusively used at night. Unlike the other meshed methods, drop nets require bait and the best, we're told, is smoked herring. Drop netting typically doesn't yield large quantities of shrimp, but it sure is enjoyable and relaxing.

The legal daily limit for shrimp is 48 quarts (heads on) or 29 quarts (heads off) per boat or seining party.

INSIDERS' TIP

It's customary to tip a guide or charter mate about the same as you would tip a server in a restaurant—between 15 to 20 percent of your total bill.

Crabbing

Despite its fearsome appearance and aggressive nature, the blue crab is greatly cherished in our Lowcountry. Many gourmets prefer the blue crab's sweet meat to all other locally caught seafood.

Males of the species can be distinguished from females by the shape of the abdomen. The male has a T-shape abdomen, held tightly against the body until maturity, when it loosens. The immature female has a triangle-shaped abdomen that is sealed against the body, becoming

Shrimp and worms are this fisherman's choice of bait on the Cherry Grove Pier.

Photo: Lisa Tomer Rentz

rounded and loose after the final molt. Large males (often called "Jimmies") usually have brilliant blue claws and legs. Mature females or "sooks" show off bright-orange tips on their claws.

South Carolina law allows individuals to fish two crab pots without a license if they are properly marked with floats bearing the owner's name. Be careful not to leave the pot in an area that exposes it and crabs at low tide, and check pots twice a day for the best yield. However, you must return a crab to the water if its point-to-point width is less than 5 inches or it is a female carrying an egg mass (sponge). Drop nets and collapsible traps (usually baited with herring) can be fished from docks and bridges. Or, you can give "dipping" a try. Dipping involves a long-handled dip net, several yards of string and a chicken neck or fish head for bait. Tie the bait to the string and throw out into the water. Once you feel a tug, pull the bait and crab close enough to quickly dip the crustacean from the water into a waiting bucket. Always keep crabs alive, cool and dry prior to cooking. A refrigerator or cooler with a small amount of ice is the best storage method. Never put crabs in a container of water; they will die quickly from lack of oxygen.

Crabs become inactive in winter when water temperatures fall below 50 to 55 degrees. The best time of the year to harvest large, heavy crabs is usually from October through December. Mature females are typically found near the ocean, while large males are most common in rivers and creeks.

Fishing Charters

When casting into the world of deep-sea fishing, we feel the need to give you fair warning. If you have never been on an offshore fishing trip, take medication to relieve seasickness the night before you leave. Even some experienced sailors have been found writhing around the deck, begging for a quick and merciful death. Once a deep-sea fishing vessel is out on an excursion, it will not turn back to shore early for the sake of one or two heaving passengers. Most local pharmacies carry motion-sickness pills—available over the counter—as well as patches that affix behind the ear.

That said, get ready for some exhilarating fishing opportunities, both inshore and in the Gulf Stream. The following charters are good bets.

North Strand

Blackfish Charter Boat
Waterfront Dr., Little River
• (843) 249-1379
With more than 40 years experience fishing

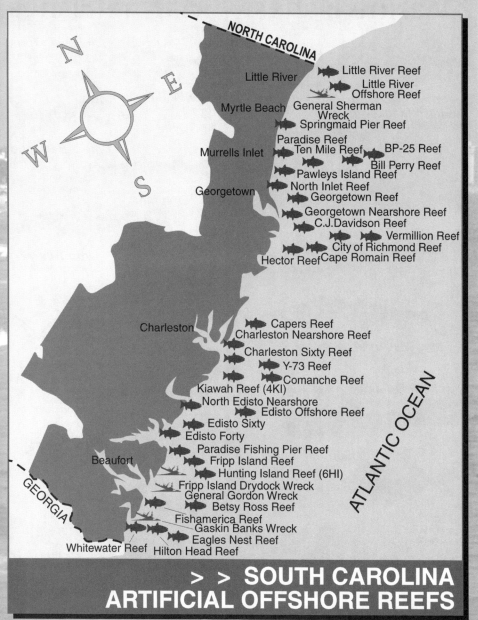

> > SOUTH CAROLINA ARTIFICIAL OFFSHORE REEFS

Credit: South Carolina Department of Natural Resources

Inshore Marine Fishes

Black Drum
Pogonias cromis
Av., 5–40 lbs.
Reaches, 180 lbs.

Spanish Mackerel
Scomberomorus maculatus
Av., 1–2 lbs.
Common, 3–5 lbs.
Reaches, 12 lbs.

Spotted Seatrout
Cynoscion nebulosus
Av., 1–2 lbs.
Common, 3–5 lbs.
Reaches, 16 lbs.

Crevalle Jack
Caranxhippos
Av., 1–2 lbs.
Common, 8–12 lbs.
Reaches, 55 lbs.

King Mackerel
Scomberomorus cavalla
Av., 6–10 lbs.
Common, 20–30 lbs.
Reaches, 90 lbs.

Southern Flounder
Paralichtyslethostigma
Av., 1–2 lbs.
Reaches, 10–12 lbs.

Florida Pompano
Trachinotuscarolinus
Av., 1–2 lbs.
Common, 2–3 lbs.
Reaches, 7 lbs.

Red Drum
Sciaenopsocellatus
Av., 5–10 lbs.
Common, 20–40 lbs.
Reaches, 80 lbs.

Sheepshead
Archosargusprobatocephalus
Av., 1 lbs.
Common, 3–5 lbs.
Reaches, 20 lbs.

Whiting
Menticirrhusspp.
Av., ½–1 lbs.
Reaches, 3 lbs.

Offshore Marine Fishes

Yellowfin Tuna
Thunnusalbacares
Av., 2–40 lbs.
Reaches, 400 lbs.

Blue Marlin
Tetrapturusalbidus
Av., 30–40 lbs.
Reaches, 180 lbs.

Great Barracuda
Sphyraenabarracuda
Av., 3–7 lbs.
Common, 10–20 lbs.
Reaches, 90 lbs.

Dolphin
Coryphaenahippurus
Av., 2–4 lbs.
Common, 10–15 lbs.
Reaches, 85 lbs.

Little Tunny
Euthynnusalleteratus
Av., 5–8 lbs.
Common, 10–12 lbs.
Reaches, 35 lbs.

Crevalle Jack
Caranxhippos
Av., 1–2 lbs.
Common, 8–12 lbs.
Reaches, 55 lbs.

Wahoo
Acanthocybiumsolanden
Av., 15–20 lbs.
Common, 30–40 lbs.
Reaches, 180 lbs.

Amberjack
Serioladumerili
Av., 10–20 lbs.
Common, 40–60 lbs.
Reaches, 150 lbs.

Sailfish
Isotiophorusalbicans
Av., 30 lbs.
Common, 40–50 lbs.
Reaches, 135 lbs.

King Mackerel
Scomberomoruscavalla
Av., 6–10 lbs.
Common, 20–30 lbs.
Reaches, 90 lbs.

White Marlin
Makairanigricans
Av., 300 lbs.
Common, 400–500 lbs.
Reaches, 1,800 lbs.

Spanish Mackerel
Scomberomorusmaculatus
Av., 1–2 lbs.
Common, 3–5 lbs.
Reaches, 15 lbs.

Credit:South Carolina Department of Natural Resource

Common Inshore Fishing Rigs

Surf fishing rig for red drum

line

improved clinch knot

–25" leader

3-way swivel

hook

clinch knot

duolock snap

pyramid sinker

Bottom rig

swivel

duolock snap

sinker

Flounder drift rig

line

barrel swivel

hook

egg sinker

leader

small cork float

Fish finder rig

line

hook

duolock snap

barrel swivel

leader

pyramid sinker

Boat rig for large red drum

line

barrel swivel

leader

egg sinker

hook

Float rig

rubber band

float

sinker

swivel

hook

local waters, Capt. Larry Long will take a party of six people on fishing excursions from Spring through Fall, specifically April through mid-November. Half- and full-day trips can be arranged, including shark fishing and trolling the Gulf Stream. As is typical for fishing charters, bait and tackle are included; food and drink are not. Trips on The Blackfish cost $450 for a half-day and $700 for the whole day. A Gulf Stream adventure is $1,100 for approximately 12 hours. Bottomfishing, trolling or shark fishing is available on each trip.

Ten-year-old Stephen Manser Jr. from Lake Norman, North Carolina, had the fishing trip of a lifetime aboard Long's *Blackfish* in July 1997. The "tug" on young Stephen's line turned out to be a 12-foot-long, 1,200 pound gray tiger shark that took everyone on the boat three hours to reel in.

Captain Danny Juel's Charter Service
Waterfront Dr., Little River
• (843) 249-4515

Capt. Juel has been a local mariner for more than 40 years, and he proudly serves as commander of the 36-foot sportfishing boat *Fish Screamer*. Danny runs charters from Easter through Thanksgiving and provides an on-board "maid" who will bait your hook, take in your catch and clean your fish for tips. A party of up to six people can book the *Fish Screamer* for a half-day for $400, all day for $600, or 12 hours in the Gulf Stream for $900. All bait and tackle are provided; bring a cooler of food and drink.

Hurricane Fishing Fleet
Hurricane Marina, The Waterfront at Calabash, Calabash, N.C.
• (843) 249-3571

Trips depart daily, March through December, from Calabash waters. Hurricane's armada includes the 90-foot *Hurricane II*, the 77-foot *Capt. Juel II*, the 45-foot *Cyclone* and the 40-foot *Party Time*.

Bottom-fishing trips range from half-day to full day in the Gulf Stream and include excursions specifically for snapper. Trolling and other sportfishing trips of 4½ to 12 hours can be arranged as well as nighttime shark fishing. Public and private charters are available. Costs start at $30 per person, and reservations are recommended. Rod, reel, bait and tackle are provided.

FISHING

One look at the smile on this fellow's face and you know it's hard to beat the singular pleasure of catching "the big one!"

Photo: Courtesy of Captain Dick's Marina

FISHING

Longway Charter Fishing
The Waterfront,
1898 N. Twisted Oaks Dr., Little River
• **(843) 249-7813**

Another boat that can accommodate parties of up to six people, *Longway* accepts both individual and group reservations. A five-hour trip costs $400; an eight-hour trip, $600; and a 12-hour Gulf Stream excursion, $900. All prices include gear and bait. Charters run from mid-April to mid-November.

The Pride of the Carolinas
B.W.'s Marina, 4495 Mineola Ave.,
Little River
• **(843) 249-1100**

Half-day and Gulf Stream fishing are the *fare du jour* here. This charter service has more than 20 years' experience trolling local waters. All summer long, night-fishing excursions are offered from 6 to 10 PM at a cost of $30 per adult or teen, $25 for kids 12 and younger. From March 1 through Thanksgiving weekend, Gulf Stream expeditions depart every Saturday from 7 AM to 6 PM—$70 for adults and teens and $65 for kids 12 and younger. In spring and fall, three-quarter-day offshore treks run every Tuesday and Thursday from 8 AM to 2:30 PM for $40 per adult or teen and $35 per youngster. Sportfishing trips for as many as six people can be chartered on the 40-foot *Sundancer*. Fuel, bait, tackle and ice plus dockage for small or large boats are available.

South Strand

Capt. Dick's Marina
4123 U.S. Hwy. 17 S., Murrells Inlet
• **(843) 651-3676 Ext. 228**

Enjoy deep-sea bottom fishing aboard the *New Capt. Bill*, *Capt. Bill III* and *New Inlet Princess*. Trips range from five to 21 hours. Rods, manual reels, bait and tackle are provided on the shorter trips; electric reels are only available for the much longer deep-sea voyages. Fishing licenses are provided for all anglers who charter from here. Air-conditioned cabins and full food service are featured on all of Capt. Dick's vessels. Fishing excursions cost anywhere from $34 to $139 per adult. Special sportfishing junkets can be booked by individuals or groups of six for a half-day, three-quarter

day or full day in Gulf Stream waters. Prices range from $425 to $1,000.

Georgetown Charters
Georgetown Landing Marina,
Marina Dr. and U.S. Hwy. 17, Georgetown
• **(843) 545-5479**

Inshore, backwater or jetty fishing excursions can be chartered here from April 1 to December 1. Parties of two to four people can be accommodated for half day trips for $250–$350, three-quarter day trip for $350–$450, and full day trips for $450–$550.

Customized touring or shelling jaunts are also available. This company does not take individual reservations; you must organize your own party. See our Boating chapter for information about this marina's facilities and hours.

INSIDERS' TIP
Don't forget your camera—and plenty of film—when going out on a charter fishing trip. You'll want to record all those near-misses and great catches.

Real Crazy Charters
Marlin Quay Marina,
1398 S. Waccamaw Dr.,
Murrells Inlet
• **(843) 651-4444**

This sportfishing headquarters offers charters any time of the year plus parasailing (see our Watersports chapter for para-sailing details). Vessels for charter include a 27-ft. Catamaran, a 43-ft. Torres and a 54-ft. Bertram.

Half-, three-quarter-, and full-day as well as Gulf Stream adventures are available. Bait, tackle, and licenses is provided. Food and drink are available on *Real Crazy IV*. Cost ranges from $350 to $1,700. Reservations recommended.

Voyager's View Marina
U.S. Hwy. 17 Bus., Murrells Inlet
• **(843) 651-7033**

Sportfishing charters can be booked here aboard the *Hats Off*, *Adventurer*, or *Point Runner*. Half-day, three-quarter–day, full-day and Gulf Stream adventures are available. Each boat is privately owned, and each captain sets his or her price for trips; prices average from $325 to $425 for half-day trips, from $450 to $650 for three-quarter-day trips, from $550 to $800 for an all-day excursion and $775 to $1,100 for a Gulf Stream trip. See our Boating chapter for information about facilities at this full-service marina.

Fishing Piers

Believe it or not, fishing piers are a major business undertaking. Recently it was reported

FISHING

South Carolina Saltwater Gamefish Records Caught in Grand Strand Waters

Common Name (AFS)—Weight (lbs.-oz.); Port, Year; Angler, Hometown

Amberjack—99-11; Georgetown, 1998; by S. Kelly, North Myrtle Beach, S.C.
Barracuda, Great—65-0; Georgetown, 1948; Henry Shelor, Sumter, S.C.
Bonito, Atlantic—7-11; Little River, 1993 ; Charles Adams, Tabor City, N.C.
Drum, Red(Ch Bass)**—75-0; Murrells Inlet, 1965; A. J. Taylor, Conway. S.C.
Flounder, Summer—3-8; Murrells Inlet,1982; J. Wallace, Charlotte, N.C.
Grouper, Snowy—30-0; Murrells Inlet, 1981; R. Perdue, Murrells Inlet, S.C.
Grouper, Speckled Hind—45-0; Little River, 1973; H. R. Murray, Little River, S.C.
Grouper, Warsaw—310-0; Murrells Inlet, 1976; C. D. Pratt, Knoxville, Tenn.
Grunt, Margate—18-8; Murrells Inlet, 1971; J. L. Flowers, Charlotte, N.C.
Hogfish—20-8; Murrells Inlet, 1988; J. Cline, Pawleys Island, S.C.
Houndfish—9-4; Murrells Inlet, 1974; W. Kirby, Pittsburg, Pa.
Kingfish(Whiting)(tie)—2-10; Pawleys Island, 1968; C. Micheau, Georgetown, S.C.
Mackerel, Spanish—11-0; Myrtle Beach, 1983; W. Deas, Jr., Myrtle Beach, S.C.
Porgy, Red **—10-8; Murrells Inlet, 1985; J. F. Duffer, Myrtle Beach, S.C.
Runner, Rainbow—14-14; Georgetown, 1985; W. D. Harder, Orangeburg, S.C.
Sailfish—75-0; Georgetown, 1968; G. A. Reid, Clinton, S.C.
Seatrout, Spotted—11-13; Murrells Inlet, 1976; A. Pendergrass, Murrells Inlet, S.C.
Shark, Shortfin Mako—302-12; Georgetown, 1978; L. F. Howell, Beaufort, S.C.
Tiger Shark—1,780-0; Cherry Grove, 1964; W. Maxwell, Charlotte, N.C.
Snapper, Red—37-8; Little River, 1964; K. Henry, Rock Hill, S.C.
Swordfish—500-0; Georgetown, 1978; B. H. Peace III, Pawleys Island, S.C.
Tilefish, Blueline—14-6; Murrells Inlet, 1982; O. Cockerfield, Ft. Wayne, Ind.
Triggerfish, Gray*—13-9; Murrells Inlet, 1989; Jim Hilton, Lake Wylie, S.C.
Triggerfish, Queen—6-5; Murrells Inlet, 2000; Alicea Novak, Matthews, N.C.
Tuna, Blackfin—37-0; Georgetown, 1998; Wofford G. Boyd, Georgetown, S.C.
Tuna, Bluefin—332-6; Murrells Inlet, 1996; Michael E. Stone, Savannah,Ga.
Wahoo—30-5; Murrells Inlet, 1998; J. Moore, Valdese, N.C.

*   Indicates a current world's record
** Currently not eligible for state record consideration due to state or federal restrictions

This info can be found on the Internet at www.dnr.state.sc.us/marine/saltrecs/saltrec.html

that a developer interested in adding a pier to North Myrtle Beach would spend between $3 million and $3.5 million just for construction. That's why a fishing pier is never merely a structure reaching into the sea from whence you cast a line. All piers on the Grand Strand offer a mixture of shops, arcades, restaurants and watersports outlets. There's enough to do to keep you occupied for a few hours or an entire day.

Make the most of your fall pier fishing excursion by casting your line from the northernmost piers, from the north side. Southward migration occurs at this time as fish of all shapes and sizes respond to shorter days and lower sunlight intensity. They reach these northern piers on the north side first. September usually yields anglers a bountiful catch of king and Spanish mackerel, mullet, menhaden, pompano, spot and bluefish.

North Strand

Cherry Grove Pier
3500 N. Ocean Blvd., North Myrtle Beach
• (843) 249-1625
Daily admission is $5 per rod. Seasonal rates are available. Holiday House Motel guests are admitted free. Pier walkers are charged 50¢.

This pier is 985 feet long and is lighted for night fishing. You'll find a full line of pier tackle plus a gift shop and restaurant. Cherry Grove is open 24 hours a day from March 1 through the Sunday following Thanksgiving.

Myrtle Beach

Apache Pier
Apache Campground, 9700 Kings Rd., Myrtle Beach
• **(843) 497-6486**

Welcome to the longest pier anywhere along the East Coast—measuring 1,220 feet in length. Accents include a bait-and-tackle shop, arcade, restaurant and aquariums filled with indigenous fish. Nightly entertainment is also part of the fun from May 30 through Labor Day weekend.

It will cost you $5 a day to fish from the pier or 50¢ to partake in the action as a spectator. Campers staying at Apache Campground (see our Accommodations chapter) pay only $4. Hours are 6 AM to midnight from spring through fall and 8 AM to 10 PM all winter.

Myrtle Beach State Park
4401 S. Kings Hwy., Myrtle Beach
• **(843) 238-5326**

A $2 parking fee is levied to anyone entering the park, except from November 5 to mid-March. Regular admission cost is $4 per fishing pole, and season passes are available. Fishing rods can be rented for $4 a piece. The pier is open to the public whenever the park is—6 AM to 9:30 PM each day. Tackle, bait, ice and a gift shop are on the premises.

Pier 14 Restaurant, Lounge & Fishing Pier
1304 N. Ocean Blvd., Myrtle Beach
• **(843) 448-4314**

More popular for the fine dining at the restaurant than for the fishing allure, Pier 14 does its rod-and-reel business from the tackle shop situated right next door. There is a $5 charge for fishing, but anyone can walk the pier or watch the angling free of charge. An arcade and an outdoor patio also are open to the public. Pier 14 is in full swing from 7 AM to midnight all summer long, continuing through mid-October. From mid-October through the second week in November, operating hours are from 8 AM to 10 PM. This pier is closed during the winter months, mid-November until mid-February.

Second Avenue Pier & Restaurant
200 N. Ocean Blvd., Myrtle Beach
• **(843) 626-8480**

Admission is $5 for a daily pass to fish, 50¢ for spectators; inquire about season passes. You'll find a full line of bait, tackle, rods and reels here plus a gift shop, arcade and full-service restaurant.

This lighted pier with T-shape end is 905 feet long. Hours are 7 AM to 11 PM daily from March 1 through the end of September or early October.

Springmaid Pier
3200 S. Ocean Blvd., Myrtle Beach
• **(843) 238-5189 Ext. 3008**

Bait and ice are sold here, and tackle is available for rent or purchase. Admission price is $6.50 per angler (spectators are free), with special weekly and year-round rates offered.

Springmaid is open seven days a week year round from 6 AM to midnight; the tackle shop closes at 10 PM during summer.

South Strand

The Pier at Garden City
110 Waccamaw Dr. S., Garden City Beach
• **(843) 651-9700**

The Pier at Garden City is open 24 hours a day, year round. Daily admission to fish is $6, and spectators are admitted free. Season passes can be purchased for $65. Bait and rental gear are available from the tackle shop.

Stop by the arcade and oceanfront deck of the Pier Cafe for before- or after-fishing activities. The cafe itself usually closes from Christmas through April 1.

Surfside Pier
11 S. Ocean Blvd., Surfside Beach
• **(843) 238-0121**

Admission to this 810-foot-long pier is $5 per angler. Spectators pay a 50¢ charge. Weekly and season passes are available. You'll find tackle, bait, and rod-and-reel rentals on the pier along with a gift shop.

The biggest tarpon ever caught from a South Carolina pier (142 pounds) was landed here in September 1995. The tackle shop and pier are open 24 hours a day from March 1 through December 15.

INSIDERS' TIP
If you're going to be fishing without a local captain or guide, check on current regulations before embarking on your fishing trip. Fines for illegal fish can be substantial.

FISHING

Bait & Tackle Shops

Like any sport, you need the right equipment to complement technique. All Grand Strand piers and fishing venues offer a smattering of outlets where you can get your hands on a rod and reel and bait. But, for the serious angler, the following bait and tackle venues offer years of experience, local tips, and top-quality gear.

North Strand

Boulineau's Foods Plus
318 Sea Mountain Hwy., Cherry Grove
• (843)249-3556

Since 1948, Boulineau's has served as one of the area's most popular suppliers of fishing equipment, hardware, cut bait—and lots and lots of free advice. The shop is open year round from 7 AM to 10 PM.

Johnny's Bait & Tackle
4377 Sea Mountain Hwy.
(S.C. Hwy. 9), Little River
• (843) 249-1288

Cornell Williamson is proud of his 20-year-old business and is about as experienced an angler as you'll ever meet. He swears by his mud minnows to catch flounder and recommends ballyhoo and rig mullet to troll for king mackerel. Both offshore and freshwater tackle are available.

Saltwater, freshwater and shrimping licenses can be purchased here. Johnny's is open every day of the year from 6 AM to 5 PM.

Myrtle Beach

City Bait & Tackle
713 Eighth Ave. N. and Alder St.,
Myrtle Beach
• (843) 448-2543

This 25-year-old family business has earned a sterling reputation among local fishing enthusiasts. Owner Roy Brigham will tell you in a heartbeat that the only advertising worth believing in is good customer service and word of mouth.

City Bait & Tackle keeps a steady supply of mullet, shrimp and squid as preferred bait as well as a wide range of tackle. Roy is always willing to inform customers where to cast their line for the catch of the day. This store is open 365 days a year from 6 AM to 7 PM.

South Strand

Cedar Hill Landing
5225 U.S. Hwy. 17 S. Bus., Murrells Inlet
• (843) 651-8706

Cedar Hill is another bait and tackle shop owned by the Nance family with a full array of live bait—oysters, crabs and shrimp—and all the equipment an angler needs to be completely outfitted. This fishing emporium is open year round, seven days a week from 6 AM to 9 PM. Johnboat rentals are available here, and we'll tell you more about that if you refer to our Boating chapter.

Fishing Tournaments

If you reckon yourself an astute angler and want to put your skills to the ultimate test, you've come to the right place. We've listed a handful of area tournaments that are open to all interested participants.

Boating tournaments, usually of the offshore variety, are relatively costly to enter, but prize purses are lucrative, typically totaling thousands of dollars. The pier fishing contests tend to be cumulative events, lasting several months; awards are less extravagant and often involve goods rather than cold, hard cash.

Regardless of the form or nature of the brass ring, the following tournaments are competitive as well as a great excuse to ply the waters along the Grand Strand.

Boat Fishing

American Red Cross
Inshore Saltwater Fishing Tournament
(843) 546-5422 (Judith Bayer-Griffith)

This is an annual team competition, focused on reeling in the biggest red drum, spotted sea trout and flounder (summer and Southern) from Murrells Inlet to Charleston. Prizes are based on 80% entry fee payback, for the first ten places, with a $1,000 minimum guaranteed to the first place winner and $100 for the largest in each species. The tournament gets underway with a captain's dinner; fishing begins the next morning at daylight. Entry fee is $85 per boat.

Evinrude Outboards
King Mackerel Fishing Tournament
• (843) 238-0485 (Donnie Griffin)

This early June tournament starts off with a

Deep sea fishing is a favorite activity among those who visit the Grand Strand.

Photo: Courtesy of Captain Dick's Marina

FISHING

multi-inlet kickoff: Boats are launched from Little River and Georgetown. Anglers compete for the $25,000 first prize, awarded to the angler who catches the biggest king mackerel. This is a $160,000 all-cash tournament, based on 250 competing boats. Entry fees are $300 per vessel.

South Carolina Governor's Cup Billfishing Series
• (843) 762-5025

This Governor's Cup tournament involves marinas from North Myrtle Beach to Edisto Island. Participants garner points during six fishing events for the biggest billfish caught; points also are awarded for the tag and release of blue and white marlin and sailfish. Each event sets its own price for entry. The average first-place purse for this event is $12,000. Participating marinas usually include the Marina at Dock Holidays in North Myrtle Beach, Marlin Quay Marina in Murrells Inlet, Georgetown Landing Marina in Georgetown, Wild Dunes Yacht Harbor in Isle of Palms Marina, Bohicket in John's Island, Charleston Harbor Marina Resort in Charleston and Edisto Marina in Edisto Beach. (See our Boating chapter for details about Grand Strand marinas.)

Besides receiving a cash prize, winners are invited to the Governor's mansion for a celebratory dinner.

Tailwalkers King Sting King Mackerel Classic
• (843)527-2495 (Stuart Ballard)

Always held the first weekend in August, this fishing competition is also a multi-inlet event, with boats departing from Georgetown. Based on the participation of at least 175 boats, the first-place catch wins a $41,000 boat, motor and trailer. The second-place angler receives $15,000 cash. The rest of the prize money is divided evenly among anglers who claim the next 30 largest mackerels. This tournament costs $375 per boat to enter, but organizers promise that almost every contestant floats away a winner.

Pier Fishing

Grand Strand Fishing Rodeo
• (843) 626-7444 (Michelle Habeck)

If you prefer to cast from one of the Grand Strand's piers, this annual tournament is for you. More than $10,000 in cash and prizes is awarded from April through October for the biggest "fish of the month." There's no fee to enter the tournament.

Pier King Mackerel Tournaments
(843) 626-7444 (Michelle Habeck)

These mid-May and early September pier tournaments are much like the Fishing Rodeo. Pay the $35 per person entry fee and cast from any pier along the Grand Strand to tempt the tenacious "kings." The total cash purse is based upon the collected entry fees and is allotted proportionally among the first- through fifth-place winners.

Official Weigh Stations

If you're a participant in one of these tournaments and want to throw your day's catch into the hat for competition, the following locations serve as official weigh stations.

On the North Strand: Cherry Grove Pier, N. Ocean Boulevard; and Harbourgate Marina, 2120 Sea Mountain Highway.

In Myrtle Beach: Apache Pier, 9700 Kings Road; Second Avenue Pier, 200 N. Ocean Boulevard; Myrtle Beach State Park, 4401 U.S. Highway 17 S.; Pier 14, 1304 N. Ocean Blvd. and Springmaid Beach Pier, 3200 S. Ocean Boulevard.

On the South Strand: Surfside Pier, 11 S. Ocean Boulevard; Marlin Quay Marina, 1398 S. Waccamaw Drive; The Pier at Garden City, 110 Waccamaw Drive S.; Capt. Dick's Marina, 4123 U.S. Highway 17 Business; Voyager's View Marina, U.S. Highway 17 Business; and Georgetown Landing Marina, 1 Marina Drive.

Boating

Boating the Grand Strand's waters is a bewitching alternative means of travel through this part of the country, foregone by most. What often gets missed in the wink-of-an-eye speeds of faster modes of transportation stretches out before you in a peaceful panorama when navigating rivers, marshes and waterways. Like the persona of area natives, the Grand Strand's seaways seem slower-moving, easier . . . belying the churning eddy of activity just below the surface.

In this coastal area, water routes once were the main arteries for the lifeblood and growth of this region and today are steeped in the history of its people. When the marshy inlets of Calabash, Cherry Grove, Murrells Inlet and Pawleys Island were fair game for anyone, their bulging beds of oysters and clams fed generations of families. There was a time when nets, pots and traps were seen dangling from almost any dock or even a tree, containing the daily catch of blue crabs and shrimp. The deep, drifting Waccamaw River made rice planters some of the wealthiest people in the world during the 1850s, as its waters fed massive rice paddies along its banks. During summers in the mid-1800s, the river was alive with barges carrying whole families and their favorite furnishings from their inland plantation homes to seasonal abodes on Pawleys Island—a cooler clime and a safe haven from "summer fever" (malaria transmitted from mosquitoes).

The historical development of Grand Strand boating routes seems as murky as the water itself. All that we know for sure is that it was a generations-long process, most likely motivated by economic need or inspired by the discoveries of maverick explorers.

Sometimes referred to as the Inland Waterway, or even Watery Route 1, the Intracoastal Waterway stretches from 23 miles north of Boston to the Florida Keys. The Intracoastal is the domain of pleasure craft, small fishing vessels and, at times, barges. It is a master of quick change: at one moment a narrow, banked channel; at the next turn, a broad, hazy inland sea bounded by gold, green and brown marsh grasses. Dredged to a 12-foot depth from Norfolk, Virginia, southward to Miami, the Intracoastal is famous for hidden sandbars along its path—the main reason smaller craft are recommended.

Because some of its northern sections are closed, mile 0 officially begins at Norfolk. The waterway's history is sketchy at best, but evidence shows it was used by Native Americans to travel the length of the coast. Around 1643 some Massachusetts colonists dug a half-mile-long canal linking the Anniquam River and Gloucester Harbor. President George Washington was responsible for surveying the Great Dismal Swamp, a 200,000-acre wilderness spanning parts of southeastern Virginia and northeastern North Carolina, in 1763. Thirty years later work finally began in the swamp to connect rivers in Virginia and North Carolina. The final portion was completed in 1936 when the federal government became involved and tied in the area between Little River and Winyah Bay in South Carolina.

Today, when it comes to boating, the Grand Strand offers practically every imaginable type of waterway, including tea-colored rivers stained by the tannins of cypress roots, briny marshes and the open waters of the Atlantic Ocean and aqua-blue Gulf Stream.

LOOK FOR:
• Rules of the Waterway
• Public Boat Ramps
• Public-access Marinas
• Boating Tours and Excursions
• Boat Rentals

Rules of the Waterway

Even though we know you wouldn't launch a boat without knowledge of safety methods and rules, we thought it important to outline your legal responsibilities as a boater. First and foremost, the operator of any vessel is required by law to file with local authorities a formal, written report of any accident. This can be accomplished simply by contacting the U.S. Coast Guard Boating Safety Hotline, (800) 368-5647, to make a verbal report and acquire a form.

Accident Reports

It is necessary to report damage to a vessel or its equipment, injury or loss of life, or any missing passenger. You must also file a report in the case of grounding, capsizing, someone falling overboard, colliding, sinking, striking a boat or propeller, swamping, flooding, fire, an explosion or the disappearance of a craft. Injury to or the death or disappearance of an individual must be reported within 48 hours, while damage to a vessel or property must be disclosed within 10 days of the incident.

Approaching Vessels and Right of Way

When approaching another boat in open waters, each party must move to the right after a short (one-second) horn signal, answered by the other vessel. If crossing paths, the boat to your right from dead ahead to two points abaft your beam has the right of way. You should sound one short blast ("I'm altering course to starboard"), two short blasts ("... to port") or three short blasts (". . . to stern").

In all situations the boat being overtaken has the right of way, even if the overtaking ship enters your danger zone. The overtaking boat is required to sound two long and one short blast if it intends to pass on the right; two long, two short blasts if on the left. If you are being overtaken, respond with one long, one short, one long and one short signal if you understand and agree.

Casting Off

Leaving a slip or dock dictates that you have no right of way until you are completely clear of the dock. It is every operator's responsibility to leave port without danger to other boats, and it's a good idea to sound one long blast as you are about to depart. All sailboats under sail alone (no motorized power) and fishing boats have the right of way and should be given wide berth. The only exception to this rule is when the sailboat is overtaking a motorboat, in which case the motorized craft maintains the right of way.

Common sense guides most boating regulations: Allow large ships with restricted maneuverability the right of way; stay away from docks, piers and swimming areas; and take responsibility for damage caused by your wake.

Life Jackets

In boats less that 16 feet in length, a wearable life vest must be accessible for each person aboard. If the boat is more than 16 feet in length, wearable life vests must be accessible, in addition to a ring buoy or other safety device that can be thrown. All children younger than 12 aboard a vessel less than 16 feet long are required to wear life jackets.

The Pilot

Anyone 16 or older can legally pilot a boat. Those younger than 16 can only run a vessel after taking a boater education course and passing a test. Courses are offered

INSIDERS' TIP

If you're left treading water on a boating excursion, fight hypothermia by keeping on all clothing to trap heat. Avoid moving as much as possible and draw your knees up while floating on your back in your life jacket. If you have a treading companion, huddle together to stay warm.

through the U.S. Coast Guard Auxiliary, U.S. Power Squadron and the Department of Motor Vehicles. The DMV issues educational handbooks for study prior to testing.

Safety First

If the wind suddenly shifts, or if lightning and choppy water are evident, there's a good chance a storm is brewing; in that case, boating is not a good idea for the time being.

Before casting off into any waters, check your vessel for the following items: a portable radio to check weather reports, a flashlight, extra batteries, matches, a navigation map of the area, suntan lotion, a first-aid kit, sunglasses, a raincoat and an extra length of tie-line. It's always best to tell someone where you're going, who is accompanying you and how long you plan to be away. Before starting the engine, open hatches, run the blower and, most importantly, sniff for gasoline fumes in the fuel and engine areas. Make sure all fishing and hunting gear is well packed—there's nothing like a loose fish hook to ruin a potentially great outing.

While cruising, change seats carefully, especially if the craft is a small one. The rule of thumb is to stay low and near the center line. Use caution when passing a powerboat, and anchor from the bow with a line that is at least five times as long as the water's depth.

Public Boat Ramps

The following sites (listed geographically from north to south) are provided by Horry and Georgetown counties to allow boaters access to waterways. None of them has been formally named, so we've provided the approximate location for each.

Hogg Inlet: in the North Myrtle Beach area between Little River and Cherry Grove Beach

North Myrtle Beach/Little River: under the bridge at S.C. Highway 9, on the Intracoastal Waterway

Ocean Drive Beach: in North Myrtle Beach, just west of U.S. Highway 17

Three in Socastee: Off S.C. Highway 544 turn into Rosewood Estates and follow the road until it ends; Peachtree Landing is located off S.C. Highway 544 at the old Socastee Bridge; Enterprise Landing is located off S.C. Highway 707 just south of the Socastee bridges.

Murrells Inlet: Highway 17 Business beside Belin United Methodist Church

Georgetown: follow U.S. Highway 701 to its southern end in Georgetown

Public-access Marinas

If you're lucky enough to own a sailing vessel, we think you'll find the following comprehensive list of area marinas useful in getting around the Strand by watercraft. It's always best to contact the marinas in advance, especially if you'll be arriving late at night or if your boat is experiencing mechanical trouble. Marina personnel usually will make sure someone is there to meet you and that the right equipment is available for repairs. All of the Grand Strand's public marinas listed here are open year round, even if hours of operation vary from season to season.

North Strand

Anchor Marina
2200 Little River Neck Rd., Little River
• **(843) 249-7899**

"Do it yourself is always welcome" is the motto of Anchor Marina, where sailors are encouraged to pull in for repairs and supplies. A 35-ton travel lift is available, and mechanics are on call 24 hours a day to fix anything from a blister to a broken propeller shaft. Anchor's staff also offer bottom painting, fiberglass work and power washing.

This 85-slip marina provides wet and dry storage, showers, bathrooms, a ship's store, restaurant and lounge. General hours for the marina and store are 8 AM to 5 PM seven days a week; the restaurant and lounge are open from 11 AM until the wee hours of the morning.

B.W.'s Marina
4495 Mineola Ave., Little River
• **(843) 280-8954**

B.W.'s, managed by Michelle Coffey, officially opened for business in April 1996, taking over for the Pier at Little River. Transient boats are allowed to tie up at the face dock, and 10 slips are available for monthly rental. Water, 110- and 220-amp. electrical hookups also are available as well as gasoline and diesel fuels. This marina is open from 7:30 AM to 6 PM with extended hours during the summer.

Nautical Lingo

While by no means a complete list, the following glossary will help keep your common boating terminology shipshape from stem to stern.

ABEAM—At right angles to the boat's center line.
AFT—Toward the back.
BEAM—The boat at its widest part.
BILGE—Lower interior areas of the hull.
BOW—Front end of the boat.
BOW EYE—Where trailer cable is attached to the boat.
BROAD ON THE BOW—Between abeam and bow.
BROAD ON THE QUARTER—Halfway between abeam and astern.
BULKHEADS—Vertical partitions.
CENTERBOARD—Plate of metal or wood, raised or lowered on pivot to control sailboat's lateral resistance.
CHART—A boater's map. Never call it a map.
CLEAT—Fittings with horns to which a line is secured.
COME ABOUT—Changing direction by bringing bow through the wind.
CURRENT—River or tidal flow of water.
DEAD AHEAD—Straight ahead over bow.
DEAD ASTERN—Straight back over stern.
DRAFT—Depth of water needed to float the boat.
EBB—Outgoing tide.
FATHOM—Six feet (a measure of depth).
FLOOD—Incoming tide.
FORE—Toward the front (bow) of the boat.
FORE AND AFT—An object that runs parallel to the keel.

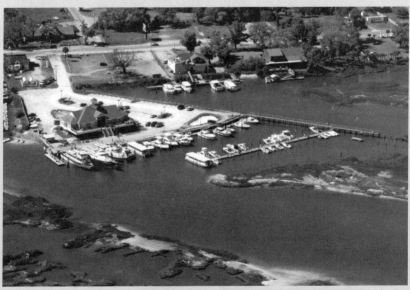

From shrimp boats to private yachts to state-of-the-art ocean-going vessels, area marinas sport a wide assortment of watercraft.

Photo: Courtesy of Brandon Advertising

GUNWALE—Upper part of the top plank of topsides.
GROUND TACKLE—All the gear used for anchoring.
HALYARD—A line to hoist a sail.
HEAD—Fore part of the boat; also, a seagoing toilet.
HELM—The steering mechanism of a boat.
HULL—Basic part of a boat consisting of the keel, frames, planking and deck.
JIB—Triangular sail set between bow and foremast.
JIBE—Sailboat changes direction by bringing the stern through the wind. This
maneuver can be dangerous.
KEEL—Major structural member of a hull.
KNOT—Measure of speed (=1 nautical mph).
LEEWARD—The side of a boat away from the wind.
LINE—Any rope that performs a function on the boat.
NAUTICAL MILE—A measure of distance (6,076.1 ft.).
PORT—Left side of a boat.
REEF—Short lengths of line spaced horizontally on a sail. The sail is dropped to
where the lines can be tied thus shortening (reefing) the sail in a strong wind.
RODE—The anchor line.
RUDDER (RIGHT, LEFT)—The rudder positioned to the right or left. Often
confused with right or left tiller. A tiller put to the right will move the rudder left.
SHEER—A line to control a sail's angle to the wind.
SLACK—Period between flood and ebb when the current is not flowing.
SPRINGLINE—A line leading from stern to forward (or on bow to aft) on dock to
prevent boat from moving ahead or astern.
STARBOARD—The right side of a boat.
STEM—The near-vertical structural member at the bow.
STERN—The back of the boat.
TACK—Sailing as near to the wind as possible. Starboard tack, wind coming over
the forward right side of the boat; port tack, wind coming over the forward left.
Also for motorboats not heading directly into the wind.
TIDE—The rise or fall of water.
TILLER—A horizontal arm extending from the top of the rudder post that is used
to steer the boat.
TRANSOM—Flat planking across the stern.
VEER—Wind direction shifts clockwise.
WINDWARD—Toward the wind.
YAW—Stern moved to either side by a following sea.

Source: *Boating Guide*, 3rd edition, Martin Frederick Inc., Snibbe Book Div.

Coquina Harbour Inc.
720 U.S. Hwy. 17 N., North Myrtle Beach
• **(843) 249-9333**

Russell Edwards manages this 113-slip marina that offers a bath house and self-service laundry facilities. Monthly and yearly slip leases can be negotiated. The marina is open year round.

Crickett Cove Marina
4483 N. Baker St., Little River
• **(843) 249-7169**

Crickett Cove opened in July 1997 and is the last such venture that will be permitted on saltwater marsh since those wetlands are a protected natural habitat. Concrete floating docks offer transient boat storage, and 73 wet slips are available for boats from 40 to 55 feet in length. Dry storage can accommodate 340 vessels as long as 35 feet. Two fueling depots, inside and outside, offer gas and diesel fuel pumps. Hookups include water, cable TV, telephone and 30-, 50- and 100-amp. electricity. Crickett Cove serves guests with showers, bathrooms and laundry facilities. Currents, (843) 280-3189, opened in February 1998, serving lunch and dinner. Currents opens daily at 11:30 AM. Marina hours are 8 AM to sunset seven days a week.

Especially during winter, the Intracoastal Waterway is filled with boats of all shapes and sizes—many of which are headed south for warmer weather.

Photo: Courtesy of Lowcountry Companion

Harbourgate Marina
2120 Sea Mountain Hwy. (S.C. Hwy. 9), North Myrtle Beach
• **(843) 249-8888**

This marina, under the Little River Swing Bridge, offers a full range of services, including repairs. You'll find cable TV, laundry facilities and showers on site. Harbourgate also boasts a well-stocked ship's store on the premises. Harbourgate Marina is the site of a 100-room Hampton Inn, (843) 249-1997, that opened April 1, 1997. Guests of the Hampton Inn receive special privileges at the marina and a free continental breakfast every morning during their stay.

Marina at Dock Holidays/ Vereen's Marina
1525 13th Ave. N., North Myrtle Beach
• **(843) 280-6354**

Wet dockage is available at one of 102 slips here, as are laundry facilities, showers, a ship's store, cable TV, water, and phone hookups. Dock Holidays offers gas and diesel fuels. Five popular restaurants and lounges are located nearby. Thirty- and 50-amp. shore power also is accessible. In 1997 Dock Holidays added a pump-out station for nautical guests. Hours of operation range from 8 AM to 7 PM, depending on the season.

Myrtle Beach Yacht Club at Coquina Harbour
714 U.S. Hwy. 17 N., Little River
• **(843) 249-5376**

Many of this club's 153 slips are designated for transient use, and boaters can enjoy convenient access to both 30- and 50-amp. power. There is a swimming pool, a pool bar and restaurant, as well as showers, bathrooms, laundry facilities, and water and cable TV hookups. The club offers diesel and gasoline fuels as well as a pump-out station. You'll find an on-site ship's store offering beer, wine and ice, and a number of first-class restaurants are within walking distance. The black-and-white lighthouse at the mouth of Coquina Harbor marks the nautical route to the club. Hours of operation are always 8 AM to dusk.

North Myrtle Beach Marina
4430 Belle Marina Rd., Little River
• **(843) 249-1000**

This full-service marina offers dry storage and crane service that can accommodate any motorized watercraft or sailboat up to 65 feet in length. North Myrtle Beach Marina specializes in service and repairs. The ship's store at this marina stocks an extensive array of boat supplies and fishing tackle. Hours of operation are 8 AM to 6 PM daily.

Myrtle Beach

Hague Marina
**#1 Hague Dr., off S.C. Hwy. 707,
at the Intracoastal Waterway,
Myrtle Beach**
• **(843) 293-2141**

George Russ manages this site. Hague offers yacht service and supplies and storage—wet or dry, covered or uncovered. Transient dockage is available for 90¢ per foot per night. Water and electric hookups plus a ship's store are available. Hague is open 8 AM to 6 PM daily spring through fall, until 5 PM during the winter months.

Osprey Marina
8400 Osprey Rd., Myrtle Beach
• **(843) 215-5353**

Osprey opened in January 1997 next door to the Waccatee Zoo (see our Attractions and Kidstuff chapters). All of Osprey's 96 slips are rented by the year only. Dry storage is available, as are cable TV, phone, water and 30- and 50-amp. electric hookups. This marina provides a pump-out station as well as gasoline and diesel fuels. Amenities include showers, laundry facilities and an on-site convenience store. Hours run 8 AM to 6 PM.

South Strand

Belle Isle Marina
Belle Isle Rd., Georgetown
• **(843) 546-8491**

Sporting both floating and fixed docks, Belle Isle provides 120 slips, dry storage, laundry facilities, showers and bathrooms and also offers diesel fuel or gasoline. A courtesy car to take customers into town is available at no charge. The marina also has a fully stocked ship's store.

In season, the marina and store are open seven days a week from 7 AM to 7 PM. When the weather gets cooler and things slow down, they close up shop at 5 PM.

Georgetown Landing Marina
**432 Marina Dr. and U.S. Hwy. 17,
Georgetown**
• **(843) 546-1776**

This 150-slip deepwater marina has both floating and fixed docks, as well as a recently completed floating linear transient dock. Gas and diesel fuels are available. The property is home to the Lands End Restaurant, popular for years with locals who come to sample the daily seafood specials. Georgetown Landing is open 8 AM to 7 PM throughout summer. In the

Many of the area's most popular cruises never leave the calm waters of area creeks and inlets—making these outings an ideal choice for young and old.

Photo: Courtesy of Captain Dick's Marina

winter hours are 9 AM to 5 PM. A 98-room Hampton Inn, (843) 545-5000, services this marina.

Marlin Quay Marina
1398 S. Waccamaw Dr., Garden City Beach
• **(843) 651-4444**

Besides running an array of charters from this marina, owner Charles Stone offers boat dockage for long-term lease. Bathrooms, showers, laundry facilities, 30- and 50-amp. power hookups and a ship's store are available as are gasoline and diesel fuel pumps. The marina does not allow "live aboards" (where people live on the boat year round) or Jet Skis. It is open year round—6 AM to 8 PM in the summer months and 8 AM to 5 PM during the winter after Daylight Savings Time kicks in.

Voyager's View Marina
U.S. Hwy. 17 Bus., Murrells Inlet
• **(843) 651-7033**

Voyager's View is a full-service marina, with slip rentals, fuel, bait, fishing supplies and dry storage for boats. Drop by and see manager Jack Sowders for assistance.

A bar and grill are on site. Grill hours are from 7 AM to 4 PM; bar hours are from 7 AM to 10 PM.

Wacca-Wache Marina
1950 Wachesaw Rd., Murrells Inlet
• **(843) 651-2994**

Wacca-Wache maintains 108 floating slips, 15 of which are available for transient vessels. This marina also offers 120 dry-storage slips and a choice of 30-, 50- or 100-amp. electrical hookups. Additional services include cable TV hookups, a pump-out station, gasoline and diesel fuel, a ship's store, laundry facilities and showers. A courtesy car is available to transient boaters for an hour at a time to boaters docked at the marina. Wacca-Wache is open from 8 AM to 8 PM during peak boating season, generally June through September.

Boating Tours and Excursions

If you don't have your own vessel and want to explore the Grand Strand from a watery point of view, check out one or more of the following trips. There is something for everybody, no matter what your age or particular interest.

North Strand

Great American Riverboats
Waccatee 200, Enterprise Rd., Socastee
Barefoot Landing, U.S. Hwy. 17, North Myrtle Beach
• **(843) 650-6600, (800) 685-6601**

The Great American Riverboat Company operates two well-appointed boats in the Myrtle Beach area. The *Queen Mary II*—an exquisite replica of the glamorous cruise liner built in the 1930s—operates from the Waccatee Zoo in the Socastee community on the south end of the Strand. The *Barefoot Princess II*—an enormous riverboat that traveled 3200 miles down the Mississippi, across the Gulf of Mexico and back up the Waterway to its current home—operates from Barefoot Landing on the northern end of the Strand. In addition to outdoor decks, both boats boast enclosed, climate-controlled decks—with snack bars, comfortable seating, dance floors, and elegant dining areas.

Both the *Queen Mary* and the *Barefoot Princess* offer daytime, sunset and dinner cruises along the Intracoastal Waterway. All cruises include a cash bar, tour narrator and live entertainment. The daytime excursion lasts 1½ hours and costs $12 for adults and $6 for kids ages 6 to 16; it's free for children 5 and younger. The sunset cruise lasts two hours; admission is $14 for adults, $7 for children ages 6 to 16 and free for kids 5 and younger. Patrons on the 2½-hour dinner cruise have their choice of a prime rib or chicken Cordon Bleu dinner for $36.50 (tax and gratuity included).

Hurricane Fishing Fleet
Hurricane Marina, The Waterfront at Calabash, Calabash, N.C.
• **(843) 249-4575**

"If you haven't experienced the charm of Myrtle Beach from the deck of one of our

> **INSIDERS' TIP**
> Drop into the Original Benjamin's seafood restaurant on Restaurant Row to see fine replicas of famous vessels. Local museum curator and shipwright Jimmy Frost displays his 35-foot-long, 7-foot-tall model of the *Queen Elizabeth* cruise ship that sailed 59 years ago. A 45-foot replica of the *Mayflower* was recently added. Frost showcases his work in the lobby of the restaurant.

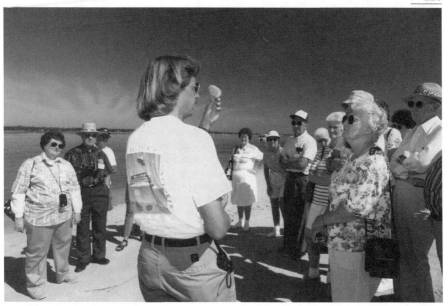

Educational cruises are a fun and easy way to sneak a little learning into your family vacation.

Photo: Courtesy of Captain Dick's Marina

cruises, you haven't experienced Myrtle Beach," is the motto referring to the Hurricane's roster of sea tours.

Hurricane's Adventure Cruises encourage passengers to join the crew for an afternoon, setting a course for the Atlantic Ocean where you'll meet up with a shrimp boat fleet and watch them ply their trade. Shrimping and watching active marine life is the theme of this jaunt, which costs $18 per person 12 and older and $15 per child 11 and younger.

Call the number listed for reservations and schedules because hours and types of cruises change periodically.

South Strand

Capt. Bill's Fleet
Capt. Dick's Marina,
4123 U.S. Hwy. 17 S. Bus., Murrells Inlet
• (843) 651-3676
Discover Murrells Inlet and the Atlantic Ocean from Capt. Dick's located on the waterfront in Murrells Inlet. Make fishing memories and experience the real thrill of catching those big ones. Longer trips travel further offshore to deeper water and produce a wider variety, greater quantity and larger fish! From the half-day Sea Bass Fishing Adventure to the All Day Gulfstream Adventure to the Sundown Fish-

ing Excursion, choices abound and range in price from $25 to $50 per person depending on age and which fishing adventure you choose.

Capt. Dick's Saltwater Marsh Explorer Adventure has long remained one of their most popular tours. Discover the area's own marine wonderland in a 2 1/2-hour boat journey guided by a marine biologist. Experience the vital, living habitat that is home to hundreds of fascinating and mysterious marine creatures. Not an artificial environment like a zoo or aquarium, this interactive tour delivers a glimpse of the real thing. Various nets and dredges are employed to retrieve specimens from beneath the water. Specimens go into onboard touch-tanks where they can be seen, observed and when appropriate, touched and held. There is also a fishing demonstration and a beach walk along a barrier island that is not accessible by car. Participants occasionally, encounter bottle-nosed dolphins—an added delight! All Explorer vessels are rest room equipped.

"Cruisin' The Beach," an ocean sightseeing cruise, is a memorable excursion suitable for the entire family. This cruise departs from the historic Inlet, passes through the tranquil natural beauty of the marsh, and ends up on the majestic Atlantic. Cruising the shoreline of the Grand Strand, the Myrtle Beach skyline is newly captivating. Call ahead for scheduling information. Rates are $14 per adult and $6 for children between the ages of six and twelve. Children under six are free.

Capt. Dick's offers more than we have room to tell you about. Dozens of tours include ecology outings, fishing and sightseeing excursions and pirate adventures. The Captain also offers boat rentals, jet ski rental, parasailing and nearly anything else you can think of. Give the Captain a call at the number listed or visit the website at www.captdicks.com.

Black River Outdoors Center
U.S. Highway 701 North, Georgetown
• **(843) 546-4840**

Unlike whitewater, the waterways along the Tideland Coast are "meandering, gentle, flowing", says naturalist and ecotourism enthusiast Bill Unger, owner of Black River Outdoors Center. All year round, Unger and his professionally trained tour guides offer kayak tours upon the area's blackwater rivers, cypress-tupelo swamps, salt marshes, rice plantation canals and creeks. A sampling of the guided explorations, designed for the adventurous types who love exploring, include the wildlife swamp preserves of the Black River, Waccamaw National Wildlife Refuge and Sandy Island, the creeks and canals of Chicora Wood Plantation, and the saltwater marshes of Murrells Inlet and Huntington Beach State Park.

The uninitiated are often surprised to learn that participation requires only a moderate level of physical fitness. Even first-timers have no trouble paddling the gentle waterways of the area. Reservations are required, and guided day tours of 3 1/2 to 4 hours are priced at a very reasonable $45 (when accompanied by parents, children under thirteen are $25). Group rates are available.

If you are hungry for a bit of solitude, you can also rent kayaks and canoes to launch your own self-guided adventure. Life jackets, paddles, cartop carriers, and safety instruction are included. Touring kayaks are available for the more experienced. Or you can rent a surf kayak to keep at your beach house for a day or a week!

Black River Outdoors Center also offers an impressive stock of kayaks, canoes, small boat trailers and paddling accessories at their retail store, open Monday through Saturday from 9 AM until 5:30 PM. Visit the website at www.blackriveroutdoors.com.

The Jolly Rover
End of Broad Street, Downtown Boardwalk, Georgetown
• **(843) 546-8822 or (800) 705-9063**

Well-suited to sail from historic Georgetown, the Jolly Rover is a tall ship schooner, the same kind of vessel once used by shifty-eyed pirates to ply our Lowcountry waterways. This ship, a 79-foot, two-masted, gaff-rigged topsail schooner which can hold 49 passengers, is a carefully and lovingly crafted replica with modern features for which Blackbeard would have yearned: a steel hull, aluminum masts and nylon sails, modern restroom facilities, an inboard engine and safety lines around the deck to keep little pirates from falling overboard.

Throughout spring and summer, the Jolly Rover will feature three tours per day, Monday through Saturday. Two hour "Pirate Adventures" at 10 AM and 1 PM feature folklore and stories told by a "real" pirate in period clothing. The young and young at heart will enjoy tales of plank walking and buried treasure. Enjoy the fine salt air on deck or relax "down below" as you sail around an uninhabited island and catch glimpses of bald eagles, sea birds and maybe even a 'gator lurking on shore. At 6 PM, also on Mondays through Saturdays, a 2 1/2-hour "Romantic Evening Sail" gives lucky guests an opportunity to experience the romance and magic of daylight disappearing over darkening waters. This tour certainly makes for a memorable end to any day!

The Jolly Rover is operated by an experienced Captain and Crew. There's an on-board Ship Store with light snacks, beverages and Jolly Rover souvenirs.

The Carolina Rover
End of Broad Street, Downtown Boardwalk, Georgetown
• **(843) 546-8822 or (800) 705-9063**

The Carolina Rover, a 49-passenger pontoon boat, offers a different kind of tour. Monday through Saturdays, three hour daily tours— at 10 a.m., 1 p.m. and 5 p.m.—focus on the Georgetown Lighthouse, shelling excursions, and the lush natural environment of the Carolina Lowcountry.

The ever-popular Shelling and Lighthouse Cruise transports its guests a dozen miles or so over smooth inland waters into the mouth of

INSIDERS' TIP

More than 1,000 people die in boating accidents every year. Fifty percent of those deaths involve alcohol. Fifty percent of drunk men who drown have their flies unzipped. Get the picture?

Don't limit yourself to beachside activities! Our rivers and waterways offer a wealth of things to do—from educational and sightseeing cruises to fishing, watersports and more.

Photo: Courtesy of Lesnik Himmelsbach Wilson Hearl & Hirsch

Winyah Bay where an uninhabited and wild-life-rich barrier island sports a historic old light-house—and more shells than most of you have ever seen. Participants are allowed to step right off the boat onto the sun-bleached shoreline to sun, stroll and pick up shells. Plenty of time is allotted for the beach, so expect to spend roughly three hours blissfully removed from civilization.

The Carolina Rover features plenty of shade, snacks, beverages and clean restroom facilities. An onboard naturalist's informative commentary is an added delight.

Lady Franada
End of Broad Street,
Downtown Boardwalk, Georgetown
• (843) 546-8822 or (800) 705-9063

For a delightful change of pace, the Lady Franada offers a selection of eco-friendly excursions that will introduce you to a treasure chest

of unique Lowcountry experiences. Comfortably seated aboard this canvas-covered, outboard-powered pontoon boat, you'll explore pockets of solitude in and around Winyah Bay, as well as in five surrounding rivers. Captain Rod, a long-time native and marvelous storyteller, delivers entertaining narrative that includes local lore, natural and American history tidbits, environmental issues and a hearty helping of good old Southern humor and hospitality.

Daily Plantation Tours allow participants to cruise peaceful, slow-moving rivers past plantation mansions, long-abandoned rice fields, majestic old oaks and a plethora of wildlife. Loved by history buffs and nature lovers, these three-hour tours are perennial favorites and attract lots of return clientele.

Lighthouse Tours cruise to a remote barrier island—past Hobcaw Barony and over the sunken remains of the USS Harvest Moon—where Winyah Bay meets the wide, blue

Atlantic. Explore a place where the sea spills its secrets and deposits an ever-changing array of shelling opportunities.

Plenty of snacks and beverages are available on board, so bring a buck or two but you need not bring anything more. There are clean restroom facilities, too.

Brookgreen Gardens
U.S. Hwy. 17 S., Murrells Inlet
• **(843) 237-4218**

Some of Brookgreen Gardens' most unspoiled vistas can be enjoyed aboard "The Springfield," a 48-foot pontoon boat that offers an up-close look at some of the Lowcountry's native flora and fauna. Several times each day, as the boat winds its way through the scenic waterways, a Brookgreen naturalist tells the story of the long-abandoned rice fields that once thrived in Georgetown County from the mid-eighteenth century until the Civil War. These tours combine the marvels of nature, the thrill of discovery and the intrigue of history. Wilderness lovers, birdwatchers, botanical enthusiasts, and history buffs will long remember this trip.

Boat Rentals

If you have a penchant to captain your own vessel or are looking to take a leisurely cruise on a pontoon boat, the following is a comprehensive listing of established, year-round outlets that offer this equipment. During the summer, you can contact any of the public-access marinas listed earlier in this chapter. Many rent watercraft during the busy season but discontinue rentals right after Labor Day. If you are on the lookout for great kayaking and canoeing opportunities, please refer to our Watersports chapter.

North Strand

Atlantic Watersports
32nd Ave. South, North Myrtle Beach
• **(843) 272-2420**

Rent kayaks or Hobie Cats or opt for a parasailing adventure. A ride on the Banana Boat is a special treat. Reservations are important, especially if you plan to parasail, so please call ahead. Atlantic Watersports opens each morning at 8:30 AM.

North Myrtle Beach Watersports
13th Ave. North, North Myrtle Beach
(at Dock Holiday's Marina)
• **(843) 281-9337**

Three-seater "Seadoos" are available for riding on the Intracoastal Waterway. Fees vary according to the length of the ride and number of people, so please call for additional information. Open from 9 AM until 6:30 PM each day.

Wind 'N Sea Outfitters
62nd Ave. North, Highway 17 Bypass, Myrtle Beach
• **(843) 692-0089**

Wind 'N Sea offers kayak rentals and guided kayak tours. Freshwater and ocean excursions are available and focus on the coast's diverse wildlife. Instruction is available, too. Reservations preferred. Call for rates and availability.

Myrtle Beach

Downwind Sails
2915 S. Ocean Sails Blvd., Myrtle Beach
• **(843) 448-7245**

Right on the beach, Downwind Sails rents 14- or 16-foot sailboats and Hobie Cats from April 1 through October 25. The general price is $35 per hour, but discounts often apply after Labor Day when business slows down. Lessons are highly recommended for novices and run $45 per hour. Downwind is open all summer long from 8 AM to 8 PM. In the fall, hours are from 10 AM to 5 PM.

INSIDERS' TIP
South Carolina is ranked ninth in the nation for its number of registered boats.

Myrtle Beach Water Sports Inc.
9915 N. Kings Hwy., Myrtle Beach
• **(843) 497-8848**
Little River waterfront
• **(843) 280-7777**

These two locations rent pontoon boats, jet skis, and jet boats and also offer para-sailing, island tours and dolphin watches. Both locations are open seven days, 8 AM until 6 PM April through October. For more information, visit www.myrtlebeachwatersports.com.

South Strand

Capt. Dick's Marina
4123 U.S. Hwy. 17 Bus., Murrells Inlet
• **(843) 651-3676**

For cruising or fishing the inlet only, Capt.

Dick's rents 15-foot fiberglass johnboats with 15-hp. outboard motors. Each boat accommodates up to four people and rents for $55 per four hours, $75 for eight hours. Life jackets, fuel, safety equipment and licenses are included in the rental package. For an additional $5, you can also rent a rod and reel for the trip. Johnboat rentals are offered Easter through Thanksgiving. Parasailing trips are an option, too.

Cedar Hill Landing
5225 U.S. Hwy. 17 Bus., Murrells Inlet
• (843) 651-8706

Cedar Hill rents 14-foot johnboats with 6-hp and 15-hp motors for $45 per half-day or $55 per full day of fishing or cruising. Fuel, fishing licenses and life jackets are included in the rental fee. Rod and reels cost an additional $8 per rig. Rentals are available year round.

Beach Information

With an average annual temperature of 74 degrees and 216 days of blue Carolina skies and bright sunshine each year, the Grand Strand's mild, subtropical climate is a mecca for sun worshipers and beachcombers alike. Even when the summer temperatures and humidity chase the majority of people into air-conditioned shelter, the beach will always carry a soft, welcoming breeze that defies the heat. The wide ribbon of sandy coast stretches for 60 miles, and the Atlantic Ocean is usually less turbulent than its West Coast cousin, the Pacific Ocean. As hundreds of thousands of locals and visitors will attest, there's nothing like a glorious day at the beach!

A Friendly Reminder about Sun Exposure . . .

There are few things in life easier to acquire and more painful to live with than a bad sunburn, and around here you can turn a good stinging shade of pink in just 30 minutes to an hour. Longer doses of sun can send sunbathers to the hospital with blisters, nausea and excruciating pain.

Don't be fooled by clouds or cool air: You can get a bad burn even on a day when you can't see the sun. Before you hit the Strand, pick up some good suntan lotion with a high sun protection factor (SPF). We suggest an SPF of 15 to begin the suntan process. Apply it an hour before you start swimming, walking or bicycling and remember to reapply it

The many piers of the Grand Strand give visitors dry access to the ocean.

Photo: Lisa Tomer Rentz

Imagination and a few plastic implements can yield the castle of a child's dreams.

Photo: Courtesy of Myrtle Beach Area Chamber of Commerce

after swimming or if you're perspiring—even if it's waterproof. Most experts recommend avoiding the sun during the hottest part of the day: between noon and 4 PM. Even under the shade, the sun can reflect off the water and sand, so you can still get a burn.

When it comes to SPFs and protecting your skin, there's safety in numbers. Ranging from 2 to 45, the SPF on a particular sunscreen tells you how many times longer (not how many hours longer) the lotion protects you from a sunburn, compared to the time it would take if you wore no sunscreen at all. So, if your skin normally reddens after 20 unprotected minutes in the sun, slathering on an SPF 15 will let you endure the rays for 5 hours (20 x 15 = 300 minutes). You can also make an educated SPF decision by keeping tabs on news reports of daily ultraviolet (UV) index numbers. These numbers range from 0 to 10+, depending on the season, cloud cover and other atmospheric conditions. On a day with a moderate UV reading of 5, wear an SPF 15 lotion and a hat; if the reading is 10 or higher, aim for an SPF of 30 and cover up.

Be sure to wear something on your head. A visor is good to protect your face, but to shield your head and hair, a full hat with a brim that's at least 3-inches wide is best. Good sunglasses that filter out ultraviolet rays should also be part of your standard beach attire. If you've got young children or a baby with you, be sure to take extra care to protect their tender skin. Make them wear hats and reapply sunscreen every few minutes. If kids are determined to stay in the ocean for hours, put T-shirts on them. Some rafts and Boogie boards will cause mild rashes on unprotected stomachs anyway, so the T-shirts will serve two purposes.

If you want to dress to beat the heat, get wise to fabric and weaves. Unbleached cotton, satiny polyesters and silk either absorb or reflect UV rays, while crepe, viscose and bleached cottons allow UV rays to pass through, making a direct hit to your skin. Look for tightly woven materials, like cotton twill, that don't allow light to pass through, enhancing its sun protection power. And, while white and pastel shades of clothing may make you feel cooler, dark tones actually absorb UV rays better.

Ocean Swimming Safety

There is nothing quite so seductive as the gently rolling waves of the Atlantic Ocean. It beckons you to walk in and float amid its briny, undulating waters. And, all at once, you're in perfect commune with nature itself. We know how easily common sense can be forgotten while riding the folds of the ocean, but you must always remember that the forces of nature are not only majestic but also unpredictable—and, at times, downright dangerous. That's why swimming is not permitted beyond 50 yards from the beach or over shoulder depth.

Lucky for us all, Grand Strand beaches are prime tourist attractions overseen by trained lifeguards. As a visitor to the area or local resident, it is always a good idea to plant your beach chair near a lifeguard stand. Before you even get one toe into the surf, these watchdogs of the shoreline will let you know the current swimming conditions by posting colored flags: yellow means use extra caution; red means NO SWIMMING! Scoping out a lifeguard-protected area of the beach gives you the peace of mind that comes from knowing you're not swimming alone, your children have an extra pair of eyes locked on them and, if anything untoward should happen, someone well-trained in rescue and CPR is on hand.

Undertow

That incredible force of water that pulls you oceanward when waves recede is an undertow. Depending on weather conditions, it can be very strong. If you find yourself caught in one, don't panic or try to fight it. Stay calm. Float with the waves and you will eventually be brought back to shore. If waves are bigger than usual, it's a good bet that the undertow will be stronger and it's best to stay in shallower waters.

Riptides

When you combine high waves, a full moon and hurricanes or tropical storms brewing in the Atlantic Ocean, conditions are rife for dangerous riptides or rip currents. "Rips" occur when two opposing currents meet, causing a swirling action that can carry swimmers from safer waters. These currents represent an overflow of water coming into shore that travels back into the ocean in a narrow current with considerable force and speed. Telltale signs of riptides are rough, choppy water that appears deeper and darker than normal, with swirling debris, kelp or sand. Since 80 percent of ocean rescues are a result of swimmers finding themselves caught in a rip current, it's wise to know how to get out of such a force. As with a strong undertow, try to relax. It's useless to fight a rip current. Go along with it and then angle yourself to swim or float parallel to the shoreline. Waves at either side of the rip current will take you back to shore.

Beach Rules

Alcohol

All Grand Strand beaches forbid alcohol consumption and possession. All open containers with alcohol are forbidden. This rule applies to all public access areas as well.

Attracting Sharks

No one is permitted to bait, fish for or otherwise attract sharks to an area within a half-mile of the beach.

Cars on the Beach

Driving on the beach is no longer allowed on any portion of the Grand Strand beaches.

Distribution of Literature/Solicitation

You might have wondered why the only advertising along the beach is by airplane banner or a lighted boat. Well, it's because other forms are against the law here. No one can distribute anything in the genre of pamphlets, advertisements, handbills or circulars. It is also a "no-no" to conduct business of any kind on the beach, including promotional devices such as free samples or admission passes.

Recumbent bikes are a fun way to get around the beach.

Photo: Lisa Tomer Rentz

Fireworks

Unincorporated areas of Horry County are the only places where fireworks are permitted (they're not allowed within any city limits). Use is restricted to private property between the hours of 10 AM and 10 PM.

Glass Containers

It is unlawful to take any glass bottle, drinking glass or other glass containers to the beach with you.

Horses

Horses are not allowed on the Strand in North Myrtle Beach. Riders in Myrtle Beach must have a permit from the city clerk. In Surfside, horses are banned from the beach April 1 through November 1, and in Horry County, horses are banned from beaches March 1 through October 31.

Littering

Although you would never believe it, considering the mountains of trash collected along the Strand every fall during Beach Sweep, littering on the beach or in the water is against the law. This includes any glass, bottles, cans, paper, garbage, waste or refuse.

Motorized Watercraft

In North Myrtle Beach motorized watercraft cannot be launched from the beach between 9 AM and 5 PM from May 15 through September 15. Vehicles must be kept at least 50 yards from

The Grand Strand
Beach Renourishment Project

There is no doubt that the Grand Strand's 60 miles of beach comprise the basis of its status as a tourism mecca. It only stands to reason that the most devastating threat to this area is beach erosion.

Even though our Atlantic beaches have been classified as "stable" (the erosion rate standing at less that a foot per year), it certainly does not mean "static." Beach sands are constantly shifting and, with time, will wash out the beach, buildings, parking lots, swimming pools and even roads.

Knowing how important the beach is to the economic well-being of the area, local, state and federal factions have put into effect a renourishment project to span the next 50 years. The total cost to bring continued and new life to 25 miles of beach from North Myrtle Beach to Garden City Beach is estimated at around $54 million. The plan is to create approximately 136 acres of new beach and widen the existing coastline by 75 to 120 linear feet. This is being done by dredging more than 5 million cubic yards of sand from four ocean-floor sites, 2 to 3 miles offshore. (The $54 million cost is an estimate for keeping the beach in good repair for fifty years. Each completed area should have a functional life span of approximately ten years before minor renourishment has to be done. Also, Surfside and Garden City Beaches were renourished in 1999.)

Renourishment of the beach has already been a factor in North Myrtle Beach with only some concern from oceanfront hotel owners about the bulldozers on the shoreline that create noise and work through the night at lighted worksites. (Beach renourishment crews work 24 hours a day, seven days a week.) But locals and tourists alike step back to admire the finished strips, and all agree that it's well worth the inconvenience. Renourished sections of the beach are wider and often scattered with seashells galore.

The renourishment project for Myrtle Beach began in April of 1997 with the

Beach renourishment projects, which utilize sand pumped from the ocean floor, protect oceanfront property and keep our beaches wide and beautiful.

Photo: Courtesy of City of Myrtle Beach

BEACH INFORMATION

intent of continuous work until completion in December of 1997. During June of that year, the construction project became such a hazard to the public use of the beach it was postponed until October. The project was completed during the Spring of 1998. This phase of the overall project cost approximately $13 million.

Two areas between North Myrtle Beach and Garden City Beach that will not be renourished are from 48th Avenue S. in North Myrtle Beach to 82nd Avenue N. in Myrtle Beach, and from 29th Avenue S. in Myrtle Beach to the northern boundary of Myrtle Beach State Park. Apparently, those areas do not meet federal requirements for public access.

swimmers. In Myrtle Beach, all motorized craft must be at least 50 yards beyond bathers; Jet Skis must be at least 100 yards away. No motorized boats are allowed at Surfside Beach.

All boats must be registered with a permit secured from a lifeguard. Boats must not be left unattended between 8 PM and 8 AM. In Horry County, boaters cannot endanger swimmers and must be at least 400 feet from the shore and 500 feet from any fishing pier.

Animal Laws

In North Myrtle Beach, Myrtle Beach and Surfside Beach, dogs in public must be kept on a leash at all times. From May 15 through September 15, no dogs are allowed on the beach between 9 AM and 5 PM. In Myrtle Beach, between 21st Avenue North and 13th Avenue South, no animals are allowed on the beach or on Ocean Boulevard at any time of year.

Rafts and Floats

In Myrtle Beach and in Horry County areas, rafts must be covered with fabric and have ropes attached to their entire perimeters.

Sand Dunes, Sea Oats and Beach Grass

It is illegal to walk on sand dunes and to pick or otherwise damage sea oats and beach grass, and sand fencing.

Sleeping on the Beach

Myrtle Beach, North Myrtle Beach and Horry County forbid sleeping on the beach between 9 PM and sunrise. In Surfside Beach, people must not sleep in or around automobiles or motor vehicles on the street, in an alleyway or at public accesses.

Swimming

Swimming in the ocean isn't the same as swimming in a lake, river or pool, so don't expect it to be. Veteran ocean swimmers don't fear the ocean, its waves or currents, but they have a healthy respect for it. Caution and common sense are the keys.

One of the most important things to remember is that the lifeguard, young and good-looking though he or she might be, has trained rigorously for this job. Listen to the lifeguard.

All Grand Strand beaches set shoulder-deep and 50 yards-offshore limits for swimmers, but the lifeguard has the authority to keep you in closer if he or she believes conditions warrant it. Disobeying the lifeguard can result in arrest and charges; fines can run from $25 to $200.

Thong Bathing Suits/Nudity

It is illegal to wear a thong bathing suit in North Myrtle Beach, Myrtle Beach and Surfside Beach. Skinny-dippers and nudists, take note: You can be arrested for public nudity on the beach or at any beach access point.

Sandcastle building remains one of the quintessential summertime pleasures for the young and young at heart.

Photo: Courtesy of Myrtle Beach Area Chamber of Commerce

Noise

It is a violation to play any radio or similar device loud enough to disturb persons in dwellings, hotels or residences. This ordinance also includes vehicles and motorcycles with loud exhaust pipes.

Beach Wheelchairs

Beach wheelchairs are available for free to handicapped persons in the Myrtle Beach area. The chairs are designed with oversize rubber wheels that make rolling on a sandy surface easy. The following beach services are responsible for the distribution and storage of the wheelchairs at the following locations:

Myrtle Beach Lifeguards, 76th Avenue N. to 69th Avenue N.; John's Beach Service, 63rd Avenue N. to 23rd Avenue N.; Boardwalk Beach Service, Ninth Avenue N. to the Myrtle Beach Pavilion; Huggins Beach Service, Seventh Avenue N. to Third Avenue N.; and Lack's Beach Service, 20th Avenue S. to 29th Avenue S.

Members of the handicapped public who wish to use one of the beach-going wheelchairs can either contact the beach service of their choice or go to one of the aforementioned locations. In the off-season, call the police department for assistance. Although there is no fee for using the wheelchair, a one-hour limit is requested, unless no one else wishes to use it. Beach-going wheelchairs must be pushed by a second party.

Jellyfish

Jellyfish visits are predictable when southeastern winds blow the live gooey masses into warm, shallow waters. Some are perfectly harmless, but the stinging variety will produce a swelling welt similar to a wound caused by the lash of a whip. And don't be fooled! They can sting even after they wash up on shore. Common symptoms from the venom of a Portuguese man-of-war, for instance, can include nausea, vomiting and muscle cramps. The man-of-war type is actually a colony of jellyfish contained below a 10-inch-long purple and blue float. Tentacles have been known to reach 20 feet and are described by experts as "self-contained, spring-loaded venom glands" that zap a swimmer or anything else that gets in the way. If you're frolicking in the ocean late in the summer and see a blue, football-shape mass floating around, get out of the way.

The sea nettle form of the medusa family is the least toxic, unless you're highly allergic to its formula of venom. Sea nettles are umbrella-shaped, usually spanning 6 inches in diameter and showing a red pigment. Their tentacles are 5- to 7-feet long, and even when beached, they can attack if their stinging cells are still wet.

Of greater concern to your general health and well-being is the small, box-shaped jellyfish called a sea wasp. It's clear, only about 3 inches long, and its tentacles hang from the side of the body, often unnoticed. Unlike the Portuguese man-of-war, no one has ever died from a sea nettle sting, but its toxins cause immense pain.

Cabbage head, or cannonball, jellyfish is the only generally harmless variety that descends upon Grand Strand shores. Clear on top with red sides, they get their name from the fact that they resemble a head of cabbage.

Since the water-based toxins of jellyfish react to proteins, meat tenderizer is the most effective way to treat stings, and it should be the first line of treatment. If meat tenderizer is not on-hand, some people use vinegar. All area lifeguards carry a specially formulated ointment (cortisone, meat tenderizer and Vaseline) for jellyfish stings and will be more than happy to share it with you. Most often, tentacles or nettles are left on the victim's skin and need to be removed. Always use tweezers or run the edge of a credit card along the area to remove nettles. Rinse the area with alcohol, then apply ointment or meat tenderizer.

Shell Collecting

Seashells are considered by many to be timeless art treasures. But unlike most objets d'art, they are created by Mother Nature, given to us by the sea and the price is right—they're free. Since the beginning of recorded time, mankind has held a fascination with seashells. They are found in excavated, ancient temples, graves and sacred statues. Native American Indians used scallop shells as dishes and made weapons from the sharp lips of others. Shell cups and ornaments were used in religious and war ceremonies as well as to top Indian burial mounds.

How We Get Seashells

It is important to note that a shell is actually the splendidly built home of a living mollusk, fashioned from lime taken from the sea water. If you collect a shell that is empty, you are justifiably taking a discarded house. But, if you snatch one from the beach that still holds a living organism, you are killing that mollusk. A mollusk's internal organs are covered by a sac of skin called a mantle, and this organ manufactures the shell by secreting a substance that mixes with lime taken from food. The richer the food source, the thicker and more colorful the shell. Shell homes are built, bit by bit, in layers. Color comes from a rhythm of pigments fed to the shell at particular times in its development. Sunlight and heat also influence color, which is why shells of the same species might vary greatly in pigment.

Collection Tips

Whenever there is turbulence in the sea from tropical storms and hurricanes, you can bet that shorelines will be stocked with shells. After Hurricane Fran thundered by the Grand Strand in September 1996, Huntington Beach State Park reported its jetties were knee-deep in whelks and Horse Conchs. Another factor greatly feeding the beached shell population is the Grand Strand Beach Renourishment Project, currently underway. From North Myrtle Beach to Garden City Beach, sand dredged from ocean floor sites will create 136 acres of new beach and widen the existing coastline by 75 to 120 linear feet. As sand is dredged, shells are loosened and sent spiraling toward the shore or scooped up and brought right to the beach.

The Grand Strand beach renourishment project has also kicked up 60-million-year-old fossils. It's true! In April 1997 a retired high school teacher identified a strange object, found by the hundreds on a North Myrtle Beach section of beach, as 60-million-year-old casts of clam shells.

They were mistaken by many as fossilized turtle heads. Richard E. Petit, a research associate with the Smithsonian Institute, checked them out and confirmed that the molds were formed inside Cucullaea, a mollusk that became extinct in this part of the world a little less than 60 million years ago. Petit explained that they look like miniature stone turtle heads due to the employ shell filling with fine silt that hardened over the millennia.

Normally the best time to search out shells is during a new or full moon and always at low tide. You'll discover the most abundant selection around jetties in Garden City Beach, Murrells Inlet and Huntington Beach State Park. If you're a serious collector, a field trip to one of the barrier islands, such as Shell Island, will reveal a treasure trove of seashells, since these keys are uninhabited, virgin territory.

To take full advantage of your seashell collecting experience along the Strand, we suggest contacting Steve Roth at Huntington Beach State Park, (843) 237-4440, or Bud Lanning, president of the Grand Strand Shell Club, (843) 238-5242. Roth is a local expert on shells and heads up an entire program devoted to mollusks. His beachcombing programs at Huntington Beach include guided tours through the shell-heaped area, and he is as free as the ocean breeze with information and expertise. Beachcombing and shell-collecting romps are offered several times each week year round and are free with paid admission to the park (refer to our Parks and Recreation chapter for details on Huntington Beach State Park).

The Grand Strand Shell Club has been in existence for nearly 10 years with the express purpose of educating the public and preserving shell species. If you would like to join Bud Lanning and the other 200 members of this shelling club, an annual membership costs a mere $5 for an individual and $8 for your whole family. The group coordinates numerous field trips every year, a Seashell Auction (the main fund-raising event) and exhibitions at area malls. In conjunction with the City of Myrtle Beach, The Shell Club has created an extensive and fascinating shell display that is housed at the Myrtle Beach Convention Center. More than five hundred shells are showcased, representing more than 140 species.

For a real treat, feast your eyes on a personal collection of more than 7,000 shells and fossils at the new Nature Center established at Ocean Lakes Campground, 6001 U.S. Highway 17 S. in Myrtle Beach. Retired minister Leonard Raker displays the result of his 40-year obsession with the sea's bounty.

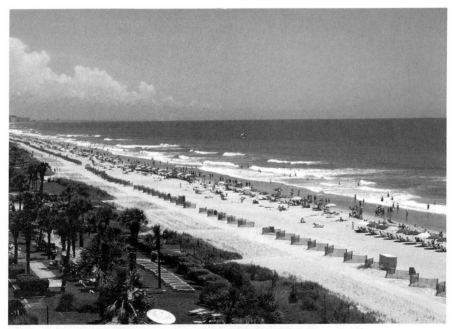

Our long, blonde beaches will always be the area's primary attraction.

Photo: Courtesy of Brandon Advertising

Actually, it's a love story. When Raker was dating his wife, he found a beautiful and rare shell and gave it to her. She lost it. The young man has been combing beaches from Prince Edward Island, Canada, to Honolulu ever since for a replacement. To this day, he hasn't found that particular shell anywhere, but he has amassed an impressive collection that includes microscopic species.

Leonard Raker receives no salary but shares his shells and fossils with the world and holds educational programs at the center. It is open Monday, Wednesday and Friday from 9 AM to noon. Admission is free.

Species along the Strand

You're in shell-collecting heaven, with more than 700 species washing up regularly on Grand Strand shores, including a host of rare, sought-after varieties. The most common classes of shells to be found are pelecypods (bivalves)—two shells that have a hinge-like closing—and gastropods (univalves), which are one-shelled creatures. Here, you'll also find an abundance of sand dollars (echinoderms), relatives of the starfish. Because Gulf Stream currents come to us from Florida, you might be lucky enough to snap up a Florida Horse Conch, the largest known univalve that grows up to 24 inches. Another shelling jackpot that can be found along the Grand Strand is the Left-handed Lightening Whelk, considered a prize since it grows counterclockwise and can reach up to 18 inches in size. Bivalves from the cockle family that regularly visit our shores are the Lemon, Prickly and Giant Atlantic shells. The Notated Clam, with its zigzag scrawling, is a fairly common find. Keep an eye out for South Carolina's state shell, the Lettered Olive. It's known for its glossy appearance caused by its owner embracing it before he or she leaves home. And our neighbor North Carolina consistently releases its state shell to us—the very beautiful Scotch Bonnet.

Hurricanes: Don't Get Caught Blowin' in the Wind

Hurricanes, tornadoes and gusty tropical storms are no strangers to Grand Stranders. Nearly every year the area is threatened to be directly hit by hurricanes. Each hurricane brings its own brand of wrath, whipping residents and businesses with high winds and teeming rains that raised roof shingles, blew away outdoor signs and bent palm trees to the ground. With every one of these storms, thousands of residents were left without power for days at a time, and flooding sent riverfront homeowners to higher ground. State officials and locals alike took fast and strong measures to protect life and property when alerted to each impending hurricane, recalling the devastation wrought when Hurricane Hugo hit the Strand in 1989. While many considered the mandatory evacuation order an extreme measure at the time, Hugo reminded folks why Hurricane Hazel claimed 95 lives in 1954, before advanced mass communication.

The September day Hugo arrived was not unlike any other beautiful fall day along the Grand Strand with blue Carolina skies, warm but not humid. Light swirls of wind blew around pieces of loose paper by late afternoon, but nothing noticeable foretold of the coming onslaught. Like many Myrtle Beach residents, we boarded and taped windows, brought in supplies and settled down for a stormier-than-usual evening. By 10 PM, calm naivete turned into abject terror as windows bowed inwards, power failure forced silent darkness, driving rains stung the skin and attempts at walking outdoors proved futile. To add insult to injury, many of those who fled inland were followed by the devilish tornadoes spawned when Hugo made landfall. Those whirling dervishes were responsible for tossing around mobile homes, selectively demolishing beach houses and snapping Carolina pines from the top, leaving behind nothing but seawater-burnt needles.

INSIDERS' TIP

Myrtle Beach has instituted an Emergency Operations Center (EOC) to address hurricanes or other disasters as they're approaching and after their impact. The general phone number for the EOC is (843) 918-1400, but it is only activated when emergency services are being used.

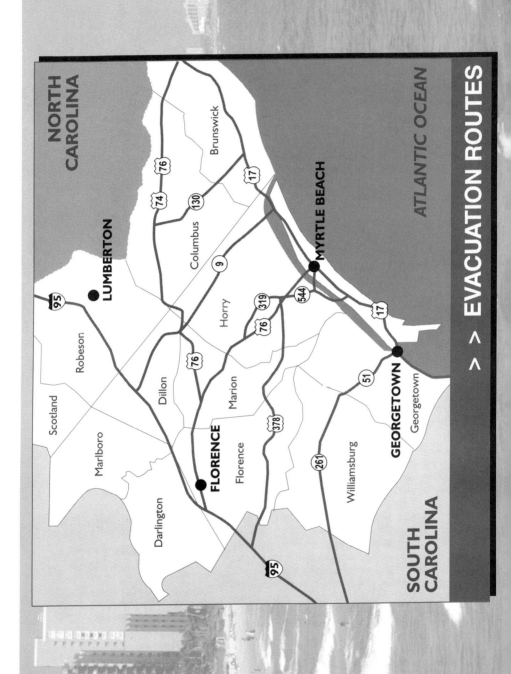

> > EVACUATION ROUTES

Take it from us, the advent of a hurricane is nothing to fool around with. We have included this special section to give you all necessary information to keep yourself and your family as safe as possible in the face of such a natural disaster.

Hurricanes, Tropical Storms and Tornadoes

Tropical storms and hurricanes that hit the eastern United States usually begin off the coast of Africa during late summer, when seas near the equator are unusually warm. A tropical depression is the first step in creating a full-fledged hurricane. Winds begin to rotate in a pattern, increasing to about 31 miles per hour as pressure drops near the center. Narrow bands of rainfall form, some resulting in heavy downpours. Tropical depressions are defined as organized, sustained winds less than 40 mph.

A definite circular wind pattern has developed by the time a tropical storm is upon us. Warm, moist air is pumped into the weather system by wind speeds of up to 74 mph, causing heavy rainfall and a pattern of squall lines. Tropical storms carry winds from 40 to 74 mph.

Hurricanes are huge atmospheric heat pumps that pull in moist air from the ocean's surface to gain power. The air converges in the center and spirals upward. As it rises, the air cools and thunderstorms form. The ocean surface under the spiral acts as a low-pressure area. Cool, dry air is cycled downward, where it is warmed by the sea and rises to continue the swirling cycle.

A hurricane's strength depends largely on the degree to which air is allowed to flow unhindered into and out of the central column, or eye. Hurricanes gain their classification when winds roar above 74 mph.

Tornadoes are funnel clouds. Scientists cannot agree on exactly what causes such a phenomenon. Some claim the origin to be vigorous updrafts in a thundercloud; others think the cause is falling hail. In any case, a spinning funnel cloud has been known to lift cars and rip apart buildings as its vacuum action sucks in air from the ground and carries it upward. The weakest type of tornado blows out from a thunderstorm, usually lasting less than five minutes with winds rarely exceeding 150 mph. Large tornadoes can stir up enough wind to travel as fast as 300 mph. In rare instances, twisters have lasted for hours, measured a half-mile wide and traveled more than 200 miles.

Advance Preparation: Surviving a Hurricane

When you live in a coastal area, you need to have an advance plan for hurricanes, just as you would for a house fire. Since inland motels fill up quickly with the warning of a hurricane, formulate some idea of where you will go if evacuation is necessary. Gather basic supplies required for securing your home and valuables now. Keep them stored in the garage or some other accessible room.

Items to keep on hand: plywood for boarding the outside of windows, tape, rain gear, batteries, rope, bottled water, canned foods (don't forget the can opener), flashlights, a battery-operated radio, candles and first-aid supplies. All of these items sell out in a hurry when a storm is coming, so it's smart to always keep them in supply.

If both parents in a household work, and if you have children who work, develop a plan of communication in the event of a hurricane warning or evacuation order. Determine where you will meet and who is responsible for what facets of your preparedness plan. Think through how you will assist an invalid or handicapped member of your family.

Evacuation shelters offer only the bare necessities. Store your valuables and irreplaceable keepsakes in empty appliances and put plastic bags over household goods such as televisions, lamps and computers. Before you evacuate, let a friend or relative outside the area know of your intended destination.

What to Do During a Hurricane Watch

A hurricane watch is issued when there is a threat of such conditions in your area within 24 to 36 hours. Begin to monitor storm reports on various radio and television stations. Rely only on facts presented by the media and emergency officials. This is the time to refill any necessary prescriptions (we suggest two-weeks worth) and fill up your vehicle's gas tank. You could lose precious time waiting in line at the gas pump, and if electricity goes out, pumps won't operate.

If you will need cash for travel, get it during the "watch" timeframe. ATMs also will have waiting lines and do not work without electricity.

Specifically, have these items stocked in your home: canned food and juices; dried fruit; bread; cookies; crackers; peanut butter and jelly; coffee and tea; enough bottled water for a gallon per person per day for two weeks; ice to cool food and charcoal (for a hibachi or grill) to cook it; a water-purification kit; disposable plates, cups and utensils; infant care items; a battery-operated radio, TV and clock; mosquito repellent; ice chest; plastic trash bags; chlorinated bleach; fire extinguisher; cleanup supplies; toilet paper, paper towels and pre-moistened towelettes.

Check mobile-home tie-downs and secure lawn furniture or other loose outdoor items. Moor small watercraft or move boats to safety. Tape, board or shutter windows to help prevent glass from shattering and wedge sliding glass doors to prevent them from lifting off their tracks. What will you do with the pets? Now is the time to determine whether you will leave them in the house or take them to a kennel. Evacuation shelters do not allow pets of any kind. For your pet's sake have the following necessities on hand: proper identification collar and rabies tag; carrier or cage; leash; water and food bowls; any medications; newspapers or cat litter; proof of vaccinations.

What to Do During a Hurricane Warning

Hurricane warnings are issued when conditions are expected in your area within 24 hours or less. Stay tuned to radio or television for official bulletins and make sure everything is boarded and taped. If you decide to stay in your home during a hurricane, understand that emergency vehicles and personnel are taken off the roads when winds reach 55 mph or more. If any member of your family has special needs, make sure your local EMS has that information.

Stay on the downside of the house away from windows, skylights and glass doors. Clean appropriate containers and your bathtub for storing water. Use the telephone only in an emergency. If you lose power, turn off major appliances to reduce damage and curtail a power surge when electricity is resumed. A hard and fast rule is never to stay in a mobile home or an area within a flood zone, under any condition, during a hurricane. Before you evacuate, shut off water and electricity at main stations and securely lock up.

Hurricane Shelters

When evacuation is imminent, keep an ear cocked to local radio and television for updated shelter locations. Locations may change or become full during the course of a storm. As of this writing, the American Red Cross reports that the following three shelters will be opened within four hours after each school closes following a voluntary evacuation request from the state's Governor: Conway High School at 2201 Church Street in Conway; Loris High School at 301 Heritage Road in Loris; and Andrews Elementary School at 13072 County Line Road in Andrews.

In the event of a Mandatory Evacuation, the following shelters will open as soon as possible: Aynor High School, 210 Highway 24 in Aynor; Carolina Forest Elementary, 285 East Perry Road off Highway 501 in Myrtle Beach; Forestbrook Elementary, 4000 Panthers Parkway off Forestbrook Road in Myrtle Beach; Green Sea-Floyds, 5265 Highway 9 in Green Sea; Loris Middle School, 3410 Church Street in Loris; Whittemore Park Middle, 1808 Rhue Street in Conway; North Myrtle Beach High School, 3750 Sea Mountain Highway in North Myrtle Beach; Forestbrook Middle School, 4430 Gator Lane off Forestbrook Road in Myrtle Beach and, in Georgetown County, Pleasant Hill High School, Schoolhouse Drive in Hemingway.

Be prepared for shelter accommodations: You will be sleeping on the floor or a cot; food might not be available; there are no provisions for medical services; and pets are not allowed. Bring pillows, blankets, sleeping bags or air mattresses, extra clothing, shoes, eyeglasses, lightweight folding chairs and cots and personal hygiene items. Have important papers and identification with you.

Contact the local Red Cross Chapter at 843-477-0020 for further information on disaster preparedness for your business and family.

Watersports

Worldwide, there are more exciting waters to explore, but for the sheer pleasure of participating in watersports, the Grand Strand has its fair share of fans. In fact, our sun-kissed area is a perfect place to learn and practice the rudiments of a particular watersport. The Intracoastal Waterway and Black River offer calmer waters to test out water skiing; there are plenty of scuba-diving courses available and some interesting underwater ledges and wrecks to explore; and the relatively less powerful breakers of the Atlantic Ocean have never discouraged a novice surfer.

Whether you're adept at a watersport or want to try one out, this chapter should drift you in the right direction.

LOOK FOR:
• Surfing
• Water-Skiing
• Scuba Diving
• Watersports Outlets

Surfing

South Carolina waters are not especially good for surfing except when a hurricane or other storm is approaching. Unlike the West Coast, our East Coast has a continental shelf more than 60 miles off the shore that forms a gradual upgrade toward the beach. By Mother Nature's design, wave swells start breaking when they hit the shelf, diminishing the seawater rollers as they travel inland.

Still, the Grand Strand has its share of avid surfers. On just about any day, you'll see people waxing their boards and rushing to the water to ride the wall or hit the lip.

An active and proud community of surfers—an interesting mix of clergy, business owners, restaurant workers and high school and college students—is alive and well along the Strand. The well-established Grand Strand District of the Eastern Surfing Association now hails more than 200-plus members, ranging in age from 4 to 52 years old. The association holds competitions throughout the year along the Strand; local amateur surfers hoping to turn professional vie for points to help them get into meets around the country. For information, call Denny Green at (843) 293-0200.

Grand Strand surfing enthusiasts all have slightly different reasons for their love of the sport: Some refer to surfing as a way of life; others cite the sport as a natural, addictive high; and some even wax spiritual that surfing is God's way of teaching love and respect for the ocean.

Whatever the motivation to engage in wave riding, the smaller, calmer swells along the Grand Strand give beginners a wonderful chance to learn the sport while developing the strength, flexibility, endurance and balance needed to do it well.

Rules of Surfing

Surfing is restricted to certain areas and times on all Grand Strand beaches. All surfers are required to wear leashes. In Horry County surfers must not endanger swimmers and must not surf within 300 feet of a fishing pier.

In North Myrtle Beach surfing and skim boarding are forbidden between 9 AM and 4 PM from May 15 through September 15, except in four areas: near Cherry Grove Pier and at 13th Avenue S., 28th Avenue S., 38th Avenue S. and 6th Avenue N.

Surfboards are not allowed in Myrtle Beach between 9 AM and 5 PM from March 16 through September 15, except in five locations: 29th Avenue S., 41st Avenue N. through 47th Avenue N., 82nd Avenue N. to the city limits, and from the south side of Eighth Avenue N. to the north end of the public boardwalk. (Last location open only from October 1 to April 15.)

In Surfside Beach surfing is not allowed from 9 AM to 5 PM except in the area between 12th Avenue N. to 14th Avenue N. and 6th Avenue S. to 9th Avenue S. For more information on regulations, call (843) 650-4131.

There are a number of shops along the Grand Strand that cater exclusively to the sport of surfing. All of these outlets carry a full line of accessories and apparel, including wet suits, booties, gloves, hoods and, of course, swimwear. (Note: Once you're outfitted and ready to hit the waves, check out this chapter's gray box on surfer lingo so you won't be mistaken for a "kook.")

North Strand

Bert's Surf Shop
806 21st Ave., North Myrtle Beach
• (843) 272-7458

Bert's can set you up with boards from the CB, Hobie, ProMotion, Robert August and Hap Jacobs lines. You can rent surfboards for five to 10 hours at a cost between $15 and $20. Bert's offers a full line of men's and ladies clothing. The shop is generally open from 10 AM until 10 PM, but seasonal schedules sometimes apply. Call ahead if you need to.

North Shore Surf Shop
201-C Sea Mountain Hwy.
(S.C. Hwy. 9), North Myrtle Beach
• (843) 249-5169
110 U.S. Hwy. 17 S., North Myrtle Beach
• (843) 280-5071

North Shore carries Wave Riding vehicles, as well as Action, Liar, and Lost boards. Kayaks, surfboards, and body boards can be rented from $3 an hour to $20 per day. Please note that the Sea Mountain Highway store is only open Fridays, Saturdays and Sundays from October 1 to March 1.

Surf City
3300 U.S. Hwy. 17 S., North Myrtle Beach
• (843) 272-1090

Surf City stocks new and used surfboards, skim boards, body boards, skateboards and other related equipment. Rental rates range anywhere from $10 to $20 per day.

Myrtle Beach

Surf City
1103 N. Kings Hwy., Myrtle Beach
• (843) 626-7919
Myrtle Square Mall,
2501 N. Kings Hwy., Myrtle Beach
• (843) 626-5412

These locations of Surf City, like their North Myrtle Beach counterpart, sell and rent surfboards, body boards, skateboards and related equipment.

South Strand

Island Surf
10080 Ocean Hwy. (U.S. Hwy. 17),
Pawleys Island
• (843) 237-1767

Island Surf is the Strand's exclusive dealer for Maya surfboards. They also carry a full line of surfing accessories. The shop is open Monday through Saturdays from 10:30 AM until 5 PM all year long.

Village Surf Shop
500 Atlantic Ave., Garden City Beach
• (843) 651-6396
2016 N. Kings Highway, Myrtle Beach
• (843) 651-8176

Established in 1969, Village Surf Shop is the oldest hard-core surf shop around. Besides crafting custom boards, this store carries Perfection, RipCurl and Sharp Eye brands.

If your passion dictates a custom-made surfboard, and your wallet is willing, this is the one and only place to visit along the Strand. Established in 1969, Village Surf Shop is the oldest hard-core surf shop around. Besides fashioning custom boards, this store carries Perfection, Rusty, Spyder, JC Hawaii, Kechele and Lost name brands.

Owner Kelly Richards is usually found next door to this shop, covered in Sytrofoam dust with rock music blaring as he shapes one of his masterpieces, called Perfection Surfboards. For nearly two decades years Richards has made boards that are better suited to surfing the East Coast, having a wider surface and heavier weight that allows for a longer ride on smaller waves. The Village also rents surfboards for $20 a day, $30 for two days.

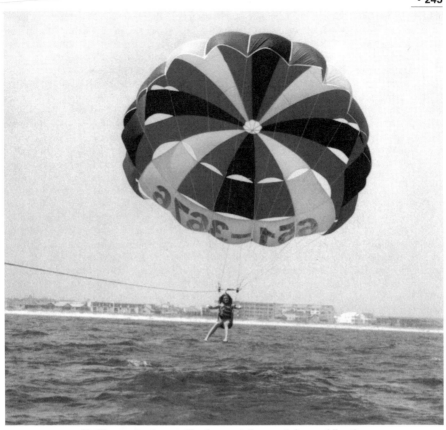

Nothing can beat parasailing for great views and sheer exhilaration.

Photo: Courtesy of Captain Dick's Marina

Water-Skiing

Especially along the Intracoastal Waterway on warm Sunday afternoons, the chugging and screeching of motors from powerboats is a familiar sound. This is when locals launch their vessels to socialize with friends, sunbathe and partake in the exciting and fun sport of water skiing.

The Black River in Georgetown is another popular water-skiing venue.

In South Carolina, water skiing is prohibited between sunset and sunrise. It is considered a three-person operation:

•The boat operator ensures the safe navigation of the vessel and skiers. He or she monitors the boat's speed, adjusting it to the abilities or desires of the skier.

•The observer, who must be at least 12 years old, takes responsibility for the skier's safety by keeping a constant eye on the person skimming across the water, the tow rope and wakes.

An alternative to an observer is a wide-angle rearview mirror adjusted so the operator can see the person in tow.

•The skier is responsible for not exceeding his or her abilities, to help ensure the safe operation of the boat and to communicate with the operator of the vessel. A ski belt or PFD (personal flotation device) must be worn unless the skier has a first-class or higher rating with the American Water Ski Association. But, even if the skier is not wearing such an apparatus, an extra PFD must be aboard.

For all water-skiing equipment and wet suits, visit The Sailing & Ski Connection at 515 U.S. Highway 501 in Myrtle Beach; or give them a call at (843) 626-SAIL.

Scuba Diving

Exploring the ocean and discovering its treasures is an unquestionably exciting experience. However, this sport, as much as any other, is inherently fraught with danger. Therefore, we urge you to educate yourself well about the rules, regulations and risks associated with scuba diving and receive proper training from a certified instructor before strapping on a tank and plunging into the ocean's depths.

No diving is allowed in any waters within the city limits of Myrtle Beach or near piers. The sport can be legally practiced in Surfside Beach, but only if the diver is equipped with a flag to mark his/her underwater location. In all cases you aren't allowed to scuba dive unless you are certified, and every body of water has restrictions on underwater hunting.

Wrecks

Along with artificial reefs—mostly created by intentionally sunken vessels—and live bottom ledges, the Grand Strand offers some fascinating dive sites. Many are historically significant. In 1942 the *Hebe*, a Dutch merchant ship, and the *St. Cathan*, a British submarine chaser, collided and sank; at the time the vessels crossed paths, the *St. Cathan* was under blackout conditions to avoid a U-boat. These two wrecks now rest a quarter-mile apart on the ocean floor, as they have for more than 50 years, providing refuge to myriad marine life. Experienced divers say it's a wonderful site to mingle with game fish and tropicals, search for historic artifacts and take underwater photographs. Two unnamed wrecks occurred in Grand Strand waters in the 1800s, one of which is a copper-clad paddle-wheel steamer. Apparently, the scattered wreckage from each is replete with historic artifacts.

In 1964, while under tow to the Virgin Islands to become a floating hotel and casino, the *Richmond*—a 261-foot, five-deck passenger ship—sank off the coast of Georgetown during a storm. Most of the steel decks and the hull had remained intact since the accident until Hurricane Hugo hit in 1989, collapsing what remained of the hull. The wreckage is scattered but is still home to a wealth of fish species, including angels, butterflies, damsels, grouper, jacks and spades.

Artificial Reefs

Since the briny waters of the Grand Strand area are underlaid by a sandy ocean floor that by nature offers little "live bottom" to attract sea life, the Grand Strand Saltwater Anglers Association, in conjunction with state and local fishing clubs, developed a program to create artificial reefs. These reefs have cultivated underwater forests where deserts formerly stood on the ocean's floor and turned salvage into ecological treasures. In short, artificial reefs provide abundant fishing and diving sites that are easily accessible to small craft.

One such reef, the Bill Perry—named in memory of a local young fisherman who died in a car accident—was built in 1992, 25 miles offshore. Sunken vessels at this spot include a shrimp boat, a tug boat and two 115-foot military landing craft containing Polaris missiles, igniters and control pads. In one year plant growth went wild. The site, a favorite for divers, resembles a thick, underwater forest with such dense fish activity that it is now sometimes difficult to pinpoint the reef. Large ivory coral is the most abundant around Bill Perry Reef.

Creating an artificial reef is not as easy as just sinking a large piece of machinery or broken-down vessel. Whatever is sunk must meet guidelines set forth by the South Carolina Department of Natural Resources. It must be cleaned, environmentally safe and stripped of all floatable material, plastic or oils. Then it must be hauled out to sea by barge and tug boat. Objects such as a cement mixer fall to the ocean floor on their own, but ships must have holes blasted in them to sink as well as to provide the new reef with ventilation and water flow. The Defense Department is the biggest contributor of materials for artificial reefs; it costs anywhere from $1,000 to a whopping $50,000 to properly prepare and sink them.

Other artificial sites that attract hundreds of divers each year include:

• the 10-mile Barge, where a 200-foot barge was sunk in 1972 in about 30 to 40 feet of water just off the Murrells Inlet coastline;

• the 11-mile Tug and Airplane, created using a 90-foot tug boat and, later, a Navy training plane;

• the BP-25, named after the 160-foot tanker *Bernard Perkins* that's sunk at the spot; and,

• the 468-foot-long WW II Amphibious Assault Troop Transport the USS *Vermilion* that was sunk in 1988. The *Vermilion* was originally dropped

INSIDERS' TIP

Always wear an effective waterproof sunscreen when playing any sport in local waters. Reapply the lotion or gel often, all over your body, even if you're wearing a shirt and shorts. When clothing gets wet, fibers relax and allow the sun a direct hit on your skin.

in 107 feet of water, but the 1989 assault of Hurricane Hugo moved the wreck a quarter-mile into 130 feet of water.

The latest, greatest dive site to hit the Grand Strand is called Barracuda Alley! In cooperation with the SC Department of Natural Resources, this 150-foot barge—outfitted with structures of various shapes and designs that attract fish—was sunk in 63 feet of water early in 2000 alongside a group of 20 armored personnel carriers. With much of the structure rising 10 to 20 feet off the bottom, and with over 100 feet of swim-throughs and a training platform, this is an excellent dive for everyone. Come and visit this site, about 10 miles from Little River Inlet, so you can see how it grows and changes throughout the years.

For further information on South Carolina's Artificial Reef Program write to: Artificial Reefs, PO Box 12559, Charleston, SC 29422-2559, or call Bob Martore (843) 762-5082 at the DNR.

Dive Shops

We suggest you contact or stop by the following dive shops to check out a good selection of scuba gear for sale or rent, to receive instruction and certification, or to book daily diving charters. All of the following shops offer PADI certification, and professional staff members can likely answer any questions you might have.

North Strand

Coastal Scuba
1626 U.S. Hwy. 17 S., North Myrtle Beach • (843) 361-3323, (800) 249-9388
Coastal Scuba brings together many years of experience from its captains, instructors and dive masters to make your diving experience the very best it can be. Every diver—from the newly certified to the seasoned veteran—will find a dive charter through Coastal Scuba; there are more than half a dozen to choose from and they range in price from $55 to $110. A variety of classes—from mini-courses to accelerated "executive-style" classes to full PADI certification and advanced instruction—are also offered.

Coastal Scuba's dive vessel is the *Safari III*, a 40-foot vessel custom made for diving. Her 14-foot beam offers plenty of room to store gear bags. The dive ladder and platform are large and strong to make entries and exits easy. She has side curtains that allow you to stay dry when waters are choppy, but allows air to circulate, too. Once your dive is over you can rinse off with a freshwater shower.

WATERSPORTS

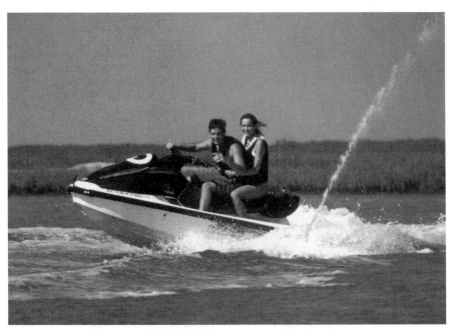

Once you've climbed aboard a Jet Ski, odds are good the thrill will have you daydreaming about owning one of your very own!

Photo: Courtesy of Captain Dick's Marina

Demand for diving is high, especially during the summer and on weekends, so please book early. Visit the website at www.coastalscuba.com for lots of additional information.

Myrtle Beach

Scuba Syndrome
515 U.S. Hwy. 501, Myrtle Beach
• **(843) 626-3483**

Certified divers can plunder the Grand Strand's offshore waters for $50 to $90 a day, depending on how far out you want to go. Renting a full set of gear costs $35. SSI classes start at $45 per person.

South Strand

Mermaid Diving Adventures
4123 U.S. Hwy. 17 Bus., Murrells Inlet
• **(843) 357-3483**

Mermaid is the only Nitrox facility in the area. (For the uninitiated, Nitrox is oxygen-enriched air that provides for longer diving times, shorter surface intervals and increased physical energy.) The PADI-certified instructors here boast that they can turn anyone onto scuba diving for life if given the chance. Individuals ages 12 to 79 have "graduated" from Mermaid's certification courses; the basic open-water course costs $165 a person.

Annual dive trips are coordinated to Cozumel, Mexico, and to Florida to meet the manatee face to face. Mermaid specializes in full-service Dacor and Oceanic equipment.

Dive charters can be booked at Mermaid on weekends during spring and fall and seven days a week during the summer months. Each junket can take along six passengers, and all leave the dock promptly at 7 AM. Charters range from $65 to $100.

Under Sea Adventures Inc.
510 Oak Ave., Garden City Beach
• **(843) 651-1290**

Under Sea specializes in custom diving packages. Choices range from lobster-hunting excursions to multiple deep-site dives and underwater tours of World War II wrecks. Be prepared to stay overnight since a number of these exciting trips last 1½ to two days. Costs start at $65 and go to $125 a person. PADI certification and equipment rentals are also available.

Watersports Outlets

Whether or not you're nautically inclined,

you shouldn't miss experiencing the incredible feeling of gliding across the waves on a windsurfer or Waverunner; paddling the back bays and estuaries of coastal inland waters in a sea kayak; or soaring, suspended in air, as you parasail above the salty ocean spray.

We include a few establishments that provide the equipment you'll need to participate in these exhilarating activities. Kayaking seems to be the new watersport of choice along the Grand Strand, following an impressive emergence of ecologically inclined tours. Kayaking is feasible for folks of almost any fitness and skill level, as it allows paddlers to explore waters and the surrounding landscape at a leisurely pace. If you're combing the area for equipment rentals during summer, you most likely will find more outlets than we've included here. That's because a number of independent business people set up rental stands at local marinas until the end of the summer. If there's a marina close by, call ahead to see if it rents your favorite type of water buggy. (Refer to our Boating chapter for a listing of local marinas.) We mention only those venues that can be contacted all year long and have an established location.

Kayaking

North Strand

Wind 'N Sea Outfitters
803 28th Ave. S., North Myrtle Beach
• **(843) 272-4420**
62nd Ave. N. and U.S. Hwy. 17 Bypass, Myrtle Beach
• **(843) 692-0089**

Home of the Coastal Canoe and Kayak Club, this outfitter runs continuous kayak excursions year round. Membership to the club runs only $5 per year and includes a monthly newsletter of events. Members don't hold regular meetings. Instead, they schedule "paddling get-togethers" to bring members to sessions, and business is conducted on-the-glide. Wind 'N Sea organizes such events as a monthly Full Moon Paddle kayak trip down the Waccamaw River that departs at midnight. It's free if you have your own equipment; $15 a person if you need to be outfitted. Every fall this outfitter coordinates and sponsors the Surf Rodeo—contestants kayak across ocean waves, perform tricks, then surf their vessels into shore! Kayak rentals are available for $15 to $35, depending upon the season and hours of use. Be sure to ask about the shuttle service to get your equipment where it needs to go.

Myrtle Beach

Sailing & Ski Connection
515 U.S. Hwy. 501, Myrtle Beach
• (843) 626-SAIL

Weather permitting, Sailing & Ski runs weekly, supervised kayak tours along the salt marshes of Murrells Inlet. If a group has a special interest, this outfitter will do everything it can to make that interest a reality. The regular salt-marsh trip—$40 per person—lasts three hours and includes munchies.

South Strand

Black River Expeditions Inc.
21 Garden Ave., Georgetown
• (843) 546-4840

By canoe or kayak, Black River Expeditions takes watery advantage of the tidelands of Georgetown, one of the largest estuarine system on the East Coast. Hundreds of miles of waterways offer something new and exciting at every turn: the Black River's cypress swamps; saltwater tidal creeks of Pawleys Island and Huntington Marsh; rice plantation canals of the Great Pee Dee and Waccamaw rivers; the Cape Romain National Wildlife Refuge; and the Francis Marion National Forest. All tours are guided and include all necessary equipment, safety instruction and transportation. The waters are known to be slow-moving. Year-round, daily morning excursions last about four hours; evening paddle cruises—Tuesdays, Wednesdays and Thursdays from April until Labor Day—last around 1½ hours.

Kayaking tours of tidal saltwater creeks start out at Huntington Beach State Park and proceed through cord grass marshes and along sandy beaches of Murrells Inlet to the causeway. Half-day guided tours are $45 for adults and teens and $25 for age twelve and under. This same trip is offered at night around periods of the full moon for the same price as the daytime treks; bring along your own food, drinks and a flashlight if going at night.

Kayak and canoe tours of the Black River follow the ancient watery route of commerce

that served rice and indigo plantations from the 1700s. These treks explore the untouched blackwater cypress swamps, alive with ducks, wild turkeys, herons, alligators and the swamp canary. Prices are the same as the previously mentioned saltwater creek trips.

Departing from East Bay Park Landing on the Sampit River in Georgetown, the Historic Harbor Paddle Cruise passes the Harborwalk, scores of fishing vessels, private yachts, the tall ship *Jolly Rover*, the Kaminski House and Clock Tower. This tour is offered on summer nights at a cost of $20 per person; children younger than 7 go for free.

If the history of rice planting intrigues you, the Rice Field Canal Paddle trip will take you to the remains of antebellum dikes and trunk gates once used to flood rice paddies. Creeks and hand-dug canals interlace the Great Pee Dee and Waccamaw rivers and showcase vast plantations that sustained an aristocratic society who made millions growing "Waccamaw Gold."

The daytime version of this trip includes a peek from the water at one of the plantation homes. This half-day excursion costs $45 for adults and teens, $20 for age twelve and younger.

Jet Skiing, Parasailing, WaveRunning and More

In this section we include personal watercraft rentals where you are at the helm of fast and slick vessels. If it's a pontoon or sailboat you're specifically looking for, please refer to our Boating chapter for related information.

Myrtle Beach

Downwind Sails
2915 S. Ocean Blvd., Myrtle Beach
• (843) 448-7245

Rentals, rides and lessons for bananas, Jet Skis and parasailers are available here. Prices vary depending on what equipment you want, the time of year and what's in stock. It's a good bet, though, that you'll enjoy significant discounts after late August, when heavy tourist traffic dies down. Downwind Sails is open April to mid-October and is right on the beach. This is a great spot to hang out during the summer, with all of the boating action plus regular beach volleyball tournaments.

INSIDERS' TIP

Personal watercraft have proven to be dangerous watersports equipment in the hands of an inexperienced or impaired operator. Every year the Grand Strand mourns deaths caused by too young, too reckless or too drunk personal watercraft drivers involved in boating accidents.

Myrtle Beach Water Sports, Inc.
9915 N. Kings Hwy., Myrtle Beach
- **(843) 497-8848**

This watersports store rents Jet Skis, pontoons and jetboats by the hour. Specials on rentals and tours are offered throughout the year, so be sure to inquire about any discounts you might be entitled to. This outlet is open 8 AM to 6 PM daily from March 1 through October.

North Strand

Atlantic Watersports
32nd Avenue S., N. Myrtle Beach
- **(843) 272-2420**

Book a parasailing adventure at Atlantic Watersports from April through October. The flight lasts 10 to 12 minutes at an altitude of approximately 500 feet. It's $50 per person, and reservations are preferred.

South Strand

Capt. Dick's Marina
4123 U.S. Hwy. 17 Bus., Murrells Inlet
- **(843) 651-3676**

Parasailing flights are booked from this marina year round, weather permitting. Bookings slow down considerably beginning in October and continuing throughout winter when winds are friskier and waters choppier. For $50 you can enjoy a two-hour boat trip and 12 to 15 minutes of soaring 200 to 300 feet above the ocean. Capt. Dick's also rents genuine Yamaha Wave Runners. Cost is $49 for 45 minutes of riding Inlet Channels out into the ocean.

Marlin Quay Parasailing
Marlin Quay Marina,
1398 S. Waccamaw Dr., Garden City Beach
- **(843) 651-4444**

This high-flying experience includes a 1½ to 2 hour boat ride in the Atlantic Ocean plus a 15-minute flight over 200 feet in the air. There must be six people per boat to make the excursion. The cost is $42 plus tax per parasailor. Trips are scheduled from March through September. Discounts for couples are available.

Myrtle Beach Water Sports of Little River
Little River Waterfront
- **(843) 280-7777 or (843) 280-5483**

Enjoy beautiful scenic views of Byrd Island from your lofty parasail perch. Reservations are required. This watersport resource also offers pontoons and Jet Skis. Open daily from 8 AM to 6 PM, March through October.

Daytrips

LOOK FOR:
• Charleston
• Conway
• Indigo Farms, N.C.
• Wilmington, N.C.

Once upon a time there were lulls of "what can we do today" for Grand Strand visitors. These were usually rainy days when the beach was less than pleasant, long days during too-long vacations that needed a break in the monotony and those disastrous days when the sun had turned the skin too lobster to handle another burning. But with the most recent growth along the Grand Strand, it is nearly impossible to find a day without some suitable activity . . . no matter what your particular interest.

In this chapter we offer suggestions for daytrips. Any one of them will give you an up-close look at Southern culture, a taste of the extraordinary beauty and history of the Carolinas' coastal region, and generally something to do if you wonder what is just beyond the Strand's offerings. Zip to Conway or Charleston in South Carolina, or Wilmington, just across the state line in North Carolina, to spend a day enjoying the sights and return; you'll be cozy in your bed before the lines shorten on Restaurant Row.

Charleston

Charleston. The very name of this beautiful city conjures up images of sprawling plantations, honey-dipped Southern belles and the sweet bouquet of magnolia floating on the ocean breeze. Charleston, a synergy of charm and cosmopolitan flair, is steeped in a history that parallels the South itself—indeed, the little city is a microcosm of the whole South. More distinctive than any other Southern city, Charleston has found its way into operas, novels, movies, television dramas and even soap operas. Simply put, there's no place like it in all the world, and you don't dare get as close as Myrtle Beach and miss out on the enchantment.

It will come as no surprise that Charleston boasts far too many enticements to mention even a respectable fraction in this chapter. If you want to know more, pick up a copy of *The Insiders'® Guide to Greater Charleston*. Cover to cover, it's packed with the particulars you'll need to know to enjoy this fascinating city to its fullest extent.

Any time is a great time to visit the area, but spring, as a whole, is remarkable with warm days, crisp nights and flowers galore. In May **Spoleto**, an international arts festival, exacts a welcome grip on the city. Spoleto, consistently a huge success, is a celebration of opera, jazz, theater, dance and visual arts sometimes categorized as classical and sometimes modern enough to cause controversy. People from all over the globe return year after year, and the numbers keep growing. For more information about the festival, write P.O. Box 157, Charleston, South Carolina 29402, or call (843) 722-2764.

In September **The Charleston Preservation Society** opens many of the city's privately owned homes and gardens during its annual candlelight tour series. This is the second of our two favorite times to visit. Many of the tours include chamber music and champagne receptions, and all are imbued with an authentic sense of yesteryear. Learn more by calling (843) 722-4630.

Many of Charleston's legendary plantations are open to the public.

All of the gardens are memorable; some are outright unforgettable. The most popular and well known of the lineup: **Drayton Hall**, (843) 766-0188; **Middleton Place**, (843) 556-6020; **Magnolia Plantation and Gardens**, (843) 571-1266; **Cypress Gardens**, (843) 553-0515, which was once part of Dean Hall Plantation; and **Boone Hall**, (843) 884-4371. Admission to the plantations and gardens is $12.50 for adults and $6 for children ages 6 to 12.

INSIDERS' TIP

If you decide to explore Charleston, be sure to leave plenty of time to stop along the way. If you are staying in Myrtle Beach, the two-hour drive south to Charleston is filled with diversions: a detour into Murrells Inlet or Pawleys Island, a tour of Hampton Plantation, roadside produce stands, historical markers. Watch for the signs!

   Charles Towne Landing, 1500 Old Towne Road, (843) 852-4200, a South Carolina state park, is also a former plantation. Today the park is dedicated to re-creating and interpreting the first permanent English settlement in the Carolinas, on this site in 1670. There's a film about the history of the Lowcountry, an animal forest, a reproduction of a 17th-century trading vessel and a colonial area where visitors can observe candle making, open-fire cooking, woodworking and the colony's first printing press. Bicycles, the best way to get around, are available for rent. Hours are 8:30 AM to 5 PM. Admission is $5 for adults, $2.50 for children ages 6 through 14 and $2.50 for out-of-state seniors. In-state seniors, handicapped visitors and children younger than 6 are admitted free.

   Nearly every school child in South Carolina has been to the **Fort Sumter National Monument** in Charleston Harbor at least once. Many know the story by heart. In 1861, Confederate soldiers fired upon Union forces stationed at the fort, and the Civil War began. You can only get to Fort Sumter by boat, but that's a big part of the fun. Catch the tour at Charleston's City Marina on Lockwood Boulevard or at Patriots Point in Mount Pleasant. Call (843) 722-1691 for more information.

   Charleston is home to **The Citadel**, 171 Moultrie Street, (843) 953-6966, once an all-male state-supported military college that has recently been the center of much controversy over the court-ordered admittance of women. If you're headed to Charleston, plan your trip to include a Friday when school is in session so you can watch the weekly dress parade; it starts at 3:45 PM.

   Charleston is chock-full of museums and carefully preserved historic homes, many of which are open to the public. The **Frances R. Edmunds Center for Historic Preservation**, 108 Meeting Street, (843) 724-8484, is a good place to start your visit. You can buy tickets here to most area attractions, and the staff will offer lots of friendly tourist advice. The center is open Monday through Saturday from 10 AM to 5 PM, and Sunday from 2 to 5 PM.

   If you're looking for excellent shopping alternatives, Charleston sports a fine array. So if your daytrip isn't full to overflowing, at least check out **King Street** and the **Old Market** area. The selections are overwhelming: old shops, new shops, food shops, open air shops. It's something you'll have to experience to understand.

   Charleston is a scenic two-hour trip from Myrtle Beach. Take U.S. Highway 17 S. Even the trip down to Charleston is a great experience. Driving through **Frances Marion National Park** shows you some of the finest coastal natural beauty in America ... and, alas, some of the most devastation to forest and wildlife areas by a hurricane (the hundreds-of-years-old trees will never recover from the damage wrought by Hurricane Hugo, and the area shows the loss).

   The historic antebellum village of **McClellanville** (also devastated by Hugo, but well-recovered) is about halfway along the route and offers some of the finest white-oak-lined streets and hanging moss in South Carolina. Just before you get to Charleston, the little village of Mt. Pleasant will amaze you with roadside huts set up to sell baskets, bowls and other carriers woven from South Carolina sweet grass—an art developed by slaves and handed down through the generations to just a handful of old women who still remember the method. These beautiful objects are also among the most utilitarian pieces you can find. Museums pay fortunes for them; here and here alone you can find them on the roadside for what'll seem like a steal.

Conway

   Conway is one of the prettiest little towns you'll ever stumble upon if you seek a typical southern small town; it's filled with friendly folks who can demonstrate the very essence of

The Lowcountry's signature sweetgrass baskets are still made by hand in Charleston, S.C.

Photo: Courtesy of Charleston Convention & Visitors Bureau

Southern hospitality. A mere 14 miles from Myrtle Beach, most people are introduced to Conway as they drive through it en route to Myrtle Beach. Most people don't realize that a few blocks east of the congestion on U.S. Highway 501 Bypass, just beyond the choke of auto exhaust, is Conway's historic section. In addition to its rich history, thanks to the extensive planting and protection of trees, Conway has been designated a Tree City, USA. However, the newest trees aren't the ones that impress visitors most; the enormous age-old oaks are what Conwayites and tourists love best. Local residents have gone to great lengths to preserve and protect their oaks. In some cases they have even constructed roads around the majestic trees! The reward is a cool canopy of shade unfurling across streets where lovely homes date back a century and more.

One of the first and finest oaks you'll see as you drive down Conway's Main Street is the **Wade Hampton Oak** in front of the Horry County Museum. A plaque on the oak commemorates the day in 1876 when Confederate Gen. Wade Hampton brought his campaign for the governorship to Conway and addressed a crowd from beneath the tree. Many years later, when construction of a railroad threatened the historic hardwood, a spirited local lady, Mary Beaty, brandished a loaded shotgun and ordered workers, "Touch not a single bough."

Just across the street from the Horry County Museum, another stately oak spills shade in the yard of the First Methodist Church. Its gnarled branches stretch over the historic graves in the cemetery. Don't miss the oak on Elm Street at Fifth Avenue around which motorists have to maneuver their cars. On Sixth Avenue, near Elm Street, the road literally splits in half to go around another tree. A monument at the foot of this tree was erected in honor of soldiers who died defending the Confederacy. The blacktop makes way for another oak at the intersection of Seventh Avenue and Beaty Street. If time permits, allow yourself the leisure to mosey along nearby streets; you'll enjoy a veritable parade of the beautiful old trees that typify the South at its finest. The Conway Chamber of Commerce publishes *A Guide to Conway's Fine Oaks,* an illustrated booklet with facts, poems dedicated to the trees and a self guided tour.

But, before you take off for a lazy amble beneath the trees, stop for an enlightening tour at the **Horry County Museum**, 201 Main Street, (843) 248-1282. Open 10 AM to 5 PM Monday through Saturday, one of the museum's most popular exhibits includes a variety of Lowcountry animals. Sadly, burgeoning development in the area has endangered many species. Those on display were accidentally killed (that's right, there is a "roadkill" display in the museum). In addition to birds, alligators and more, you can see everybody's favorite: an enormous 300-pound black bear that was hit by a car on U.S. 501 many years ago. The central theme underlying all of the exhibits is the wide range of environmental conditions found in Horry County and how its inhabitants, from prehistoric times to the present, have adapted to these local conditions.

If yours is a spring vacation, Conway is a not-to-be-missed excursion. Flowers begin blooming as early as March and usually flourish throughout most of April. Tulip trees and Japanese magnolias are particular favorites. They're complemented by quince, daffodils, narcissus, goldenrod, white and purple wisteria, crape myrtle, flowering cherry trees, Bradford pear trees, pink and white dogwoods and thousands of azaleas in vivid, delicious colors.

Conway is the county seat of Horry County. Plans for the town, originally known as Kingston Township, were drafted around 1734. The first settlers arrived a few years later. (It wasn't until the early 1900s that Conway residents began to build vacation cottages at New Town, the summer retreat now known as Myrtle Beach.) As the area's primary transportation route, the Waccamaw River was absolutely vital to early life in Conway. For many, many years, the town's economy centered on by-products gleaned from the thick pine forests that surrounded the city. Many businessmen found wealth selling lumber, tar, pitch and turpentine.

Your best bet is to enter Conway over the Main Street Bridge. (The bridge has been restored to look like it did when it was first erected.) The **Conway Chamber of Commerce**, 203 Main Street, will be the first building on the left. Do yourself a favor and take a few minutes to stop and ask questions. And be sure to get a copy of the "Conway's Historic Tour" brochure so you won't miss a single one of the city's beautiful and significant buildings, many of which are on the National Register of Historic Buildings. The self-guided tour also features a number of distinctive homes including Snow Hill, at the corner of Kingston Lake and Lakeside drives, and the Arthur Burroughs home just across the street.

Conway City Hall, on the left at the foot of the bridge, was designed by Robert Mills, who also masterminded the Washington Monument and several other public buildings in our nation's capital. Constructed in 1824 or 1825, the building was the area's first courthouse. The city clock, which has become a Conway trademark, was added more than a century later in 1939. In recent years, since the city became part of the Main Street USA program, Conway's once-sleepy downtown has been transformed by a host of extensive renovations. Buildings, most of which were built in the early 1900s, have been restored to their original appearances. Numerous businesses have opened and flourished since the restoration began 11 years ago. A host of department stores, speciality shops and antiques markets now line the historic streets.

For a town of modest size, Conway has a surprising number of excellent restaurants. A popular spot with locals is **The Trestle**, 308 Main Street, (843) 248-9896. Fresh pastries are featured every morning. A doughnut or a cinnamon twist with a cup of coffee will start your historic tour off right. Lunchtime fare includes stuffed potatoes, chicken salad and a delectable club sandwich made extraordinary by fresh-baked sourdough bread. Other lunch suggestions include **The Sidewheeler**, 110 Main on the Riverfront, (843) 248-7048, and **Chan's Garden**, 1117 Third Avenue, (843) 248-9182. **Wayne's Restaurant**, 1127 Third Avenue, (843) 248-2951, a longtime local favorite, will serve up a sampling of the South's finest: Southern fried chicken, chicken bog (also known as chicken pilau, pronounced "per-low"), corn bread, Southern-style vegetables, collards and creamy banana pudding.

Conway initiated development of its riverfront area several years ago, and the improvement has been phenomenal. For a change of pace, check out the boats at the city-owned **Conway Marina** at the end of Elm Street. Take a stroll along the scenic river on the updated 850 foot boardwalk. For an especially tranquil day, rent a canoe or pontoon boat at the marina and disappear down the river or into the swamp off **Kingston Lake**. Canoes and pontoons can be rented for a half-day or full day. If you can, talk marina operator Dick Davis into serving as your guide. He also rents fishing boats and might be willing to show you where to catch "the big one."

Another of the marina's options is to take a riverboat cruise on the **Kingston Lady**, and on several nights during the summer you can catch a live-play murder mystery on board, courtesy

DAYTRIPS

The battleship USS North Carolina is a must-see when you visit Wilmington.

Photo: Joe Swift

DAYTRIPS

of the world-renowned Vagabond Players. Otherwise, a two to four hour tour down the uncharted Waccamaw is enhanced by a narrated history of the beautiful blackwater river that's estimated to be 5 million years old. You're sure to catch a glimpse of the river's abundant wildlife, including alligators, otters, turtles and majestic blue herons. A two-hour sunset cruise is especially romantic and often features live entertainment. Call the Conway Marina and Kingston Lady at (843) 248-4033 or (800) 361-6058 to set up your river adventure.

Conway is the undisputed heart of Horry County's thriving tobacco industry. Each year, in a little more than three months, the Conway market pumps about $40 million into the economy. Many visitors to Conway enjoy the unique experience of a tobacco auction. The tobacco market typically opens in mid-July and closes toward the end of October. Conway's warehouses include **Coastal Farmer's** on Cultra Road off U.S. Highway 501 W. at El Bethel, and **New Farmers** at 2401 Main Street. Tobacco isn't sold every day during the marketing season, and the order of the sale rotates. Before you head for the warehouses, get a sales schedule from the Conway Chamber of Commerce. The prattle of the auctioneer sounds like a strange language to the uninitiated, but any of the friendly farmers will be glad to give you a quick lesson in growing, grading, stabilization regulations and "turning the tag."

Conway boasts several popular annual events. The **Rivertown Jazz Festival**, sponsored by the Conway Main Street program, draws thousands to the riverfront beneath Main Street Bridge. Usually scheduled for May or early June, this event showcases plenty of outrageously delicious food, jazzy toe-tapping tunes, entertainment for kids and pretty river scenery to boot. Best of all, the festival is free and appropriate for all ages, so bring lawn chairs or a big blanket, stretch out comfortably and relegate your cares to some other day.

Riverfest is another much-anticipated annual event. Best wear your swimsuit; to truly enjoy this festival, you have to get wet. Events include Waccamaw raft races for all ages, crafts, concerts, lunch and scads of children's games. The day's most unusual event is undoubtedly the Jell-O Jump. Adventuresome kids actually leap into a chilled vat of Jell-O to recover marked golf balls. Ball markings determine the prizes to be won, including items such as soft drinks and free passes to area attractions. But the grand-prize winner gets cold, hard cash. Riverfest is typically held on the Saturday that falls closest to the Fourth of July and features an explosive fireworks finale.

On the first weekend in December, the riverfront is the focus of another colorful event—the **Christmas Boat Parade**. In 1992 Conway had its first nighttime boat parade. The aquatic procession features boats of all sizes—bedecked in Christmas regalia. The '92 occasion was an immediate hit, and it has become a much-loved annual event.

The Conway Area Chamber of Commerce offers popular bus tours of Conway's historical areas each year in conjunction with **Canadian-American Days Festival** in March (see our Annual Events chapter for details). Call (843) 248-2273 for more information. Another favorite Canadian-American event is the **Taste of Conway**. Not surprisingly, it's held along the riverfront and always draws eager crowds to sample the fine cuisine of Conway's restaurant owners and chefs. Delectable samples of appetizers, entrees and desserts range from about $1 to $3.50.

To get to Conway, take U.S. 501 from Myrtle Beach, S.C. Highway 90 from North Myrtle Beach and S.C. Highway 544 (or U.S. 17 Bypass to S.C. 544) from the South Strand. Or, you might want to ride the Coastal Rapid Public Transit Authority bus; call (843) 626-9138 for schedules and fares. (See our Getting Around chapter for more information.)

Indigo Farms, N.C.

Daytripping to Indigo Farms is a simple jaunt into the farm country that surrounds Myrtle Beach. The farm actually straddles the border between the Carolinas and gets its name from the blue crop that originally made this region famous. It's just a quick left then a right out of North Myrtle Beach; take S.C. Highway 9 to Loris and turn right onto S.C. Highway 57, (Indigo Farms billboards will be around) then drive straight 'til you see the farm on the side of the road. Be sure to call (843) 399-6902 first for hours, which vary, and in-season crops, which vary too.

For locals Indigo Farms is a gardening (especially for their large and priced-right ferns) and produce resource. Everything is grown on the actual farmhouse grounds or in the surrounding fields. The complex has an extensive greenhouse with a few permanent, beautiful specimens of palms growing against the roof (unfortunately, not for sale) among the lush geraniums, lantana, mandavilla and everything else that's in season. The palms look like they've been around almost as long as the Bellamy family, who runs Indigo Farms, has worked this land. The storefront extends to include an eat-in bakery and cafe with pies galore, some locally made crafts that are on display and the produce market when the merchandise is meant to be squeezed and admired.

Still owned and operated by the latest generation of Bellamys (the exact count is in dispute by family members), on the day that we visited we found Mrs. Bellamy herself operating one of the cash registers in the produce market, helped out by one of her daughters-in-law. The Bellamys seem to want to share the best way to view a farm, which is from the middle of a field. At Indigo they grow quite a few pick-it-yourself crops, from strawberries and blueberries to tomatoes and peaches. Besides being a twist on the usual shopping experience, picking your own fruits and veggies brings out more flavor to enjoy.

As you would expect, fall harvest is a busy time at Indigo Farms. In addition to the usual farm activities, Indigo hosts two fests: **Farm Heritage Day** and **Pumpkin Day**, both in October. Both festivals turn the hard-working farm into something of a handmade amusement park that even the cows can enjoy.

Farm Heritage Day explores the area's original economic

DAYTRIPS

and domestic roots. Admission is free to events; children and adults alike can pet all the usual farm animals and some not-so-usual farm animals like emus. Members of the Bellamy family and their friends provide demonstrations of crafts, usually something the demonstrator specializes in or just needs to get done: candle making or wool dyeing with indigo, which is actually another color before it hits the air and turns blue. There's a lot to learn. Traditional activities include apple bobbing, hay rides, scarecrow making, potbelly pig races and tours of the farm facilities. Cornstalks are turned into mazes and tipis for the kids. Pumpkin Day is in preparation for Halloween, of course, and children are invited to draw on their pumpkins.

Throughout the year Indigo Farms is also available for school tours, picnics, open-air parties and oyster roasts. The Bellamys are contemplating a Christmas event, so keep an eye peeled for their changing, seasonal schedule.

Wilmington, N.C.

Wilmington is a beautiful and historic seaport that affords residents and visitors the very finest opportunities for shopping, dining, culture and art. Truth is, there's far too much to see and do in a single day, but if you choose carefully and plan your trip before leaving the Grand Strand, you can cover a lot of interesting territory in a short period of time. For a complete guide to this intriguing Southern city, buy yourself a copy of *The Insiders'® Guide to Wilmington and North Carolina's Southern Coast*. Additionally, you might give the folks at the **Cape Fear Coast Convention and Visitors Bureau** a ring, (800) 222-4757; they're well-equipped to answer any of your questions.

Wilmington boasts the largest urban registered historic district in the entire state of North Carolina. Indeed, it boasts one of the largest districts listed on the National Register of Historic Places, with homes dating from as early as the mid-1700s. Meticulously restored Victorian, Georgian, Italianate and antebellum homes—from grand mansions to cottages—attest to the perseverance of Wilmingtonians. The area considered historically significant covers 200 city blocks, but much of the fun and captivating charm of Wilmington is concentrated on and near the riverfront. An architecturally unique historic district highlights the downtown area, with a scenic riverfront park overlooking the USS *North Carolina* battleship.

Follow U.S. 17 N. from the Grand Strand to Wilmington. Guide signs are posted to point you downtown where a deep harbor, restaurants, shops and impressive homes await. The harbor itself offers surprises. With a little luck, a Coast Guard ship or other vessels will be docked there, allowing visitors to board and browse.

As in many historic Southern cities, a good way to begin your Wilmington adventure is with a horse-drawn carriage tour along the riverfront past stately mansions and beautifully restored homes. Various tours, including walking and boat tours, are available at the foot of Market Street by the river. They are well worth the reasonable prices as they provide lively narratives of the area's history and point out attractions you might want to return to on your own. Two popular boat tours on the Cape Fear River are aboard the *Captain J.M. Maffitt* and the *Henrietta II*. The *Henrietta II* bills itself as North Carolina's only true sternwheel paddleboat. Sightseeing cruises offer opportunities to view real plantations. The Maffitt also offers sightseeing cruises on the Cape Fear River. Special fall cruises are a real treat.

During the summer months, the Maffitt serves as a river taxi to ferry people to the **USS North Carolina**. Once the most powerful battleship in the world, the North Carolina now rests majestically in the harbor and is easily seen from Water Street; but to drive to it, you have to go to U.S. 17 S. and circle the city. (If you save the battleship for your last stop before heading back to the Grand Strand, it will be right on the way home.) If you want to stay downtown for shopping and supper, take the *Maffitt* instead of driving. For more information, call (800) 676-0162.

The USS *North Carolina*, a 15-story battleship that is two city blocks long, is Wilmington's most popular attraction. Dedicated to the 10,000 North Carolinians who sacrificed their lives during World War II, the USS *North Carolina* participated in every major naval offensive in the Pacific Ocean. But, here's a word of warning. If you have a physical handicap, claustrophobia or any ailment that remotely resembles vertigo, tuck your greenbacks back in your pocket and move on. Only the main deck is handicapped-accessible. One staircase after another requires careful maneuvering, and there are 5- to 6-inch ledges to finesse at every door. There are more

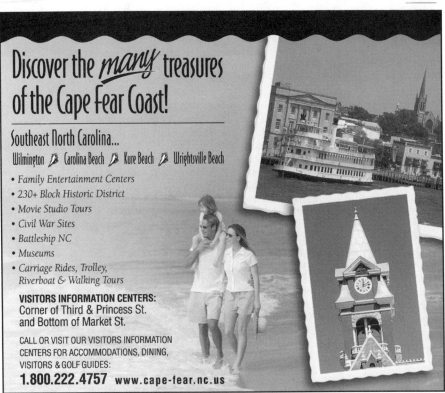
than a few tight spots. Granted, you don't have to climb into the turrets, but if you tour the lower deck, you're already into the tight spots before you realize you need to turn back. The brave souls who decide to go ahead will enjoy a wonderful history lesson.

The adventure begins with an orientation film about the battleship and its escapades during World War II. After orientation, choose from two self-guided tours. One tour can take as long as two hours. Winding through the ship's bowels, you'll see the cobbler shop, sailors' quarters, officers' quarters, galley, bake shop, kitchen, dining areas, engine room, laundry, print shop, dark room, a doctor's office and dispensary, an operating room, an isolation area, a financial section, a supply office and more. It's awesome! A second tour eliminates much of the climbing and takes in fewer decks; it takes approximately an hour.

The ship is open daily from 8 AM until sunset May through September and until 5 PM for the rest of the year. Admission costs $8 for adults and $4 for children ages 6 to 11; kids younger than 6 get in free.

Let's head back downtown for some shopping. In most cases, downtown stores are independent specialty stores that brim with surprises from upscale to whimsical. One of Wilmington's brightest stars is the recently revived **City Market**. (You can enter on South Front Street or Water Street.) The market has fresh fruit and vegetables, a variety of tempting home-baked treats, jellies, honey and plenty of handmade crafts. On the northern end of the riverfront, **The Cotton Exchange** is another not-to-be-missed shopping stop. It's at the corner of Water and Grace streets, (910) 343-9896. (You can also enter at 313 N. Front.) An old cotton warehouse that's been converted into a mall of sorts, The Cotton Exchange houses more than 30 businesses on three levels. Even if you don't like to shop, it's worth the stop to see the displays of cotton bales, weighing equipment and photographs that recount the building's evolution. At last count, there were four restaurants at The Cotton Exchange, so don't worry when hunger assails you. **Chandler's Wharf,** an equally charming but smaller shopping complex, is on the extreme southern end of the riverfront. It, too, definitely merits a stop.

If there's any time left in your day, other attractions include **St. John's Museum of Art**, 114 Orange Street, (910) 763-0281 or (910) 341-7981, with three restored, architecturally distinctive buildings united by a sculpture garden and a collection of works from some 80 contemporary North Carolina artists and craftspeople; **Orton Plantation**, off N.C. Highway 133 at Winnabow, (910) 371-6851, an old rice plantation where the gardens are open to the public; and the **Wilmington Railroad Museum**, 501 Nutt Street, (910) 763-2634, a kind of fun house for folks fascinated by trains and train culture.

Wilmington's biggest shindig of the year is the **Azalea Festival**. It's held in April and includes a parade, street fair, and home and garden tours. For more information about the area or the festival, call the Cape Fear Coast Convention and Visitors Bureau, (800) 222-4757.

And, one last note, you might want to call ahead to see if **Thalian Hall Center for the Performing Arts**, 310 Chestnut Street, (910) 343-3664, has a performance scheduled during your visit. Full-scale musicals, light opera and internationally renowned dance companies are part of Thalian's consistently high-quality programming. Thalian Hall is the only surviving theater designed by John Montague Trumble, one of America's foremost 19th-century theater designers. Historic tours are offered. Tickets are $5 for adults and $3 for children younger than 12; group rates are available. Call (910) 343-3660 in advance for reservations and exact tour schedules.

Because of the large international film industry headquartered in Wilmington (Coleco's DeLaurentis studio is there, and several major films have come from Wilmington including *The Crow, Blue Velvet, Cape Fear, King Kong* and others), there is a large artsy avant garde community. Walk along cobblestone Front Street any night to sip espresso at the coffeehouses, listen to live music in the bars or enjoy New Age cuisine in one of the cozy little restaurants. Oh, and don't forget to smile and say hello to any of the visiting movie stars who might be there on location.

Real Estate

LOOK FOR:
• Residential
  Developments
• Real Estate
  Agencies

If you choose to visit the Grand Strand in the early spring, you'll probably be surprised at how early the flowers blossom—and by how much construction is going on. For spring fix-up (as opposed to spring cleaning), Grand Stranders get out their hammers and wrenches, nail guns and compressors, bulldozers and cranes to prepare for the busy summer months ahead. In 1999, 7,307 building permits were filed; for residents and visitors alike, the continuous development that Myrtle Beach has experienced in the last four years has been continuously exciting.

The Strand's permanent population has tripled in the last 30 years. Horry County is one of the nation's fastest-growing retirement communities. In fact, almost 15 percent of the population in both Horry and Georgetown counties is older than 65. That figure can be compared to only 9 percent in 1980.

With a relatively low cost of living (despite regressive state sales tax on food, clothing and housing), the Myrtle Beach area appeals to active retirees, singles and new families. Residential opportunities abound: golf course villas, country clubs, sprawling residences with amenities, smaller sheet-rock neighborhoods, friendly mobile-home communities and condominium villages.

As is the case in many resort areas, real estate scams have posed problems in Myrtle Beach. Federal consumer watchdogs have done pretty well in helping to close down many timeshare and other real estate shams in the past few years.

Do be careful before you sign on the dotted line. But don't fret; with a little research and homework, you should do fine. Take time to analyze your real estate purchases carefully, whether for investment or permanent occupancy. You should consider the long-term potential of the property. Is high tide already lapping at the back deck? Is insurance a manageable expense? Is an oceanfront view worth it, or should you consider a purchase off the beach . . . on a lake, the Waccamaw River or a golf course? Do zoning ordinances protect the long-term integrity of your investment? And, don't forget to inquire about homeowner association fees; these are not included in your mortgage but are assessed monthly or annually—and can increase rather considerably, and unexpectedly, as well.

Myrtle Beach boasts many reputable and well-established communities. Historically, these areas tended to be concentrated on the North Strand. That is changing, albeit slowly. Enduring communities such as The Dunes, Pine Lakes and anything on Ocean Boulevard from 30th to 80th avenues N. will certainly prove a strong purchase. In these areas, zoning laws are already in place to protect the value of your purchase. As a result, such properties come with a hefty price tag. But there are plenty of newer developments all over the Strand that are well worth considering. One of the most exclusive addresses in America, with residents including Amy Vanderbilt, professional football player Michael Fox of the Carolina Panthers, the CEO of NationsBank and other luminaries, is the South Strand neighborhood of DeBordieu (locally pronounced "debby-doo"). Remember, these days a place "at the beach" doesn't necessarily mean "on the beach."

The subsequently listed developments represent a few of our favorite communities. These are followed by a sampling of the dozens of real estate agencies with strong reputations.

Residential Developments

North Strand

Lightkeeper's Village
U.S. Hwy. 17, Little River
• **(843) 249-5720, (800) 344-1604**

Overlooking the Intracoastal Waterway and adjacent to Coquina Harbor, this 35-acre community offers three types of properties: Lighthouse Pointe, Watchmen's Cottages and Yacht Club Villas.

Lighthouse Pointe, priced from $196,900, includes waterway villas. Three-bedroom floor plans prominently feature natural light. The neighborhood boasts a waterfront pool with spacious sun decks and a waterfront clubhouse with a bar, sitting areas and a fitness room.

Watchmen's Cottages, priced from $115,900, feature elegant and finely detailed two- and three-bedroom homes. The single-level design was created specifically with retirees in mind.

The two-bedroom, two-bath Yacht Club Villas are priced from $127,900. Residents enjoy the tennis court, putting green, three pools, sun decks, two clubhouses and Waterway and Harbourside boardwalks. Boat slips also are available.

Tidewater Golf Club & Plantation
4901 Little River Neck Rd.,
North Myrtle Beach
• **(843) 249-1403, (800) 843-3234**

Like more than a few residential communities in this area, Tidewater is probably best known for its golf course. This community offers homes on-course or off-course.

Developers at Tidewater carefully planned this community to preserve and protect the area's dense maritime forest and to offer homeowners spectacular views of saltwater marshes, freshwater ponds and the Atlantic Ocean. You'll find luxurious condominium villas, custom-finished homes and spacious court-

yard houses. Each of the residential districts at Tidewater features its own distinct architectural style and landscaping. Villas range from $130,000 to $165,000, and homes with lots start at $150,000 and range to more than $400,000.

Tidewater sports its own swim and racquet club with a junior Olympic-size pool, kiddie pool and tennis courts.

The Waterfront at Briarcliffe Commons
U.S. Hwy. 17, Briarcliffe
• **(843) 361-8877, (888) 272-8700**

Briarcliffe is a pleasant stretch of tall pines between North Myrtle Beach and Restaurant Row that can be easily overlooked as you zoom in your car by on Highway 17. Residents like their community that way; green and relatively undisturbed.

The Waterfront at Briarcliffe Commons makes the most of this enticing location by offering 188 condominiums between Highway 17 and the Intracoastal Waterway. Buildings overlooking the waterway are five stories, and the lake and lagoon view buildings have three levels. The development also includes a pool and hot tub complex overlooking the waterway, two levels of terraced walkways, bridges, gazebos, fishing pier and a secure entrance.

The floor plans offer three bedrooms (one as an alternate den/office) 9-foot or vaulted ceilings, walk-in closets and large screened verandas. Prices start at $105,900 and extend to $159,000 for the prime waterway view.

The allure of this location is compounded by a highway front commercial center containing a Copeland's New Orleans restaurant, a Fuddruckers, and a Marriott Courtyard hotel. Not only is this center convenient for residents, but it also serves as a buffer to the gates of one of the North Strand's most enticing condominium communities.

Myrtle Beach

Dunes Country Club
9000 N. Ocean Blvd., Myrtle Beach
• **inquire through local Realtors**

If living among the local ruling class and

INSIDERS' TIP

Unless you've lived along the Grand Strand for a while or visited often, don't jump into buying a home just because the market's hot and houses seem to sell quickly. Rent first to avoid making a hasty decision that you might later find difficult to live with. That will give you time to explore all the real estate opportunities here.

REAL ESTATE

Many area real estate companies also offer vacation rentals.

Photo: courtesy of Kimberly Allyson Duncan

the old money is important to you, this is the place to choose; there are not many *nouveau riche* here. The homes, sold through various Realtors, are quite beautiful—though many are older than you might expect. Appropriately, the upscale Dunes Golf Club anchors this community. Many homes feature golf vistas; a precious few feature ocean views.

Buying a home here doesn't qualify you to enjoy the many amenities; memberships are additional, and the dues are steep. Home prices at Dunes start around $200,000 and climb up and over $750,000.

Heritage Communities
4728 Jenn Dr., Myrtle Beach
• (843) 449-6200, (800) 489-5661
Heritage Communities is developing four of Myrtle Beach's finest and bestselling communities. Magnolia Place at Myrtlewood Golf Club sold 700 units in 31 months. Magnolia Place, The Gardens at Cypress Bay Golf Club and Riverwalk at Arrowhead all offer luxury golf villas. Azalea Lakes in Socastee provides condominiums more conducive to full-time living, with garages and extra storage space. All four communities have swimming pools, fitness centers and soothing water views.

The $60,000 to mid-$70,000 one- and two-bedroom brick villas of Magnolia Place fea-ture 9- and 12-foot ceilings, tiled floors and palladium windows. Magnolia Place has a convenient location on the U.S. 17 Bypass with Broadway At The Beach in sight.

Situated in the Villages at Arrowhead, Riverwalk is a development of brick golf course villas overlooking the Intracoastal Waterway just minutes from Waccamaw Pottery and U.S. Highway 501 to Conway. Prices start in the $60,000s.

The Gardens at Cypress Bay Golf Course, in peaceful Little River, offers studio villas starting at $32,900 and two-bedroom homes starting at $71,900. And finally, Azalea Lakes condominiums are highlighted by 9-foot and cathedral ceilings; the one-bedroom units range from $54,000 to $57,000, the two-bedrooms units from $68,000 to $72,000.

Kingston Plantation
9770 Kings Rd., Myrtle Beach
• (843) 449-6400, (800) 382-3332
Kingston Plantation is 145 heavily forested, parklike acres with freshwater lakes and a half-mile of secluded beach. Expect to see wildlife, including black swans, egrets, mallard ducks and sea turtles.

A $4 million health club features an indoor pool, three squash and racquetball courts, an aerobics studio, weight-training and cardiovas-

REAL ESTATE

cular equipment, a sauna, whirlpool and locker room facilities. There's even a professional masseuse on staff. Outdoors you'll find a junior Olympic-size pool and exceptional tennis facilities. (See our Parks and Recreation chapter for related information.) In addition, each of Kingston's different communities typically feature unique amenities.

From luxury oceanfront residences to clusters of lakeside villas and townhomes, Kingston has a home to suit virtually any taste, with 90 different floor plans in all. Prices vary dramatically—from roughly $120,000 to $450,000.

Plantation Point
3800 U.S. Hwy. 17 Bypass, Myrtle Beach
• **inquire through local Realtors**

Plantation Point is well known as one of the more expensive communities in the Myrtle Beach area. Just off the By-pass in Myrtle Beach, it's right in the heart of the action. The Myrtlewood Golf Club wraps around the development. Some lots and homes flank the Intracoastal Waterway.

There are many different residential options at Plantation Point, and what you choose determines what amenities you may access. Charleston Place is the newest offering, with single-family brick homes fronting the course. Options in Plantation Point include lots, estate homes, single-family homes and townhouse communities in a range of prices—from around $100,000 for a modest townhouse to $350,000 or more for an estate home.

Seaside Village
27th Ave. S., Myrtle Beach
• **(843) 626-8270**

Conveniently located at the south end of Myrtle Beach from 25th to 29th avenues S., Seaside Village is two blocks from the ocean and just as close to the city's Whispering Pines Golf Course. The development of single-family dwellings offers eight model homes with custom design in mind. The community abounds with family-neighborhood charm; a white picket fence surrounds the community, and there is a swimming pool and cabana area. Constructed by Carrell and Associates from

Little River, homes here range in price from $133,900 to $159,900.

South Strand

DeBordieu
129 Luvan Blvd. (U.S. Hwy. 17),
Georgetown
• **(843) 546-4176**

DeBordieu is a private oceanfront residential community encompassing 2,700 acres of age-old oaks and pines, tidal marshes and creeks with access to the Atlantic Ocean. This might be the most prestigious address on the South Strand. Justifiably so, DeBordieu bills itself as a purveyor of "splendid isolation."

This community offers a variety of homesites and villas with ocean, forest, marsh and fairway views, and all are served by central water and sewer systems and underground utilities.

DeBordieu Club's golf course has been nationally acclaimed as one of Pete Dye's best. The colonial-style clubhouse is spectacular. The Beach Club, with its lovely pool overlooking the ocean, offers superb dining. And the Tennis Center boasts eight composition courts and an excellent pro shop. Access to DeBordieu is controlled by a security entrance that is staffed 24 hours a day.

Living here is a pricey proposition, but if money is not an object and you don't mind the half-hour drive to Myrtle Beach, there's no prettier place or better investment. Homesites range upward from $65,000 to beyond $150,000 (no, that doesn't include the house!).

Heritage Plantation
U.S. Hwy. 17, Pawleys Island
• **(843) 237-9824, (800) 448-2010**

Blessed with a unique combination of 300-year-old oaks, giant magnolias, scenic rice fields and Waccamaw River vistas, Heritage Plantation features a clubhouse with a 75-foot heated pool and Jacuzzi, lighted tennis courts, a fitness center, card room and a social area for entertaining. Property owners enjoy abundant golfing opportunities, including special privileges on six of the Grand Strand's top-rated

INSIDERS' TIP

The city planning offices of Myrtle and North Myrtle Beach are vaults of information for prospective homebuyers and current homeowners. City planners and building inspectors are on hand to offer advice concerning everything from flood zones to future developments. These factors and many more affect everything from your insurance rates to future land values.

courses: Oyster Bay, Marsh Harbour, all three Legends courses and The Heritage Club itself, where members get reserved tee times. The beaches of Pawleys Island are only 3 miles away.

Homesites at Heritage Plantation range from $40,000 to $290,000. Homes start around $180,000.

Indigo Creek
9557 Indigo Club Dr.,
off U.S. Hwy. 17 Bypass S., Murrells Inlet
• (843) 650-9475, (800) 654-9202

Indigo Creek is rich in natural beauty, thick with forest and sprinkled with lakes. It's a breeze to reach Myrtle Beach on U.S. Highway 17 Bypass from Indigo Creek, which is less than a five-minute drive from restaurants, entertainment, shopping, medical facilities and beaches.

Indigo Creek boasts the features of a community committed to preserving long-term value: privacy, attractive landscaping, well-lighted streets with curbs and gutters, underground utilities and an architectural review board. Even when the local real estate market was sluggish and slow, Indigo Creek was setting sales records.

An 18-hole championship course designed by Willard Byrd offers an indisputably challenging game of golf. There's a private pool complex too.

Lots at Indigo Creek are priced from $35,000, and homes begin at about $121,000.

Island Green Country Club
S.C. Hwy. 707, Myrtle Beach
• (843) 650-1652, (800) 992-9775

Island Green Country Club is southwest of Surfside Beach between S.C. 707 and the Intracoastal Waterway. Pleasantly removed from the mainstream bustle but just minutes from everything you'd like to do in the Myrtle Beach area, Island Green has been successfully selling real estate (and attracting golfers to its course) for about a decade. It is currently the seasonal home of a number of "stars" of local theater.

For now, Island Green features two properties: Green Tree Condominiums and Green Gate Villas. As an incentive, free golf memberships accompany every purchase.

One- and two-bedroom units at Green Tree Condominiums feature fabulous golf course views from expansive screened porches. These units are touted as ideal second homes and are reasonably priced from the low $40,000s to the mid-$60,000s.

Green Gate Villas, Island Green's newest patio-home development, offers spacious single-family homes along curbed streets on individually deeded lots. Choose from five floor plans; prices range from $88,000 to about $110,000.

Oceanfront communities with conscience marry preservation with residential opportunities.

REAL ESTATE

In addition to its 27 golf holes and a well-appointed clubhouse, Island Green's amenities include a large outdoor pool and a health spa with Jacuzzi and exercise equipment. You'll also find outdoor pools as well as lighted tennis courts.

Litchfield by the Sea
U.S. Hwy. 17 , Pawleys Island
• **(843) 237-4000, (800) 476-2861**

For nearly 40 years The Litchfield Company has been developing private seaside communities amid beaches, marshlands and lush Lowcountry golf courses. Amenities include pools, spas, tennis and volleyball courts, bike paths, fishing opportunities, picnic areas and three of the finest golf clubs in the Lowcountry.

Throughout this spacious resort, you can choose from homesites, single-family homes and a variety of quality townhomes or villas overlooking miles of clean, white sand beaches, marshland, lakes or golf course fairways. Prices range from around $125,000 to more than $1 million.

Pawleys Plantation
U.S. Hwy. 17, Pawleys Island
• **(843) 237-7884**

Pawleys Plantation is a world-class golf and country club built on 582 acres of natural wetlands, salt marshes, lakes and rolling green fairways. Bordered on the south by a 645-acre nature preserve, this private community offers homesites and golf villas for purchase as well as accommodations and golf packages for those who want to vacation in the country club atmosphere. The Pawleys Plantation golf course is an 18-hole championship layout designed by Jack Nicklaus. Among its most unforgettable features are a tremendous double green, a dramatic split fairway and breathtaking lake and marsh views. An antebellum-style clubhouse ranks with the finest club facilities in the Southeast. (See our Golf chapter for more detailed information.)

Neighborhoods of villas throughout the plantation offer comfortable year-round living or a perfect getaway house for the second-home buyer. Lots feature a variety of views. Homesites start at about $20,000, and villas start around $106,000.

INSIDERS' TIP
Rentals, whether weekly, monthly or annual, are big business on the Strand. If you're house shopping, consider letting next year's vacationers pay a good chunk of your mortgage— look into multifamily structures.

Prestwick Country Club
S.C. Hwy. 544, Surfside Beach
• **(843) 293-6000, (800) 521-8522**

Prestwick is situated around a private, $6 million Pete and P.B. Dye-designed golf course (see our Golf chapter). Prestwick Country Club also boasts one of the Strand's finest tennis complexes—11 clay courts, two hard-surface courts and a stadium court (see our Parks and Recreation chapter). You'll also find a health club facility with a sauna, whirlpool, exercise areas and indoor and outdoor pools. Security is provided 24 hours a day.

Prestwick features condominiums and homes, with direct fairway or lake views, ranging from $120,000 to $400,000. Custom-built residences are also available. Homesites run from approximately $45,000 to $90,000. Patio homes are priced from $130,000 to more than $180,000.

Wachesaw Plantation
Wachesaw Rd., Murrells Inlet
• **(843) 357-1263, (800) 373-1263**

Wachesaw Plantation has an interesting history: it's built on the site of old Native American burial grounds that later became flourishing rice plantations. Ancient moss-draped oaks characterize this private community.

Amenities include a clubhouse, equestrian center, eight tennis courts, a swimming pool and a Tom Fazio-designed private golf course. A beautiful dining facility offers expansive views of the Intracoastal Waterway. Homes are priced from $234,900; cottages from $127,500; homesites from $27,500.

Wachesaw Plantation East
U.S. Hwy. 17, Murrells Inlet
• **(843) 357-5260, (800) 451-0115**

Wachesaw Plantation East, a more recent development phase, offers a semiprivate golf course, a private residential community and a host of amenities. Homes are carefully situated to capture views of the semiprivate golf course, lakes and the natural beauty of the surrounding landscape. Though just a 15-minute drive south of Myrtle Beach, Wachesaw Plantation East remains worlds apart from Myrtle's fray yet is conveniently near shopping, dining and medical facilities.

The Clyde Johnston-designed golf course,

which opened for play in fall 1996, offers a hint of Scottish-links influence—accented by freshwater wetlands and lakes. (See our Golf chapter for details.)

The community features fitness and biking trails and a clubhouse complex that includes a health club, swimming pool, guest inn and conference center.

Homes of 1,700 to 3,500 square feet are priced in the $150,000s. Condominiums—1,100 to 1,800 square feet—are priced from around $79,900.

Willbrook Plantation
U.S. Hwy. 17, Litchfield Beach
• (843) 237-4000, (800) 476-2861

The natural profile of Willbrook Plantation has changed little since it operated as three colonial rice plantations. Deer and fowl remain abundant, as do towering cypress trees, Carolina pines and age-old oaks.

Half-acre lots, from $68,000, are currently for sale throughout Willbrook Plantation. Single-family homes are available in a pleasant community called Allston Point.

Centex Builders developed the newest community within Willbrook. Called The Tradition, this community is built around a new 18-hole championship golf course. Several different single-family floor plans are offered, starting at $130,000 (including homesites). Willbrook Golf and Country Club offers half-acre lots starting at $68,000.

In addition to swimming, tennis and the extensive clubhouse, all Willbrook residents can take advantage of the amenities at Litchfield By The Sea. Private beach access, a beach club, tennis and bike trails set the stage for a lifestyle that's tough to beat.

Real Estate Agencies

As you drive along the Strand, it might seem that there's a real estate office on every corner. Since you have a plethora of choices, you should give much time and consideration to choosing your agent. More often than with many other occupations, people enter the real estate field from widely disparate backgrounds. Consequently, the first salesperson you stumble across might or might not be a good fit for you. Scan first, then narrow down. Interview dif-

ferent people and choose someone with whom you're truly comfortable. After all, this is probably one of the biggest investments you'll ever make, and you deserve someone you can speak with honestly, confide in frequently and respect without reservation. If you're coming from another area, speak with a real estate agent you know and trust back home. Often, agents have contacts in the industry that will help you zero in on the perfect person.

When looking for the perfect property, *The Sun News* can be a primary resource. In particular, every Sunday paper delivers a comprehensive insert called *Real Estate Plus*. It is estimated that at least a third of realty transactions begin with a newspaper ad. Realtors use it religiously—though not always to advertise their best buys. (Can't tip off the competition!) They usually advertise a broad and respectable selection of their listings, hoping to attract prospective buyers for the hidden bargains.

Listed subsequently are some area real estate agencies whose brokers can help with the purchase of a new residence or an investment property. Please consider that the Strand has dozens and dozens of professional Realtors, many of whom are not detailed here. This list is in no way meant to reflect upon the qualifications of the real estate professionals not included here. If you'd like further information about other companies in the area, call the Grand Strand Board of Realtors at (843) 272-6113, or the Association of Coastal Carolinas Realtors at (843) 626-3638.

North Strand

Century 21
Coastal Carolina Properties Inc.
1908 U.S. Hwy. 17 S., North Myrtle Beach
• (843) 272-6754, (800) 328-9008

Coastal Carolina Properties was founded in August 1973 as a general brokerage and development agency. In 1978, a decision was made to concentrate on general brokerage, and Coastal Carolina Properties joined the renowned Century 21 system. It has grown to employ approximately 25 agents and staffs a property management division. In 1996 the company earned Century 21's Quality Service

> ## INSIDERS' TIP
> If you are relocating here from another state, many real estate agents advise that you start home-buying proceedings before you move and while you have an existing, long-term job. Banks are more likely to lend to someone with that security than to someone who has just moved.

Award and was one of the top-21 producing companies in the Carolinas.

Crescent Realty
710 17th Ave. S., North Myrtle Beach
• (843) 272-6753

Crescent Realty takes its name from the beach community it has been operating from since 1977. Broker-in-charge Rachel S. Thompson and her associate, Helena Gray, have 49 years of combined experience in the business. Both Rachel and Helena live in North Myrtle Beach and thus have firsthand knowledge of that Grand Strand community.

Crescent Realty also works with North Carolina properties.

RE/MAX Southern Shores
100 U.S. Hwy. 17 S., North Myrtle Beach
• (843) 249-5555, (800) 729-0064

With offices throughout North America, RE/MAX serves residential, commercial and investment needs. The Southern Shores agency and has just completed eight successive years of record sales, making it one of the leaders in residential sales from Calabash into Myrtle Beach. Currently, RE/MAX Southern Shores staff has 12 agents.

Myrtle Beach

Century 21 Boling & Associates
7722 N. Kings Hwy.,
Myrtle Beach
• (843) 449-2121,
(800) 634-2500

This Century 21 office opened for business in 1986. In five years, Penny I. Boling, broker-in-charge, helped the company—at the time, one of the least productive in the region—become one of the leading Century 21 offices in South Carolina. Boling & Associates controls 200 or more listings at any given time, including condos and townhomes, residential, commercial and multifamily structures as well as land—all properties in various price ranges.

This agency thrives on a team-players concept. The majority of the sales associates have been with the company for more than five years. A property management division is available to coordinate annual rentals.

Century 21 Broadhurst & Associates Inc.
3405 N. Kings Hwy., Myrtle Beach
• (843) 448-7169, (800) 845-2055

Century 21 Broadhurst & Associates, owned by Myrtle Beach City Councilwoman Rachel Broadhurst, is a full-service real estate company with more than 30 professionally trained property specialists. In business since 1974, this firm is one of the largest Century 21 offices in the Carolinas, with agents in Murrells Inlet and Calabash as well as Myrtle Beach. Serving clients in all phases of real estate, Broadhurst & Associates offers one-stop shopping for residential, vacation, commercial and investment properties. In 1997 Broadhurst earned Century 21's Quality Service Company award.

Chicora Real Estate & Development
10225 U.S. Hwy. 17 N.,
Myrtle Beach
• (843) 272-8700

Chicora maintains three other offices throughout the Strand: 2812 U.S. Highway 17 S., Garden City, (843) 651-9300; 7508 N. Kings Highway, Myrtle Beach, (843) 449-4404; and A101 A Place at the Beach V, Shore Drive, Myrtle Beach, (843) 449-9494. Chicora also has sales centers at Myrtle Pointe, Southcreek, SouthWood, Covenant Towers, Ashton Glenn, Ashley Cove and Eastport.

To maintain this coverage, Chicora staffs more than 60 agents and offers residential, resort, commercial and industrial properties. This company also has annual- and vacation-rental departments, offers homeowner association management and cultivates its own new developments.

ERA Callihan, Teal, Skelley & Associates
357 Lake Arrowhead Rd., Myrtle Beach
• (843) 449-8900, (800) 833-6330

ERA Callihan, Teal, Skelley & Associates is an 9-year-old agency with a strong reputation in both South and North Carolina. This three-

INSIDERS' TIP

If you're interested in buying a home in a planned community that assesses a monthly homeowner's fee, investigate the terms thoroughly. Such fees can be raised without notice at any given time. Find out the original and current fees. Ask if the fee covers home insurance, pest control, outside irrigation and lighting or landscape maintenance. If you're paying a hefty fee just to support ever-increasing liability insurance for the community pool that you rarely use, a home in that community might not be worth it to you.

REAL ESTATE

partner firm has 10 offices along the Grand Strand from Calabash, North Carolina, to Pawleys Island, South Carolina. It employs approximately 50 agents who specialize in general real estate, vacation and annual rentals and planned residential communities, for which the firm is probably best known.

In past years, ERA Callihan, Teal, Skelley & Associates handled more transactions than any other ERA company in the nation.

Fitzgerald Realty Inc.
900 Gilead Dr., Ste. 101A, Murrells Inlet
• **(843) 293-7053, (800) 395-6610**

Established in 1985, Fitzgerald Realty has approximately 20 full- and part-time agents. This real estate firm specializes in residential and resort properties in the Grand Strand area.

The company prides itself on a "no surprises" sales process—from home selection through the final closing.

Coldwell Banker Leonard-Roberts Real Estate
3501 N. Kings Hwy., Myrtle Beach
• **(843) 626-7676, (800) 280-7676**

Two of the Strand's most prominent real estate firms merged in 1997 to form a single, dynamic company with offices in Myrtle Beach (see listed address) and at 14792 Ocean Highway, Pawleys Island, (843) 237-1686.

In the past individually—and now together—the associations have been developing and marketing some of coastal South Carolina's most notable communities, including Indigo Creek Golf Plantation in Murrells Inlet (see previous entry) and SpringLake at Carolina Forest. The company has established a positive reputation for its integrity, performance and professionalism.

Leonard-Roberts offers a range of real estate services—brokerage, consulting, market research, development, marketing, and property management—and is a leader in residential, resort and commercial real estate.

LITUS* Properties - Joe Garrell & Associates
1551 21st Ave. N., Ste. 1, Myrtle Beach
• **(843) 449-9000, (800) 285-5634**

LITUS* Properties has been in business for more than 20 years, and its experience is renowned. LITUS* staffs more than 50 agents in numerous departments that handle commercial sales, business properties, resort properties and general brokerage. The company is distinguished by a sales staff that collectively holds more certifications and accreditations in real estate and business-practice brokerage than any other agency in North America.

Merrill Lynch
600 27th Ave. N., Myrtle Beach
• **(843) 946-2000, (800) 937-0848**

Merrill Lynch is considered a top-notch finance firm on Wall Street and an industry leader among peers. Employees are trained to take great pride in principles and client commitment. This office has been in the Myrtle Beach area since 1988 and is the working home to approximately 15 brokers.

Pavilack Realty & Rental Corp.
603 N. Kings Hwy., Myrtle Beach
• **(843) 448-9471,**
(800) 868-9471

Pavilack is a small company that offers clients personalized service in the sale or purchase of commercial real estate. Owner Harry Pavilack works closely with his associates, bringing his legal expertise to all transactions.

Robert E. Powell – Better Homes & Gardens
4757 U.S. Hwy. 17 Bypass S., Myrtle Beach
• **(843) 293-7778, (800) 868-7778**

This firm has served the beach since 1976 and has been affiliated with Better Homes & Gardens since 1981. This is the only Better Homes & Gardens franchise on the Strand. Formerly Berry Realty, this agency's territory ranges from the North Carolina state line to Winyah Bay in Georgetown.

With approximately 15 agents, Powell specializes in residential properties—primary, secondary and investment. This company also staffs a property management division that orchestrates annual rentals and is particularly proud of its in-house training program.

The Prudential Burroughs & Chapin Realty Inc.
7421 N. Kings Hwy. Myrtle Beach
• **(843) 449-9444, (800) 277-7704**

Anyone who knows anything about the history of Myrtle Beach will recognize the names Burroughs and Chapin. The parent company has been around for more than a century. With 24,000 acres, this company is one of the largest landowners in Horry County. The firm owns numerous office buildings and retail complexes, including Broadway At The Beach, Myrtle Square Mall and Myrtle Beach Pavilion.

Recognized as No. 1 in Prudential Southern

residential sales in 1996, Burroughs & Chapin Realty has 38 agents. All have garnered more than $2 million in sales, making this one of the most productive firms in the Grand Strand area.

South Strand

Garden City Realty Inc.
608 Atlantic Ave., Garden City Beach
• **(843) 651-2121, (800) 395-5930**

Since 1973 Garden City Realty has been a focal point for South Strand real estate deals and has earned a reputation for scrupulously fair dealing. This comprehensive agency's six agents can handle a range of real estate needs—buying, selling or renting. The experienced, well-trained staff has access to more than 4,500 listings of Myrtle Beach-area homes, condos and land parcels. Garden City Realty offers nearly 400 rental properties on the South Strand.

Pawleys Island Realty Company
88 N. Causeway, Pawleys Island
• **(843) 237-2431, (800) 937-7352**

Pawleys Island Realty Company provides eight professional associates who can answer any questions you might have about any property in Georgetown County, including all the developments. The specialty at this agency is the resort real estate market. Pawleys Island Realty also prides itself in being the largest vacation rental company in its area, with a large inventory of homes in Pawleys Island and Litchfield Beach.

Rose Realty
1711 U.S. Hwy. 17 S., Surfside Beach
• **(843) 650-9274, (800) 845-6706**

Rose Realty is the exclusive property management company of the huge development known as Oceanside Village, a planned community of more than 900 modular beach homes and cottages; half are occupied by owners, and the others are available as rentals. Like the Ocean Lakes community of Myrtle Beach, residents of Oceanside Village get around in golf carts and enjoy the safety and security of 24-hour, on-site security systems. Amenities include swimming pools, lakes stocked with game fish, tennis courts, a volleyball court, softball diamond, huge clubhouse and planned activities.

Senior Scene

The Grand Strand and retirees have a passionate love affair going. And, this perfect coupling is not only compatible, but also seems to be intensifying every year as more and more active seniors come south to embrace the comfortable coastal lifestyle. Between 1980 and 1990, the number of retirees in Horry County alone increased 103 percent. Regional planners estimate the current over-55 population at approximately 50,000.

Who can blame them? They're finished with the workaday world but not with life. They come to get ultimate quality out of the golden years under the warm Carolina sunshine. Many of our retirees hail from colder regions to the north where they spent many a winter shoveling snow, wrapping kids in knitted scarves and navigating icy roads. Here seniors can enjoy the freedom of a temperate climate, partake in the luxury of walking barefoot along a sandy coast and, for the most part, get far more purchasing mileage out of their dollar.

In turn, they have wooed and won the hearts of Grand Stranders with the skills and experience they apply to local civic groups, churches, the arts and governmental entities. Retirees have become and will remain an integral part of this community. As one 69-year-old widow put it, "I moved to Myrtle Beach four months ago and have a busier schedule than ever before. No one needs to be lonely in Myrtle Beach. There's just too much to do." Echoing this sentiment, the October 1996 issue of *Money* magazine's *Money Extra: America's Top Places to Live Today* cited Myrtle Beach as one of the 20 most desirable retirement meccas in the nation. And, just one week following that accolade, the Southeast Journal edition of *The Wall Street Journal* ranked the Grand Strand as one of the dozen hottest retirement spots in six Southeast states: "If a community with 100 golf courses, 1,500 restaurants and 10 theaters featuring entertainers such as Johnny Mathis is NOT a retirement spot, something's wrong."

Many retired folks volunteer at area schools and hospitals. They serve on boards and councils, operate community projects, head up fundraising drives and participate in cultural programs. The Long Bay Symphony can credit its very existence to retirees who worked in the music business and performed with symphonies in larger cities. The over-55 set have their own acting troupe, the Grand Strand Players, which puts on three productions a year. The Waccamaw Carving Club, the Waccamaw Arts and Crafts Guild, the Grand Strand Concert Band and the Long Bay Photography Club would all have slim membership rolls without retirees.

Horry's seniors have their own newspapers, *Fifty Plus* and *Carolina Seniors*; their own annual trade show, The Lifestyles Expo, held each winter in the Myrtle Beach Convention Center (see our Annual Events chapter); and their own production company that puts together a 30-minute program each month for Cox Cable TV.

The Grand Strand also entices migrant retirees, usually referred to as "snowbirds," who follow the sunshine south to escape the harsh northern winters. They rent houses and apartments or stay in hotels, taking advantage of lower winter rates. Around March or April, when temperatures start to rise, they head home. No one seems to have a good grasp of

LOOK FOR:
- **The Single Senior Set**
- **Active Senior Centers**
- **Educational Programs**
- **Independent-living Communities**
- **Assisted-living Communities**
- **In-home Healthcare Options**
- **Senior Services Directory**

just how many snowbirds winter along the Grand Strand, although estimates range upwards of 50,000.

The Carolinas are perfectly positioned to attract the new generation of retirees. Younger, more active seniors are choosing destinations like South Carolina because it is at least a day closer to their northern homes than Florida, offers a break from relentless heat and humidity, and provides plenty of activities beyond shuffleboard or a dip in the pool.

Jobs and entrepreneurial opportunity are also high on the list of desirable qualities, since many of today's retirees want to continue to work at least part-time or wish to start their own businesses.

The Single Senior Set

A recent census report tells us that 23 percent of Horry County's population is over the age of 65 and living alone. Many of these single seniors are satisfied with their new-found life of freedom and take up traveling and exercising lifelong passions that have laid dormant for years.

Of course, tried and true ways to meet new friends are through attending your church or synagogue, becoming a member of a local senior center, enrolling in special interest courses and joining volunteer organizations. But, in this section of Insiders'® Guide, we pass along some formal and informal settings guaranteed to put you in the mainstream of local, active seniors that you probably wouldn't find until you had lived here awhile.

One 68-year-old widow in Surfside Beach has taken up globe trotting and suggests booking on the annual group excursion coordinated every February by Surfside Travelers, 825-A Surfside Drive, (843) 238-2838. The trip is usually a cruise or other all-inclusive package. Past destinations have been Alaska, Cancun, Acapulco and Puerto Rico. Although you don't have to be a senior to travel with this group, 95 percent of the group passengers are retired.

The VFW Post 10420, 4359 U.S. Highway 17 Bypass in Murrells Inlet, (843) 651-6900, is a hot spot for the older set when it comes to dining and dancing. It's open every day for lunch and dinner with live bands performing on Friday and Sunday nights from 6:30 to 10:30 PM. Music ranges from big band tunes to beach music and the dance floor is usually packed.

Mall-walking clubs have become serious programs for health and socializing among the 50-plus circle. Before stores open at 10 AM, the empty aisles are alive with the sounds of chitchat and padding Reeboks as hundreds of participants log in mall-miles. All of the Grand Strand malls offer a walking club, and all are thriving. The Colonial Mallwalkers operate out of Colonial Mall, 10177 N. Kings Highway.,

Seniors shaggin' on the Strand.

Photo: Lisa Tomer Rentz

Myrtle Beach and is sponsored by Grand Strand Regional Medical Center. Applications and fliers can be picked up anytime at the guest services booth near JCPenney and the food court, or call Hugh Brown or Dee Knight at the hospital, (843) 839-6015.

Instep is the name of the club at Inlet Square Mall, U.S. 17 Business in Murrells Inlet. Applications are available near the entrance to JCPenney or by contacting Debi McKenzie of Georgetown Memorial Hospital by phone at (843) 527-7105. Grand Strand Regional also sponsors the Myrtle Square Milers at Myrtle Square Mall, 2501 N. Kings Highway, Myrtle Beach. Fliers and applications are ready for you at the bulletin board near Kay-Bee Toys.

Active Senior Centers

To offer a central meeting spot and support to our ever-growing senior population along the Grand Strand, a number of centers have sprung up all along our shoreline. All are staffed by full-time activities personnel and operate Monday through Friday only. If you're a regular participant in these arenas of action, you'll need the weekends to rest up!

North Strand

North Strand Senior Center
2290 S.C. Hwy. 90, Longs
• (843) 399-7130
About 30 to 35 people hook up at this center every day, to join in on a laid-out format of programming. Mondays offer educational forums on nutrition and various subjects of interest to the group. Tuesday is bingo and cards day. Wednesdays are for fellowship with sing-a-longs and Bible study. Arts and crafts is the fare for Thursdays, and Friday is the day that the group is taken to various area stores for shopping excursions. A hot lunch is served each day at this center for donations only. Membership is $3 per year. Hours are 9 AM to 2 PM.

Myrtle Beach

Grand Strand Senior Center
1268 21st Ave. N., Myrtle Beach
• (843) 626-3991
The Horry County Council On Aging realized the fruits of its labor in 1995 when this senior center opened its doors. This $1.4 million project offers seniors 16,000 square feet of space including an auditorium, kitchen, dress-

ing rooms and meeting chambers. Open Monday through Friday from 9 AM to 4 PM, the senior center plays host to a dizzying schedule of events: tole painting, bridge, dance aerobics, yoga, mah-jongg (a game of Chinese origin similar to dominoes), bingo, health screening, ballroom dancing, calligraphy, art classes, chess, language lessons, oil painting, support groups, quilting . . . let us catch our breath . . . French lessons, support groups, seminars and tax-preparation instruction. You would have to have the energy of two preteens on summer vacation to keep up with all of the center's activities! The Seniors for the Performing Arts theatrical troupe performs full-production plays in the auditorium that have become very popular with senior center members and locals alike. Regular luncheons are also part of the center's monthly agenda. Membership is $15 a person and allows access to all senior center activities plus a monthly newsletter. New volunteers are always welcome.

South Strand

Georgetown Senior Center
2104 Lincoln St., Georgetown
• (843) 546-9410
The Georgetown center offers an agenda of things to do including crafts, exercise programs, quilting, card games and day trips to such attractions as Brookgreen Gardens. There are about 30 active members. Lunch is served each day for 30¢ per person. You can join this senior center for a mere $2 a year. This program operates from 10 AM to 2 PM.

South Strand Senior Center
1032 10th Ave. N.
(behind Giants Beachwear), Surfside Beach
• (843) 238-3644
South Strand has 100 members with an average of 45 people coming to the center daily. A van service is available for seniors without transportation. A different roster of events is coordinated for each day, keeping things hopping with speakers, daytrips, games, ceramics and exercise. Hot lunches are served five days a week for donations. Membership cost is $4 a year. South Strand is open from 9 AM to 2 PM.

Educational Programs

Since the pursuit of knowledge spans every generation and one is never too young nor too old to learn, the Grand Strand has enjoyed a recent proliferation of educational programs

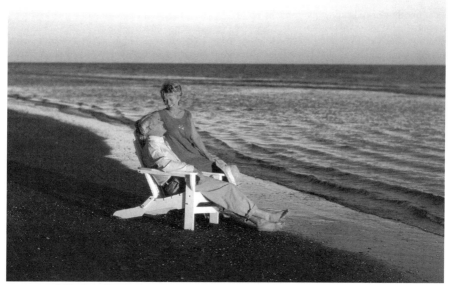

With views like these, it's easy to understand why the Grand Strand's retirement population has more than doubled in the past decade.

that enroll seniors by the hundreds. With time on their hands and minds as sharp as tacks, many of our older citizens have quit marking off days on the calendar . . . they're too busy organizing their lives by semester.

Campus Brookgreen
Brookgreen Gardens,
1931 Brookgreen Dr., Murrells Inlet
• (843) 235-6001

Through an ever-growing array of courses, workshops and trips, Campus Brookgreen's "Nine-Week Sessions" offer many opportunities to explore and enjoy a wide range of activities. Courses are designed for adults for the pure pleasure of learning. There are no exams or grades, nor any educational prerequisites for participation. Course topics include; Fine Arts Classes, such as sculpture, watercolor, tole painting, and polymer clay; Lowcountry Studies, including environmental issues, plantation archaeology, African American and cultural studies, as well as history related classes; and Weekend Workshops with a variety of special interest classes.

Classes are held at various locations in Brookgreen Gardens. Course tuition ranges from $35 to $150 for a Brookgreen member.

(Some courses are higher due to supplemental materials, field trips, visiting lecturers, or equipment requirements.) Courses are open both to members and non-members. To register for Campus Brookgreen classes, or to request more information, please call 235-6001.

Horry-Georgetown Technical College Continuing Education
Conway Campus,
U.S. Hwy. 501 E., Conway
• (843) 349-5363
Grand Strand Campus,
Woodlawn Park School, 743 Hemlock Ave.
• (843) 477-0808
Georgetown Campus,
4003 S. Frasier St., Georgetown
• (843) 546-8406

All campus locations of Horry-Georgetown Technical College, including the Grand Strand campus on the former Myrtle Beach Air Force Base, encourage and support a wide range of courses and special programs that attract senior students due to their scope, convenience and affordability. Every semester, a good number of continuing-education courses are designated as senior citizen specials. If you are at least 60 years of age, a South Carolina resident and neither yourself nor your spouse is employed full time, you may qualify to receive a total tuition waiver to take a particular course, or be eligible for a 50 percent discount of the tuition fee.

Continuing education courses included topics such as financial and business training; computers and the Internet; construction and home repair; health and wellness-related; arts and crafts specialties; and languages.

The cost and hours of each course do vary. Each campus of Horry-Georgetown Technical College is happy to send you their current schedule and updates if you give them a call. Preregistration is required for all classes.

Lifelong Learning Society
Coastal Carolina University, Conway
• **(843) 349-2665**

University faculty and professionals from the community teach a variety of intellectual, cultural and social classes. No formal papers or exams are required of the senior students. A $25 membership fee to join the Lifelong program entitles participants to use of the campus facilities, free admission to the college's athletic events and student rates on tickets to shows at Wheelwright Auditorium. Members also have the opportunity to attend special workshops, travel-study programs and sessions at the university. Some of the courses offer include computers (beginner to web page design); art classes; finance; Spanish, French and German conversation; Russian history; the President's Series; Waccamaw-Chicora Indian history; literature; writing workshops; a variety personal enrichment selections; bridge; holiday event planning, etc. Check out learning possibilities at www.coastal.edu/learn.

Other workshops include a creative writing and a learning-by-doing investment session. Course fees range from $20 to $59 and are normally offered Mondays through Saturdays.

Independent-living Communities

Although there are several very nice residential areas exclusively for retirees, many choose to live amidst the rest of the population. In fact, retirees can be found in just about every Grand Strand neighborhood. And, if the residential community is governed by a homeowners' association, you can bet concerned and conscientious seniors will be involved. Here is a listing we put together of beautiful, safe and active retirement-living communities.

North Strand

Country Lakes
4353 Erie St., Little River
• **(843) 399-2333, (800) 238-6565**

The Jensen family has added Country Lakes in the north end of the county, which is smaller than its Garden City cousin. A small pool and clubhouse grace the grounds. For security, an electronic bar crosses the road to keep uninvited guests out and protect residents and their properties. There is an on-site sales office. Home costs run from the mid-$70,000s to $110,000.

Myrtle Beach

Covenant Towers
5001 Little River Rd., Myrtle Beach
• **(843) 449-2484**

Covenant Towers offers a simple and unique opportunity for independent adult living in an upscale development. Located in the residential north end next to prestigious Pine Lakes Golf Course, the nine acre campus has 159 independent living condominium residences and even a few two-bedroom plus den/study residences.

Occupants must be 55 years old or older and ownership is deeded fee simple. In addition to being equipped with an emergency call system, each residence boasts a balcony, full kitchen and one, two or three full baths. On-site amenities include a swimming pool, library, dining room, coffee shop, craft/game room, mail room, banking, beauty/barber shop, fish ponds and gardens/grounds with walking paths. Nestled in a quiet, established residential neighborhood, Covenant Towers enjoys easy access to the beach, shopping, golf restaurants and all the wonderful opportunities the Grand Strand offers.

Numerous services and activities are available to homeowners. Dinner is available in the dining room Monday through Saturday evenings, and a full lunch is available on Sunday. A full time activities staff coordinates recreational activities, i.e. water aerobics, sittercise, bridge, bowling, golf, bingo, crafts, etc., as well as opportunities to enjoy shows, concerts, lectures, shopping and the many restaurants along the Grand Strand.

SENIOR SCENE

Residents also enjoy the convenience of housekeeping service, weekly linen service, water and sewerage, insurance coverage on the structures(s) and maintenance on the buildings and grounds included as well. The convenience of a small 25 bed, private, fully licensed, skilled nursing unit allows homeowners the comfort of a quick skilled response to an emergency call or care by familiar professionals should a resident need respite or long term care. Covenant Towers does not provide assisted living services.

Homeowner residents elect the Board of directors that govern the association with the guidance of a licensed administrator and professional property management company. They have proven themselves to be good stewards of their assets over the past fifteen years and bring a wealth of professional and life experiences to this democratic process. Residences range in price from the low $40,000 to approximately $150,000 for the largest floor plan. Information is available on site Monday through Friday and by appointment on the weekends.

Myrtle Trace
506 Sand Ridge Rd., East Conway
• (843) 347-6637, (800) 227-0631

As motorists pass the Myrtle Trace sign on U.S. Highway 501, they don't get a hint about the magnitude of what lies beyond that sign and the wooded area that buffers the community from traffic. But pull in and take a look around; you'll be stunned to find about 500 homes in three unique communities. Myrtle Trace is about 15 years old and has a maturity that some newer developments lack. It is immaculately manicured and features lakes, golf course lots, a clubhouse and swimming pool.

Most of the people who buy at Myrtle Trace move in while they're still in their late 50s or early 60s, and they give new meaning to the words "active retirement." Residents band together to plan activities that range from all kinds of card games to theatrical performances. There is a bowling league, and of course, golf is king. Between 20 and 30 residents work several days a week at area golf courses as starters and rangers to earn a few dollars and, mostly, to secure golf privileges. About 50 of Myrtle Trace's

women work as volunteers at nearby Conway Hospital.

Buyers can select a house design from 16 floor plans, and a staff designer is available to adjust the plans to suit the owner. A homesite and house range from $133,000 to $175,000, depending on the location and floor plan selected. Myrtle Trace is now within 1 mile of a new shopping center off of U.S. 501, which offers a grocery store, pharmacy, shops and restaurants. The sales office is on site, and models are open every day except Sunday.

South Strand

Jensen's Inc.
3196 Moonshadow Ln., Garden City
• (843) 651-2520, (800) 238-6565

In accordance with federal guidelines, Jensen's has restricted its manufactured-housing development to people 55 and older. Initiated in the early 1970s, this development is currently home to about 575 families. Existing-home resales account for about 55 contracts per year. At Jensen's, residents lease their lots and buy their own homes. A senior can move into a double-wide abode for between $35,000 and $80,000. There is also a section of homes closer to traditional mobile units that cost between $15,500 and $27,000. Jensen's is quiet and well-manicured and bubbles with small lakes and canals. Residents plan their own activities through the Jensen's Activity Club (JAC), which distributes a monthly newsletter chockfull of things to do. There's a sales office on site.

Ocean Lakes
6001 U.S. Hwy. 17 S.,
Surfside Beach
• (843) 238-3446

Ocean Lakes is billed as the Largest Oceanfront Campground on the East Coast, and although it serves as a typical campground during the tourist season, it also has about 400 year-round residents, mostly retirees. In 1999, the National Association of RV Parks and Campgrounds nominated Ocean Lakes as the number one large RV park in the United States. The campground is on the ocean and has a recreational building where residents can work on crafts or meet for a variety of activities. An indoor pool was recently added. An activities director makes

INSIDERS' TIP

If you're retired and an avid golfer, you can save a lot of money on tee times if you're willing to do a little work. A number of area golf courses trade out playing privileges with seniors who relieve the regular staff by working golf carts or acting as starters.

sure residents stay busy with everything from shopping and trips, to miniature golf tournaments. A year-round chaplain works to meet residents' spiritual needs, providing Sunday worship services in an outdoor amphitheater when the weather permits and indoors when it doesn't.

Homes at Ocean Lakes are mostly small mobile units, some of which showcase a more permanent appearance with added rooms and porches. However, with the housing boom along the Grand Strand this year, a large number of two-story beach homes have been added to the landscape.

Ocean Lakes is a guarded community, and security staff stationed at the gate make sure only residents, their guests, registered campers and people attending worship services get in. As added security, Ocean Lakes instituted a 24-hour patrol of the grounds.

Few people use their cars inside Ocean Lakes. Instead, you'll find their transportation much slower and more relaxed—golf carts work just fine, thank you! At any given time, there are about 130 sites for sale, ranging from $35,000 for a camper home to $300,000 for some oceanfront beach houses.

Assisted-living Communities

Myrtle Beach

Alterra "Sterling House" of Conway
872 Singleton Ridge Road, Conway
•(843)347-3050

Alterra is one of the largest and most experienced providers of assisted living services for older adults and the nation's largest operator of freestanding memory care residences for individuals with Alzheimer's disease or other memory impairments. Headquartered in Milwaukee, Wisconsin, the company operates nationwide with over 450 residences in operation in 29 states. Since its founding in 1981, the Company's purpose has remained steadfast: to maximize the quality of life and dignity of older adults. Alterra has long been recognized for its innovative approach to caring for the elderly.

Alterra's local facility, Sterling House of Conway, provides specialized services to meet the needs of older adults. Although residences vary in design and purpose, they share a common trait—a caring and dedicated staff committed to maximizing the dignity and quality of life of those they serve. From Alzheimer's care to daily assisted living services, residences are purposefully designed to meet the changing needs and abilities of residents. Sterling House of Conway's goal is to provide the ideal combination of services, housing and lifestyle. To accomplish this goal, they combine state-of-the-art programming, a holistic approach and a variety of residence models, each designed to meet the acuity level and financial ability of their customers.

Supportive services include assistance with personal care and hygiene, an emergency response system, professionally trained 24-hour staff, three daily meals, snacks and beverages around the clock, housekeeping and laundry services, medication management, life enrichment activities and outings and so much more. Call for more information or visit Alterra's website at www.assisted.com.

The Lakes at Litchfield
120 Lakes at Litchfield Drive,
Pawleys Island
•(843) 235-9393

The Lakes at Litchfield is much more than a place to live. Residents and families take comfort in knowing the community offers a continuum of care that meets needs and provides a seamless transition as needs change. It's a community that takes pride in offering the setting, support and services necessary to ensure residents' comfort and security.

The Lakes at Litchfield features a range of elegant residential choices that offer every comfort and convenience. Lovely two and three bedroom homes feature bright Carolina sun rooms, fireplaces, nine-foot ceilings and quality appliances. Each home has its own garage, a cart for community travel, and a 24-hour emergency call system for safety. Meals in the elegant Charleston Dining Room, maid service, all maintenance, taxes, insurance, utilities, scheduled transportation and more are all included in a reasonable occupancy fee. Plus, should you ever decide to leave The Lakes at Litchfield, a substantial amount of your initial investment will be returned. Spacious one and two-bedroom apartments (with no up-front investment) are also affordable options. Plus, the community is thoughtfully designed to embrace the natural charm of Pawleys Island with lakes, courtyards, fountains, as well as a gazebo and clubhouse.

In addition to single-family homes, garden homes and apartment homes, The Lakes at

SENIOR SCENE

Litchfield Assisted Living and Special Care Communities provide state-of-the-art services for those needing special attention and care. Per month costs start at around $2,000 and go up to around $3,000 for dementia care. Both centers offer incomparable care in a truly caring community. See for yourself what makes The Lakes at Litchfield so special.

Myrtle Beach Manor by Marriott
9547 N. Kings Hwy., Myrtle Beach
• **(843) 449-5283**

Myrtle Beach Manor offers services for people in all phases of their senior years. There are 60 apartments, ranging from studios to one-bedroom units. These are rented on a monthly basis to people who want to live independently but like the security of knowing someone is nearby to watch out for them. The 104 beds in the healthcare center are designed for those who need to be regularly looked in on. The manor also houses a secured Special Care Center and full rehabilitation department that includes occupational and physical therapy. An activities' director makes sure that residents have something to do seven days a week. The 30-year-old establishment has six lovely manicured acres, and a sunny day will bring many manor residents outside to enjoy the scenery and a view of the Intracoastal Waterway. Monthly costs at Myrtle Beach Manor begin at $1,950. A daily rate of $105 to $128 applies to those residents who require substantial healthcare services.

Pinedale Residential Center
1201 Creel St., Conway
• **(843) 248-2087**
2902 S. Island Rd., Georgetown
• **(843) 527-1797**

When Dale Hudson, a psychologist from Camden, South Carolina, began work on Pinedale, he deemed it would be most appealing to prospective residents if it looked and felt like a real home. Housing 98 beds in Conway and 32 beds in the Georgetown location, Pinedale centers look like a home, with screened-in porches and swings overlooking a quiet yard. Residents choose from private or semiprivate rooms, furnished or unfurnished, depending on their wishes.

Four levels of care are offered: ambulatory care for individuals who want safety and companionship; assisted care for seniors who need

24-hour protection, help with bathing, dressing, diets, medications and safety; Alzheimer's care for those who suffer any stage of the disease, needing long-term or adult day care; and respite care for people who need short-term care while recuperating from an illness or injury. Also, recreational, social, worship and counseling services are a part of Pinedale's comprehensive program. Costs at Pinedale range from $1,000 per month for a semiprivate room for an ambulatory resident to $1,750 for an Alzheimer's patient requiring a private room.

In-home Healthcare Options

When a parent, aunt or other older relative becomes ill or infirm, it's not surprising that concerned family members look to a nursing home for care. But, according to the South Carolina Budget and Control Board, Office of Insurance Services, a nursing home is often the most extreme option.

In order to keep loved ones in their own homes with their pride intact, there are other options to consider. We discuss some of those options in the following section, outlining the positive and negative aspects of each in a realistic manner.

Family Home Care

If you, your siblings or other caring relatives live within reach, you could consider family home care. Modifications to the ailing person's home may be needed, modifications like installing a ramp near the entrance for wheelchair access and rearranging furniture to accommodate the chair or a walker. It might also be necessary to rent or purchase special equipment such as a hospital bed or oxygen tank. Everyone involved should decide who will do the cooking, cleaning, laundry and shopping. And, most of all, each helper must honestly evaluate his or her ability to do these chores.

The positive side to this arrangement is that it costs nothing but time, and in many cases, patients recover best in the comfort of familiar surroundings. It can also be a way to strengthen family relationships, providing the time required does not become a strain.

INSIDERS' TIP

If you're 55 years of age or older, always ask about available senior discounts whenever you shop, dine out or purchase a good or service. Many Grand Strand businesses offer the senior set special price reductions.

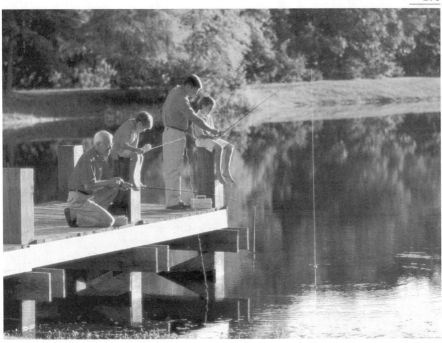

*Because the area is a veritable treasure chest of things to do, the area's burgeoning retirement
population is well positioned to entertain visiting family members.*

Photo: Courtesy of Lesnik Himmelsbach Wilson Hearl & Hirsch

On the negative side, family members usually are not healthcare professionals. Albeit with the best intentions, family members might tend to pamper a relative, rather than insisting, for example, on a prescribed daily walk.

Private Nursing

This arrangement intrudes the least on the lives of other family members, including a spouse. A private nurse can be hired to care for someone in the comfort of home. Private nurses can be found through nursing placement services, home-health agencies or discharge services of a hospital. Every hospital staffs a discharge nurse who can provide this information.

Some private nursing fees are covered by Medicare or the sick relative's supplemental insurance. For the most part, however, this is a very expensive care option, since most private nurses charge by the hour.

Home-care Services

Overall, this care option compromises between the relatively high cost of a private nurse and the difficult task of being sole caretaker of a sick relative.

Generally, you arrange for a nurse to stop in for a few hours, two or three times a week, depending on the person's needs. Along with this, a nurse's aid is hired to come in on a particular schedule to bathe and groom the relative. Physical or occupational therapists can also be attained. Discharge services at your hospital can usually provide you with a list of qualified professionals or, in some cases, make all of the arrangements for you.

Medicare covers the costs of an agency-approved visiting nurse, nurse's aid and therapist for up to eight hours a day for 21 consecutive days or as long as the relative's doctor deems necessary. Medicare coverage stops when the doctor says the nurse is no longer needed for care. At that point, if you want the nurse's aid to continue, you foot the bill.

Care Management

This is a variation on home-care services, usually employed by relatives who don't live near the person requiring help. An elder-care agency or geriatric-care manager evaluates what the patient needs, develops an appropriate healthcare plan and hires the necessary personnel. The program is overseen by the manager, who is available 24 hours a day to handle problems or emergencies. Care managers usually receive $150 to $300 an hour for the initial consultation and to monitor the person's care regularly. You must also pay the fees for all personnel hired to care for the relative. Medicare and supplemental coverage does kick in for this service, but every condition is different.

Besides the Eldercare Locator number listed in this chapter's subsequent "Senior Service Directory" section, you can also contact the National Association of Professional Geriatric Care Managers in Tucson, Arizona, (602) 881-8008. This association publishes a directory of geriatric-care managers nationwide. For additional information, contact the local chapter of the AARP (refer to the "Senior Service Directory") and ask for the free booklet Care Management: Arranging for Long-term Care.

Senior Services Directory

The following agencies and information clearinghouses could come in handy as resources for seniors.

North Strand

North Strand Senior Health Center
427 River Hills Dr., Little River
• **(843) 281-2778**

As an outpatient department of Grand Strand Regional Medical Center designed to meet and simplify the healthcare process for seniors, the brand-new North Strand Senior Health Center targets the needs of the senior population. The staff has been specially trained in the needs of senior citizens and will help patients assess, manage and prevent health-related problems. On-site services include medical exams, lab work and EKGs. The center welcomes Medicare assignments. Non-health services include assistance in locating community resources to addressing legal, financial and housing concerns.

Myrtle Beach

American Association of Retired Persons (AARP) Resource Center
In Myrtle Beach
• **(843) 232-1111**

Devoted to the needs of senior adults, the AARP sponsors an employment program that includes job training and, in some cases, placement for older workers with limited incomes. Call the office nearest you and ask about the Senior Community Service Employment Program (SCSEP). Office hours are 9 AM to 3 PM, Tuesday, Wednesday and Thursday.

Fifty-Five Alive Mature Driving
Grand Strand Senior Center,
1268 21st Ave. N., Myrtle Beach
• **(843) 626-3991**

This refresher course consists of eight hours of classroom instruction that stresses safe, defensive driving skills. Those who take the course get a 10 to 15 percent discount on auto insurance. Cost is $10 per person. The program is sponsored by the AARP.

Grand Strand Retirement Club
• **(843) 448-5670**

For $5 a year, any permanent and retired resident living east of the Intracoastal Waterway can join this social club, which meets regularly for lunch. Members perform some charity work but primarily meet to network with one another or play in the club's bowling league. Please call ahead for reservations.

National Association of Senior Friends, Grand Strand Chapter
Grand Strand Regional Medical Center,
82nd Avenue Pkwy., Myrtle Beach
• **(843) 692-1634, (843) 692-1645**

This nonprofit organization offers members educational and social activities, discounts, free cholesterol screenings, flu shots and various other services. The official office for the chapter is located in the main lobby of Grand Strand Regional Medical Center.

Senior Advisory Committee of Myrtle Beach
Myrtle Beach Convention Center,
Oak St. and 21st Ave. N., Myrtle Beach
• **(843) 497-8501**

This committee was organized through the City of Myrtle Beach to address specific needs of senior citizens such as larger print on road signs, longer crosswalk signals and noise ordinances.

Service Corps of Retired Executives (SCORE)
• **(843) 449-8538**

Calling all retired business people and executives . . . This volunteer corps offers free counsel to individuals who want to go into business as well as to businesses experiencing problems. Retired executives and professionals are encouraged to donate their skills and background to the cause.

Senior Golfers Association and Senior Golf Journal
3013 Church St., Myrtle Beach
• (843) 448-1569

The Senior Golfers Association and its publication, *Senior Golf Journal*, include members and subscriptions from virtually every town and city across the United States. Golf tournaments and the journal are coordinated here, but interest is national.

South Strand

Fifty Plus
1432 Seahouse Court, Surfside
• (843) 215-4118

This newspaper, expressly printed to suit senior citizens and retirees, is published monthly and distributed all along the Grand Strand from the North Carolina border to Georgetown and Conway, South Carolina. For home delivery, subscriptions cost $18 per year; or pick up a free copy at newsstands.

Georgetown County Council on Aging
Georgetown
• (843) 546-8539

This agency can provide referral services for local seniors.

Surfside Beach Fifties-Plus Group
Surfside Civic Center,
829 Pine Dr., Surfside Beach
• (843) 913-6339

This active social group is for older couples and singles. Fifties-Plus members get together for a meeting on the third Monday each month. A potluck luncheon is held the first Monday of each month, and planned activities range from bowling to games to trips.

Beyond the Strand

Elderhostel
Coastal Carolina University, Conway
• (843) 349-2665

Participants in this exciting program get an opportunity to take up to three noncredit courses in liberal arts and sciences from a host institution in the United States or abroad. This program is offered at more than 1,600 locations internationally.

Horry County Council on Aging Inc.
2213 N. Main St., Conway
• (843) 248-5523

The Council on Aging acts as an information and referral service for all senior citizens and their families. Staff provide up-to-date information on everything from home-delivered meals to living wills. This agency also performs the daunting task of managing eight area senior centers. In September 1997, this agency began publishing the monthly *Senior Life & Times* tabloid, which is distributed through the Council on Aging membership and its senior centers. *Life & Times* is full of tips, medical advice and event calendars. To contact the publication, call (843) 236-5151.

Horry County Veterans Affairs Office
211 Beaty St., Conway
• (843) 248-1291

This agency provides services to veterans and their dependents or survivors. It also operates as an intermediary between veteran patients and the VA hospital.

Senior Friends and Volunteer Service
• (843) 692-1645

Chapter meetings, luncheons and day trips are just a few of the fun activities orchestrated by this organization. Call for the ever-changing details.

Seniors Helping Seniors
• (843) 449-8318

A division of Senior Peer Counseling Service, this agency is a marvelous resource for the senior set.

Social Security Administration
905 Third Ave., Conway
• (843) 248-4271, (800) 772-2121,
(800) 772-1213

This agency provides information on social security benefits, including Supplemental Security Income (SSI) and disability. According to a recent report from SSI, retirees younger than 65 may earn $8,640 a year before their Social Security benefits would be reduced. Those between the ages of 65 and 69 years may earn as much as $13,500. There is no limit on those 70 or more years old.

Office hours are 7 AM to 7 PM Monday through Friday. For more information, visit www.ssa.gov.

South Carolina Employment Security Commission

• (843) 248-4289

Many Grand Strand companies readily employ older citizens. Contact this agency about job opportunities. Ask for Norma Hoffmaster regarding the special Title Five program for retired workers.

South Carolina Services Information Systems

• (800) 922-1107

Any senior who endures the misfortune of being disabled should call this toll-free number. South Carolina Services provides information on a variety of specialized resources for those in need.

Child Care & Education

LOOK FOR:
• Child Care
- Day-care Options
- Babysitting
  Services for
  Visitors
• Education
- Public Schools
- Private Schools
- Higher Education

Grand Stranders take great pride in their reputation as a beach community where family concerns receive their full attention. For example, parents here take education very seriously. In fact, in the fall of 1999, 83 percent of parents and guardians attended a personalized learning conference on behalf of their children, and 78 percent of parents and guardians officially pledged to be active in their child's education.

The fine schools of the Grand Strand—from private religious schools to technical academies—make good use of the amazing resources available in this area. For example, Horry Telephone Cooperative, a local connectivity provider, helped get the schools online. The tools are in place for the next generation of Grand Stranders to be able to read, write and compete with their peers nationwide. As a result, Horry County school district was chosen to be a recipient of the "What Parents Want" award, as presented by School Match, an independent educational consulting firm. More than 60,000 parents were surveyed nationally to determine the criteria for this designation, and only 14 percent of schools nationwide qualified.

The Horry County school system serves over 28,000 students. Horry County ranks first in the state for in-migration; by 2003 enrollment is expected to reach 30,542, representing an 11 percent increase from 1998. While South Carolina schools as a whole have not ranked very high in the nation, Horry County scholastic statistics rate higher and are improving. The county completed a $104 million overhaul in 1997, and has many plans for the future already underway: On November 2 of 1999, 77 percent of voters gave support to area schools by voting for the school district's $150 million bond referendum. As a result, the school district plans to build ten new schools and make additions to nine existing schools over the next four years to help relieve current crowding and to make way for impending growth.

The Horry County school district is the fifth largest of 91 state districts, and still maintains a relatively low dropout rate of 3.1 percent, with 65 percent of graduates going on to higher education. Fifty-one percent of the teachers in this county hold advanced degrees. The board of education is elected democratically, hires a superintendent, and works with the National Education Association. Class sizes in grades kindergarten through eighth have been limited to 25 or less, and four schools in the area have been named National Blue Ribbon Schools by the U.S. Department of Education. Achievement scores have been low in the recent past, but new curriculum standards and teaching models are beginning to show results: Second graders climbed 13 points in reading and 14 points in math in 1999, placing them in the top third of the national average. A new literacy model helped Horry County students top the state average in English language arts. Efforts also include such practical measures as placing a school resource officer or a security guard on campus, and full-time drug and weapon canine surveillence teams in all high schools, middle schools and career centers.

The first portion of this chapter discusses child care for the youngest of your gang. Then we move on to discuss primary- and secondary-education options.

Child Care

Day-care Options

Although word of mouth has always been one of the best ways to zero-in on reliable child care, newcomers don't have the benefit of an established network of reliable parents and other adults for advice. So, if you're new to our area, we suggest you request information from the Family Information Network. This computer database, part of the Clemson University Extension Service system, provides information about day-care centers, including adult care, throughout the state. Extension offices are at 1949 Industrial Park Road, Conway, (843) 365-6715, and at 1837 N. Frasier Street, Georgetown, (843) 546-4481.

The Family Information Network can provide data on pricing and child-to-staff ratios as well as information about meals, transportation services and other specifics you'll want to know about any center you're considering. It can also offer helpful hints on selecting the right day-care option for your child. Get the complete scoop on child-care laws and child-service agencies too. If you'd like to use the computer yourself, call for an appointment. If convenience is important to you, just call and ask for county agent Debbie Strickland in the Conway office or Barbara Lambert in Georgetown. They'll be happy to sift through a veritable mountain of information and mail you a printout of the centers in your area as well as any additional data you request. Best of all, there is absolutely no charge for this service.

The South Carolina Department of Social Services is responsible for licensing all day-care centers in the state. The Conway office, 1951 Industrial Park Road, (843) 365-5565, can provide you with a list of approved centers, including for-profit and nonprofit centers, as well as the names of individuals licensed to keep children in their homes.

Increasingly popular AuPairCare is an option. AuPairCare matches American families with child-care providers from all over the world, ages 18 to 25, who are interested in spending a year in the United States. Au pairs are thoroughly screened, and host families can choose for themselves a provider who best suits their personal needs and collective personality. Despite one recent tragedy that made national news, au pairs have been relied upon for generations.

INSIDERS' TIP

The mall-size Barnes & Noble bookstore on U.S. Highway 17 Bypass is the perfect place to take the kids. In addition to a truly staggering collection of children's literature, there are frequent storytelling hours and other activities for tykes. Call (843) 444-4046 for details.

Unlike a paid employee for whom you have to report income, an au pair essentially becomes a member of the family: The individual lives in your home, participates in household chores, shares your meals and your celebrations. In exchange for room, board and a salary-like weekly allowance, the au pair offers constant care for one or more children. During the program year, local or regional AuPairCare counselors provide support to both the families and the au pair. For more information, call (800) 4AUPAIR.

Mother's Day Out (MDO) is a "playgroup" program offered by the First Presbyterian Church in Myrtle Beach that allows mothers to "escape" from their little ones for a few hours without resorting to an all-day day-care situation. The program is always up and running from May through September. Frequent special summer programs are available as well. There are always at least four staff members on duty.

The program operates weekdays from 9 AM until noon, with extended care offered until 5 PM. Mornings are reserved for children from just-walking age through 3 years old. In the afternoons, all children 5 and younger are welcome to participate. Director Sherry Clardy describes the

Numerous private schools flourish along the Grand Strand.

Photo: courtesy Kimberly Allyson Duncan

program as "semi-structured play time." There's time for crafts, for videos, for snacks, reading and more.

Although the program is church-sponsored, parents do not have to be church members to use the service; however they should expect Christian values and education. MDO has met with such success, parents must contend with a long waiting list. Preregistration is held in February for church members and the first week of March for the public, but you can call Ms. Clardy anytime, (843) 626-3883, to get your name on the waiting list.

St. Philip's Lutheran Church in Myrtle Beach also offers a Mother's Morning Out program that runs through May and June to supplement their extensive day-care program, which includes kinder-music and gymnastics. Contact Jeanie Stetzer, (843) 449-4322, for an application.

Be sure to read the Kidstuff and Attractions chapters for fun and educational activities to occupy your brood's time.

Babysitting Services for Visitors

With the heavy influx of families visiting this area, there are frequent inquiries about babysitting services available to nonresidents. After all, time-starved moms and dads deserve a break from the family rat-race every now and again!

If you'd consider leaving your child with a sitting service, read on. The following businesses cater primarily to the tourist market but serve a few locals as well. Although they can sometimes accommodate parents on short notice, officials suggest calling at least 24 hours in advance, especially during the busy summer season. Most of the sitters are mature women, many of whom are 30 or older. All are thoroughly screened. Sitters provide their own transportation and will accept jobs from North Myrtle Beach to Garden City Beach.

Resort Babysitting, (843) 280-9613, has been in operation in the Myrtle Beach area since 1982. Rates are $5 per hour for one child, $6 for two children, $7 for three and $8 for four. After four children, compute your charges by adding $2 per hour for each additional child. There is a $6 transportation charge and a three-hour minimum for babysitting.

Grandmother's Sitting Service, (843) 236-3811, is another of the area's time-tested babysitting services. Owned by soft-spoken Grandmom Extraordinaire Evelyn Todd, this service has been in operation for approximately 20 years. Although Ms. Todd charges $7 per hour (cash only; $1 per hour for each additional child), there is no additional charge for transportation. Like Resort Babysitting, Grandmother's Sitting Service requires a three-hour minimum.

Education

Public Schools

The Horry County School District's student services begin with an early childhood program for 4-year-olds with developmental and learning difficulties. Kindergarten for 5-year-olds is a standard part of the statewide school curriculum and is available throughout the district.

Summer Success School is offered to students who need additional help between terms. Summer Success helps students acquire skills they missed during the standard school year and provides additional reading and math instruction to students who need just a little extra help. This program often enables students to advance to the next grade level instead of being retained for an entire year.

Every elementary school offers the PELICAN program for gifted and talented students. PELICAN provides enrichment activities one day a week that foster critical-thinking skills and encourage creativity.

Middle schools offer basic classes as well as honors programs. Similarly, all seven Horry County high schools provide a basic curriculum plus college-preparatory and honors classes. Advanced Placement classes afford students who pass standardized tests possible exemption from certain introductory college classes.

One unique feature of the Horry County schools is Playcard Environmental Center, a nature preserve in the western portion of the county. The center not only gives urban and suburban kids a taste of rural life, but also teaches all children a healthy respect for the earth's resources. Students learn about Native American and pioneer cultures and the ecosystems of a thriving

Horry County's population is soaring; modern, new schools are being built to accommodate the influx.

Photo: courtesy of Horry County Schools

blackwater swamp. The pristine preserve features a collection of farm and domestic animals, a nature trail with labeled flora and fauna, an old rope swing in a forested area and a real beaver dam.

School officials assert that Playcard is unique in South Carolina and perhaps the United States. The 200-acre preserve also provides a site for observation and study in various scientific disciplines. The program is sponsored by both the community and the school district and is governed by an advisory board made up of representatives from Coastal Carolina University, Horry-Georgetown Technical College, and community and business members.

Conway is the district's largest high school, with more than 2,000 students. Socastee, the South Strand's high school, ranks second.

The school district also offers the Aynor/Conway Career Center, the Finklea Career Center and the Academy of Arts, Science and Technology—formerly the Grand Strand Career Center—that collectively provide high school students with vocational, technical, occupational and academic training. The Conway School of Nursing, housed at the Aynor/Conway Career Center, is a two-year program that prepares students for careers as licensed practical nurses (LPNs). The Academy of Arts, Science and Technology offers instruction in new programs such as graphics, video/audio technology, pre-engineering, golf course technology (that's right, the academic study of golf courses!), dance and hospitality services (also known as hotel management). For more information, contact Horry County Schools at (843) 248-8500.

Private Schools

With the exception of some day-care centers and preschools, all of Horry's private schools are church-affiliated and basically Christian, reflecting a regional tradition of fundamental Christian morality, beliefs and culture (see our Worship chapter).

North Strand

Risen Christ Lutheran School
10595 U.S. Hwy. 17 N.,
North Myrtle Beach
• (843) 272-8163

Risen Christ was established with the primary stated goal "of preparing each child for a happy and fruitful life." In keeping with their interpretation of such a lofty goal, a number of developmental categories are emphasized: intellectual, spiritual, emotional, social and physical. Risen Christ staff believe that administering to students on these levels helps children grow into well-rounded and successful adults.

Risen Christ is dedicated to bringing up children "in the way of the Lord" (which presumably does *not* mean that all the students become carpenters and deliver impromptu speeches in temples). Along with providing spiritual training, Risen Christ strives to maintain high academic standards. The school belongs to the Lutheran Education Association

and is one of more than 3,000 Lutheran schools in the United States. Curricular areas of study include religion, English, spelling, writing, math, social studies, science, computers, art, music and physical education and Spanish (grades 6, 7 and 8).

Risen Christ offers pre-kindergarten and kindergarten classes as well as primary grades 1 through 8. Additionally, it offers before- and after-school child care for pre-kindergartners through 5th-graders. A summer camp also is offered for students.

Myrtle Beach

Calvary Christian School
Dick Pond Rd., Myrtle Beach
• (843) 650-2829

A ministry of Calvary Bible Church, Calvary offers preschool programs for youngsters 3 through 5 years of age and regular classes for 1st through 12th graders in a distinctly religious setting. In its second decade of operation, this is the Strand's oldest Christian school, although officially all denominations are welcome in a student body of approximately 350. The elementary classes are known for their strong phonics program. According to standardized achievement test results, Calvary rates more than a year ahead of national grade-level averages. Similarly, SAT scores rank ahead of both the state and the national average.

INSIDERS' TIP

Horry-Georgetown Technical College offers a degree in golf course management. The two-year program started in 1972.

Grand Strand Academy
2756 Howard Pkwy., Myrtle Beach
• **(843) 477-1448**

Sponsored by the Cathedral Bible College (also profiled in this chapter), Grand Strand Academy is a school with strong academics and a strong religious emphasis. The academy uses the advanced A Beka curriculum for 4-year-olds through 12th graders. The school's active fine arts program includes chorus, orchestra, art appreciation, even Latin and Greek on the high school level.

St. Andrews Catholic School
3601 N. Kings Hwy., Myrtle Beach
• **(843) 448-6062**

St. Andrews is supported by tuition and parish subsidies. Class sizes range from 25 to 30 students, and faculty positions total approximately 14. The program is enhanced by an active PTO and Mother's Club. Consequently, parent volunteers contribute significantly to the overall quality of their children's educational experience.

Christian education at St. Andrews is designed to educate the child as a whole—intellectually, morally, physically, emotionally and socially. Students enjoy a high level of interaction with teachers and classmates. St. Andrews strives to develop leadership through classroom activities, school worship, liturgies and extracurricular activities. The educational program is designed to foster academic excellence, emphasizing basic skills as a strong foundation. And the program's success is evident in standardized test results and in the number of students admitted to advanced-placement high school programs.

Classes are offered from kindergarten (5-year-olds) through 8th grade, and after-school care is available for students.

South Strand

Pawleys Island Montessori Day School
9305 Ocean Hwy., Pawleys Island
• **(843) 237-9015**

Approximately 50 students, from 2-year-olds to 6th graders, attend Pawleys Island Montessori Day School. The curriculum, as the name indicates, is based on the world-renowned Montessori philosophy of education, where instructors respect each child's pace of learning and encourage students to follow their own interests. Emphasizing "concrete manipulations" (a.k.a. hands-on activities), the school

has a student-teacher ratio of 10-to-1 or less. Established 13 years ago, the school operates nine months of the year, has playground facilities, is developing expansion plans and welcomes new students. Contact Dr. Pamela Ness at the listed number for an application.

Beyond the Strand

ATC Christian School
1672 S.C. Hwy. 905, Conway
• **(843) 365-6800**

An affiliate of The Prayer Center, ATCCS offers A Beka classes for 4-year-olds through 8th-graders. A preschool program for 2- and 3-year-olds is also available. Education is administered in a Christian environment, which school officials believe is vital not only for developing character through moral training, but also for reaching an outstanding level of academic excellence.

Conway Christian School
1951 Riverside Dr., Conway
• **(843) 347-7041**

The primary goal of Conway Christian School is to provide quality education with a Biblical perspective in a distinctly Christian atmosphere of discipline. The school's academic priority is teaching fundamental skills. An affiliate of Grace Presbyterian Church, Conway Christian offers preschool classes for 4- and 5-year-olds and uses the A Beka curriculum, including French and Spanish, for students in the 1st through 12th grades.

Higher Education

Myrtle Beach

Cathedral Bible College
2756 Howard Pkwy., Myrtle Beach
• **(843) 477-1448**

Cathedral Bible College offers a Master of Theology degree, with majors in ministry, missions, Christian education, church administration, counseling and music. The college, which occupies the site of a former U.S. Air Force base, enrolls approximately 100 students.

Fortune School of Real Estate
350 Wesley St., Unit 305, Myrtle Beach
• **(843) 236-1131**

Fortune School of Real Estate trains new agents, existing agents and aspiring brokers in preparation for the state licensing exam.

Webster University
4589 Oleander Dr., Myrtle Beach
• (843) 497-3677

Webster University is an independent, non-denominational, multi-campus international business college offering a graduate program at its Myrtle Beach campus. Webster prides itself on offering degree programs that many schools in the area do not, including Management, Human Resources and Clinical Psychology. Classes are conveniently scheduled to attract students from up to 2 hours away as well as working professionals. In response to increasing enrollment, Webster built a new and upgraded facility in 1997.

Graduate programs in business, human resources development, management and clinical counseling are all accredited by the North Central Association of Colleges and Schools. Admission to the MA and MBA programs is open to all students who hold an undergraduate degree from a regionally accredited college or university.

In a nutshell, Webster offers education tailored to busy professionals. The distinction of Webster's whole approach is that of its commitment to education and to the community. This motto has created distinct advantages for adult students—fulfilling the wish list of anyone who wants to change careers, retool in the wake of cutbacks or closings, or advance in his or her current situation.

Beyond the Strand

Coastal Carolina University
U.S. Hwy. 501 E., Conway
• (843) 347-3161

Coastal Carolina is a comprehensive liberal arts institution offering baccalaureate degrees in 33 major fields of study as well as master's degrees in education. The university is committed to excellence in teaching, research and public service.

Canvassing 244 wooded acres just minutes from the Atlantic Ocean and the resort area of Myrtle Beach, the Coastal Carolina campus is home to more than 4,500 students from South Carolina and 40 other states as well as 26 foreign countries.

A Coastal Carolina education offers a hands-on, personal educational experience. More than 200 faculty members bring impressive credentials from universities throughout the nation. Select faculty have been awarded Fulbright grants for research projects and study in such countries as New Zealand, Kenya, Colombia, Poland and China. In addition, students can interact with worldwide experts on a variety of topical issues through the advanced technologies of long-distance education and online computer services.

Coastal Carolina's academic programs often are supplemented with field experiences and "real world" applications. Students have the chance to participate in faculty-led travel to a pristine barrier island on the South Carolina coast, the Grand Canyon, archaeological digs in surrounding historical settings, Fortune 500 companies, the marbled chambers of the United States Supreme Court, Oxford University and East Africa.

A reciprocal student-exchange program with Nene College in North Hampton, England, has been established through the Palmetto Partnership for International Exchange, a partnership headed by Coastal Carolina with the College of Charleston and Lander and Winthrop universities.

The university's four applied research centers help students realize the practical applications of classroom theory and the importance of university-community relations.

University programs that serve the community include continuing education; Lifelong Learning Society, an academic program for those 50 and older (see our Senior Scene chapter); and cultural events including live arts performances.

Coastal Carolina athletes participate in NCAA Division I, with 14 varsity teams competing in the Big South Conference.

Coastal Carolina is accredited by the Commission of the Southern Association of Colleges and Schools to award the baccalaureate degree and the master's degree in education.

INSIDERS' TIP

From June 7 to August 27, Myrtle Beach Golf Holiday has organized single-day tournaments through the Strand to double as family fun and as lessons in good sportsmanship. The format is two person teams, Captain's choice (scramble). No established handicap is needed. There is no age minimum, so this tournament is great for beginners. Per day, the cost is $25 for adults and $17 for youths, which includes greens fees, electric carts and prizes. Call (800) 845-4658 for more details.

In 1954, when a group of concerned citizens met in the Horry County Memorial Library to discuss a daring proposal—the creation of a local college—the foundation was laid for Coastal Carolina to provide quality education for its students. For more than 40 years, the university has been building a tradition of excellence. In 1994 it broke from the University of South Carolina system in a major political battle over endowments; it seems that Coastal officials felt that they were at the bottom of the priorities list for fund-raising expenditures. Since the split, Coastal Carolina has begun major expansion, and the Golf Course Management program has come to be recognized as one of the nation's finest.

and Associate in Science to a varied technical and business curriculum. In addition to the two-year degrees, HGTC has several transfer agreements with other South Carolina colleges and universities that allow students to obtain four-year degrees. Furthermore, HGTC has 74 courses guaranteed to transfer for full credit to any public higher-education institution in South Carolina. Its thriving Continuing Education program and intensive on-site industrial training program—serving more than 75 businesses, industries and organizations each year—round out HGTC's educational opportunities.

Horry-Georgetown Technical College is accredited by the Commission on Colleges of the Southern Association of Colleges and Schools.

Horry-Georgetown Technical College
2050 U.S. Hwy. 501 E., Conway
• **(843) 347-3186**

Horry-Georgetown Technical College, established in 1966, currently boasts an annual student enrollment of more than 3,200. Combined with the Continuing Education Division of HGTC, which provides skill enhancement and specialized job training, that number reaches 14,000. The college continues to grow and prosper while serving Horry and Georgetown counties as well as surrounding communities.

HGTC is in the business of cultivating excellence across three campuses, with convenient sites in Conway, Myrtle Beach (now also on the former Air Force base) and Georgetown. The college offers more than 40 degrees, diplomas and certificates—from Associate in Arts

North American Institute of Aviation
1700 Airport Rd., Conway
• **(843) 397-9111, (800) 345-6152**

This private international institute operates out of the Conway/Horry County Airport. Students—approaching nearly 100 at any given time—train to become commercial airline pilots. After a six-month course, pilots return to their home countries to accumulate flight time. Once they have logged 1,500 flight hours, they return to Conway to earn an Airline Transport Pilot designation.

Most of the students come from Scandinavian countries and live in dormitories at the airport.

The school moved to Conway from the Northeast about 18 years ago because officials preferred the area's geography and mild weather.

Healthcare

For the benefit of any visitor to the Grand Strand, this chapter will give you pertinent information about regional medical services, clinics and hospitals. Healthcare services listed here should be able to handle anything from a severe sunburn to debilitating pain.

The Grand Strand has recently witnessed an incredible growth in healthcare services and specialists. Rapid growth, ideal locations for golf and attractions, and what one physician called "a doctor-friendly environment" have brought a weighty influx of medical expertise to the area. Over the past two years, Loris Hospital has added 10 doctors (making a staff of fifty full time doctors), and in the past four years, Grand Strand Regional Medical Center has doubled its staff of full-time doctors, making a staff of 200 physicians. Conway Hospital has grown by nearly 25 doctors since 1998.

Besides the less stressful lifestyle and heralded Southern hospitality enjoyed by many of these practitioners, the need for doctors who practice geriatrics, rheumatology and endocrinology has soared in direct proportion with the number of senior citizens relocating to the Grand Strand.

If you are about to become a resident or have just moved into our area, the referral services can quickly put you in touch with a new family doctor or specialist.

LOOK FOR:
• Referrals and
  Free Advice
• Regional
  Healthcare
  Facilities
  - Walk-in Clinics
  - Hospitals
  - Mental Health/
    Addictions
  - Health-related
    Associations and
    Support Groups

Referrals and Free Advice

Physician Referral Source
• (843) 692-1052

Especially if a medical specialist is needed, this service will give you all the necessary referral information, including a doctor's hours. Physician Referral represents more than 100 physicians on Grand Strand Regional Medical Center's staff and more than 25 medical specialties and sub-specialties. This service is available 8:30 AM to 5 PM, Monday through Friday.

Doctors Referral Service
• (843) 716-7000 Ext. 6410

Sponsored by Loris Community Hospital, referral to conveniently located physicians who meet a person's medical needs can be accessed by this service.

Doctors Referral Service is available Monday through Friday from 8:30 AM to 5 PM.

Regional Healthcare Facilities

Walk-in Clinics

Visitors who need to see a doctor but aren't sick enough to go to a hospital emergency room can save themselves time and money by seeking care at one of the Grand Strand's walk-in medical clinics.

These clinics take patients without appointments, but most of them don't take insurance, Medicaid or Medicare, so be prepared to pay when you go. Costs run anywhere from $55 to $75 for an average visit, and some healthcare providers accept traveler's checks, in-state personal checks or credit cards as methods of payment (as noted in each write-up).

Clinic doctors routinely treat sunburn, heat rash, heat exhaustion, cuts, sprains, broken bones, jellyfish stings and sore throats. And some facilities offer more complex services, including X-rays and stabilization of patients who have had heart attacks. Here is a listing of walk-in clinics representing each area of the Strand.

North Strand

Access Medical Care
3816 U.S. Hwy. 17 S., North Myrtle Beach
• (843) 272-1411

Access Medical Care offers minor surgery, X-rays, electrocardiograms and complete laboratory services as well as a pharmacy. With the exception of Blue Cross/Blue Shield, insurance is not accepted, but office workers will fill out Medicare and Medicaid papers for people who live in South and North Carolina. Access will file workers' compensation claims. The clinic is open Monday through Friday from 8 AM to 8 PM, and on Saturday and Sunday from 9 AM to 6 PM.

Doctor's Care North Myrtle Beach
1714 U.S. Hwy. 17 S., North Myrtle Beach
• (843) 361-0705

Doctor's Care medical clinic provides primary and urgent care, including X-rays, stitches and stabilization of heart attack patients. The clinic accepts regular patients for family practice and can also handle minor lab work. Emergencies will be sent to the nearest hospital. The cost for a typical non-emergency office visit ranges from $59 to $65. The North Myrtle Beach clinic is open from 8 AM to 8 PM, Monday through Friday and from 8 AM to 6 PM on Saturday and Sunday.

Myrtle Beach

Doctor's Care Myrtle Beach
1220 21st Ave. N., Myrtle Beach
• (843) 626-9379

The Doctor's Care medical clinics provide primary and urgent care, including X-rays, stitches and stabilization of heart attack patients. Doctors here accept regular patients for family practice. The clinics also handle minor lab work. Emergencies are sent to the nearest hospital. The center is open from 8:30 AM to 6:30 PM Monday through Friday, and 9 AM to 5 PM on Saturday and Sunday. The cost for a typical non-emergency office visit ranges from $59 to $65; if you return to the clinic, the cost is reduced. Doctor's Care dispenses common medications to its patients.

Family Health Center
4810 N. Kings Hwy., Myrtle Beach
• (843) 497-7131

Access Medical offers minor surgery, X-rays,

electrocardiograms and complete lab services. Access also operates a limited-medications pharmacy. Insurance is not accepted (except Blue Cross/Blue Shield), but office workers will fill out Medicare and Medicaid papers for people who live in South and North Carolina. Access will file workers' compensation injury claims. The clinic is open Monday through Friday from 8 AM to 6 PM.

Myrtle Beach Medical Center
504 D, 27th Ave. N., Myrtle Beach
• (843) 946-9690

ASAP Medical Clinic has been at the Grand Strand since 1992. It's open Monday through Friday from 8:30 AM to 5 PM. Doctors handle minor medical emergencies including sunburn, fire-ant stings and cuts. The clinic can also perform drug and alcohol screening for business and industry. One of the most common services provided is replacement of prescriptions for travelers who have left their medications at home. Life-threatening emergencies are sent on to a hospital.

ASAP accepts credit cards, traveler's checks and in-state checks. Costs start at about $55 and range upward, depending on the services provided. The clinic is also working to develop a local clientele among area industries, providing pre-employment physicals for workers' compensation. For this service, ASAP will accept Medicare, Champus and some city and county insurances.

South Strand

Doctor's Care
Surfside Medical Center,
1600 U.S. Hwy. 17 N., Surfside Beach
• (843) 238-1461

This Doctor's Care clinic, like its counterparts in North Myrtle Beach and Myrtle Beach (see previous entries for details), provides primary and urgent care and handles minor lab work. The Surfside Beach clinic is open seven days a week from 8 AM to 8 PM.

MedPlus
997 U.S. Hwy. 17 Bus., Surfside Beach
• (843) 238-3685

Resident physician and clinic owner Dr. James Turek takes care of patients at MedPlus. This walk-in clinic, across from Wild Water Waterpark & Family Fun Center (see our Attractions chapter for details), also serves regular patients by appointment.

MedPlus conducts allergy tests as well as

bone-density tests to determine early signs of osteoporosis.

From mid-June through Labor Day, MedPlus is open Monday through Saturday from 8 AM to 8 PM. During the rest of the year, it's open Monday to Friday from 8 AM to 6 PM and Saturday from 9 AM to 1 PM. The cost of a first-time urgent-care visit starts at $55, while established patients pay $44.

Hospitals

It's heart-wrenching when you, a loved one or friend needs hospital attention, but you can take comfort in the care and professionalism found at the following medical facilities. Scanning through this section, you should be able to get a good idea of the specialty services offered by each, just in case you need to make a quick decision about where to take someone for medical attention.

North Strand

Loris Community Hospital
3655 Mitchell St., Loris
• **(843) 716-7000**

Some visitors at the northern end of the Grand Strand might find it quickest to visit Loris, an acute care, nonprofit community hospital. Loris has a capacity of 105 patients, all in private rooms. The hospital also runs a separate 88-bed, skilled nursing assisted facility known as the Loris Healthcare System Extended Care Center.

Loris Hospital offers 24-hour emergency service, cardiac rehabilitation services, same-day surgery, a modern intensive-care unit, ultrasound, magnetic resonance imaging (MRI), a CT scanner, nuclear medicine, extensive outpatient services, an obstetrics unit with childbirth and breast-feeding classes, and nutritional counseling.

Recent expansion has included the construction of a 26,000-square-foot center for health and fitness that houses cardiac rehabilitation, physical therapy, hydrotherapy, exercise programs and meeting facilities. Regular classes focus on smoking cessation, weight loss and low-fat cooking. Unlike other hospital-sponsored wellness programs, Loris Community offers use of its fitness facility to the public in an effort to keep people out of its beds through prevention.

The fitness center offers a variety of aerobic classes including Seniorcize and water aerobics, plus cardiovascular and strength-building equipment. In fact, the center quickly earned a local reputation as an "unofficial" community spot, being selected by community members as the site for wedding receptions, gatherings and programs.

In December 1995, Loris Hospital began offering after-hours primary care in the emergency room. This service, called Fast Track, gives patients the option of seeing a physician's assistant for medical care that is urgent but not an emergency. Fast Track services are available from 3 to 11 PM Friday through Monday.

Loris Hospital also has opened a full complement of medical offices in North Myrtle Beach as well as the LCH Family Health Center clinic. One such outlying medical bureau that opened in 1997 is the North Myrtle Beach Physical Rehabilitation Center, which offers treatment for neurological, orthopedic and developmental problems. Here, patients can be evaluated and treated for accidents and strokes, muscular-skeletal injuries, strength and range of motion limitations, balance and coordination deficits, and gait and postural problems. Speech therapists are on duty to evaluate and treat speaking, language and swallowing difficulties.

Myrtle Beach

Grand Strand Regional Medical Center
809 82nd Pkwy., Myrtle Beach
• **(843) 692-1000**

Grand Strand Regional Medical Center is a 190-bed acute-care facility that offers an array of medical services on both an inpatient and outpatient basis. The medical staff numbers more than 750 with more than 200 physicians on call.

Grand Strand Regional has the county's only comprehensive cardiac program, with two operating rooms dedicated solely to open-heart surgery, angioplasty and other heart-related procedures. The hospital is noted for its state-of-the-art cardiac catheterization and diagnostic laboratory, stents and cardiac rehabilitation. A rehabilitation center now houses exercise equipment and supervised programs for cardiac patients that includes fitness, nutritional counseling, education and risk education.

Prior to the birth of Grand Strand's cardiac surgery program in April 1995, the closest places performing open-heart surgery were Charleston and Florence, South Carolina, or Wilmington, North Carolina. For many, an hour or more was too long a jaunt for cardiac treatment and angioplasty. The need for local services was apparent: Heart disease is the leading cause of death

HEALTHCARE

in South Carolina and accounts for 35 percent of all deaths statewide. Grand Strand Regional Medical Center in Myrtle Beach answered that need by building a 14,600-square-foot, $5.9 million surgical addition to the hospital that includes an eight-bed surgical intensive-care unit and two new operating suites. A satellite pharmacy services the operating rooms and the surgical intensive-care unit.

The Emergency Department is a designated trauma center using electronic technology that includes a hyperbaric chamber commonly used in treating diving accidents, wounds and burns. Emergency also offers Care Express to treat minor injuries and illnesses for anyone without a local physician. Care Express is open to new residents and visitors alike. Grand Strand Regional emergency services is also the proud owner of HeartLink, a cardiac transport ambulance for those in need of acute care. All of Grand Strand's emergency department physicians are board-certified in emergency medicine. For added convenience, an outpatient pharmacy is open to the public from 7 AM to 7 PM every day of the week.

Grand Strand Hospital has the only accredited community cancer program in Horry and Georgetown counties. It is also a member of the National Consortium of Breast Centers and has on staff one of the leading experts in the field of breast cancer. Mammography is available at the hospital and at diagnostic centers in Little River and Surfside Beach. Grand Strand employs advanced breast biopsy instrumentation (ABBI) for breast biopsy, which is a stereotactic technology that targets tissue within 1 millimeter of accuracy and greatly minimizes the amount of healthy tissue taken. ABBI can be performed under a local anesthetic, allowing a patient to resume normal activity in a few hours.

An 18-bed Extended Care Unit at Grand Strand provides transition from acute hospital care to intensive rehabilitation services. Extended Care has on staff dedicated physical and activity therapists, nurses, social workers and dieticians.

Hospital officials work especially hard at preventive care and community education through an annual health fair held on the first Saturday in February, and a cardiac wellness program that includes the Mall Walkers' Club, the Cardiac Lifelong Program and ongoing community cholesterol screenings.

Other community programs include prostate cancer screening and a teddy bear clinic for children—an annual event at Grand Strand Regional aimed at allaying children's fears of hospitals. Preschoolers bring their "injured" teddy bears into the emergency room where doctors and nurses apply bandages, splints, stitches and the odd button.

South Strand

Georgetown Memorial Hospital
606 Black River Rd., Georgetown
• **(843) 527-7000,**
(843) 626-9040 (from Myrtle Beach)

This is a private, nonprofit acute-care medical facility that is currently licensed for 142 beds. More than 50 physicians representing 20 areas of specialty practice are members of the active medical staff.

Medical services include ambulatory surgery; birthing suites; cardiac diagnostics, catheterization and rehabilitation; full emergency and lab services; MRI; pathology; radiology; renal dialysis; and respiratory therapy. The hospital also offers cholesterol screenings, dietary consultation and discharge planning. Throughout any given year, Georgetown Memorial holds various educational programs and events.

Established in 1950, Georgetown Memorial has consistently expanded services to keep up with the needs of the community. Most recently, the hospital added pre-op bays, a fifth surgical suite and a diagnostic imaging center.

Beyond the Strand

Conway Hospital
300 Singleton Ridge Rd., Conway
• **(843) 347-7111**

Conway Hospital, a private, nonprofit institution, was in downtown Conway for more than a half-century before a large, modern facility was built outside the city limits between Conway and Myrtle Beach.

The hospital opened in 1982, and today approximately 125 physicians make rounds among 160 modern, private rooms. The building itself has three stories, with patient rooms occupying the top two floors. Conway Hospital has 80 medical/surgical beds, 29 obstetrical/gynecological beds, 18 for pediatrics and 10 equipped for intensive and coronary care.

Services include 24-hour emergency and urgent care, one-day surgery, chemotherapy, CT scanning, MRI, lithotripsy, maternity care, pediatric care, mammography, cardiac rehabilitation, nuclear medicine, physical therapy, respiratory therapy, home healthcare, surgical care, ultrasound, intensive care and progressive care. A new generation of echocardiographic equip-

---

ment, as well as CT scanning, MRI, digital substraction angiography, blood gas analysis, impedance plethysmography, advanced telemetry techniques and cardiac catheterization allows for state-of-the-art diagnostic and treatment capabilities. The hospital is also certified as a Level III trauma center as well as Level II perinatal center.

Conway Hospital recently became the world's first to receive the Spectron Hip Reconstruction system. In August 1996, Dr. James Yates performed the sixth autologous chondrocyte transplant in the United States at Conway Hospital. The procedure is noted for producing remarkable results for young patients suffering from knee cartilage injury.

Patients requiring dialysis during their hospital stay are served at the facility through an inpatient dialysis unit. In addition, the adjoining Medstar subacute care building provides care to individuals in transition from intensive services to home, at a significantly reduced cost.

Adjacent to Conway Hospital is Kingston Nursing Center, an 88-bed long-term nursing home owned and operated by the hospital. And, through the efforts of a joint venture, Conway Hospital works with American Home Patient, a company that supplies home infusion services, home respiratory services and home medical equipment.

In spring 1996 Conway Hospital opened its 39,000-square-foot wellness and fitness center. This center includes a swimming pool, racquetball courts, an indoor track, basketball court, weight room, his and hers saunas and locker rooms. Aerobics classes are scheduled as well. Memberships to the wellness facility are open to individuals, patients and corporations, and a variety of rate packages is available. For more information, call (843) 347-1515.

In 1997 the AVX Corporation provided Conway Hospital with a $100,000 grant to put a 24-foot mobile health van on the road. Now, health screening services are available throughout Horry County to meet the needs of medically underserved people in the area.

Other Regional Facilities

McLeod Regional Medical Center
555 E. Cheves St., Florence
• **(843) 667-2000**

About 75 miles from Myrtle Beach is McLeod Regional Hospital, a regional referral center for 12 counties in southeastern South Carolina. McLeod was established in 1906 as a small infirmary; today, it's a large high-tech

medical center, with 331 beds and a variety of services. Many Horry County residents depend on McLeod's neonatal intensive care unit to tend to premature babies and full-term babies born with special problems.

The hospital's breast-imaging center helps doctors detect breast cancer in its early stages. McLeod has the state's first permanent MRI system, a high-tech machine that uses a magnetic field to see into the body in a much clearer way than other scanning machines allow.

McLeod also provides comprehensive inpatient, outpatient and diagnostic facilities, including an extensive 24-hour laboratory, computerized tomography, angiography, computer-enhanced nuclear medicine, ultrasound, echocardiography, mammography, EEG, EKG, a vascular laboratory, osteoporosis screening, a sleep center and 24-hour emergency care. The Florence hospital is the state-designated regional trauma center.

The facility added a five-story freestanding Women's Pavilion connected to McLeod. The pavilion houses a mammography unit, outpatient surgery rooms and a special section for labor and delivery or Caesarean section.

At the Pediatric After-Hours Care Center, children 16 and younger can receive treatment for about 40 ailments. The After-Hours Center takes over when the doctors' offices close, handling minor cuts and scrapes, ear aches, tummy aches, even coughs and fevers. Nine pediatricians work in rotation from 6:30 to 10:30 PM. It is also far less expensive than an emergency-room visit.

A range of support departments buttress the hospital's services. These include rehabilitative services, pain management, cardiac rehabilitation, respiratory services, counseling and discharge planning, hospice, infection control, pastoral services, patient representatives, volunteer services, computer services and marketing.

Mental Health/Addictions

South Strand

The Waccamaw Center for Mental Health
164 Waccamaw Medical Park Dr., Conway
• **(843) 347-4888**
2710 Highmarket St., Georgetown
• **(843) 546-6107**

The Waccamaw Center is a public, nonprofit agency that handles any sort of mental health issue on an outpatient basis. Fees are established on a sliding scale; you pay only what you can afford based on income and expenses, and most insurances are accepted. Staff is on call 24 hours a day, seven days a week to respond to emergencies and crises. Both clinics offer adult services, child and adolescent therapy, alcohol and drug abuse counseling, programs for the chronically mentally ill and emergency stabilization.

The center is continuously developing special community programs to institute prevention of growing mental health problems. The school-based program operates out of a number of Grand Strand schools, offering on-site help to children and their families. An Employee Assistance Program offers mental health services to business and industry on a contractual basis. The Waccamaw Center also will refer clients to an appropriate inpatient facility if it is necessary.

INSIDERS' TIP

Nearly all Grand Strand hospitals now have impressive wellness centers with exercise equipment, aerobics classes, swimming pools and a host of heath-related programs. Membership is open to the public, making them an alternative workout spot to gyms, aerobics studios and fitness venues. Trained professional staff is a must for all hospital wellness programs.

gram. Regular outpatient services are available Monday through Thursday from 8:30 AM to 7:30 PM, and on Friday from 8:30 AM to 5 PM.

The Commission on Drug and Alcohol Abuse also operates a 24-hour residential center that can accommodate 10 patients at any given time. The agency works with managed-care programs and provides Employee Assistance Program contracts to area business and industry.

This agency accepts Medicaid, Medicare and most commercial insurances as methods of payment. MasterCard and Visa are also accepted. No one is denied needed services due to indigence, but the commission does require that a fee schedule be signed with a client prior to therapy.

Beyond the Strand

Charter Sands
152 Waccamaw Medical Park Dr., Conway
• **(843) 347-7156, (800) 922-0742**
   Coastal Carolina is a specialty hospital that provides both inpatient and outpatient psychiatric and chemical dependency services. Outpatient assessments and therapy cover almost any problem from marriage and family conflicts to drug and alcohol treatment. Coastal is best known for its inpatient services, including acute psychiatric treatment for adults and children plus detoxification and a residential treatment center for adolescents. Coastal's help-line is available 24 hours a day, seven days a week (note the listed toll-free number). Coastal accepts commercial insurance, Champus and Medicare. Visa and MasterCard also accepted.

Horry County Commission on Alcohol and Drug Abuse
1004 Bell St., Conway
• **(843) 248-6291**
   This commission deals specifically with addictions, devoting a lot of time and money to prevention. Treatment services include detoxification, family programs, individual and group counseling, and an intensive outpatient pro-

Health-related Associations and Support Groups

Alzheimer's Support Group
• **(843) 347-0407, (843) 756-2106**
   This group provides a listening ear, encouragement, coping techniques, moral support and practical information. Respite services are also available, including adult day-care programs, home-health aides and short-stay nursing home programs. Monthly meetings are held at Myrtle Beach and Conway locations. At Conway Hospital, this support group meets the second Thursday of each month from 7 PM to 9 PM in the private dining room. Call Judy Swanson at the first number listed above or Kay Sendry at the second number.

American Cancer Society
2410 Hwy. 501 W., Conway
• **(843) 213-0333**
   The local chapter of the American Cancer Society is a busy one, sponsoring three Reach To Recovery support and counseling groups every month. Breast cancer support sessions are held on the second Wednesday of each month at 2 PM at the Grand Strand Senior Center, 1268 21st Avenue North in Myrtle Beach. Another group gathers on the fourth Tuesday of the month, and you must contact the cancer society to reserve a

seat for this one. A general cancer support group meets on the first Monday each month in Conway Hospital's auditorium at 6 PM.

Due to insurance issues, our local cancer society had to discontinue loaning wheelchairs and walkers to those fighting the disease. At the time this edition of *Insiders'® Guide* was on the presses, the society also had to put its transportation program on hold. A spokesperson informed us that a concerted effort was being made to reinstitute its transportation services, but it would be best to call ahead to find out for certain.

Arthritis Foundation
1314 Spring St. N.W., Atlanta, Ga.
• **(800) 283-7800**

The Arthritis Foundation provides a toll-free number to answer questions about various types of arthritis and, when appropriate, refers callers to community organizations. The foundation is also prepared to help clients and their families with financial support.

Better Breathing Club
300 Singleton Ridge Rd., Conway
• **(843) 347-7111**

This support group is specifically designed for those who have a lung disease. It is a cooperative efforts between American Home Patient, represented by Kim Sansbury; Conway Hospital, where Russ Siders works in the Respiratory Department; and the American Lung Association.

Better Breathing meets on the third Wednesday of each month from 1 to 3 PM at the Conway Hospital Wellness & Fitness Center in the conference room.

Department of Health and Environmental Control
303 Hazzard St., Georgetown
• **(843) 546-5593**
101 Elm St., Conway
• **(843) 248-1500**
107 Hwy. 57 N., Little River
• **(843) 399-5553**

DHEC provides pregnancy tests, blood tests, immunizations, family planning and tuberculosis screening. The agency can provide healthcare to the homebound, depending upon the particular circumstances. This department is always happy to provide the larger community and schools with health promotion and educational programs.

Diabetic Outreach/Multiple Sclerosis Support Group
300 Singleton Ridge Rd., Conway
• **(843) 347-8108**

A registered nurse and dietitian are on hand for this group's monthly meetings, held the first Thursday of every month at 2 PM in the Finlayson Classroom of Conway Hospital. In the hospital's auditorium, on the second Wednesday of each month, the Multiple Sclerosis group meets from 7 to 9 PM.

Joint Replacement Education Group
300 Singleton Ridge Rd., Conway
• **(843) 347-7111**

If you're anticipating knee replacement surgery, you may just want to look this group up for information. Meetings are held on the first Tuesday of the month from 10 to 11:30 AM at

HEALTHCARE

With the Waccamaw Same-Day Surgery Center, surgical procedures that once required a hospital stay now take minutes in the morning.

Photo: courtesy of Kimberly Allyson Duncan

the Conway Hospital Wellness & Fitness Center. Topics covered during the meeting include preparation for surgery and what to expect during the operation, during recovery, and during rehabilitation.

Mended Hearts
300 Singleton Ridge Rd., Conway
• (843) 347-8153

Mended Hearts is a group for anyone diagnosed with heart disease and the individual's family members. Meetings are held the third Thursday of each month from 7 to 9 PM in the Conference Room of Conway Hospital's Wellness & Fitness Center. For more information, contact the Cardiac Rehabilitation Department at the number above.

Ostomy Support Group
300 Singleton Ridge Rd., Conway
• (843) 236-7829

The ostomy group meets on the third Thursday of the month at 7 PM in Conway Hospital's dining room. Refreshments are served. For more information, contact Jaci Morgan at the number above.

HEALTHCARE

Media

Grand Stranders could not live without the media. Literally. When Hurricane Hugo thundered into town in September 1989, the radio became our nearest, dearest and most trusted friend. We found ourselves again beholden to the radio during fall 1996 with stormy visits from hurricanes Bertha and Fran. Even when power outages shrouded us in darkness and rudely shut off the television set, local radio stations such as WYAV-FM and WYAK-FM kept us informed. A number of local radio and television newscasters braved the swirling, high winds on Ocean Boulevard to give us up-to-the-minute reports, while newspaper reporters left the safety of their own homes to get the story from shelters and police outposts.

Besides comforting us through natural disasters, the media helps us digest the burgeoning amount of local goings-on. The Grand Strand has become a veritable boom town. Without media reports and newspapers, we would have one heck of a time keeping up with the daily opening and closing of businesses, entertainment venues, new housing developments and retailers.

In an area that is frenetically attracting national franchises, recording artists and movie stars, the sense of the Grand Strand as a community would be lost in the shuffle without media stories about the people we know—our neighbors.

One thing is sure: The Grand Strand media will keep you in-touch and up-to-date. Figuring out where to go on the weekend is easy when you pick up a copy of *The Sun News* on Fridays and rifle through the "Kicks!" insert. Every festival, arts event, feature movie, new restaurant, entertainer and venue is listed.

You can even start making plans while driving into town by surfing the channels of your car radio. Especially from March through September, radio airwaves are packed with announcements from nightclubs, restaurants and shops. Nightclubs generally advertise what's happening that evening for entertainment plus food and drink specials. In fact, your night's itinerary can be set even before you check into your hotel room.

With that in mind, get in touch with the Grand Strand by lending your eyes and ears to the local media.

Newspapers

Dailies

The Sun News
914 Frontage Rd. E.,
Myrtle Beach
• (843) 626-8555

Established in 1961, *The Sun News* is the only daily newspaper along the Grand Strand. It provides comprehensive local and international news, stock market reports, weather forecasts and a classified advertising section. On Fridays, the paper includes the "Kicks!" section, which offers information about upcoming entertainment as well as reviews. In 1997 *The Sun News* began a Saturday insert magazine, rotating the subjects of Health & Fitness, Senior Living, Outdoors, Technology & Computers and Homes & Gardens. The Sunday edition is

LOOK FOR:
• **Newspapers**
• **Magazines**
• **Radio Stations**
• **Television Stations**

Radio stations provide coverage and often sponsor local events and fundraisers.

Photo: Courtesy of WWXM-FM 97.7

chock-full of extras, including a separate real estate section, TV guide, coupons and *Parade* magazine. Circulation figures hit a high of 60,000 in February, 1999.

Daily delivery subscriptions for a full year are $142 or $116 if you just want delivery on Friday, Saturday and Sunday. A 13-week daily subscription runs $39.50; for weekend editions only the cost is $29.

Non-dailies

The Myrtle Beach Herald
• (843) 626-3131

Found mainly in area bookstores and grocery stores, this broadsheet newspaper comes out every Thursday morning. Editorial coverage investigates the Grand Strand from Little River to Murrells Inlet. A newcomer to the area, the *Herald* started rolling the presses in 1994. Individual issues are 50¢ a copy. Subscriptions within Horry County cost $25 a year; out-of-state subscriptions are $30.

The Times
• (843) 249-3525

Published on Wednesdays, *The Times* at-tempts to zero in on Grand Strand-related issues, such as the local option sales tax and further development of the local transportation infrastructure. You can find it at bookstores and in brochure racks at local restaurants and businesses for 50¢ each. Subscriptions run $30 for the year.

Coastal Observer
• (843) 237-8438

This weekly newspaper hits the streets on Thursdays and covers the region known as the Waccamaw Neck: DeBordieu, Pawleys Island, Murrells Inlet, Litchfield Beach and Garden City Beach. The *Observer* has been the recipient of numerous awards presented by the South Carolina Press Association for feature writing, sports coverage, layout and design. It can be found in businesses and boxes throughout the Waccamaw Neck region at a cost of 25¢ per issue. Subscriptions are $14 a year.

The Georgetown Times
• (843) 546-4148

A well-established local newspaper, *The Georgetown Times* is published on Mondays, Wednesdays and Fridays and covers events in

Georgetown and its surrounding communities. Special and favorite sections that come out in the Times at least once a year include the "Newcomer's Guide," "Bridal Guide," and "Hunting Guide." You'll find copies in news racks throughout the county for 25¢ apiece. Local subscriptions run $24 per year.

Magazines

Alternatives NewsMagazine
• (843) 444-5556

Alternatives is considered a magazine by content only, since an issue is actually slightly smaller and glossier than a broadsheet newspaper. Articles focus more on ideas or concepts than on reporting news. Local cultural events are always listed thoroughly in *Alternatives*. The publication features a roster of eclectic columnists who give opinions on various subjects—even a psychiatrist's view of the human condition. *Alternatives* is a freebie and is available all over the Grand Strand—in offices, businesses, magazine racks and restaurants. It's published twice a month, every other Thursday.

Pee Dee Magazine
• (843) 448-9141

Pee Dee is a slick, glossy publication, found only on magazine racks for $3.95. Published bimonthly, it provides extensive coverage of personalities, issues and the history of the Pee Dee region, which includes the Grand Strand and Florence, South Carolina, areas. Popular features of *Pee Dee Magazine* include the recipe section, book reviews, featured homes of architectural or historical interest and travel scoops covering an interesting daytrip or extensive trek to a foreign land. Subscriptions run $18.90 for a year.

Radio Stations

As in most any area with a largely tourism-driven economy, the Grand Strand's world of radio is an ever-changing, volatile industry. Local radio personalities are in a constant state of flux: in and out of town, changing stations, switching formats and showing up at different time drives. On any given day, your favorite country-music DJ might disappear from the airwaves, only to be heard farther down the dial hawking the latest rap tunes.

But if you're here long enough, you can place a face to almost every voice you hear on the radio. Businesses, restaurants, nightclubs and entertainment theaters are always booking radio personalities to perform on-site "remotes." These are hard-working people, ladies and gentlemen. Many local radio personnel start their days on-air at 5 AM, then spend the evening promoting a club act.

A 1997 study independently conducted by Young & Rubicam found that radio rules in the Myrtle Beach and Florence markets. The analysis set out to determine how much time American adults spend watching television, reading newspapers and magazines and listening to the radio. Out of the 211 markets across the nation used in the study, Myrtle Beach and Florence ranked No. 7 for radio loyalty. Apparently, our adult population listens to the radio an average of three hours and 26 minutes each day. The national average for tuning into the radio is three hours and nine minutes each day.

We are confident that you will find the music that you love to listen to on at least one of the stations listed here.

INSIDERS' TIP

So your favorite musical group is coming to town and you don't have enough money for advance tickets? Keep your ears tuned to the radio and your finger on that rapid-dial touchtone phone. Most area concerts are promoted by one radio station or another with a free ticket giveaway contest. If you're the right caller of the hour, you could be on your way to the concert with primo seats.

Adult Contemporary
WMYB-FM 99.5 (Soft rock)
WNMB-FM 105.9
WGSN-AM 900

Adult Urban Contemporary
WDAI-FM 98.5

Contemporary Hits
WWXM-FM 97.7

Country
WEGX-FM 92.9
WGTN-FM 100.7
WGTR-FM 107.9
WJXY-FM 93.9
WYAK-FM 103.1
WLSC-AM 1240

Easy Listening
WJYR-FM 92.1

MEDIA

Gospel
WLMC-AM 1470
WPJS-AM 1330

Jazz
WLGI-FM 90.9

Oldies
WSYN-FM 106.5
WVCO-FM 94.9
COOL-FM 104.9

Rock
WYAV-FM 104.1
WKZQ-FM 101.7/AM 1450
WSCA-FM 93.7
WWSK-FM 107.1

Talk Radio
WRNN-FM 94.5
WGTN-AM 1400

Television Stations

First things first. In order to find your favorite program on a particular network, you need to know which cable company is servicing your area. TV guides will give you a lineup of what channel you should turn to, in accordance with the designated cable delivery company you're hooked up to. This listing should set your remote control straight. Warning: If you're a channel surfer, ignore this section and simply proceed as usual.

North Strand

Horry Telephone
1608 N. Main St., Conway
• **(843) 365-2151**
This cable provider jumps around Horry County, but exclusively services the northern Longs region and its surrounding communities, including Carolina Forest, Little River Inn, The Spa at Little River, The Preserve and Colonial Charters.

Myrtle Beach

Time Warner Cable
1901 Oak St., Myrtle Beach
• **(843) 913-7940**
You are in Time Warner country if you are living or staying in Myrtle Beach proper, Little River, Atlantic Beach, North Myrtle Beach, Briarcliffe or any Myrtle Beach hotel or condominium. TV guides use "TG" to designate the Time Warner service in the areas of Georgetown and Andrews.

Time Warner officially acquired Jones Intercable in mid-1998. This cable company serves three-fourths of all customers in Horry and Georgetown counties. At the same time, its delivery system is being upgraded, at a cost of $15 million, to install fiber-optic cable and new converters. To the customer, this means greater channel capacity, improved picture and sound quality and increased reliability. High speed cable modems will offer Internet access.

South Strand

Cablevision
9261 S.C. Hwy. 707, Myrtle Beach
• **(843) 650-7450**
Cablevision services the Briarcliffe area, the Forest, Arcadian section, Shore Drive section and county regions of Surfside Beach, Litchfield Beach, Hagley Estates and Pawleys Island.

Network Affiliates and Local Satellites

ABC Affiliates

WWAY-TV 3
WCIV-TV 4
Local Satellite: WPDE-TV 15
Founders Center, 2411 Oak St., Ste. 206, Myrtle Beach • (843) 448-9733, (843) 946-6689 (Weather Center)
News channel 15 boasts an impressive weather and environmental team and offers newscasts at 5 and 6 PM daily. Gordon Barnes has more than 40 years of weather-forecasting experience under his belt and the notoriety of having worked closely with Walter Cronkite; and Chief Meteorologist Ed Piotrowski has been voted the state's No. 1 weathercaster by the Associated Press of South Carolina for three years running. Channel 15 is also locally noted for its quarterly "Health Digest" and "Always Kids Network" programming. Half-hour segments investigate and report on significant issues related to health and viewers 16 and younger. All of our ABC stations bring you *Good Morning America* at 7 AM and air *All My Children, One Life to Live* and *General Hospital* from 1 through 4 PM. Other ABC programming varies from channel to channel during the time-blocks of morning talk shows and evening sitcoms.

Subscribers to Time Warner Cable can access ABC programming on Channel 9. TV 4 is on Channel 4. Horry Telephone service is on Channel 9 as well. Cablevision airs Channel 4 on Channel 57; Channel 9 stays the same.

CBS Affiliates

WCSC-TV 5
Local Satellite: WBTW-TV 13
101 McDonald Ct., Myrtle Beach
• (843) 293-1301

Like the weather team of WPDE-TV 15, WBTW Chief Meteorologist Don Leuhrs has received accolades from public and press alike for his outstanding coverage of weather conditions during Hurricane Fran in September 1996. TV 13 offers a local segment during its morning news broadcast that is one of the best venues for exposure in town. Approximately 31,000 viewers from the Grand Strand and as far away as Florence, South Carolina, tune in regularly. All CBS affiliates air the news at 5 and 6 PM. Between 12:30 and 5 PM, CBS offers an impressive lineup of soaps: *The Young and the Restless, The Bold and the Beautiful, As the World Turns* and *Guiding Light*. Daytime programming ends at with the *Oprah Winfrey Show*.

CBS carries some of the best tried-and-true shows, such as *60 Minutes* and *Chicago Hope*. New hit programming includes *Touched by an Angel* and *Early Edition*.

TV 13 has originated news and programming from the Myrtle Beach area for 14 years now and prides itself on being an integral part of the Grand Strand community. During Halloween, the station works with local Holiday Inns to provide barrier-free trick or treating to special-needs children. WBTW TV-13 also sponsors a Senior Fair each year and projects that honor outstanding local teachers, students and athletes. Joining forces with Crime Stoppers and regional law enforcement, Channel 13 airs *Carolina's Most Wanted* every Sunday at noon. This program has been responsible for apprehending 60 percent of the criminals featured since viewers are able to give information and tips anonymously.

All CBS programming is found on Channel 13 for Time Warner customers and Horry Telephone viewers. Jones Intercable and Cablevision customers may select either channel 5 or 13.

INSIDERS' TIP

If you find that weekends are the only time you can leisurely read the paper, *The Sun News* has a special circulation package for you: a weekend subscription. Call (843) 626-8555 and sign up to have Friday, Saturday and Sunday papers delivered to your doorstep.

NBC Affiliates

WECT-TV 6
WIS-TV 10
WCBD-TV 2

These NBC stations offer a popular programming roster. *Days of Our Lives, Another World, Montel Williams* and *Oprah Winfrey* round out daytime viewing from 1 to 5 PM. Two hours of award-winning news follows, and then come some of the best sitcoms TV has to offer, including *Home Improvement, Friends, Seinfeld, Caroline In The City, Frasier* and *Mad About You*. NBC introduced us to new shows such as *3rd Rock From the Sun, Men Behaving Badly* and *Suddenly Susan*. These affiliates also bring you the *Tonight Show* every night of the week plus *ER, The Pretender* and *Profiler*.

Time Warner Cable gives you NBC on channels 6 and 10 as does Horry Telephone. The network is found on channels 6 and 62 with Cablevision.

Fox Affiliates

WFXB-TV 43
WTAT-TV 24

A deal cut in October 1996 officially awarded Myrtle Beach's only independent television station, WGSE-TV 43, the Fox Broadcasting Company affiliation for the Florence and Myrtle Beach markets. Fox programming began on WFXB in January 1997, right around the date of the Super Bowl, which the station carried. Until then, WGSE-TV 43 aired only family and religious programming.

Besides major sporting events, Fox's programming includes *The X-Files, Star Trek, Melrose Place, Sliders* and *Millennium*. Fox programming can be found on Time Warner Channel 4. Cablevision airs Fox on channels 24 and 26 and Horry Telephone subscribers need to switch to Channel 7.

United Paramount Affiliate

WWMB-TV 21

No matter what local cable service you subscribe to, WWMB programming is found on Channel 16, except for Cablevision, which carries it on Channel 60.

This is the only network affiliate on the

Grand Strand that airs the popular series *Baywatch, Baywatch Night, Tales From the Crypt* and *Kung Fu: The Legend Continues.*

Educational

WITV-TV 7
WHMC-TV 23
WJPM-TV 33
WUNJ-TV 39

All of these education-oriented stations offer programming for the entire family. All are good morning channels for kids; catch *Barney & Friends* or *Sesame Street.*

The *NewsHour* with Jim Lehrer airs every evening at 7 PM, followed by a variety of instructional and investigative programming.

Time Warner customers can find TV 7, TV 23 and TV 33 on local Channel 17, while WUNJ-TV 39 is on Channel 3. If you're staying in a Myrtle Beach hotel, the channel will be 21. The Horry Telephone channel is 8 and Cablevision is Channel 7.

Scroll Channels

Time Warner Cable and Waccamaw Cable

Scroll channels offer a constant listing of local information and public service announcements accompanied by easy-listening music.

These channels are widely accessed by hotel guests since they supply Grand Strand visitors with plenty of updated information and complete community calendars.

Local Feature Shows

The talk show *Southern Style* has featured local guests since its inception in 1985. "Hostess with the mostest" Diane DeVaughn Stokes invites a variety of people with stories and passions to her hour-long program, which airs twice daily at 10 AM and 7:30 PM on Time Warner Cable, Channel 5. Diane's spots are always upbeat, like the hostess herself—whether on or off the air. Time Warner also produces *Now This Week In Coastal Entertainment*, hosted by Richard Green, that highlights some aspect of local living. *This Week* is cablecast on Channel 5 four times a week—Sunday and Thursday at 2 PM and Saturday and Tuesday at 8 PM. And, if you're looking for a home along the Grand Strand, tune in to *Coastal Carolina Real Estate,* which airs on Channel 5 at 7 AM, 11 AM, 6:30 PM and 1 AM every day.

Both the Travel Vision Group, Beach TV 45 of South Carolina and *Grand Strand Video Magazine* offer viewers cable programs that speak specifically to the tourism market. Programs take you to attractions, restaurants and theaters—and even provide golf tips.

MEDIA

Volunteer Opportunities

LOOK FOR:
- Countywide
- Myrtle Beach
- South Strand

Want to get the pulse on a seemingly erratic resort area in a hurry? Become a volunteer! We highly recommend this pastime as one of the best ways to become entrenched in the community. Whether you're a newcomer to the Grand Strand or have chosen this sandy coast as your retirement home, joining a volunteer corps can open an insightful window to local politics, culture and people.

For those who are coming into town to tackle a new job assignment or career, a number of area businesses encourage volunteer activity by paying club membership dues for their employees. Civic, which means "of citizenship," organizations can often plug you right into a networking circuit of business contacts. Even *Fortune 500* magazine cites volunteer experience as a highlight many American corporations look for on resumes.

On a purely social level, civic involvement in a specific club will serve you up a slice of local life. Each organization presents its own microcosm or cross-section of Grand Strand citizenry, where you're bound to meet an interesting friend or two and, perhaps, the man or woman of your dreams. For singles, we can assure you that meeting locals through volunteer activities will beat a werewolf lifestyle of moonlight bar stalking.

Volunteer opportunities abound up and down the Grand Strand strip and in its pockets of subcommunities. To get a fairly comprehensive listing of volunteer outlets, we suggest dropping into the main office of the Myrtle Beach Area Chamber of Commerce on Oak Street to pick up the free-to-the-public guide *Civic & Service Organizations of the Myrtle Beach Area*. You can also get updated volunteer information from *The Sun News:* Civic and support-group meetings are announced in Sunday's "Coastal Living" section.

Included here are some volunteer organizations to start with that we know would gratefully welcome your help and/or participation.

Countywide

Big Brothers and Big Sisters of Horry County
- **(843) 248-0164**

Big Brothers and Big Sisters is a nationwide, not-for-profit youth service organization. The mission of Big Brothers and Big Sisters is to "make a big difference, one child at a time" in the lives of at-risk children. Through professionally-supported primarily one-to-one mentoring re-lationships with caring adults, and to assist the children in achieving their highest potential as they grow to become confident, competent, and caring individuals. Big Brothers and Big Sisters of America has matched millions of children in need with caring adult mentors since 1904. Research shows that children with Big Brothers and Big Sisters are less likely to use drugs and alcohol, skip school, and exhibit violent behavior.

Big Brothers and Big Sisters are caring adults who are mentors to children, often from single-parent homes. Men and women from all backgrounds help guide their little brothers and little sisters toward bright futures by sharing life experiences. "Bigs" and "Littles" enjoy school work, sports, recreational activities, movies, museums, and just talking together. In a nutshell, a "Big" is a friend.

Horry Cultural Arts Council
• (843) 248-7200

Arts enthusiasts are invited to volunteer with this council at any time. The Arts Council operates year round and needs plenty of help with bulk mailings and phone-a-thons in order to recruit new sponsors and members. The fall is a very busy time for staff and volunteers of the council, with their major arts festival VIVACE! staging performances all over the Grand Strand. Volunteers work in every capacity during VIVACE!; from taking tickets at shows to placing props. See our Arts chapter for more on the event.

Horry-Georgetown County Guardian Ad Litem Program
Horry County Offices, Third Ave., Conway
• (843) 248-7374

Volunteers in this program are specially trained to become advocates for abused and neglected children, representing the child's best interests through the Family Court system. This is interesting, viable work and a wonderful opportunity to learn the legal system firsthand while helping a child in need.

As of October 1997, there were 41 trained guardians in Horry County and six in Georgetown county. However, as coordinator, Robin Poston declared, "we never have enough." Guardian Ad Litems are appointed by the court. They conduct interviews with the child and other sources deemed necessary to a case, collect records and documents, seek recommendations and advice from experts and monitor agencies and persons who provide care or service to the child. All of this data is reported as findings to the court.

We must tell you that the situations guardians encounter are often not at all pleasant, and some cases of abuse and neglect are downright ugly.

This program asks for a one-year commitment from its volunteers to handle one or more cases at a time, depending on your available time to give. You must apply and undergo a criminal check through the State Law Enforcement Division and the central registry at the Department of Social Services. Volunteers ini-

tially receive 15 hours of free training and must observe a court hearing. Ongoing training is constantly in the works.

Literacy Council of Horry County
• (843) 248-6140

How can you measure the contribution to a life when you teach someone who is illiterate how to read? Nita Brown and the literacy council are always eager to recruit volunteers to this task and the council offers a comprehensive training program. Teaching materials are given to every volunteer, and placement with a wishful reader is almost immediate. Literacy tutor training is held almost every other month at different locations around the county.

Mercy Hospice of Horry County
• (843) 236-2282

Hospice volunteers lend an extra pair of hands to help, extra ears to listen and a heart to love and console. A training course is required to become a Hospice volunteer, since you will be working with a person suffering from a terminal, incurable condition and his or her family. Volunteers are considered to be dedicated, loving friends who often provide relief for the caregiver. Volunteers also assist Mercy Hospice with office duties and fund-raising activities. Call Elizabeth Mazurkiewicz at the number above about getting involved.

Mobile Meals
• (843) 651-7734

"Waste not, want not" is the motto of this group, and its active volunteers don't believe in squandering a minute when it comes to delivering food to hungry people in need. Dozens of volunteers race hot lunches every day of the week—regardless of weather—to homebound citizens from the state line in Little River as far south as Brookgreen Gardens in Murrells Inlet. More than 40,000 meals are delivered. These volunteers are so dedicated, they even made deliveries on Christmas Day and New Year's Day. With so many meals to deliver to so many needy folks, Mobile Meals more than welcomes another pair of helping hands, so call Bob Kohrumel at the number above or Charles Smith, who also coordinates volunteers, at (843) 449-9141.

Optimist Clubs
• (843) 238-1559

Call Phil Cox for referrals to any Optimist Club operating along the Grand Strand. Optimists meet morning, noon or night in a variety of places, so you should be able to find a chap-

Brookgreen Gardens boasts a very active volunteer program.

Photo: courtesy of Brookgreen Gardens

ter that suits your schedule. Cox is a member of the Grand Strand Optimist Club, but chapters are also available in North Myrtle Beach, South Strand and the Waccamaw Neck area. Calling themselves the "Friends of Youth," Optimists are the official area sponsors of the "Just Say No" program to discourage the use of drugs and alcohol by school-age children; they also sponsor sports teams through the YMCA.

Annual Optimist fund-raisers allow the clubs to donate money to such helping organizations as the Horry County Shelter Home for children, the Boys and Girls Club and the Big Brother program.

Volunteer Rescue Squads
In Myrtle Beach
• **(843) 626-7352**
In Murrells Inlet
• **(843) 651-9170**
In North Myrtle Beach
• **(843) 272-3144**

Yes, the Grand Strand has a complete emergency ambulance service run solely by volunteers. Not one paid employee works at any of the area rescue squads. They operate from 7 PM to 7 AM, seven days a week, responding to emergency 911 calls dispatched from police departments. Volunteers serve as drivers, crews and trained medical assistants. You must be 18 or older to volunteer.

Myrtle Beach

American Red Cross
2795 Pampas Dr., Myrtle Beach
• **(843) 477-0020**

If you prefer hands-on, in-the-trenches work, volunteering with the Red Cross could be just the ticket. This national community-assistance organization needs people to teach CPR courses, assist with Bloodmobiles, work in hurricane shelters, train for emergency disaster relief and help to coordinate the annual Community Christmas Dinner. Contact Rick McDow for more information.

City of Myrtle Beach
921-A Oak St., Myrtle Beach
• **(843) 918-1000**

If you want to get right in the thick of things, consider volunteering for the city. Take surveys, coach a youth sports team or perform a number of office duties. Volunteer positions are available in the departments of planning, construction, police, finance, engineering, public services and parks and recreation, so you can certainly find a suitable and enjoyable alternative. The City of Myrtle Beach also recruits active volunteers by the score for Chapin Library. Each department and facility accepts, screens and trains volunteers to its specifications.

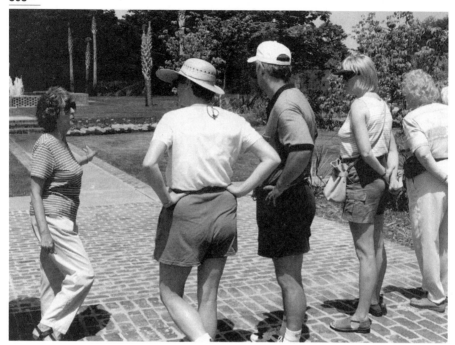

Participants in the volunteer programs sponsored by Brookgreen Gardens are trained and utilized for all sorts of tasks.

Photo: Courtesy of Brookgreen Gardens

Civitan Club
• (843) 650-4006

These "builders of good citizens" primarily focus on projects that deal with youth. Civitans are the official local sponsors of Special Olympics for physically and mentally challenged children. The club currently has 30 to 35 members and meets at 1 PM on the second and fourth Tuesdays of each month at The Dunes Golf and Beach Club. Call TeAnne Oehler for more specifics.

Another Civitan Club started up at the north end of the Strand, headed up by Alston Pittman, (843) 249-5666 or (843) 249-2917. This group meets on the first and third Thursdays of the month at Billy the Kid's Restaurant on S.C. Highway 9 in North Myrtle Beach.

Grand Strand Regional Medical Center Auxiliary
• (843) 692-1634

Volunteers are used in every department and on every floor of this major hospital. If you're interested, book an appointment to obtain more information or apply for volunteer work. Individuals are matched to particular positions at the hospital according to their backgrounds and skills.

Orientation and training are provided. Talk to Gay Cooke, CDVS, to get involved.

Grand Strand Humane Society
10th Ave. N. Ext., Myrtle Beach
• (843) 448-5891, (843) 448-9151
409 Bay St., North Myrtle Beach
• (843) 249-4948

This is definitely the right place for animal lovers to donate their time and energy. People are needed to assist in the care of animals in the North Myrtle Beach and Myrtle Beach shelters and to help with fund-raising and community-awareness programs. Volunteer coordinator Sue White can be reached at (843) 448-4904.

Habitat for Humanity of Horry County
• (843) 916-8815

Dedicated to providing adequate housing for needy families, this local chapter of Habitat for Humanity is currently building six homes. Volunteers for Habitat assist in a variety of ways: The entire construction of a home is done by volunteers and the soon-to-be-homeowners; others help to raise money for the organization through Habitat's thrift shop, concession stands at major events and gift wrapping at local malls during the Christmas shopping season. All Habitat committees, including Site Selection, Family Selection, Legal Affairs and Surveying, are composed of volunteers. The only restriction is that a volunteer must be at least 14 years of age to work on a construction site. Call Judy Swanson at the number above if you want to pick up a hammer and join.

Hi Newcomers
• (843) 215-1538

As the name suggests, this 300-member-strong organization is for those who have taken up permanent residency in the Grand Strand area within the last year (a.k.a. newcomers). From September through May, members meet for coffee and informative luncheons as well as to organize charity functions. Members are allowed to participate for three years and then are invited to join Newcomers Alumnae of the Grand Strand (NAGS). Gail Crooks takes calls at the number above.

Kiwanis International
• (843) 448-5123

A group for men and women 18 and older, Kiwanis clubs worldwide are mandated to serve their communities. They run four or five major fund-raisers each year, and all monies raised must be donated or spent in the hometown. The group does a fine job supporting many area services such as Helping Hand and meals-on-wheels. Franklin Long will answer other questions you may have.

INSIDERS' TIP

Becoming a volunteer often uncovers hidden talents in people. Through civic participation and community projects, we've seen meek personalities turn into strong leaders, tongue-tied stutterers become inspiring public speakers and people struggling with insecurities leave dead-end jobs to start their own businesses.

The Myrtle Beach Jaycees
• (843) 650-6252

The Jaycees is definitely a "doers" club, relying far more on member participation than on fees to run the organization. At present count, the group has a membership of about 55 men and women between the ages of 21 and 40 and runs upward of 30 projects and programs every year, covering a wide range of activities from charity fundraising to public speaking competitions. This is a good club to join not only to socialize, but to foster people-management skills as well. Anyone is welcome to attend any of their meetings, which are held on the second and fourth Mondays of every month at 7 PM.

South Strand

Fire Departments
Surfside Beach Fire Department
115 U.S. Hwy. 17 N., Surfside Beach
• (843) 238-2314
Murrells Inlet Fire Department
3641 U.S. Hwy. 17 S., Murrells Inlet
• (843) 651-5143, (843) 651-5273

Here's your chance to live out that childhood dream of riding along in a screeching fire-engine, wearing a shiny red hat and big boots, with your arm slung around a dalmatian . . . OK, it's not really all fun and games. But volunteer firefighters are always needed, and the department requires no previous experience; training is provided.

Worship

One local, albeit cynical, restaurant owner once commented to us, Visitors don't come here to think, they don't come to read and they certainly don't come here to go to church." He, of course, was alluding to the party-all-the-time image so often associated with Myrtle Beach. But despite his analysis and pronouncement, the Grand Strand is part of, and the vast majority of its visitors are from, the heart of the southern God-fearing Bible Belt. And one thing about Southerners is that regardless of how hard they party, they tend to be spiritual with the same vigor.

Consequently, the denominational makeup of the area traditionally has been largely Protestant and more than a little fundamentalist in nature; South Carolina voters elected the only Christian Coalition-affiliated governor in the nation. Furthermore, this region's churches reflect its history: All Saints Episcopal Church on Pawleys Island celebrated its 233rd birthday in 2000, and Prince George Winyah Church in Georgetown is one of South Carolina's few original colonial church buildings still in use. Conway's historic district is home to two more distinctive churches— Kingston Presbyterian and First United Methodist.

Nonetheless, with the large numbers of northern retirees and a more diverse population becoming year-round Grand Strand residents, the religious scene has come to include plenty of players in addition to Presbyterians, Methodists and Baptists. Longtime resident, newcomer or visitor, you can be assured of finding almost any congregation of your religious philosophy on the Grand Strand. Here's an abbreviated list of choices: Charismatic, interdenominational, nondenominational, Apostolic, Assemblies of God, Bible Church, Free Will Baptist, Independent Baptist, Southern Baptist, Catholic, Christian Non-Denominational, Christian Science, Church of Christ, Community Church, Disciples of Christ, Episcopal, Evangelical, Jewish, Jehovah's Witnesses, Antiochian Orthodox, Greek Orthodox, Russian Orthodox, Latter-day Saints (Mormon), Lutheran-ELCA, Lutheran-LCMS, Methodist, United Fellowship of Metropolitan Community Church, African Methodist Episcopal-Zion, Nazarene, Pentecostal Holiness, Presbyterian-ARP, Presbyterian-PCA, Presbyterian-USA, Religious Society of Friends (Quakers), Salvation Army, Spirit-Filled Evangelical, Unitarian and Unity.

So diverse has the area become, there are television Christian ministries here, a 1,000-seat Charismatic Christian church, even an Indian-mysticism retreat, Meher Spiritual Center, on the oceanfront just to the north of Myrtle Beach (a retreat often visited by well-known rock 'n' roll musicians from the United States and England).

For the tried-and-true, born-and-raised Grand Strander, church is often at the center of social, family and political life. And a large number of locals find it hugely important to be considered "Christian," however nebulous the term might be. Allegiance to a particular place of worship is not demonstrated merely by regularly attending Sunday services or tithing. Your children attend the church's day-care program. You are dedicated enough to serve as director of a church-sponsored board. You or your spouse teach Sunday School classes. And you would never consider playing in a softball league that is not sanctioned by your church.

All Saints Episcopal Church in Pawleys Island is over 230 years old.

Photo: Courtesy of Brookgreen

Indeed, for many native Stranders, the church weaves the very fabric of their lives.

There are simply too many churches to mention them all; so please check a phone book to find listings and worship times. The Myrtle Beach Area Chamber of Commerce, (843) 626-7444, also prints a free list of area churches and synagogues, and *The Sun News* runs a church directory every Saturday.

WORSHIP

Index of Advertisers

Index